Causality, Determinism and Prognosis in Criminology

by

József Vigh

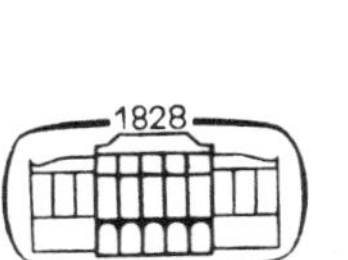

Akadémiai Kiadó, Budapest 1986

This is a translation of the revised original,
Kauzalitás, determináció és prognózis a kriminológiában,
Akadémiai Kiadó, Budapest

Translated by
Árpád Erdei

Translation editor:
Geoffrey Thompson

ISBN 963 05 3976 4

Printed in Hungary

Contents

Part Three

The Interpretation of Determinism Existing in Human Behaviour

Part Four

The Role of Prognostication in Criminal Behaviour

Part Five

Putting the Principle of Determinism into Effect in the Establishment of Criminal Responsibility

Introduction

In spite of its history of development over more than a hundred years, criminology has not yet reached the point of setting up a uniform explanatory principle embracing all aspects of the nature of criminal human behaviour and the character of the establishment of criminal responsibility. The lack of such a homogeneous explanatory principle may be traced back partly to the fact that criminology has an interdisciplinary character, so that its development is closely related to the development of other disciplines concerned with human behaviour. Another partial explanation is that these disciplines, concerned with human behaviour, particularly philosophy, sociology, psychology, neurophysiology and pedagogy, are not adapted to the requirements of criminology to the extent that they should be integrated into one homogeneous system. Starting from the lack of a *homogeneous explanatory principle,* some scholars doubt the *raison d'être* of criminology as an independent discipline and instead of insisting on an explanatory principle, they approach criminal behaviour from the viewpoint of either sociology or psychology, thereby simplifying reality. In my opinion, this tendency of onesidedness can be traced back primarily to the fact that the causitive determination of criminal human behaviour is not yet adequately explored, and, consequently, neither the individual process of becoming a criminal, nor the fact that crime is a mass phenomenon, is explained unambiguously.

It was more than ten years ago that András Szabó wrote in his work entitled *The Issues of Principle of Criminological Research:* "It is beyond doubt that in the course of criminological research we see social and psychological phenomena, so that causality appears on different levels of the dynamics of reality. What has been said in the literature of criminology about the problem of causality so far, is essentially the repetition of theses of philosophy, of epistemology. The significance of this is not to be belittled, naturally, since socialist criminology expresses its deterministic theoretical foundations in this way. However, it is evident that from the moment when criminology can demonstrate the determination of criminality — in other words, criminology finds an explanatory principle instead of mere description — the problems of causality appear in a different way, on the level of explanatory theoretical theses. The *criminological adaptation* of the philosophical issue of causality has not yet taken place in socialist criminology and this is what we consider a first step. When criminological studies reach the phase of explaining the phenomenon of crime, and not only describing and recording it, then the issues of causality will not appear as epistemological generalities but as tangible criminological generalities, forming an immanent part of the theoretical formula explaining crime."[1]

This correctly formulated requirement is still valid although during the last decade we have advanced toward our aim. A particularly significant step has been taken by V. N. Kudriavtsev, the noted Soviet criminologist, in his book dealing with the problem of causality.[2] And his path is the same that we intend to proceed on with this study. In my opinion, there is no other discipline apart from criminology that could demonstrate the causative determination of criminal human behaviour, that could answer the questions of *criminal behaviour, of criminality.* Neither psychology nor sociology, nor their variants qualified as "criminal", can solve alone the theoretical problems concerning crime. Only the discipline that adapts and comprises the achievements of all disciplines concerned with human behaviour and the factors influencing it, using any kind of approach, is able to form a homogeneous explanatory principle. It is my conviction that without a comprehensive theory concerning crime it is impossible to create an effective system of criminal justice which serves the interests of prevention and it is impossible to understand fully the necessity of the perpetrator's criminal behaviour and, consequently, to take adequate preventive measures.

It was primarily in order to promote the elaboration of such a comprehensive theory that I have attempted to contribute to the development of the criminological adaptation of causality, determination and prognostication in this study, to introduce the causative determination of criminal human behaviour on a general level, and to clarify the contradictions and the differences in the interpretation of the theoretical issues of the administration of criminal justice.

It is not practicable, however, to speak in general only of the administration of criminal justice, since nowadays significant differences in the theoretical foundations are apparent. For this reason I wish first to point out that some Western criminalists (criminal lawyers, criminologists, etc.) speak about a crisis of criminal law. They say that criminal law based on retribution and repression cannot satisfy modern requirements, and is not in accordance with the present state of the disciplines concerning human behaviour and with social development in general.[3]

They urge the reform of criminal law and the introduction of kinds of punishment which have preventive and educative aim, or the addition of these kinds to the

[1] A. Szabó, "A kriminológiai kutatások elvi kérdései" (Theoretical Issues of Criminological Research), *Állam- és Jogtudomány,* 3 (1963), p. 323.

[2] V. N. Kudriavtsev, *Pritshinnost v Kriminologii,* Moscow: Yuriditsheskaya Literatura, 1968.

[3] E. Cséka, "A Nemzetközi Büntetőjogi Társaság budapesti kongresszusának várnai és freiburgi előkészítő kollokviuma" (The Varna and Freiburg Preparatory Colloquium of the Budapest Congress of the AIDP), *Jogtudományi Közlöny,* 4 (1974).

existing ones. In certain countries (e.g. in the Scandinavian states, in Holland, in England) this approach has already gained a broad acceptance or become predominant and this fact is manifested in various institutions. This process of administration of justice, which is frequently described as "humanized" or "democratized", follows more closely in my opinion, the laws of human behaviour than the earlier, so-called classical, system of administration of justice.

The feeling of crisis can perhaps be traced back to the tension caused by the contradiction between practice and theory of the administration of justice. Thus, it is not an exaggeration if we say it is not as much a crisis of the practice of criminal law and the administration of criminal justice as the crisis of the theoretical foundations, the doctrines of criminal law and the views on criminal responsibility.

It seems to me that the theory of criminal liability, in spite of significant development in the last decades, is still too strongly embedded in the fabric of legal dogmatism and is not concentrated adequately on causal and probable interrelations in the process of determination the result of which is the criminal offence and by changing which the criminal offence would be avoidable.

It is a fact of history that criminal justice systems based on retribution and repression found their theoretical ground in idealism, in indeterminism. The system of repressive punishment, proportional to the deed, is a necessary consequence of the doctrine of divine free will and of formal bourgeois legal equality gaining dominance. The practice of the administration of justice, however, is more and more abandoning this theoretical basis nowadays and it is the principle of determinism that is more and more strongly expressed, independent of whether this fact is admitted by the bourgeois criminalists, or not. Marc Ancel, the prominent representative of the theory of the new Social Defence (which, in my opinion, is one of the most progressive schools of bourgeois criminology), for example, sharply criticizes the retributive institutions of punishment but, at the same time, he positively denies the principle of determinism and adheres to the conception of free will, in other words, to the theoretical basis that the much criticized retributive institutions have been built on.[4]

The situation is quite different in the socialist countries where the acceptance of the principle of determinism in the domain of criminal responsibility is a necessary consequence of the dominance of the materialist Weltanschauung. For this reason, not even the thought of a crisis does arise; this, however, is far from meaning that our system of establishing criminal responsibility is perfect and does not require modernization. In spite of the fact that in Hungary, as in other socialist countries, the theoreticians of criminal law admit the reality of the principle of determinism, there are significant differences in its interpretation. There are scholars who, while theoretically admitting the principle of determinism and causality, deem the main-

[4] M. Ancel, *Social Defense. A Modern Approach to Criminal Problems,* London: Routledge and Kegan Paul, 1965.

tenance of the old practice natural and believe that the ideas of retribution and education are compatible within the penal system. Others believe that the principle of determinism is compatible with the doctrine of free will and speak about relatively free will or moderate determinism. This theoretically unclear state of the basis of criminal responsibility prompted me to make an attempt at interpreting correctly and understanding better the principle of determinism and at outlining a system of establishing responsibility which, in my opinion, is a logical consequence of the acceptance of the determinist conception.

The third factor inducing me to expound theoretically the three large topics together, is that criminological prognostication is theoretically unacceptable if we do not accept the law of causality and determinism as a basis. Criminological prognostication which deals with the future tendencies of crime and criminal behaviour is inconceivable without knowing and making use of the laws of causality. The laws manifest in perpetrated crimes, in the sphere of causality, define the probability of future events and make the preparation of prognoses possible. In this way our knowledge of the real past and the image of the future anticipated through the laws are connected through the chain of cause and effect and form the foundations of the planned measures to be taken in the present and the future. The validity of our prognoses, their coming true or their faults, thus serves as a check on our conception of causality. The experience of criminological prognostication proves that it is the prognoses of scientists with a conception of causality most closely reflecting reality that come true with the highest probability. Or, formulating it in a different way, a good prognosis is dependent on the right conception of causality. This recognition also led me to make an attempt at writing a theoretical work which presents the determination of criminal behaviour both in its past and future forms.

The principle of determinism at the present is not only a theory built on hypotheses but proven reality. Beyond everyday experience, the operation of electronic machines producing almost incredible results, the flights of rockets in space and many other scientific accomplishments prove beyond doubt the existence of causal and probability relations, the determinative processes of phenomena, and the correctness of the principle of determinism. Due to the development of science and technology, the universe reveals itself to humanity. It becomes evident for more and more people that it is not the Earth and mankind that is the centre of the universe, and that on Earth and on other planets it is not according to divine free will that things happen but according to laws, the laws of the internal dynamics of matter. Man, however, as a conscious being, is able to adapt to laws and to modify the effects of laws by changing the causes and conditions. All this does not mean, of course, that human activity is not subordinated to the laws of causality and that the operation of human consciousness is above causal relations.

In the last decade the struggle for the acceptance of the principle of determinism gained new strength in criminology and in the theory of penal law. It was at the turn of the century, in the period of the battle for the reform of penal law, that a similar struggle was fought in Hungary. At the time the struggle ended with a compromise: legislation, due to the prevailing religious outlook, remained on the ground of indeterminism theoretically, but particular provisions of penal law reflected the principle of determinism (e.g. penal law concerning juveniles, the expression of the idea of education in the penal system to a certain extent.) At the present time the conditions for winning acceptance of the principle of determinism in the administration of justice are incomparably more favourable. In the socialist countries the indeterministic theory has been kept in the background and since the prevailing ideology is historical materialism, it is the deterministic view that is accepted.

Many people ask the question whether it is possible to create an effective system of administering criminal justice which is based on an indeterministic ideology. It is not without precedent that people professing idealism as their conviction proposed or sanctioned measures with preventive aims and educative means. In cases like this it is not a consequence of their conviction but is due to the requirements of everyday practice which is in conflict with their ideology, and this fact probably does not even reach their awareness since their ideology is the product of traditions and not the result of their professional conviction. In reality, however, it is difficult for people with an indeterministic outlook accepting retributive punishment, proportional to the deed, as just, to put into practice a system of the administration of justice which is not aimed at retribution and taking vengeance but at taking educative measures in the broadest sense in order to avoid behaviour harmful to society. The indeterministic theory and deterministic practice can hardly coexist in the long run.

The social structure of our age demands the most exact exploration of the laws of human behaviour and the practical use of these laws. It is only in this way that a framework of coexistence, including the system of administration of justice, can be created, which is able to ensure, together with other factors, obedience to social norms. The Belgian Quetelet's ideas, written more than a hundred years ago—that human behaviour seemingly regulated by free will is as much dominated by laws as the world of natural phenomena—may be a motto for the administration of justice.[5] And these laws are discoverable and must be discovered so that we are able to create an effective system of administration of justice and take effective preventive measures in order to decrease crime.

To understand criminal behaviour and crime, a certain knowledge of psychology, sociology and, last but not least, philosophy is needed. In writing this study I strove to make broad use of the achievements of these disciplines but only to the necessary extent. The priority of the outlook of philosophy follows from the topic. Yet, when exploring particular categories of philosophy I did not engage in philosophical debates but accepted the view prevailing in Marxist philosophy or the one which seemed the most suitable to explain crime and criminal behaviour. The same is true

[5] A. Quetelet, *Sur l'homme et le développement de ses facultées ou essai de physique sociale,* Paris, 1835.

of other disciplines as well. In cases the accepted philosophical or other scientific views did not provide the necessary guide-lines or starting point, I attempted to find the solution on the bases of facts and information.

In studying causality, determination and prognostication and their practical application I tried to connect inductive and deductive inferences. I tried, if it was possible, to check the inferences based on theories by the analysis of facts. I tried not to form conclusions that I did not see proven or verified with a high degree of probability.

I did follow the widely accepted method of presenting all the various scholarly views related to the issues examined and forming my own opinion through the comparison and evaluation of the significant or less significant differences of these views. I employed the method of describing some typical (or what I thought typical) opinions and stated my own after that, trying, at the same time, to prove its correctness with the information available to me.

Making use of the achievements of other disciplines, as is natural in criminology, involves certain dangers as well as indisputable advantages. This danger appears in two forms. The first is apparent when the achievements of other disciplines are adapted together with the use of their own phraseology in order to ensure that mistakes are avoided. This, in general makes the full understanding of the work difficult since most of the readers cannot be equally knowledgeable in all the related disciplines. The other form of danger appears when we attempt to formulate the achievements of other disciplines in the terminology of our own and we take the risk of certain simplifications. I have selected this latter, which is, in my opinion, the lesser danger of the two, because clarity, at least on a professional level, is a very important requirement for me. I should like to make sure that all the experts who read my study understand completely what I have written and perhaps even what I would have liked to write but could not because of the demands of conciseness. I have tried to express my ideas clearly and to employ clear terms. I used particular care when discussing problems of a philosophical nature to avoid a complicated phraseology and preferred to express my views at possibly undue length rather than allow any ambiguity to arise.

In additon, I should mention that this study is primarily of a theoretical nature but has not been written for theoreticians only. I believe that practical experts can also find it useful, for it may help them to understand better the theoretical background of their practical activity. The ideas to be found in the book, as with anybody else's ideas, are the reflection, the reproduction, of objective reality. How consistent this reflection or reproduction is with the original depends primarily on the intellectually adapted knowledge and individual experience, on the ability of reproducing that has been formed individually by external factors acting on inborn and acquired biological conditions. I hope that the reproduction provided by me, or my production, is basically consistent with reality, although certain differences may appear in the details. I did not and could not aim at either perfection or completeness, and, taking into consideration the nature of my topic, the available time and other circumstances, I set the aim of writing for those dealing with criminal matters a work which helps them to understand better the essence of criminal behaviour and crime and to find better solutions for the problems of criminal justice.

Finally, I should point out that the manuscript of the book was ready and sent to the publishers in 1977. Its assertions and conclusions were aimed at providing a theoretical background for the new Hungarian Penal Code which was put into force on the 1st July, 1979.

Part One

The Causality of Criminal Offences and Crime

I On the Concept of Crime and Criminal Offence

It belongs to the essence of the criminological approach that criminal offences and crime are regarded as effects and the basic task of criminological studies is to explore and formulate all the causes and conditions that determine the genesis of criminal offences and crime. Precisely for this reason, the clarification of the problems of causality (or an attempt at that) demands the correct interpretation of these concepts as phenomena having the role of effects in the sequence of causality. Considering the present abundance of the definitions of concepts, it is almost impossible to present our position concerning any basic issue without defining the concept of crime and criminal offence that we accept or regard as correct.

1 The Concept of Crime

Since the collection of statistical data concerning crime and the administration of justice was introduced in a number of European countries in the 1820s, the totality of criminal offences has been given a new meaning. As a result of the work of the Belgian A. Quetelet, one of the prominent pioneers of criminology, who was the first to make use of the data of official criminal statistics, it has become clear that viewing the measurable and actually measured mass of criminal offences, i.e. crime, is not the same as viewing individual offences. Even the most detailed knowledge of an individual offence, a criminal case or a criminal, does not make it possible to recognize the characteristics and laws that dominate crime. To use an analogy: even the most exact description of a tree or a few trees in a forest cannot provide enough information for perceiving the forest, for knowing its characteristics, dimensions, structure, changes and its relative position among other features on the surface of the Earth. Examining one criminal offence, we may have a glimpse of crime but it is no more than seeing the ocean in a drop of water. The ocean is of the same material but it is still different since in the drop of water the dimensions, pressure, depth, whirling and the waves of the ocean are not present. In some ways it is the same with a criminal offence and crime. Crime comprises criminal offences and their perpetrators, in the same way as a forest consists of trees or the ocean of drops of water, but it is a concept of a different level and it has different features beyond the fact that its main characteristics are formed by features comprising the nature of the individual elements. As a forest or the ocean are perceivable in their full dimensions if they are seen from above or from a distance, crime may be seen only if examined on a different level. It is, however, by the thorough examination of the constituting elements that the exploration of the internal characteristics is possible.

Criminal offences, if they occur in a high number, form a statistical mass, a set having new qualitative characteristics, namely crime. The relationship of the two phenomena is a good example of quantitative growth changing into a new quality. This dialectic relationship makes it evident that the universal causal relations appear in different forms on the level of the individual and on the level of mass phenomenon consisting of individual phenomena.

As a matter of fact, the views accepted by present day criminology and particularly by criminology of a sociological approach, originate from this originally statistical mass concept. According to the most general view, crime is a social and criminal-legal mass phenomenon which changes historically and consists of the totality of criminal offences.[1] As far as the definition of the concept is concerned, it is only the views regarding crime as the totality of acts, that of criminal offences, that we comment upon.

It is a general phenomenon even nowadays that criminalists speaking or writing of crime mean primarily the totality of criminal offences, those dangerous and harmful to society, and damaging social interests to the extent and in such a way that they are, at the same time, unlawful under penal law. This outlook originates simply from the fact that it is against this type of behaviour that society defends itself; they are prosecuted, the responsibility of the perpetrators for them is established and, first of all, punishment is imposed according to the gravity of the act, according to the measure of the harm or detriment caused by it.

As a result of criminological studies and views, in addition to the dangerousness of the act to society and its evaluation, the administration of justice pays more and more attention to perpetrators, their personalities and their social and biological characteristics. This is a natural process since the establishment of responsibility, the sentence, and the implementation of punishment are directed at the perpetrator in order to achieve special prevention, and, in order to achieve general prevention, they are directed also at people in general. It is not infrequent that whether an act which is dangerous to society would qualify as a criminal offence or not, depends on who the perpetrator is — in other words, what social, psychological or biological characteristics the perpetrator has (whether he is a recidivist, a child, feeble-minded, etc.). Thus, the concept of crime includes more and more also the perpetrator. István Vavró writes correctly that "neither criminal offences nor perpetrators considered separately can give a reliable picture of crime. Thus, crime is a special social mass phenomenon the basic unit of which, as of a statistical mass, is the

[1] N. F. Kuznetsova, *Prestuplenie i Prestupnost,* Moscow, 1969, p. 173.

criminal offence committed by a person having criminal responsibility or, inversely, a person committing an act to be punished under the law, who has all the special features that allow us to regard him as a person having criminal responsibility. This dual quality of responsibility is decisive in the examination of stochastic relations..."[2]

It seems to me, too, that crime cannot be described, particularly not criminologically, only by the characteristics of the criminal offences. And, from the point of view of etiology and prevention, it is simply indispensable to approach crime, as a social mass phenomenon, from the side both of the perpetrator and the act, and, besides, it reflects reality better. If we accept this, crime cannot be regarded merely as the totality of offences but the totality of the perpetrators also has to be understood by the term. To formulate it from a different aspect: crime, as a mass phenomenon, is manifested in such special statistical masses as the mass of acts unlawful under criminal law and that of their perpetrators. Consequently, we have to consider two elements also on the individual level: one of them is the violation of the interests protected through penal law by the given society and the other is the person committing the violation, i.e. the perpetrator. In my opinion the question of who commits offences is not less characteristic of a crime than what offences are committed, and what interests are violated by criminal behaviour. It is not only according to the structure of criminal offences that the higher or lower degree of dangerousness to society is reflected but also according to the structure of the mass of perpetrators. And from the point of view of causality and prevention, it is necessarily the perpetrators' characteristics that have primacy. Precisely for this reason, in my opinion, *crime is a historically changing, social and criminal-legal mass phenomenon which comprises the totality of criminal offences and their perpetrators in a given period of time and in a given area.*

We have to make several remarks concerning one or other terms of this definition. As far as the statistical outlook of sets, the totality of the units is concerned, one frequently reads in various professional publications that crime is not simply the totality of its constituting individual elements but it is their complex. This phraseology is used also by the university lecture notes.[3] The term is in fact suitable, since crime really is a composite whole, a statistical mass consisting of heterogeneous individual elements and subgroups, but it is not special in this respect because it is the totality or complex of criminal offences and perpetrators in the same way as the population is that of the citizens or the forest is that of the trees. Thus, the requirement that crime should not be regarded as a numerical sum total of its constituting

[2] I. Vavró, "Kauzalitás a kriminológiában" (Causality in Criminology), *Jogtudományi Közlöny,* 11 (1969), p. 611. See also J. Földvári and J. Vigh, *Kriminológia* (Criminology), Budapest: Tankönyvkiadó, 1968. p. 7.

[3] See Földvári and Vigh, *op. cit.,* p. 8., I. I. Karpets and A. R. Ratinov, "A jogtudat és a bűnözés okai" (Consciousness of Law and the Causes of Crime), *Magyar Jog,* 9 (1969), p. 559.

elements, is right, but it is no more than the requirement set in the case of all mass phenomena that may be considered as a statistical mass. A statistical mass consists not only of numerical but also material definitions, including, in addition to the numerical sum total of the individual elements, their most essential material traits characteristic of all elements. The material element of the mass presupposes a definition expressing adequately the nature of the unit. The sphere, the dimensions of crime are formed by units defined in the above way. The quality and structure of crime may be approached through a classification based on marks of differentiation, on the criteria of difference.[4]

The reason why many fear to identify the concept of the mass with the totality of the units and use the term complex is to avoid even the semblance that crime is understood as a mere quantitative accumulation of criminal offences (or their perpetrators). The outlook of statistics, however, is a guard against such a misunderstanding. In statistics, a totality or a mass has necessarily traits that the units do not have separately. Every statistical mass has its dynamism, its structure, it has a stochastic relation with other mass phenomena. It is necessary to mention also that a statistical mass is not identical with a mathematical total or number. Mathematical numbers are abstract values which may be displaced by any specific value while a statistical number always has a specific meaning, a specific content, it is always related to somebody or something. Thus the sum of criminal offences or their perpetrators may never be a mathematical, abstract number since it does not relate to anything but to criminal offences or their perpetrators and, for this reason, it is not possible to perform any optional operation with the sum. So in the formulation according to which crime is not simply the mathematical sum total of criminal offences but their complex, a conceptual paradox is manifested. Besides, I have never met the assertion of the thesis in the literature, only its negation. In my opinion it is needless to negate a thesis asserted by nobody. This negation is not justified by the supposition that someone might think of it. I believe that the explanation of the content of the concepts makes avoidable the incorrect assumptions leading to conceptual confusion. A remarkable conceptual model of

[4] The interpretation of crime as a statistical mass does not mean, of course, that there are no other criteria that could be defined for a better understanding. We speak, for instance, of forms of behaviour satisfying social needs, and of forms of problem-solving behaviour; value-oriented and value-denying, destructive forms of behaviour. I think, such characteristics cannot be compressed into the definition of the concept without damaging its clarity.

We attempted to create a concept of criminal offence that is more detailed and expressing the content better, in addition to the penal law concept of the offence. "The criminological concept of intentional offence could be formulated as an act which is dangerous to society, ordered by the law to be punished and which is a manifestation of the perpetrators' antisocial views or attitudes; it is the confrontation of individual needs with social requirements and social possibilities." J. Vigh, "Kauzalitás a kriminológiában" (Causality in Criminology), *Jogtudományi Közlöny,* 11–12 (1968), p. 574. In my opinion, crime is the statistical mass of units (acts and perpetrators) complemented or complementable with such or similar interpretations.

crime, aimed at exactness, can be found in the book of Zoltán Borsi and Kálmán Halász. According to them, the theoretical model of crime may be given as follows:

$$C = \begin{matrix} C_f = \Sigma C_n + C_l \leftrightarrows E \\ \uparrow\downarrow \leftrightarrows \uparrow\downarrow \leftrightarrows \uparrow\downarrow \\ C_s = \Sigma d_n + d_l \leftrightarrows E \end{matrix}$$

In the formula C = crime; c = criminal offences; d = perpetrator; E = effect; n = known; l = latent. For the act within crime C_n represents the discovered criminal offences; C_l represents latent criminal offences; C_f stands for completed crime; C_s means the criminal's personality (subject); the perpetrators, d_n represents the violators of penal norms who are detected; d_l represents latent perpetrators. The aspect of both the act and the person signify the quantitative and qualitative criteria. E includes, on the one hand, the social and economic interrelations independent of criminal offences and the personality of perpetrators (on the side of act); on the other hand, it includes the interrelations between the perpetrators and the effects of the micro and macro social and economic environment operating through the personality of the offenders (on the side of the persons).[5]

This theoretical model, apart from the printing errors of the symbolic transcription, demonstrates correctly that crime is the statistical mass of the known and latent criminal offences and their perpetrators. (In my opinion, the symbol of effect, while it belongs to the description of crime, is not a necessary criterion of the concept but falls in the sphere of causality. I do not consider it, however, as my task to give a conceptual interpretation in this chapter.)

It follows unmistakably from the theoretical model that the evaluation of the dimensions of crime may influence our causal approach significantly. When speaking or writing about crime, criminalists usually think of crime as measured by statistical data. Nowadays, when the graphs of discovered and statistically surveyed crime show a strong increase in the capitalist countries and they do not always decline even in socialist countries, the problem comes to the fore of the crime which exists but does not appear in the statistics — in professional terms latent crime.

According to certain bourgeois authors latent crime and crime outside the scope of criminal statistics (mainly criminal offences committed by statesmen and political leaders) have grown to the dimensions that discovered crime constitutes only a small rate of crime as a whole.

Where the problems of latent crime are studied, the results of Wallenstein's probe are mentioned in almost every publication. This study, which was published in 1947, used a questionnaire concerning 49 different criminal offences, including homicide. The questionnaire was answered by 1020 men and 678 women with a clean record.

[5] Z. Borsi and K. Halász, *A bűnözés megismerésének statisztikai módszerei* (The Statistical Methods of Studying Crime), Budapest: Közgazdasági és Jogi Könyvkiadó, 1972, pp. 52–53.

91 per cent of the interviewed persons stated that they had committed one or more of the named offences. In the case of men 18, in the case of women 11, different criminal offences had been committed by 77 men and by 74 women, and bodily injury had been caused by 49 men and 34 women.[6] Similarly remarkable data, although of a different character, were published by Dr. Wehner in the Federal Republic of Germany in 1957.[7] He drew up charts where he supplied the number of discovered criminal offences and the estimated data concerning the latent cases of the same offence in minimum and maximum values. According to the tabulations, the number of known homicide cases (including murder and infanticide) was 1029 in 1956, while the number of undiscovered homicide cases was minimum 3087, i.e. three times as many as the number of known cases, and maximum 6174, i.e. six times as many as the known number. In other words, the number of homicide cases (known and unknown together) was minimum 4116 and maximum 7203; the mean counted from the two extremes was 5659. In the case of abortions, the minimum number of the undiscovered cases was one hundred times as many and the maximum five hundred times as many as the number of the known cases. To summarize: the actual number of the committed offences is minimum twice and maximum four and a half times as many as the number of the known cases. Thus, the number of the registered criminal offences in the FRG in 1956 was 1 630 675, while the number of latent offences was minimum 3 602 398 and maximum 10 748 737. Therefore the actual number of criminal offences was not less than 5 233 073; the mean, as the most probable value, was 8 806 241, as compared to the 1 630 675 known cases.

Accepting these estimations as realistic, certain authors conclude that it is not correct to classify people as criminals and non-criminals, it is much closer to reality if people are categorized as convicted and non-convicted persons. Fritz Sack, for example, made the following statement concerning the dimensions of the criminal population: "About 80–90 per cent of the members of a society commit some act punishable under the law at least once in their life. At the same time only a very small part of these acts is ever ground by the millstones of sanctions."[8] A similarly high ratio of latent crime is reported by Inkeri Antilla on the basis of studies conducted in the Scandinavian countries.[9]

Eysenck's opinion concerning the distribution of crime is also worth mentioning. According to him:

"Criminality is obviously a continuous trait of the same kind as intelligence, or height, or weight. We may artificially say that every person either is or is not a

[6] M. Lopez-Rey, *Crime: An Analytical Appraisal,* London: Routledge and Kegan Paul, 1970, p. 15.

[7] Lopez-Rey, *op. cit.,* p. 10.

[8] F. Sack, "Neue Perspektiven in der Kriminologie", in: F. Sack and R. König, *Kriminalsoziologie,* Frankfurt am Main: Akademische Verlagsgesellschaft, 1968, p. 463.

[9] I. Antilla, *Unrecorded Criminality in Finland,* Kriminologinen Tutkimoslaitos, Helsinki, 1966.

criminal, but this would be so grossly oversimplified as to be untrue. Criminals vary among themselves, from those who fall once and never again, to those who spend most of their lives in prison. Clearly the latter have far more "criminality" in their make-up than the former. Similarly, people who are not convicted of crimes may also differ widely in respect to moral character. Some may in fact have committed crimes for which they were never caught or, if they were caught, perhaps the court took a rather lenient view. Others have never given way to temptation at all. From a rational point of view, therefore, we cannot regard criminals as being completely distinct from the rest of the population. They simply represent the extreme end of a continuous distribution..."[10]

The problem of latent crime also occupies the interest of the criminologists and criminal-statisticians of the socialist countries. The differences between the organization, social structure and equally the system of registering property and citizens of the socialist and capitalist countries, make the assumption probable that in the socialist countries not only discovered but also latent crime has lower rates than in capitalist countries. Only a few numerical, even if estimated, data are available concerning latent criminality in Hungary. As far as I know, only one, never completed, attempt was made to estimate the number of criminal offences committed by people not convicted for them, and this attempt, precisely because it was not completed, shows merely that latent crime exists in Hungary, and that its volume is not less than that of discovered crime, though its significance is much less, since it consists mainly of criminal offences of lesser gravity, prosecuted mostly on private complaint.

The remarks on latent crime are aimed only at forming a correct view of crime. Disregarding the numerical data provided by the various estimations and considering only the fact that a significant volume of crime exists apart from statistically registered crime, we may conclude that the dividing line between criminals and non-criminals, between convicted and non-convicted persons, is not as sharp as it appears when various operations are performed with the data of criminal statistics. Although it is only the discovered criminal offences and their perpetrators that can be studied, we have to keep in mind that this is only a part of the social mass phenomenon that we want to know, the causes of which we study and that we want to decrease and even to eliminate in certain spheres. Latent crime is fully latent only from the point of view of the agencies of crime control and administration of justice, or, more precisely, of criminalistics. People learn about a smaller or greater proportion of this part of crime and it seems to certain people that it is precisely the unscrupulous elements, the real exploiters of society, who are never brought before a court, while, on the other hand, it is frequently people merely gone astray and opposing social requirements stupidly who are convicted.

To avoid any misunderstanding, we emphasize that our intention is not to acquit latent offenders by this chain of thought. We deem it necessary and indispensable to

[10] H. J. Eysenck, *Crime and Personality,* London: Routledge and Kegan Paul, 1964. p. 74.

establish the responsibility of such persons. We demand the intensification of the activity aimed at the discovery of criminal offences so that no criminal offences and offenders should remain undiscovered. But, at the same time, we endorse the idea that it should be kept in mind when justice is administered that there are convicted and not convicted perpetrators as well. And it is particularly important to consider this when first offenders, persons who committed lesser offences for the first time, are to be judged.

In addition to the relation between known and latent crime and its evaluation, the definition of the sphere of known crime is a source of a number of problems which cause much debate, and taking a position in this debate influences the view of causality to a certain extent.

It is a generally accepted view among socialist criminologists that the subject matter of criminological studies is known crime. Crime includes only the acts (and their perpetrators) representing a danger to society that the law orders to be punished, or more precisely, to be punished with a criminal punishment. This view expresses a closed logical system, for if criminology equals a discipline concerned with crime and if crime equals the total of criminal offences and their perpetrators, then the subject-matter of criminology cannot be anything else but crime in a legal sense, i.e. types of human behaviour declared to be criminal offences.

There is, however, another view, which interprets crime in a broader sense and allows the concept of crime to embrace the acts representing a danger to society that are prosecuted under the law of administration and not under penal law. Since this problem is closely related to the concept of criminal offence, it will be discussed under that title.

2 The Criminological Concept of Criminal Offence

The concept of crime as a statistical mass is preconditioned by the exact definition of the concept of the units, valid for every unit and, consequently, it necessarily means the material definition of the total of the units. The material definition of the concept of crime is possible only through the definition of the concept of criminal offence and perpetrator.

The concept of criminal offence, as it is defined by penal law, is sharply criticized by certain western criminologists who regard it unsuitable for the aims of criminological studies and therefore try to formulate a so-called criminological concept of criminal offence. This trend is not a new one. During the history of the development of criminology it has frequently been demanded that a concept of criminal offence should be formulated which would embrace all kinds of antisocial behaviour independent of their evaluation under penal law, precisely for their antisocial nature, in the notion of "natural crime".[11]

[11] G. E. Gomez, *Introduction a la Criminologia,* Caracas, 1964.

Nowadays broadening the concept of criminal offence, or more correctly, the concept of crime, to embrace the full scale of "natural crime", or using the term of modern sociology, the aggregate of deviant behaviour, is a clear tendency.[12]

In the Hungarian literature one can find opinions which do not approve of "the creation of such a concept" but find it possible to formulate a criminological concept of criminal offence in the future which would be different from the legal concept, would be broader than that and would serve the aims of prevention and not that of the administration of justice.[13]

László Viski definitely opposes the criminological notion of crime and is for the legal concept. "It is criminal offences as defined by penal law that have to be the subject matter of criminology as an independent discipline, under any circumstances, at least as long as it is not proven that types of behaviour regarded legally as criminal offences and non-criminal but 'related antisocial acts' have some kind of common traits existing in reality and not only in the evaluation of the behaviour, and these traits can be demonstrated with a scientific exactness. And this, in our opinion, is not going to happen. What is studied by criminology beyond criminal offences is not studied as its own subject matter, it is studied to understand its own subject matter better, and criminology is not in fact limited in defining the scope of such studies."[14] In forming my own opinion I have started from objective reality, namely that society necessarily defends itself against all phenomena dangerous or harmful to it. If this harmful phenomenon is the consequence of natural forces (e.g. flood, lightning), society attempts to avert or prevent the danger by studying the causes and laws of the phenomenon and by using the proper means (construction, safety measures, etc). If the harmful phenomenon is a human act or its consequence, society cannot do anything else but explore the laws and causes of such acts in order to prevent them.

Nowadays clear statutes and moral norms define the kinds of behaviour that are harmful and represent a danger to society. Society takes various measures against people displaying such behaviour. The basis of the differentiated measures are the characteristic differences in the extent of the damage or injury caused by the act, on the one hand, and in the differences manifest in the perpetrators' personalities, on the other. A different measure is taken against the perpetrator of an act representing a minor danger to society and against the perpetrator of act causing grave harm.

On the basis of the present general knowledge and Weltanschauung, society holds that against the perpetrators of acts representing a grave danger to society, it is only

[12] Th. Sellin, "A Sociological Approach to the Study of Crime Causation" in: M. Wolfgang, L. Savitz and N. Johnston, *The Sociology of Crime and Delinquency,* New York—London: John Wiley & Sons, 1962.

[13] J. Molnár, *Galeribűnözés* (Juvenile Gang-Crime), Budapest: Közgazdasági és Jogi Könyvkiadó, 1971, pp. 74–75.

[14] L. Viski, *Közlekedési Büntetőjog* (Traffic Criminal Law), (Ph. D. Thesis), Budapest, 1972, pp. 654–655.

by special penal measures involving a significant legal detriment that the interest of society and citizens can be effectively protected. Therefore these types of behaviour are declared to be criminal offences and ordered to be punished with proper penalties. Thus, there are certain acts representing a danger to society, namely the gravest ones, which are declared by society to be criminal behaviour and their perpetrators are proceeded against accordingly.

From this train of thought it follows that the concept of crime may logically not be extended beyond the sphere of "crime in a legal sense"; in other words, my position is the same as Viski's. If the notion of crime were extended to embrace other forms of behaviour representing a danger to society, crime would lose its criminal nature. It is beyond doubt, however, that as a consequence of the development of criminology and other disciplines dealing with human behaviour, it is more and more evident that criminal offences and other acts dangerous to society and the establishment of responsibility for them form a far less closed system than was thought even in the first half of this century. Particularly in the socialist countries prosecution for criminal offences may take place in the form of administrative law or even socially. And, the other way round, for a non-criminal act the legal detriment may be graver than one applied for a criminal offence (e.g. the amounts of fines imposed in administrative proceedings for infractions and fines as criminal penalties.) In spite of all this, for the time being and in the foreseeable future, we have to regard the sphere of human behaviour declared, or possible to be declared, criminal, as a unit.

The issues of the subject-matter of criminology and the scope of criminological studies are closely related to the above. Many scientists are of the opinion that the scope of criminological studies may not exceed the limits of crime, and perhaps this is why they attempt to extend the notion of crime or to dissolve it in the concept of deviant behaviour. It follows from the essence of criminology that it does not study crime alone but together with its origin related to human personality and society and in its determination. Thus, e.g. during the examination of causality, the perpetrators' state of consciousness, social relations, and perhaps biological traits, have to be studied.

Similarly, if we presume that decreasing the number of administrative infractions serves the aim of preventing crime, administrative infractions may be the topic of criminological studies in order to create the proper foundations necessary for the various proposals of preventive measures.

The extension of the scope of criminological studies is justified from the point of view of causality primarily by the fact that the perpetration of criminal offences, i.e. acts involving an intensive danger to society, is frequently preceded by less antisocial forms of behaviour. It is precisely these behavioural forms that are the most certain symptoms of the process of turning into a criminal. On this level the system of subjective causes, i.e. motivation, has a very different structure than in the case of "real" or habitual offenders. It would be, however, an error to conclude that a theft involving a value of 900 forints (nowadays about $ 25) can be traced back to different causes than in the case of a theft involving 1100 forints, merely because under Hungarian law the first is only an administrative infraction and the second is a criminal offence. The difference cannot be seen clearly unless antisocial human acts are studied in large numbers or in their totality.

Thus, there are socially dangerous but non-criminal acts that do not differ from criminal offences in their character and it is only differences in evaluation, in appearance and form, depending frequently on chance, that make the dividing line between criminal and non-criminal conduct. Such may be e.g. the forms of administrative infraction or the criminal offence of minor significance in the case of theft where the distinction depends merely on the monetary value involved, or the forms of administrative infraction and criminal offence of hooliganism, prostitution or avoidance of work. This difference may not always apply since there are criminal offences (e.g. a theft involving 1200 forints and one causing particularly grave damage) which differ from each other in terms of dangerousness to society to a much greater extent than certain criminal offences from administrative infractions (e.g. a theft involving 1200 forints and one involving 900 forints). There are acts dangerous to society which are of minor gravity and which constitute criminal offences only because of the perpetrators' behaviour in the past (recidivism)—in other circumstances these acts would constitute only administrative infractions.

The differences in the degree of the acts' dangerousness to society do not necessarily represent a real difference, particularly because the value limit defining the qualification of the acts as a criminal offence is frequently changed. Let us suppose, however, that satisfying needs through the violations of norms, which is the common trait of the groups of acts, is not a characteristic of existence, and it is not a characteristic of evaluation; we are still dealing with a homogeneous mass which may be included in one unit examinable within the scope of one discipline. This discipline, however, would no longer be criminology and it would not be a criminal science. So that a discipline dealing with all types of antisocial behaviour with the same intensity could be created, the number of acts representing a serious danger to society, i.e. the number of acts called criminal offences at present, should decrease significantly and at the same time penal law should also be transformed profoundly, a significant part of it should be "degraded" to the system of liability under administrative law. I agree with József Molnár but should emphasize that criminology alone cannot follow this path, it can do it only together with other disciplines concerned with crime.

It is, however, a fact that criminology, by its nature, is able to adapt to the permanent change of reality better than penal law. Theoretically, criminology is able to realize the changes occurring among acts dangerous to society or related to them, almost as soon as the changes occur, while to change the norms of penal law is practical only after certain periods of time. Precisely for this reason, it may be one of the basic tasks of criminology to study the changes occurring in the objective sphere of society and in the thinking of people from the point of view of crime, and to recognize the future trends manifested in the changes. Based on this, proposals can be made to narrow or broaden the domain of criminal offences, to change the treatment of convicts, to make preventive measures more effective in general. Apart from all this, we emphasize, however, that as long as criminal law and criminal punishment are significant means of forming social coexistence, criminology has to be bound to criminal acts.

Of course, these bounds do not exclude that criminology should study certain types of behaviour endangering society in an integrated way (e.g. the administrative infraction and criminal offence forms of hooliganism together) and give a definition of these forms of conduct, perhaps differing from the concept of criminal offence, which reflects better their social content. Such a definition may serve as a guide-line to the modification of the definition of criminal offence and for creating a more effective way of prosecution. It is through such and similar studies that criminology explores the interrelations that make it possible for penal law and the measures taken to prevent crime to be better adapted to the nature of social development and to the nature of human conduct harmful to society and deserving punishment.

Taking such a position means from the point of view of causality that etiology has to study primarily the circumstances that elicit the acts qualifying as criminal and as antisocial behaviour of lesser significance. We have to admit that the causes of the two types of antisocial behaviour are frequently the same. In most cases, however, there are considerable differences between the two types as far as the subjective and objective causes are concerned since a significant part of the perpetrated criminal offences have no less antisocial antecedents. Consequently, the socialization or resocialization of persons having a different level of antisocial tendencies requires different measures. In terms of the mechanism of causality, there is, of course, no difference between the two groups, but in this respect there is no difference between the causative mechanism of socially useful and harmful acts either.

We expect that education, instruction and everyday social influences will make people law-abiding citizens. But against persons (or, to be more precise, in their own and society's interest) in whose case these influences (or the lack of such influences) elicit antisocial, criminal behaviour, measures are needed. By exploring the causes and conditions of such behaviour, criminology creates a possibility for limiting criminogeneous social relations on the one hand, and, precisely from the knowledge of the causes, for taking proper penal measures on the other. Consequently, if we take the position that criminology has to be connected with "crime in the sense of criminal law then criminology has to accept the concept of crime as formulated by criminal law" (it does not necessarily have to approve of that, it may put forward proposals to modify the concept).

3 The Concept of Criminal Offence in Penal Law

Since the principles of *nullum crimen sine lege* and *nulla poena sine lege* came into use penal codes have defined the concept of criminal offences as an act ordered to be punished by law. Socialist penal codes make this definition reflecting an omnipotence of law more realistic and more objective by using the concept of dangerousness to society, i.e. a criminal offence is an act which is dangerous to society and is ordered by the law to be punished. Usually within the same article, the perpetrator is also mentioned, as far as a criminal offence may be committed intentionally or (if the perpetration of the act by negligence is punished by the law) negligently.

Similar definitions of the notion of criminal offence are criticized nowadays even by those cultivating the dogmatics of law. Since it is not my intention to deal with the dogmatic problems of the concept of criminal offence, I only refer to Géza Tokaji's study published a few years ago, which discusses the topic on the basis of a comprehensive analysis, as a most typical work striving to formulate a concept of criminal offence by employing more criteria related to the personality, having the aim of serving the ends of the administration of justice but going beyond the other existing formulations. Tokaji starts his study with the paragraph: "In our opinion, when defining a concept related to our topic, we have to strive to formulate a concept of criminal offence (in harmony with the general principles of legal liability) materially able to integrate all the scholarly achievements concerning crime and crime control both at the present time and in the foreseeable future that renders it possible for socialist penal law to fulfill its humanistic tasks toward society as a whole and, at the same time, toward individuals not prevented from turning into criminals. We intend to give a definition according to which: a criminal offence is a) an act, which is b) objectively dangerous to society c) subjectively blameworthy and which—on the basis of deserving punishment due to all this—is ordered by the law to be punished."[15]

It is clear from Tokaji's opinion that he does not deem it necessary to create a separate criminological notion of the criminal offence instead of the criminal law concept appearing incomplete, but he wishes to integrate the results of criminological studies into the legal concept. We agree with this intent and strongly approve of it. Also, we approve of the demand manifest in the theses of Tokaji's dissertation, that the development of criminology and that of the theory of penal law have to converge, the dogmatics of penal law has to make use of the results of criminological studies, and, in turn, criminology has to take into consideration the constructions of dogmatics.[16] This necessary convergence and mutual dependence

[15] G. Tokaji, "Adalékok a bűncselekmény-fogalom felépítéséhez" (Contributions to the Formulation of the Concept of Criminal Offence), Acta Universitatis Szegediensis de Attila József Nominatae, *Acta Juridica et Politica,* Tomus XIX, 1972, p. 3.

[16] G. Tokaji, *Adalékok a bűncselekmény-fogalom felépítéséhez* (Contributions to the Formulation of the Concept of Criminal Offence), (Ph. D. Thesis), Szeged, 1972, pp. 18–19.

may not exclude, of course, that criminology should complete the concept of particular criminal offences or their group for the purposes of causality or prevention, with criteria not serving directly the aims of the administration of justice and are thus not necessarily included in the concept of the criminal offence. These criteria, however, may not be formulated instead of legal ones but only together with them, in addition to them. We have already attempted to create such a concept in outlining the causative pattern of intentional criminal offences[17] or in giving the conceptual definition of criminal offences of violence.[18]

The fact that we approve of criminology concentrating on "crime in a legal sense", of criminology being related to criminal acts, does not necessarily mean that it has to operate with the present concept of criminal offence, since the legal concept includes only acts violating a penal norm that are dangerous to society on the objective side, and blameworthy on the subjective side, in other words, where no circumstance excluding punishability exists.

These traits of the subject, however, may be established only in the case of detected offenders, in other words, in the case of acts violating discovered penal norms.

In the case of unknown perpetrators or undiscovered violations of norms it is impossible to establish which has been committed by persons not punishable on the grounds of one or other cause excluding punishability. It follows that this group of violations of penal norms may not be declared to be criminal offences completely.

In principle, of course, it would be possible to take the position that criminology should study only the acts that are qualified by penal law as criminal offences. This would however be contrary to the approach of criminology and everyday practice. Criminology has always regarded offences committed by children as belonging to the domain of crime, although the violation of a penal norm by a person less than fourteen years old does not constitute a criminal offence under Hungarian penal law. Taking a different approach, the approach of criminal policy or criminal statistics, we regard acts violating penal norms whose perpetrators are unknown as criminal offences and perhaps even the thought does not occur to anyone that a part of the criminal offences counted in this way might not be criminal offences at all in the sense of penal law. In practice we identify the concept of criminal offence with the concept of conduct violating a penal norm. One of the most significant steps taken by criminal statistics is precisely that it measures crime from the aspect of act in the first approach by the number of the discovered criminal offences. It is a choice for criminology that it either interprets the concept of crime in the legal sense, restricting it to acts that qualify as criminal offences under penal law and to their perpetrators or, following the present practice, it concentrates on discovered

[17] J. Vigh, *op. cit.*, see note 4.

[18] J. Vigh, K. Gönczöl, Gy. Kiss and Á. Szabó, *Az erőszakos bűncselekmények és elkövetőik* (Violent Crimes) Budapest: Közgazdasági és Jogi Könyvkiadó, 1973.

criminal offences and their known perpetrators, independent of the establishment of responsibility or the various forms of establishing responsibility.

My opinion is that it is better if criminology studies criminal acts and their perpetrators in the widest range and the causes excluding punishability, liability, and the ways of establishing responsibility serve only as the basis for the classification of the acts and their perpetrators. I could hardly imagine that we should refrain from qualifying an undefinable part of acts of unknown perpetrators violating penal law or that we should give up the criminological category of childcrime. And we could go on enumerating the cases that are excluded by the criminal law concept of offence from among the violations of penal law declared by criminology, criminalistics and public opinion as criminal offences.

The most important argument for the above opinion is, however, the intensive satisfaction of the requirement of prevention. From the point of view of society, it is not the method of establishing responsibility but the prevention of acts violating penal norms and dangerous and harmful to society that is the most important. And criminal liability is only one, even if extremely important, of the means of preventive measures.

II On the Justification of Criminal Etiology

Even if it seems strange, the issue is a current one because there are some criminal jurists and criminologists nowadays who question or deny the justification for studying the causes of criminal human behaviour. This sceptical or negative attitude is manifest first of all on the part of certain experts of capitalist countries but the evaluation of the problem is controversial in the works of socialist experts as well. For this reason, it is necessary to comment briefly on this issue.

At the end of the last century, when criminology became an independent discipline, it was able to gain its independence precisely because it started studying new aspects of crime and criminal human behaviour, the causal relations, the causes of the emergence and existence of crime and on the basis of all this, the possibilities of prevention. According to the general opinion, etiology is still a basic sphere of criminology, criminology is still striving to find an answer to the question why Mr. Jones committed a criminal offence or rather, why Joneses commit criminal offences at all, i.e. why crime exists and why it changes its ways as it does, and, starting from that, how it can be changed in such a way that it would represent a slighter danger to society both in its volume and structure.

1 Bourgeois Criminological Views Concerning the Futility of Etiology

Let us see the starting point of those denying or questioning the existence of causality. Robert MacIver, for example, writes in one of his studies:

"It is in vain to seek the cause of crime as such, of crime anywhere and everywhere. Crime is a legal category. The only thing that is alike in all crimes is that they are alike violations of law. In that only cause of crime as such is the law itself. What is a crime in one country is no crime in another; what is a crime at one time is no crime at another..."

Then he goes on:

"It has no inherent quality or property attaching to it as such, attaching to crime of all categories under all conditions. If indeed we do raise the question: Why crime? We are asking merely why people are so constituted that they violate laws under any conditions whatever. The question has no more specific significance than the question: Why human nature?"[1]

It is really an absurdity to speak of causality where it is penal law itself that is named as the single cause of criminal offences. If we accepted this "interrelation" as a fact, crime would be very simple to liquidate. It could be done by a single act of legislation. Only penal statutes should be revoked and no criminal offence would occur anymore. Or simply the machinery of the administration of justice should be stopped. This upside down attitude cannot be explained by anything else but that the person promoting this view sees only a violation of law in the formal sense, in a criminal offence. The real content of the criminal offence, i.e. the dangerousness to society, is restricted to the background or cannot even be perceived. In my opinion, if the original function of criminology is to be maintained, it has always to be kept in mind that criminal offences (forms of behaviour dangerous to society to a high degree) do not exist because the law declares an act to be a criminal offence, but because the state classifies certain forms of human behaviour as acts to be prosecuted in a particular way, in other words, to be criminal offences, because they represent a danger to society and the assumption is that the most effective way to fight them is the use of the special means of penal law. We have to look for causality between criminal offences and the phenomena that initiate and make possible the occurrence of forms of behaviour which are dangerous to society and are punished by penal law.

From the second part of the quotation it is evident that, according to the author, the causes of criminal offences are to be found in human nature. This criminological conception of causality, which is very far from the sociological aspect, is regarded as obsolete not only by socialist criminologists but also by the majority of bourgeois criminologists.

As a matter of fact the author takes the position of denying causality because of the legal concept of criminal offence which changes in time and geographical area. Other bourgeois criminologists also hold that the legal concept of criminal offence is useless in criminology. According to Thorsten Sellin, the acceptance of the legal notions of criminal offence and offender makes criminological studies superfluous, and criminology has to free itself of the fetters forged by criminal law. According to this author the criminal and non-criminal acts cannot on causal grounds be segregated from one another with any accuracy, the result, i.e. the criminal act, being void of any precise notion.

Sellin doubts that causality has a nature of law not only for this reason but also in general. According to him, science has already given up the concept of cause. Where

[1] R. MacIver, "Social Causation" in: M. Wolfgang, L. Savitz and N. Johnston, *The Sociology of Crime and Delinquency,* New York—London: John Wiley & Sons, 1962, p. 73.

it can be employed at all is the field of functional relations between elements and facts.[2]

I believe it is enough to quote Manuel Lopez-Rey to illustrate the negation of causality. He writes in a work of his, published several years ago, which, besides, contains excellent empirical data:

"As a rule crime is still regarded as a causal entity the causes of which will eventually be persistent criminological research and eventually suppressed or considerably reduced. My contention is that crime is a conceptual and not a causal or natural entity, i.e. it is what, at a historical juncture, is defined as such by the legitimate order in accordance with a changeable but always fundamental system of values and the structure and aims of a given society... As a conceptual entity the meaning and extent of crime changes more in accordance with the evolution of fundamental values and socio-economic, as well as political aims than as a result of the discovery of its 'causes'... Contemporary criminology tries unsuccessfully to avoid this conceptual character of crime by using such vague concepts as deviant or deviance or by styling itself a meta-science entitled to coin its own definition of crime."[3]

It may be seen clearly from the presented views that in the case of certain bourgeois criminologists, the negation of the causality of criminal human behaviour is a consequence primarily of the legal, "theoretical construction" nature of the legal concept of criminal offence. The fact that the concept of criminal offence and the domain of phenomena declared to be criminal change frequently in both time and space, creates the impression among criminologists that they are not dealing with a natural phenomenon of causality but with one which is dependent on the legislation of the given period, i.e. it is the consequence, the "effect" of legislation. The representatives of this idea are right in the sense that the notion of criminal offence, even the notion of crime, has a legal character and has socio-political content. This, however, does not exclude that criminal offences and crime are real and existing, nor does it question that the violation of the requirements of a society in a given period also belongs to the system of universal causality, in other words, that behaviour violating penal norms also has its causes and conditions. In my opinion it has never been and should not be the task of criminology to find the causes of crime independent of penal law. The task of criminology, for example, is not to study the causes of bodily injuries inflicted upon persons by others but only the causes and conditions of inflicting bodily injuries on persons in a manner violating penal law

[2] Th. Sellin, "Sociological Approach to the Study of Crime Causation" in: M. Wolfgang, L. Savitz and N. Johnston, *op. cit.*, p. 5. On bourgeois theories concerning the causality of crime see: G. Raskó, "A szociológia és a kriminológia" (Sociology and Criminology), *Kriminológiai és Kriminalisztikai Tanulmányok,* 10 (1973).

[3] M. Lopez-Rey, "Crime and the Penal System", *Australian and New Zealand Journal of Criminology,* March (1971).

and representing a danger or harm to society. It is in this way that the activity of the operating surgeon may be separated from the behaviour of the rowdy person causing bodily injury. Or let us take another example: causing certain minor damage to social property in order to prevent significant damage. In this behaviour the protection of property is manifested as contrasted with the activity of damaging it.

The question that has to be answered by criminal etiological studies first of all is, why a group of people (the group of offenders) violate penal norms in one way or other, why they do not adapt to social requirements. It would be the denial of reality if we stated that the violations of requirements manifested in penal norms have no cause, they are causeless forms of human behaviour. Such a view is contrary to the materialist conception of determinism, and it is precisely this conception, in my opinion, that has to be the basis of socialist criminology.

2 The Role and Interpretation of Etiology in Socialist Criminology

Causality and the importance of its study is generally admitted in the criminological literature of the socialist countries. Causal relations are regarded as an objective category, relations that exist independent of our consciousness among both natural and social phenomena and thus, between criminal human behaviour and objective phenomena determining it.[4] Debate and difference of opinion among socialist authors exist primarily in the interpretation of causality. There are authors who recognize only the dynamic form of causality and deem superfluous the "introduction" of the concept of statistical, stochastic relations in criminology.[5] Others believe the laws of a statistical nature to be dominant in the domain of crime.[6] Certain authors conclude that because of the material shortcomings of the doctrine of causality, it is advisable to set less ambitious aims than etiological studies: the task should be studying the process of turning into a criminal.[7] According to József Molnár, studying the process of becoming a criminal may be distinguished from etiological studies. "Criminal offences appear in any kind of etiological study not as abstractions of unlawful human behaviour but as specific human acts. After the perpetration of the offences, studies have to be directed

[4] M. Vermes, *The Fundamental Questions of Criminology*, Budapest: A. W. Sijthoff, Leiden— Akadémiai Kiadó, 1978; J. Vigh, "Kauzalitás a kriminológiában" (Causality in Criminology), *Jogtudományi Közlöny*, 11–12 (1959); L. Viski, *Road Traffic Offenders and Crime Policy*, Budapest: Akadémiai Kiadó, 1981.

[5] P. Simor, "Szocialista nézetek a bűnözés okairól" (Socialist Views on the Causes of Crime), *Kriminalisztikai Tanulmányok*, Vol. 7.

[6] V. N. Kudriavtsev, "Problemi pritshinnosti v kriminologii", *Voprosi Filosofii*, 10 (1971).

[7] See: J. Molnár, *Galeri bűnözés* (Juvenile Gang-Crime), Budapest: Közgazdasági és Jogi Könyvkiadó, 1971; A. Szabó, "A kriminológiai kutatások elvi kérdései" (The Theoretical Issues of Criminological Research), *Állam- és Jogtudomány*, 3 (1963).

precisely at the exploration of what the factors were in the presence of which the specific process of determination had taken place."[8]

Criminology definitely has to study the process of determination of a given criminal offence, but, in my opinion, criminology is destined for more than that. It should not be content with exploring and formulating individual causality but also has to examine what is common in the many individual specific causal relations, what is general and what is characteristic also of the whole, i.e. crime itself. It is in this way and only in this way that the laws of crime as a social mass phenomenon may be discovered, the laws which make the future movement of the units and the frequency of their occurrence probable to a smaller or greater extent. It is upon these laws that the prognosis of crime needed for planned prevention and effective prosecution of crime may be based. Thus, criminology should not be content with the individual approach dominating the administration of justice but beyond that, perhaps primarily, it has to approach crime as a mass phenomenon and has to study the law of crime as a whole. Another material problem of etiology is mentioned in László Viski's doctoral dissertation.[9] Viski attempts to outline an omnifactorial integrated field theory of crime, or a method. The adjective "omnifactorial" in his study means that all factors playing a role in the perpetration of criminal offences have to be taken into consideration. Integration has the basic meaning that in studying the criminal offence, a combined legal, sociological and psychological approach is applied. By the word field, the author refers to the fact that it is in different spheres of life that criminal offences are perpetrated.

These fundamental theses or requirements are right in general and reflect reality, in my opinion. As far as the details are concerned, however, the situation is different. In socialist criminology, or putting it more precisely, in Hungarian criminology, these ideas have been given expression even if not with the same content and under the same title, but simply without labels.[10] (It is quite possible that a lack of labelling is a mistake but it is not at all certain that Viski's labels are the best.) Viski's ideas about the relations of criminology and the integrated theory of crime demand attention and, in my opinion, a clearer and more precise formulation. However, within the scope of this study, we cannot discuss all the issues of Viski's study deserving approval or criticism, so we concentrate on the problems concerning causality. I quote the following: "Concerning the etiological approach, the integrated theory of crime has to regard the concepts of the criminal offence and the criminal as unacceptable abstractions in which the only common trait that can be generalized is the criminal unlawfulness of the displayed behaviour. As regards the particular types of behaviour, however, provided that typization is

[8] J. Molnár, *op. cit.* p. 115.

[9] See the relevant part: L. Viski, "Integrált bűnözéselmélet és közlekedési kriminológia" (Integrated Crime Theory and Traffic Criminology), *Jogtudományi Közlöny,* 9. (1973).

[10] See J. Földvári and J. Vigh, *Kriminológia* (Criminology), Budapest: Tankönyvkiadó, 1968, p. 46.

'systematic and realistic' it is imaginable that unchanging and uniform theories of causality may be formed, which also get rid of the absurdity of the wide eclecticism.+ It is therefore meaningless to explore in general the 'causes of criminality': "Criminality has no more causes than human behaviour in general. Or more exactly: the causes of criminality are identical with those of human behaviour".++ In addition: "The forcing of the phenomenon of criminality into the Procrustes' bed of cause and effect is a theoretical error: The exclusive application of the causal analysis includes the same logical error as the anthropocentric explanation of animal behaviour".+++"[11]

This quotation, which is composed of the words of others, is not clear, it is difficult to understand.

According to the last thought in the quotation, it is a mistake of principle to force the phenomenon of crime completely into the Procrustean bed of cause and effect. Indeed, it is not the only characteristic trait of crime that it fits into the system of universal causal relations (the same as all other phenomena), it has other material traits also, e.g. it has dynamics and structure. Therefore the observation is right. But, as far as the socialist literature is concerned, I have never read and have never heard that anyone identified knowledge concerning crime with etiological views. And as far as modern bourgeois criminological views are concerned, certain authors come to the conclusion (see Viski, op. cit. Note 12) that studies concerning the causes of crime should be prohibited because they identify the causal relations, the causative mechanism, "the" causality, with causality operating among the phenomena of mechanics and, therefore, they have every right to protest against attributing general validity to "cause and effect".

In the domain of human behaviour, and consequently in the domain of criminal human behaviour, other relations of causality can be found which are characterized not only by the relation of cause and effect but by integration. Thus, causal analysis has a different meaning. It would have been proper if Viski had referred to these facts in his article, as he correctly mentioned them in this dissertation where he did not allow the reader to conclude that the author agreed with the quotation in the part that is relevant here.

In the Hungarian literature of criminal law, however, doubts are expressed concerning the validity of causality in criminal human behaviour. I quote a part of Imre Békés' dissertation, as an example: "The question of whether an individual can be made *morally* responsible for the faults of his abilities (the faults of attention, foresight, etc.) or for the defects of his will, for the bad structure of his personality (in other words, human beings do not live their life but have their causal fate),

[11] L. Viski, *op. cit.*, p. 450. Notes to the quotation: +G. B. Vold, *Theoretical Criminology,* New York: Oxford University Press, 1958. p. 314. ++N. Morris and G. Hawkins, *The Honest Politicians' Guide to Crime Control,* Chicago—London: The University of Chicago Press, 1970, p. 47, pp. 50–53. According to these authors the exploration of the causes of criminality should be prohibited.

cannot be answered on the basis of evidence. In my opinion, as long as natural sciences cannot convince mankind (not legal scholars but the widest public) that thinking and psychological processes in general have a causal nature, as long as people attribute a moral value to their own and everybody else's behaviour, as long as the human illusion "I could have done something else" and the feeling of guilty conscience exist, lawyers have to recognize the individual's co-authorship in the formation of his own life, intellectual and emotional world, in the development of his character and in his actual behaviour."[12]

The fact that Békés confronts the life of the human being with his causal fate and that he does not see the existence of causality in criminal behaviour as provable by evidence, is due, in my opinion, to the wrong interpretation of causality, the identification of mechanical causality with causality in general. Without discussing the issue here in detail I only refer to the fact that the pattern of causality in conscious human behaviour, the mechanism of causality, is essentially different from the causal mechanism existing in mechanics or generally in nature. Among the subjective causes of acts (criminal offences included) performed by human beings, there are always end-causes, anticipated images of future behaviour suitable for satisfying needs. As Engels wrote: "In one point, however, the history of the development of society proves to be essentially different from that of nature. In nature—in so far as we ignore man's reaction upon nature—there are only blind, unconscious agencies acting upon one another, out of whose interplay the general law comes into operation. Nothing of all that happens—whether in the innumerable apparent accidents observable upon the surface, or in the ultimate results which confirm the regularity inherent in these accidents—as a consciously desired aim. In the history of society, on the contrary, the actors are all endowed with consciousness, are men acting with deliberation or passion, working towards definite goals; nothing happens without a conscious purpose, without an intended aim."[13] This is the new element in the principle whereby causality in social life differs from causality in nature. Consequently, from the point of view of the struggle against crime it is not the negation of causality, the "prohibition of etiological studies" but the correct interpretation of causality and the more and more exact exploration of causal factors that is needed.

The second point in Viski's quotation I want to comment on is that to study the causes of crime in general is meaningless, since the causes of crime are the same as the causes of human behaviour.

During the development of criminology, when the aim was putting the most general causes of crime in a formula, it was a rather frequently made mistake that the

[12] I. Békés, *A gondatlanság a büntetőjogban* (Negligence in Criminal Law), Budapest: Közgazdasági és Jogi Könyvkiadó, 1974, pp. 382–383.

[13] F. Engels, *Ludwig Feuerbach and the End of Classical German Philosophy,* Moscow: Progress Publishers, 1964, (Fourth printing), p. 48.

causes of crime were given a formula on the level of general human behaviour. Ferri, when he created his three-factor theory, i.e. when he traced back criminal offences to the effects of 1. anthropological factors, 2. social factors and 3. physical environment, formulated the causal factors of human behaviour in general. Similarly, Liszt's endogenous and exogenous factors are not causative factors specifically of crime but of all human behaviour. Keeping in mind the connection between crime and causative factors on this level, we can easily understand the observation that "crime has no more cause than human behaviour in general has", or more precisely, the causes of human behaviour are the causes of crime.

This linking is, however, logically incorrect, since the causes of human behaviour and the causes of crime should not be identified with each other for they are phenomena of different levels. Criminal behaviour forms only a part, a subgroup within human behaviour as a whole, and this is separated from other (non-criminal) forms of human behaviour through the use of the adjective "criminal", as a distinctive mark. Consequently, it is not the full range of phenomena (human behaviour as a whole) that is examined but only a group of it (criminal acts); we have to distinguish between the causes of the full range and the causes of its parts. In other words, it is also necessary here to distinguish groups according to certain criteria within general causes: biological, social and physical factors. This is a basic requirement of statistical grouping. All this means for criminology that it is not enough to trace the causes of crime back to the effects of biological, social and physical factors in general, but it also has to be stated what biological, what social and what physical factors may be regarded as causative factors. In this way it becomes clear that on the level of mass phenomenon, law-abiding behaviour expressing the interests of society generally has causes different from the causes of criminal behaviour disregarding others' interests.

It is, of course, true that in studying the causes of crime we cannot discover causes existing only in the case of offenders. In my opinion, however, it does not follow from this that studies concerning the causes of crime should be prohibited (this conclusion is inconsistent anyway), for such causal factors cannot be found in the case of types of offence either, although etiological studies and the development of theories of causality concerning them are possible, according to the quotation.

Nowadays it is a generally accepted view that criminal offences are caused by the combined effects of several factors (causes and conditions), by "omnifactors", and not by a single one. So the repeated occurrence of criminal offences is not the result of the repeated effect of a single cause but the result of the constellation of causative factors.[14] From all this, however, it does not follow that the elements (causative factors) of the constellation leading to the perpetration of the criminal offence never occur in a causative constellation resulting in non-criminal human behaviour. On the other hand, what does follow from this is, and this is verified by criminological

[14] The "constellation theory of causality" will be discussed in detail later on.

studies, that there are causative factors which are present in causative constellations leading to criminal offences more frequently than in constellations producing non-criminal human behaviour.

According to present criminological views, these causative factors, appearing not exclusively but with a significant frequency, that lead to the perpetration of criminal offences, are called criminogenic factors. And, unlike some bourgeois criminologists, we find sense in naming these factors, especially if we can also state what other factors accompany them, i.e. what constellations leading to criminal offences occur most frequently.

Against this argument it is, of course, easy to mention the one according to which the frequency of occurrence of the so-called criminogenic factors has not been proven by a complete survey. Indeed, I have never heard of a survey and most probably there has never been a survey which included the totality of offenders and, as a control-group, the totality of non-convicted persons. There are, however, data available concerning certain factors, such as the proportions of illiteracy, wrong attitudes toward work, within each group. No doubt, a complete survey in this strictest sense of the term could be interesting and more exact than any previous one. In my opinion, however, demanding such a survey would be unrealistic and perhaps it is not needed. The representative surveys involving control-groups conducted up to now[15] prove that the sample populations represent excellently (with only a few per cent difference) the full population. And the surveys prove that the causative factors of criminal and non-criminal human behaviour have a different structure and significantly different proportions.

From the opinion formulated above, my comment concerning the third point of the quotation follows logically. In my opinion, the notions of criminal offence and offender are not unacceptable abstractions even from the point of view of etiology, if the concept of crime is linked to space, time and a specific system of penal law. In this case it is precisely the exact definition of criminal offence and offender that makes it possible to count criminal offences and their perpetrators, in other words, to study crime as a social mass phenomenon. Certain bourgeois criminologists do not regard unlawfulness under criminal law as a criterion of all criminal offences, as compatible with etiology because in that case we should not have to study the causes of murder or theft, but the causes of violation of norms in general. According to them, in the field of crime, we can only find differences of evaluation between criminal and non-criminal behaviour. This is a fact. This social and legal evaluation, however, reflects objective realities and material differences even if the dividing line between criminal and non-criminal behaviour is artificial and the differences are not marked near this dividing line. It has always to be kept in mind that the types of

[15] See surveys conducted by the Hungarian National Institute of Criminology and Criminalistics concerning recidivists in the volumes of *Kriminalisztikai Tanulmányok:* or Sh. Glueck and E. Glueck, *Unravelling Juvenile Delinquency,* Cambridge, Mass.: Harvard University Press, 1950.

criminal human behaviour form a continuous line between the purely positive and negative poles, and condense toward the negative pole. It is precisely this continuity that requires the careful drawing of the dividing line, the precise definition of the concept of criminal offence and perpetrator.

From the point of view of causality, this chain of thought means that in etiological studies concerning crime as a whole the question really is why perpetrators violate the norms of penal law, why they do not comply with social requirements, what causative factors or causative constellations lead most frequently to the perpetration of criminal offences. When the internal structure, the types of criminal offences, are studied, the question, of course, is not only why the violation of a norm of penal law occurred but also why the given type of norm-violation occurred, and this is the primary question. But even on this level, on the level of the typical, one cannot find a causative factor or causative factors which could be found with all criminal offences falling within this range, with no exception. On the other hand, it is true that the significance is higher here as compared to non-criminals, than in the case of criminals in general. However, it is accepted in etiological studies on both levels that it is causative factors occurring with a high frequency that are considered as characteristic of the mass (the whole or the type). (It is not a requirement that such a factor should occur in every case without exception.) These significant causative factors or causal relations define the laws of crime and these laws are projected from the past onto the future, i.e. these laws form the basis of the preparation of prognoses and make it possible to work out the necessary (possible) preventive measures.

In my opinion, the "great, comprehensive" but usually monocausal theories appear in bourgeois criminology because certain parts of reality have to be described in an exact manner but, instead of accepting and making use of a materialistic conception necessary for synthesization or integration, for the formulation of the laws, the results of the partial studies of the scholars are generalized and the multi-sided causal relations may be obscured in this way. But we who cultivate socialist criminology may say openly and unambiguously that even in the range of criminal human behaviour, it is the law of universal causality that rules. Due to the differences of phenomena, causal relations may have different forms, but their existence cannot be denied. I believe that the Soviet philosopher I. S. Ladenko is right in observing that admitting the universal nature of causality presupposes the conception of determinism while denying it presupposes an indeterministic view. The latter is based on a faulty logical deduction.[16] Our methods of study may be good or less good, but they have to be built on the methods of dialectics. The value and usability of criminological theories of causality depend primarily on how exactly they can formulate the real laws of causality of crime, how well they can

[16] I. S. Ladenko, "Universalnost printsipa pritshinnosti i ee logitsheski analiz", *Sovremenny determinizm i nauka,* Novosibirsk: Izd. Nauka, 1975, Vol. 1. pp. 244–266.

demonstrate the mechanism of causative determination in the determination of criminal behaviour.

By introducing and evaluating these problems of causality selected at random, my intention has been merely to suggest that the issue of causality in criminology is a crucial one and is still a problem not explored adequately. The fact that some bourgeois criminologists, noted and respected scholars among them, deny the existence of causality or doubt the importance of studies concerning the causes of crime does not mean, of course, a crisis in the principle of causality. But it certainly means that we have to pay more attention to the study of this problem and to clarifying the concepts. The same is suggested by the fact that even socialist scholars who admit the existence of causality in criminal behaviour and who regard the exploration of the related problems as important have different opinions in the interpretation of the concepts which, I think is a consequence of a conceptual confusion and inaccuracy of concepts. We regard etiological studies as studies of reality, of actually existing interrelations in every sphere of natural and social phenomena and, therefore we deem necessary the examination of the causes of crime and the clarification of the issues of causality.

III The Causality of Criminal Offences and Crime

1 On the Concept of Causality

In philosophy, the concept of causality and its interpretation is a much discussed topic even nowadays. In the past few decades, it has particularly been among physicists, and concerning the laws and behaviour of elementary particles, that the views denying causality and dynamic laws have become stronger. According to Heisenberg, the main representative of the so-called Copenhagen interpretation of quantum-mechanics, in the world of elementary particles it is not objective effects but "observation that has the decisive role in the process, and reality is different depending on whether we observe it or not."[1] Although philosophers of a materialistic outlook[2] prove with facts the existence of objective causal relations independent of our mind, the subjectivist view on the relations of phenomena still has an influence on judging social phenomena, crime among them. Specialists who have a non-materialistic ideological conviction are frequently apt to mystify to a certain extent phenomena whose occurrence cannot be explained in an exact way on the level of our present knowledge or whose dynamics or changes cannot be adequately explained.

"Causality" has been given more than one meaning during the development of philosophy. The concept may denote a category which equals concrete causal relationships; it may denote a principle which includes the law of causation, namely that the same causes always produce the same or similar effects; and finally, it may denote a doctrine according to which everything has its cause and there is nothing without a cause and anything produced has been produced by necessity.[3]

All these conceptual interpretations are also used in criminology. It is a generally accepted view in socialist administration of justice that crime, as well as individual criminal offences, have their causes and these causes under the proper circumstances will produce criminal human behaviour. It is usually formulated in the literature of

[1] W. Heisenberg, *Válogatott tanulmányok* (Selected Studies), Budapest: Gondolat Kiadó, 1967, p. 96.

[2] I. V. Sachkhov, *A kvantummechanika materialista értelmezéséről* (On the Materialist Interpretation of Quantum Mechanics), Budapest: Gondolat Kiadó, 1961.

[3] M. Bunge, *Az okság* (Causality, the Place of the Causal Principles in Modern Science), (in Hungarian), Budapest: Gondolat Kiadó, 1967, pp. 23–24.

criminology that criminal human behaviour is determined by objective and subjective causes and conditions. The concepts of causality and determinateness are frequently mixed, although the two concepts are not identical. According to the generally accepted philosophical view: "In reality, the determinacy of objects and phenomena is richer than the determination of causality or law. Thus, we may speak, apart from causality and law, of interaction, the relation between the part and the whole, quality and quantity, internal and external contradictions as the particular forms of determinancy."[4] According to Bunge, "The principle of causality is a particular case of the principle of determinacy, it exists essentially when determination exists only in one way or in an unambiguous way, due to external conditions."[5]

When causality is mentioned in philosophy usually the form of mutual relationship is meant, where in the network of multi-sided relations certain phenomena qualify as effects while other qualify as their causes. The study of mutual relations is performed on the level of the individual, on the level of concrete phenomena, although in recent literature causal relations are discussed together with the probabilistic relations manifest in mass phenomena. Causality, however, is restricted primarily to genetic (creative) relations manifest among individual phenomena.[6]

Causal relations may perhaps be defined most simply as relations between the cause and effect. This interpretation is too narrow for criminological aims and it is usuallly not only the relation between cause and effect that is understood as a causal relation but also the conditions allowing the causes to exert their influence and the effects to occur. In other words, if the causes and conditions are called collectively causative factors, then the notion of causal relation used in criminology may be precisely described as the relation between the causative factors and the effect. Such an interpretation of the causal relation explains partly the identification of the notions of causality and determination with each other. However, the content of the two concepts is still different. Causal relations exist only in connection where certain phenomena are *in a direct relation* (action, interaction) as causes and conditions with the effect. On the other hand, determination as a process includes *all the previous causal relations,* chains of cause and effect, through which the studied effect has been produced, has been determined. In fact, causal relations may be interpreted as links in the chain of process of determination.

If we take the concept of determination from any source of Marxist literature, the central attribute is always causality and law.

[4] T. Földesi, "A jelenségek egyetemes összefüggése és hatása" (The Universal Interrelations of Phenomena and their Interactions), in: *A dialektikus materializmus* (Dialectic Materialism), University Textbook, Budapest: Tankönyvkiadó, 1972, p. 134.

[5] Bunge, *op. cit.,* p. 51.

[6] See: J. Fodor, *A determinizmus-koncepció fejlődése és kapcsolatai a kvantummechanikával* (Development of the Conception and its Connection with Quantum Mechanics), Budapest: Akadémiai Kiadó, 1972.

In the university textbook entitled *Dialectic Materialism,* for example, the following may be read: "If the universe is interpreted as a set of material phenomena moving and changing incessantly, and homogeneous also in its infinite multifaceted form it follows logically that the genesis, existence and change of phenomena are determined by causes, conditions and laws belonging to this realm, and there are no mystical things and phenomena which cannot be explained in principle."[7] That is, determination, the process of determination, occurs due to causes, conditions and laws. Or, let us take the dictionary: "determinism: 1. a doctrine of the necessary causal relationship of occurrences and phenomena."[8] A similar interpretation is expressed by the first sentences of the *Dictionary of Philosophy:* "determinism: a doctrine of the universal determinateness of natural, social and psychological phenomena. The idea that everything is born and dies following laws and due to defined causes, is ancient; it is linked to the first attempts at waking people to the consciousness of the interrelations of things."[9] "Thousands of years have passed since the idea of the 'links between everything', the idea of the 'interconnection of causes' was born. The comparison of the interpretations of these things during the history of human cogitation would result in a gnoseology with the power of absolute proof."[10] In my opinion, the system of ideas concerning causes and causality is a fundamental criterion of gnoseology even at the present time.

But it is not only in these "compressed" or simplified formulations that causality is taken as the "backbone" of determination but also in analytical works of philosophy discussing details. I refer only to the Soviet philosopher M. A. Parnyuk's view: according to him "determinism answers the questions why a thing came into existence, what created it and what defined its existence, why it changes and what becomes of it."[11] It is beyond doubt that in the process of the genesis of phenomena, causal relations have a decisive role or, as the author puts it, "causality is the central point of determinism."[12] Furthermore, the principle of determinism is equally valid for the occurrences of the past, the present and the future. The causal relation, since it exists between cause and effect, always presupposes a past time. For this reason, the principle of causality is also based on past, completed phenomena. (These problems will be discussed later on.)

As can be seen from this short comparison and from the mentioned conceptual definitions, causality and determination are not identical concepts; causality forms the central nucleus of the process of determination.

[7] Földesi, *op. cit.,* p. 121.

[8] *Magyar Értelmező Kéziszótár* (Dictionary of the Hungarian Language), Budapest: Akadémiai Kiadó, 1972.

[9] *Filozófiai Kislexikon* (Dictionary of Philosophy), Budapest: Kossuth Könyvkiadó, 1972, p. 60.

[10] V. I. Lenin, *Collected Works,* (Fifth Edition), Moscow, Vol. III, 29, pp. 336–337.

[11] M. A. Parniuk, "Kontseptsia determinizma v dialekticheskom materializme", *Sovremenniy determinizm i nauka,* Vol. 1, Novosibirsk, 1975, p. 9.

[12] Parniuk, *op. cit.,* pp. 17–18.

From the point of view of cognition, the study of causal relationships, and interconnected causal relations (links of a chain) has a fundamental importance for all disciplines, including criminology, since the cognition of causal relations means the cognition of the essential. Lenin recognized that "on the one hand, the cognition of matter must be deepened to the cognition of the essential, in order to find the causes of phenomena. On the other hand, the real cognition of causes means the deepening of cognition from the surface toward the essence."[13]

The cognition of the essence of the genesis of the causal relations in criminal offences leads us to the exploration of the laws ruling the sphere of causality. It is very important in criminology that, in addition to studying the causes of individual criminal offences, we should study the causal problems of crime as a social mass phenomenon.

The question arises in the form, what causal relation is manifested on the level of the individual crime and what on the level of crime as a mass phenomenon and what causal laws may be found in the movement and change of the two different phenomena.

The answer to the questions is not an easy one since the theory of causality of philosophy generalizes primarily on the basis of the interrelations and laws of the causal relations of physical phenomena. Its phraseology is taken basically from there. It is difficult to find works dealing with causality which study the sphere of human behaviour, and criminal human behaviour in particular.[14]

My study referred to in the footnote distinguishes between two forms of causality existing in the realm of crime, namely functional and stochastic causality. At present, it seems that the distinction is not adequate either from the point of view of the terms or materially. Even the modified approach presented here is only an attempt at the generalization of the causality of criminal offences and crime, or rather, at putting general philosophical theses into concrete form, and may need verification in problems of detail.

2 The Causality of Actual Criminal Offences (Individual Causality)

In the description of causal relations the starting point are usually empirical facts. In physics and particularly in mechanics, an effect is produced by one cause, by the so-called dominant cause. For this reason, in the view of mechanical philosophy, the essence of causal relations is an unambiguous connection within which a single cause, i.e. external factor, produces the effect, usually the change of place of the

[13] V. I. Lenin, *op. cit.*, pp. 142–143.

[14] V. N. Kudriavtsev, *Pritshinnost v kriminologii,* Moscow: Yuridicheskaya Literatura, 1968; J. Vigh, "Kauzalitás a kriminológiában" (Causality in Criminology), *Jogtudományi Közlöny,* 11–12 (1959).

thing, its dynamism, and in the case of repeated occurrence the same cause produces the same effect.

Different criminological studies, however, prove beyond doubt that criminal offences can be traced back to more than one causal factor, easy to recognize and separate; in other words, a criminal offence, as an effect, has more than one cause. On the basis of studies, it has become evident that these causes accompanied by the proper condition or conditions, produce the offence of necessity.

It may happen, of course, that one of the causes producing the criminal offence has such a dominant role that the others almost fade away as compared to it and it seems that the relation is that of one cause and effect. This, however, is indeed only an appearance, because there are always other factors, in addition to the dominant cause, which have a role in the generation of the offence, even if their intensity is smaller or minimal. It follows from these facts that in the causal relations of criminal offences a multitude of causes and conditions produce the effect.

The real relation, of course, is always richer than the causal relation examined and emphasized by us, since one or other cause appearing in our causal relation may have a role not only in the causation of one single effect but also in that of others, perhaps other criminal offences among them.

For criminology, however, only those effects represent an interest that qualify as criminal offences and only those causative factors are examined in criminology that produce criminal offences. Criminology does not deal with the effects either, or at least not in the sphere of causality, that are the effects, the consequences, of criminal offences.

The several (or many) causes and one effect, as a general scheme, however, involves in principle the relationship of one cause and one effect; this relationship becomes predominant or perhaps an exclusive one if other relations remain permanent or are fixed. In physics, this relation is well demonstrated by the rise of temperature influencing the pressure of gas naturally, if the volume is not changed, i.e. under the same conditions. The appearance of such relationships in human behaviour is extremely rare and even if they occur it is mostly a dominant relationship and not an exclusive one. According to Bunge "in many cases simple causality is indispensable, even valid approximately, but it is never true in the strictest sense."[15]

a) We have spoken of phenomena or factors producing criminal offences as *causes and conditions* so far. The definition of causes and conditions or, rather, their distinction, is a much discussed issue of criminology even today. Criminologists generally admit that the solution of this problem is not only of theoretical importance but is important also from the point of view of practice, for the prevention of crime requires the delimitation of causes and conditions. This is so because the requirements are not identical concerning the liquidation of the causes

[15] Bunge, *op. cit.*, p. 193.

and conditions in the struggle against crime. In our opinion, it is not primarily against the external objective conditions of the perpetration of criminal offences that measures are needed but against the factors forming the antisocial personality and eliciting criminal decision. For this reason, we attempt to draw the line more or less precisely between causes and conditions.

The latest edition of the *Dictionary of Philosophy* reflects the general view of philosophy concerning the issue. "Complete and specific causes are distinguished. The complete cause is the totality of all conditions in the presence of which the effect occurs by necessity. The specific cause is the totality of several conditions the presence of which (if a number of other conditions are already present in the given situation and make possible the operation of the cause) elicits the effects. The exploration of the complete cause is possible only in relatively simple cases; the task of scientific studies is usually the discovery of the specific causes of the given phenomenon. This is so because the specific cause unites in itself the elements of the complete cause that are the most essential in the given situation, while the remaining elements operate only as the conditions of the given specifics."[16] There are two arguable issues in the quotation. The first is the interpretation of causes and conditions, the second is the task of science in the study of causes, given such an interpretation of cause and condition.

As far as the first issue is concerned, this definition, in my opinion, may be accepted for criminological aims only with certain modifications.

The general view of philosophy is acceptable to the extent that it is right to divide the totality of factors eliciting the effect into two groups according to their functions in the process of determination, namely *cases* and *conditions*. This coincides with the widely accepted view in criminology according to which, among the factors producing a given criminal offence, there are causes which have elicited the criminal offence and there are conditions which have made it possible for the causes to exert their influence.[17] It is hardly possible, however, to agree with the opinion that it is the most important determining factors that belong to the group of causes while the less essential or insignificant factors fall into the group of conditions. There is no doubt that the functions of the causes and conditions are different, but this is, in my opinion, a difference in functions and not in importance, at least as far as concrete human behaviour is concerned. According to experience, favourable conditions may play an extremely important, even dominant, role in the perpetration of a certain criminal offence. Unfavourable conditions or the lack of conditions may prevent the criminal offence. Precisely for this reason, I regard the distinction by importance as unnecessary in criminology.

It is the classification of causative factors by their functions that expresses the

[16] *Filozófiai Kislexikon* (Dictionary of Philosophy), op. cit., pp. 261–262.

[17] J. Földvári and J. Vigh, *Kriminológia* (Criminology), Budapest: Tankönyvkiadó, 1968, p. 94.

difference that it is advisable to consider in the causality of criminal behaviour and in taking preventive measures.

In criminology, it is the concept of causative factors or circumstances that is used as the collective term for causes and conditions. In my opinion, these concepts are not contradictory to the categories of causality in philosophy, they are only terms accepted for certain realms of objective reality that may perhaps add to the stock of notions of causality in philosophy based on causality in physics.

The practice of the administration of justice proves that the factors producing the criminal offence may be separated from each other by the above functions. We feel it necessary to note that this separation is possible only in connection with the perpetration of a concrete criminal offence, for the same phenomenon or a phenomenon of the same type which serves in a criminal offence as a cause, may serve as a condition in other cases and vice versa. Let us take an example. If a member of a juvenile gang is incited by his fellow gang-members to engage in disorderly conduct, it is beyond doubt that the friends of the juvenile become the dominant cause of the offence. But if the same juvenile gang is used by a person not belonging to the group for the perpetration of a burglary planned by him a long time ago, the juvenile group qualifies as a condition of this person's criminal behaviour.

Such an interpretation of the causes and conditions can be found in the works of Soviet and Bulgarian criminologists[18] and also of Hungarian etiologists.[19]

The division of causative factors into causes and conditions in concrete cases is expedient because for the aims of special prevention different measures are needed where favourable conditions make it possible for otherwise minor causes to become dominant, and different ones again where the effects of intensive causes are considerably mitigated by unfavourable conditions, where perhaps under the influence of the intensive causes it was the perpetrator himself who created the conditions for the perpetration of the criminal offence. But the distinction between causes and conditions is needed also from the point of view of general prevention. It must be clear that the conditions for the perpetration of criminal offences cannot be eliminated and such aims should not be set. Preventive measures may be aimed at the elimination of only the most conspicuous conditions. It is impossible, for example to organize the protection of social property or public places so that no opportunity or condition for perpetrating a criminal offence could occur at all. It is rather in the sphere of causes we may put forward the demand theoretically that they should be eliminated to the greatest possible degree.

The second issue in the quotation are the tasks of scientific studies in the exploration of causes. We agree that causes and conditions in their manifold and complex

[18] D. Fidanov, "Sluchainiat prestupnik", *Izvestiya na Mezhduvedomstveniya Sovet za Kriminologicheski Issledovaniya 2,* Sofia, 1972.

[19] L. Kesztyüs and J. Sós, *A kórélettan tankönyve* (Textbook of Physiopathology), Budapest: Medicina Könyvkiadó, 1971.

relations can hardly be more than the exploration of the essential factors. In our interpretation, however, essential factors are not only those that play the role of causes but those that may also be found among conditions. Criminological studies have to extend their scope over both causes and conditions even if not with equal intensity. In the perpetration of casual or occasional criminal offences conditions have an extremely important role.[20]

b) *External and internal factors.* It is an essential element of the philosophical view of causality that genetic changes should be produced by external factors, in other words, a phenomenon displaying changes should be under the influence of the environment. Bunge, for example, speaking of the dominance of causality, emphasizes, almost as a precondition, "the overwhelming role of external factors" contrasted with internal ones.[21]

From the point of view of criminal offences and crime this could mean that causes should be found in the objective, external environment and one may speak about causal relations if these external factors exert a strong impact on the occurrence of the criminal offence. Here we face again a special problem. A criminal offence as an effect is a conscious human act, a human manifestation. The external influence affects a person as an aware and self-conscious being and it is through him that criminal behaviour is manifested. Marxist philosophers usually call attention to the fact *that in the evaluation of the causal relation, the phenomenon affected by the cause should not be left out of account.* "In reality, one should never consider the phenomenon affected by the cause as a separate thing because this phenomenon in some way also contributes to the result. This law is valid even in the case of the simplest examples of mechanics. The result, for example, will be quite different if we want to move an iron ball with a mass of half a kilogram or the same mass of liquid with the same energy. The real significance of the law is manifested, however, on the level of the higher order forms of movement where the phenomenon affected by the causes has an increasingly significant role. Among animals, one can observe that an animal responds to the same causes in different ways at different times (e.g. because it has formed a new conditional reflex, has acquired new experience) and, for this reason, it is far from possible to calculate the effect from the cause. It is even less possible in the case of a human being, where external causes are screened by the mind; a human being is not a passive object of the external effects but decides and acts consciously. For this reason, in causal relations, the intermediary link that may play different roles in the occurrence of the effect must always be taken into consideration."[22]

A similar experience and approach may be found in biology, e.g. in the field of physiopathology. The relation between pathogenic causes and illnesses caused by

[20] See Fidanov, *op. cit.*,

[21] Bunge, *op. cit.*, p. 423.

[22] Földesi, *op. cit.*, p. 134.

them is not always plain, not always mechanical. Even the strongest virus may not cause illness in certain people while others can be made ill by a weak virus.[23]

From the point of view of criminal offences, this principle means that the so-called external criminogenous factors or circumstances do not lead to the perpetration of criminal offences in the case of every person. In someone's criminal offence, not only external influences but also his personality and his state of mind have an important role. There are criminal offences which are the consequence not so much of external circumstances as of the perpetrator's personality status. It is frequently such facts that suggest the views according to which human acts, criminal behaviour included, have their own laws, are the consequences of "self-determination" or "free will". These facts, however, are not contradictory to the universal validity of causality. Only the mechanism, the chain of links through which causality takes effect, has to be explored. Taking into account the importance of the role played by the perpetrator's personality in the genesis of the criminal offence, the general scheme of causality may be drawn in the following way:

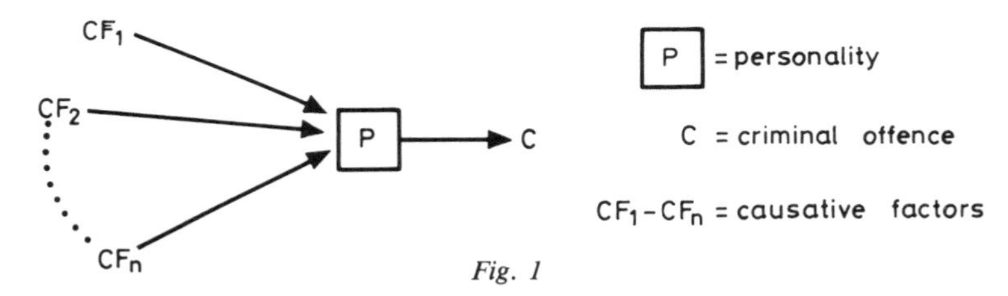

Fig. 1

The scheme reflects well the intermediary and transforming role of the perpetrator. It shows, however, at the same time, as is natural, that the criminal offence is related directly to the personality and the actual objective influences are reflected through, and adjusted to the personality.

Causality existing in human behaviour, criminal behaviour included, is not mechanical and it does not reflect a one-way effect but *an interaction is expressed by it.*

The scheme in this form demonstrates only the causal relation directly connected to the criminal offence. But if we want to express also the reality that the personality is the effect of some kind of influences, we have to modify it to a certain extent. This modification may be executed on the basis of the theory according to which the state of *personality is ultimately defined by material objective relations, the personality is the effect of influences that existed objectively.* In other words, it is the past objective relations of the individual that are subjectivized in the personality. In psychology, the state of the personality at a given time is called *actual personality.* This notion is becoming more and more generally used also in criminology. *The perpetration of a criminal offence is elicited partly by the actual personality reflecting past objective relations, partly by objective causal factors affecting the actual personality.* The complex of these actual causative factors is usually called the

[23] Kesztyüs and Sós, *op. cit.,* p. 42.

situation, the objective situation preceding the perpetration of the criminal offence. The determination of criminal offences by the objective relations on these two levels may be shown by the next scheme:

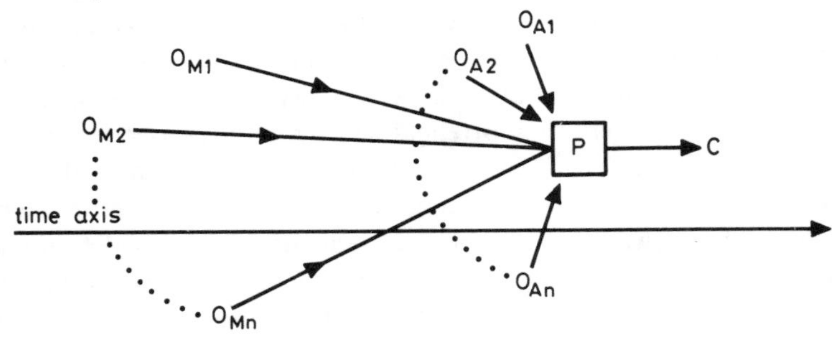

$O_{M1}-O_{Mn}$ = objective relations of the past, forming the personality

$O_{A1}-O_{An}$ = objective relations affecting the actual personality (situation)

Fig. 2

Our causal or determination scheme (not causal relation!), however, is not complete yet: the aspect of human *purposeful action,* foreseeing and anticipating the future, is still missing.

According to Marxist philosophy, purposefulness is a certain aspect of complex causal relations. The possibility of purposefulness rests on the law that the effect has an impact on its cause.[24]

The interaction between cause and effect, consequently, is not a form of determination mutually excluding or separate from each other, as is pointed out by Bunge: "...in the sphere of society the dominant category of determination is more interaction than causality."[25] It is only one of the forms of interaction when the effect as a new element of objective reality has an impact on the cause. In the case of purposeful activity, the effect, even before it is elicited, affects the personality, in the form of an intellectual mental image, as the purpose of the action. Engels writes aptly, as quoted earlier: the causes of human acts appear in the form of human aims and wishes. This is the new element the principle by which causality in social life differs from causality in nature.[26]

The aim, as a specific part of human mental life, is defined by the organic nature

24 M. G. Makarov, "A cél" (The aim). *Szemelvénygyűjtemény a filozófia szakosító hallgatói részére. Dialektikus materializmus* (Selected Passages for the Students of the Specialization Course in Philosophy. Dialectic Materialism), Budapest: Kossuth Könyvkiadó, 1969–1970, pp. 201–209.

25 Bunge, *op. cit.,* p. 204.

26 Engels, *op. cit.,*

and its bases are formed by physiological mechanisms, complex conditional reflex connections. These reflex connections are the reflections of the general inter-relations of reality. The mental image of the future phenomenon, i.e. the subjective aim influencing human activity, appears through them. If this image of the future is suitable for satisfying needs, it incites to action; if not, to refraining from action. Thus, in the general causal relation of human activity, purposeful relations also find their place, i.e. the intellectual, mental image of the effect which has not occurred yet becomes a direct cause in the process that creates the effect. Using the terms of cybernetics, a human being may be interpreted as a system of communication, as a channel between the physical source of information and the product of the action, where two information flows passing through the cognition of the need and the possibility are united in the human aim.

Since the image of the aim is the mental form of the recognized needs and possibilities, of their mental formation, objective reality may be regarded as effect and, as a subjective cause, it participates in the initiation of human behaviour. "This relation of cause and effect is mediated: aim reflects the external conditions creating it only through intermediary psychological links, individual and social experience". (In our terms, the external conditions are the causes.) "The character of the aim playing the role of the effect depends to a great extent on the internal conditions of the consciousness, in the prism of whose totality the operation of the external causes is refracted."[27] Human consciousness anticipates not only the aim to be achieved but also the expectable objective relations existing before, during and perhaps after achieving the aim. Thus, the means, methods and conditions of the perpetration participating in the achievement of the aim take shape in the mind.

This philosophical sketch, if specified for criminal human behaviour, means that the image of the aim, as a subjective factor, is also present in the perpetration of all the criminal offences where the anticipated image of the unlawful behaviour has appeared with its advantages, with its suitability for satisfying some need.

As can be seen from the above, the acceptance of the principle of causality in criminology means the recognition of causality existing in the sphere of criminal human behaviour and not the recognition of mechanical causality.

In spite of the differences in the mode and form of the genesis of the effect, it is a *fundamentally common characteristic of every causal relation that the causes and conditions define the genesis of the effect by necessity.*

In the causality of human behaviour, in its determination, the image of the aim, the awareness of one's own aim, has a particular significance. This awareness, however, appears in one way in the case of an intentional criminal offence and differently in the case of a criminal offence by negligence. Criminal law distinguishes between criminal offences by intention and by negligence, or, to be more exact, between the degrees of culpability, precisely according to the perpetrator's psycho-

[27] Makarov, *op. cit.,* p. 207.

logical relation to the offence, i.e. whether the anticipated image of a socially dangerous act, of the criminal offence, appeared in his mind, or not.

Criminological studies and, accordingly, criminological views, have frequently been directed at intentional criminal offences without distinction, and usually at their typical, frequently occurring forms, and the theorems, or laws, put even in the most general terms, are to be understood as valid for criminal offences committed intentionally. It is only recently, due to the significant increase in the rates of offences of negligence, that it is being realized that criminology is not and should not be the same as the system of knowledge concerning intentional crime but has to include the experience and theoretical conclusions of studies concerning crime by negligence.

We find an essential difference between the causal mechanism of intentional criminal offences and offences by negligence, since in the case of intentional offences the purposive behaviour constitutes the criminal offence directly, while in the case of criminal offences only if it is followed by a socially harmful consequence that could have been avoided, had the perpetrator displayed the socially expected care. Because of this structural difference we shall discuss the causality and the actual causal relations of criminal offences committed intentionally separately from those of offences by negligence.

c) *The scheme showing the causal relation of an intentional criminal offence* taking purposive human activity into consideration, may be drawn in the following way:

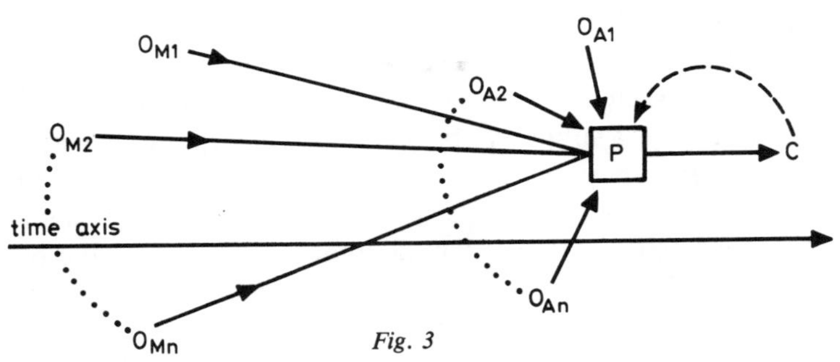

Fig. 3

The scheme drawn above illustrates the objective genesis of an intentional criminal offence. In the case of direct intention, this picture fully coincides with the subjective image formed in the perpetrator's mind before the perpetration of the act. (This coincidence concerns, of course, only the essence of the anticipated criminal offence, its dangerousness to society and its quality, and not necessarily the form of appearance in minute detail.) The situation is different in the case of *dolus eventualis.* In this case the criminal offence is not the aim of the perpetrator but he is aware of the fact that the harm to the social interest protected by criminal law is a *possible consequence* of his behaviour and resigns himself to it, and is indifferent to such consequences.

In other words, the anticipated image of the criminal offence, its contingency, does not make the perpetrator abandon or change his conduct and avoid the commission of the offence in this way.

For this reason, the subjective picture of the causal scheme can be drawn as follows:

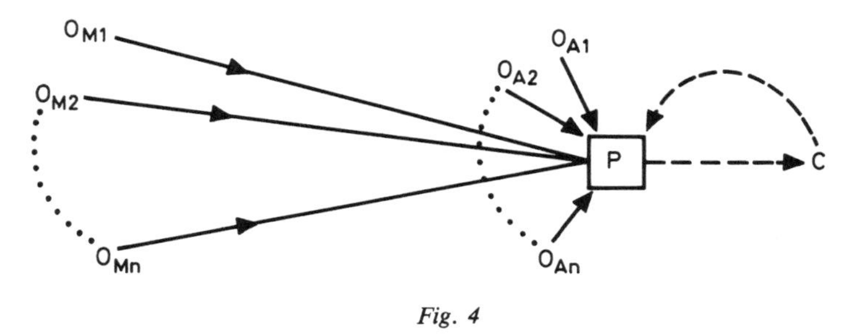

Fig. 4

The objective scheme of the criminal offence committed with *dolus eventualis* is identical to the scheme of the offences committed with direct intention since the anticipated image of the criminal offence has reached the level of awareness in the personality and has been accepted as a contingency.

d) The essence of *criminal offences of negligence* from the point of view of purposiveness may be summarized by saying that the intended, conscious activity of the perpetrator is not directed at the perpetration of a criminal offence and the acceptance of a socially harmful consequence does not even arise. The perpetrator's behaviour, which is faulty in a different way, however, together with other causal factors, not foreseen, i.e. not realized on the conscious level, produces a result harmful to society.

The scheme of these causal relations may be drawn as follows:

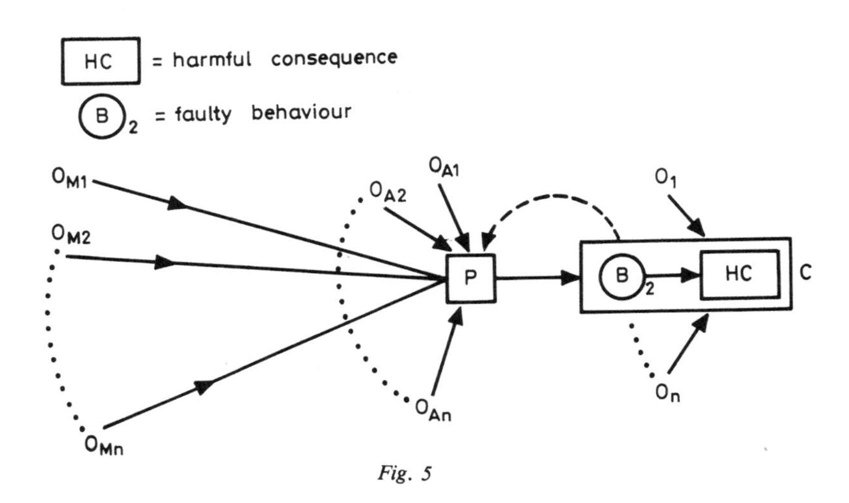

Fig. 5

Behaviour M_2 in the scheme, as one of the causal factors of criminal offences by negligence, represents the violation of care expected by society or of other requirements, and it is frequently manifested in the conscious violation of low-level norms. In other words, non culpable but otherwise faulty behaviour, together with other factors, produces the harmful consequence and, thus, a criminal offence is committed. It also happens, however, that the harmful result is the consequence of a criminal offence, when the criminal offence has been intended but certain consequences not intended by the perpetrator have also occurred and his negligence concerning them may be established. The causal scheme of such criminal offences (criminal offences *praeter intentionem)* is similar to the causal scheme of offences by negligence, with the difference that the causal factor of non culpable but otherwise faulty behaviour may be replaced with the symbol of culpable behaviour.

In criminal law, two forms of negligence are distinguished, so-called conscious negligence *(luxuria)* and carelessness. The subjective picture is different from the above schemes in both cases.

A person commits a criminal offence through conscious negligence if the possibility of the harmful consequence arises in his mind but he trusts that the consequence will not occur since in objective conditions similar to the given situation harmful consequences usually do not occur, or, at least, not to the perpetrator's knowledge. For this reason, the perpetrator considers the occurrence of the criminal offence improbable, or he may know that the occurrence of the harmful consequence has a certain probability, but he takes the risk.

The subjective picture of conscious negligence may be drawn as follows:

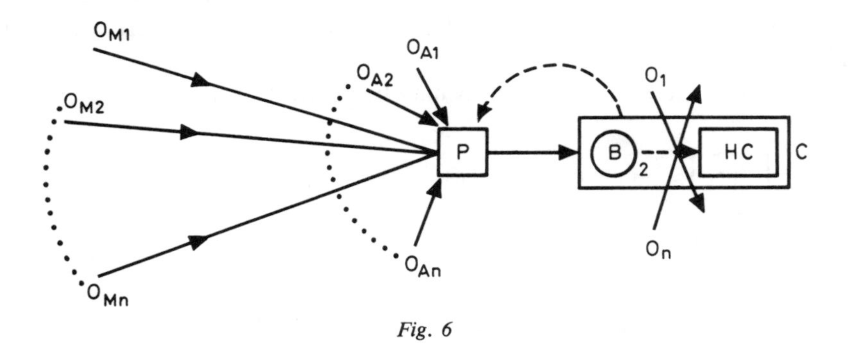

Fig. 6

The objective picture is the same as the general scheme drawn earlier.

The other form of negligence is carelessness, in the case of which the possibility of the criminal offence does not even arise in the consciousness or there is no psychological relation between the perpetrator and the harmful consequence. The harmful consequence occurs independently of the perpetrator's will and consciousness. The subjective picture in this case embraces only the faulty behaviour that produces the criminal offence together with other causal factors.

The scheme:

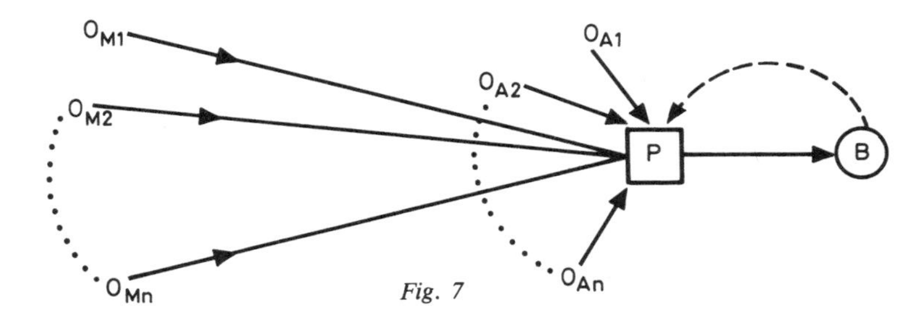

Fig. 7

The scheme is similar in its structure to the subjective picture of a criminal offence committed with direct intention, with the material difference that the possibility of socially harmful consequences does not even arise in this case, while it is the aim in the case of direct intention.

The schemes drawn here and aimed at illustrating the objective situation, reflect the mechanism of the perpetration of a particular criminal offence.

If, however, the genesis of a criminal offence is viewed not only statically, backward from the time of the perpetration, but also dynamically, as the events move, we may see that as time passes, the actual causal factors pass into the realm of the objective factors of the past, and even the effect itself, the criminal offence as objective reality, first exerts its (not necessarily criminogenic) impact as an actual objective factor on the subjective, and on objective relations connected to the subjective, and then it becomes an objective factor of the past.

It is not a one-way relation that characterizes the relation of the personality and objective processes, but interaction. Man is in permanent interaction with his environment. The environment forms the person, the person changes his environment. Interaction is realized through human acts, criminal acts among them. Every human act changes reality, even if imperceptibly in many cases, becomes part of it, and, as part of objective reality, exerts an influence on the subject, on the performer of the act.

Kudriavtsev developed a graphic figure to illustrate the genesis of criminal offences:[28]

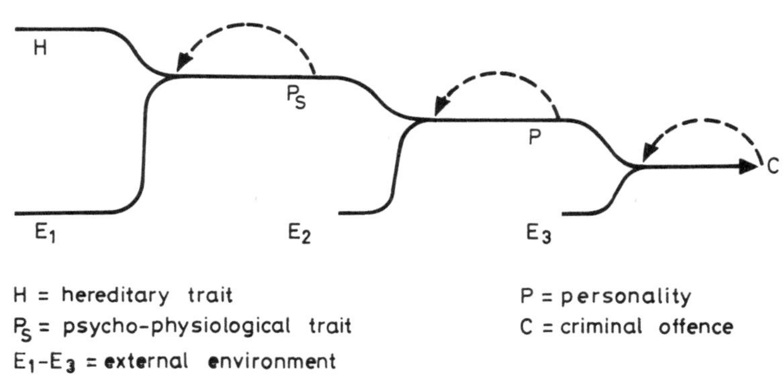

Fig. 8

[28] Kudriavtsev, *op. cit.*, p. 21.

In fact the figure is a schematic picture of the perpetrator's course of life up to the perpetration of the offence. As a result of biological traits and environmental influence, psycho-physiological traits develop, on the basis of their interaction with the environment the personality develops, and, finally, as the result of the interaction of the personality and the environment, the criminal offence occurs.

It seems necessary to note that the various elements and parts of objective reality have different effects on human beings. In the initial phase of the ontogenetic evolution it is immediate life conditions that exert the greatest influence; later our own acts gain an increasingly important role since our needs are satisfied through them, and the influence of the macro-environment increases in the same way. The objective factors can be divided into three groups, according to their relevance to us: 1. our own acts, 2. micro-environmental and 3. macro-environmental factors. The importance of this classification will be shown in the part discussing the material issues of causal relations. Here we point out only that in the case of our own acts, and from the point of view of criminology in the case of criminal acts, what is decisive is whether they, considering their effects, incite us always to the same act or not.

e) From the presented schemes, the *chain of causality* is clear, it can be seen that the personality is present in criminal behaviour between the external objective environment and the act, as a "prism" as a "communication system". It is the criminal offence and the actual objective circumstances of which we can have knowledge relatively easily and exactly in these schemes. We know much less of the personality, psychological processes and their physiological basis. Precisely for this reason, personality is called by some authors the black box of the causal mechanism.[29] What is known for certain is that there is a chain consisting of needs and opportunities (which then become motives), opinions concerning the consequences of the contemplated criminal act, the decision itself to commit that act, followed by the crime itself if extraneous circumstances allow.

It is one of the fundamental achievements of socialist criminology that it finds the connection between the perpetration of criminal offences and objective reality, above all social relations, through the personality. Socialist criminology created the notions of subjective and objective causes in the initial phase of its development and it formulated the thesis that the objective causes exert their influence indirectly, only through the personality. In the light of this train of thought, the fault of a factor theory attempting to demonstrate the direct connection between various objective factors and criminal offences is clear.

The above schemes explain not only the existence of subjective causes and their place in the causal relation but also indicate that a criminal offence as an effect is not produced by a single cause and effect relation but through a chain of causes and effects.

[29] See Kudriavtsev, *op. cit.*

The chain of cause and effect, as a general category of philosophy, means in criminology that starting backward from the criminal offence we find such causal relations of phenomena where cause/effect relations follow each other. Formulating perhaps more clearly: the subjective and objective causes producing the criminal offence also have their own causes, i.e. in a different causal relation these causes themselves are the effects of other causes.

For criminology and criminal etiology it is extremely important to study the cause/effect sequence, since its exploration explains the perpetration of the criminal offence. The causal scheme itself reflects an abstract causal chain consisting of two links, namely the impact of past relations on the formation of the personality, then the joint impact of the personality and the situation on the genesis of the criminal offence. In the *first link* of the causal chain the actual personality is the effect, and the functions of causes and conditions are discharged by the relations of the past. This link of the chain is composed of many cause/effect relations following each other in time and relatively independent of each other.

It includes all the effects and consequences that have happened to the person —the offender in our case—in his life and have formed the actual structure, the content of his personality.

The symbolic indication of the causal factors of the past in one chain-link is only an abstraction, the generalization of particular cause/effect relations which made the perpetrator what he is; made him the kind of person he was directly before the offence. In the narrower sense, it is the totality of the cause/effect relations which have formed the perpetrator's views, characteristics and habits that are harmful to society or depart from social requirements. The causal scheme we have drawn to illustrate the causality of a given criminal offence may as a matter of fact, be made suitable for all previous behaviour and, through this, it may become even clearer that the actual personality is nothing but the permanent interaction of the objective conditions, the person's own acts and the personality, from the person's birth to the studied (in this case: criminal) behaviour.

The second link in the causal chain implies the causal relation where the actual personality and the situation play the role of causative factors and the criminal offence is the effect. Here, in addition to the subjectivized situational factors, personality includes the aim conceptions that have been formed of the criminal offence as a phenomenon which has not occurred yet, in an anticipated form.

From the point of view of the establishment of criminal responsibility, the emphasis and study of a *third link* is also very important. This is the connection between the criminal activity and the consequence, i.e. the link called causality in criminal law.

The study of the first and second link in the causal chain preceding the perpetration of the criminal offence is the task primarily of criminology. The exploration of the laws dominating this realm requires broad psychological, sociological and philosophical knowledge. Historical experience proves that one-sided, or only psychological or socio-economic studies have never been able to give a comprehensive explanation of the nature, causality and prevention of criminal offences and crime. It is our conviction that the right path for criminology to follow is to study human criminal behaviour through the causal chain, on the basis of the scheme of causality, to explore the particular real phenomena whose movement and interaction produce the perpetration of criminal offences.

(As far as the figures showing the causal schemes are concerned, we have to note that of necessity they simplify the system of complex interrelations. In spite of that, I believe they suitably illustrate the skeleton of the interrelations and help in the better understanding of the essence. I regard the disparaging statements concerning "causal bundles" as underrating the clear way of conveying information.)

It is, however, a frequently raised question, how far it is practicable to go back in the causal chain since these chains are infinite and have many ramifications.

If the general causal scheme is split as going backward, the causal scheme may perhaps be shown as follows:

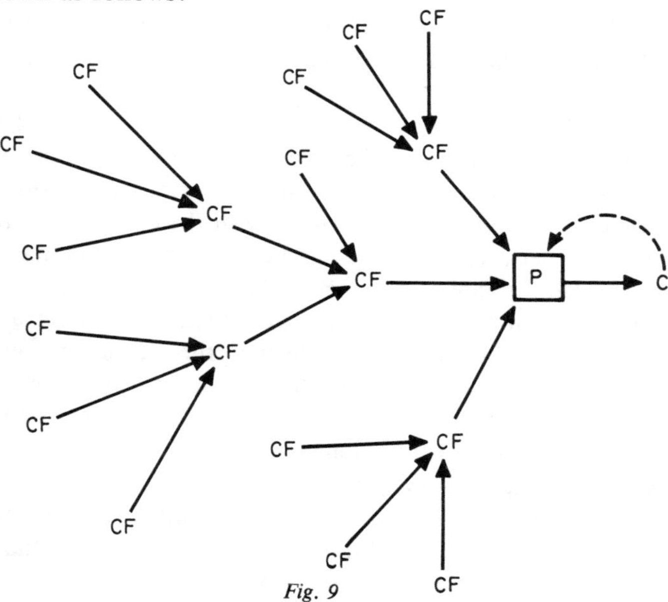

Fig. 9

The three groups of causes do not indicate the actual number of causes, they only indicate that all effects are caused by several causes. The most exact cognition possible of the causal relations of the actual personality, the objective relations affecting it and the conception of the aim (needs, possibilities) and criminal offence, as an initial link of the chain, is a fundamental requirement. The criminal offence and the situation are relatively easy to study. The problem arises when the examination of the connection between the personality and the objective relations forming it is studied. As we have mentioned, this link of the chain is the totality of many cause/effect relations following each other in time and relatively independent of each other. These concrete cause/effect relations are always connected to the personality since we consider only the causal chains that have affected the personality or, rather, its unfavourable formation, or the amplification of some antisocial motives.

Since the multitude of causal chains cannot be grasped in its completeness, in criminological studies or in the course of the administration of justice the realistic requirement may not be more than to explore the relations of the causal chain *that render it possible to understand the necessity of the genesis of criminal behaviour.*

f) Although it is not the problem of causality appearing on the level of individual, concrete phenomena, we discuss here the *causal relations of* "passive" elements, the causal relations of consequences, criminal offences, due to the lack of something, since such phenomena occur daily in the practice of the administration of justice. There is a possibility for misunderstanding in the interpretation of the mechanism of causality if we do not make our position clear concerning the productivity of the causes in the causal relation. The principle of productivity (or genetic principle) means that one of the material marks of causal relations is the active genesis, the active influence of the causes.[30]

Criminal and non-criminal human behaviour form a homogeneous set, a homogeneous system, namely the set or system of human behaviour. Similarly, their causative factors form a homogeneous system, the system of life conditions, that of the objective parameters and relations of man and his environment. In this relatively closed system, criminal and non-criminal behaviour are notions complementing and excluding each other. In the case of the same person, one of them means the negation of the other, the lack of the other. The situation is similar concerning causative factors, too. In a certain criminal volition the victory of criminogenic motives necessarily means the defeat of law-abiding motives and vice versa. Thus, the same causal relation may be formulated from both the negative and positive aspect. The presence of criminogenic factors means a certain lack of positive factors. In his monograph on responsibility, Gy. Eörsi also considers the defeat of law-abiding motives or their complete lack as a psychological cause. "If contradictory motives clash in the mind, the defeat of motives harmonious with the legal norm is the psychological cause that requires influencing through the applications of the means of responsibility and, in this way, the strengthening of such motives, and, if the struggle of motives did not even develop because the social motive never appeared in the mind under the given circumstances, the psychological cause lies here. The lack of the emergence of the social cause, however, as a psychological cause, is again an expression of what happened in reality, amalgamated for legal evaluation."[31]

[30] Bunge, *op. cit.,* p. 50.

[31] Gy. Eörsi, *A jogi felelősség alapproblémái. A polgári jogi felelősség* (The Basic Problems of Legal Responsibility. Responsibility under Civil Law), Budapest: Akadémiai Kiadó, 1961, pp. 157–158.

The pair of counter-theses may also be formulated in a similar way, even if not with the same exactness, in the sphere of objective causes. Where we find circumstances favourable from the point of view of social requirements, criminal offences do not occur, as a rule; in turn, where criminogenic circumstances dominate, criminal behaviour is natural. The presence of one of the groups of causes means at the same time the absence of the other. This contrast is valid, however, only for the extreme poles. In reality positive and negative causes cannot be found as a rule in such pure groups in the conditions of life of people, they mix in different proportions. That is the reason why convicted and non-convicted people on the one hand and offenders and honest citizens on the other hand must not be rigidly separated from each other, as has been mentioned in the part discussing the concept of crime. The continuity between criminal forms of human behaviour and their causes indicates that these phenomena form a homogeneous system within which the absence of something indicates the presence of its counterpart. Regarding the totality of social relations from the point of view of the elimination of crime, it does not make any difference how we formulate: crime exists in a certain society because there are still criminogenic factors or because it is not yet positive conditions of life that exist exclusively. Criminology, particularly socialist criminology, is able to point out the circumstances that lead to the perpetration of criminal offences with a high probability and also the circumstances that make probable the observance of social requirements. An expansion in one of the factor groups means necessarily a decrease in the other.

In the present stage of our social evolution, the possibility of eliminating criminogenic circumstances or creating completely positive circumstances does not yet exist. We know, for example, that criminal, alcoholic parents or those who grossly abuse their children exert a criminogenic effect on their children, and if the children commit criminal offences these traits of the parents are among the causes with a high probability. But we also know that the opposite, namely the law-abiding, cultured behaviour of parents who love their children, encourages children to observe social requirements. May we formulate, after all, that a juvenile commits a criminal offence because his environment is not law-abiding, the parents are not cultured and they lack love toward their children? As a matter of fact, the same traits of parents may be expressed in both a negative and positive form. This means that even if we formulate it in a positive form, we know what is lacking, since a criminal cannot be law-abiding and vice versa. From the establishment of the lack of a trait one may infer with high probability the existence of the opposite. But the frequently quoted classical example of the carelessness of the mother causing the death of her child is similarly graphic. It could also be expressed in the form that the death of the child has been caused by the lack of care expected of parents by society. Kudriavtsev positively states that the functions of causes can be fulfilled also by "passive" factors or by the lack of factors. According to him, lacking phenomena have the significance of causes in the formation of the personality since they create a "vacuum", which can be filled with criminogenic effects, and, at the same time, they have a character of real information. The lack of something is a bit of information of exactly the same nature as the presence of one or other social fact; everything depends on the content of the given phenomenon and not on its form. For this reason, the cause must always be considered in the system that constitutes reality. The "passive" behaviour of a person should be admitted as the cause of a certain result if the particular person is one of the elements of the system.[32]

We find references also in the works of other authors to the fact that they regard the lack of something as the cause of criminal offences. Karpets and Ratinov, for example, in their article entitled "The awareness of law and the causes of crime", enumerate the undeveloped state of legal awareness, its gaps, i.e. the lack of the proper awareness of law, among criminogenic causes.[33]

We agree with Kudriavtsev and everybody else representing a similar view to the extent that it is also possible to demonstrate the causal relation within a system with the "lack of something". However, in our opinion, considering the principle of the productivity of causes, criminology has to strive to describe the causal relation with existing and not lacking factors. Lacking factors are less tangible as their existing counterparts. Although it is possible to infer the lacking from the existing with a high probability, it is not possible with certainty. The existing phenomenon, its inner structure, may be examined with greater precision than it is possible to infer from lacking phenomena. For example if the lack of parental love and care is found to be the dominant factor of a criminal act committed by a juvenile, we still do not know the forms of its manifestation; abuse, neglect of care or leaving the child without supervision. Since criminal offences and crime are negative phenomena and are judged negatively it is also more justifiable logically to define the negative causative factors than the absent positive ones. This approach does not mean, of course, that the establishment of the absent positive factors is not important in the process of studying criminal human behaviour. It is precisely replacing the existing negative factors with the absent positive ones that is demanded by the interests of prevention, because it is in this way that the negative effect, the criminal offence, may be avoided. The creation of positive factors, positive conditions of existence, belongs to the essence of preventive means. The comprehensive study of causal relations between positive factors and positive behaviour, however, exceeds the scope of criminology and it falls primarily in the realm of other disciplines.

[32] V. N. Kudriavtsev, "Problemy Pritshinnosti v Kriminologii" *Voprosy Filosofii,* 10 (1971).

[33] I. I. Karpets and A. R. Ratinov, "A jogtudat és a bűnözés okai" (Legal Awareness and the Causes of Crime), *Magyar Jog és Külföldi Jogi Szemle,* (1935), p. 560.

3 The Causality of Crime (Mass Causality)

Criminology regards crime as a statistical mass, as a mass phenomenon, and crime as such has all traits characteristic of mass phenomena in general, namely it has dynamism and structure and is in a stochastic relation with other mass phenomena. From the point of view of causality, thus, the question is justified of whether or not causal relations producing crime and defining its changes are different from individual causality discussed above, i.e. from causality prevailing on the level of concrete criminal acts. Philosophy does not answer adequately this question even on a general level. Although in the literature of philosophy one may read of "causal and probability relations" the problem of mass phenomena appears only in connection with laws.[34] Here one finds innumerable views concerning the nature of dynamic and statistical laws and particularly their relations to each other.

To examine the issue, the most practicable way seems to start from the principle professed unanimously by Marxist authors according to which causality is universally valid and for this reason it may be discovered in the sphere of mass phenomena as well as among individual phenomena. If crime as a mass phenomenon, as an independent system, is regarded—as with criminal offences—as an effect, then this phenomenon also has its causes and conditions which define its existence and dynamism by necessity. Here I should start by saying that when a phenomenon has the role of an effect, it is always a consequence having already occurred. From the point of view of causality it is the crime of a past period or periods of time we may speak about.

Speaking about the causality of crime, the question poses itself whether the causes of crime are identical with the totality of the causes of individual criminal offences and what phenomena are in a causal relation with crime. The answer is supplied by empirical studies, first of all, but it may be derived also by a deductive method from the connection of the notions of criminal offence and crime. If crime is the statistical set of criminal offences and their perpetrators, the causes can only be the individual phenomena and their sets that produced the individual criminal offences.

The causes of individual criminal offences are, however, various in their individuality. Due to random effects, we may find causative factors which have appeared only in a single or in a few cases and if criminal offences are examined in a large number, i.e. on the level of mass phenomenon, these extreme causative factors become characterless.

For this reason, the causes and conditions in practice are the causative factors occurring in a large number that constitute a mass phenomenon, a statistical mass, themselves. Thus, the essence of the causality of crime is defined by the causative factors that occur on the level of mass phenomenon.

The distinction between causes and conditions in the causality of crime is not as

[34] Bunge, *op. cit.*, p. 168.

unambiguous as in the case of individual criminal offences. While on the individual level, on the level of concrete criminal offences, causes and conditions may be separated in a relatively exact way, in the case of crime the distinction can be made on the basis of the *frequency of occurrence* of the causitive factors. Only those phenomena are regarded as the causes of crime that have appeared as causes in a high number of individual criminal acts or that have appeared mainly as causes. And in the same way we regard as conditions the phenomena that have played the role of conditions in the perpetration of concrete criminal offences. Let us see an example: a criminal environment or, in the case of a juvenile, alcoholic parents appear in most of the cases as causes and for this reason we may consider them as causes of crime as well. Similarly, the lack of guarding or checking serves mostly as a condition of the perpetration of criminal offences; for this reason the lack of guarding or checking, as a mass phenomenon, may be regarded as a condition of crime. These examples are taken from the sphere of objective phenomena but we may mention examples taken from subjective causes, such as wrong attitudes toward work or social property, which may be still found in the case of many people and which also promote the existence of crime against property.

According to all this, the causal scheme of crime is somewhat different from the causal scheme of individual offences. Since crime forms a statistical mass, i.e. it is the aggregate of units relatively independent of each other but homogeneous from one aspect, the causative factors appear also in the form of statistical masses, i.e. above all mass phenomena, in addition to factors appearing infrequently or in a low number, as is illustrated by the next scheme: (See Fig. 10.)

It can be seen from the figure that if crime is regarded as a whole, it is characterized by a "several and one effect" relation in the same way as in the case of any individual offence. The totality of causative factors defines by necessity the volume and structure of crime and, in the same way, the changes in causative factors define the changes in the volume and structure of crime. This form of causality is valid also for the sub-masses of crime, in other words, for groups formed by differentiating marks as far as they still constitute a statistical mass. (E.g. crime by violence, recidivism, crime against property, etc.)

On the basis of the scheme sketched by us, the view represented also by Bunge seems inaccurate, namely that multiple causality turns into statistical determination if the possible causes reach a high degree of complexity and particularly if all the causes are of the same kind and the magnitude of their intensity is the same.[35]

According to our evaluation, mass causality is not distinguished from individual causality by the complexity of the causes but by the specific causal relation of mass phenomena.

[35] Bunge, *loc. cit.*

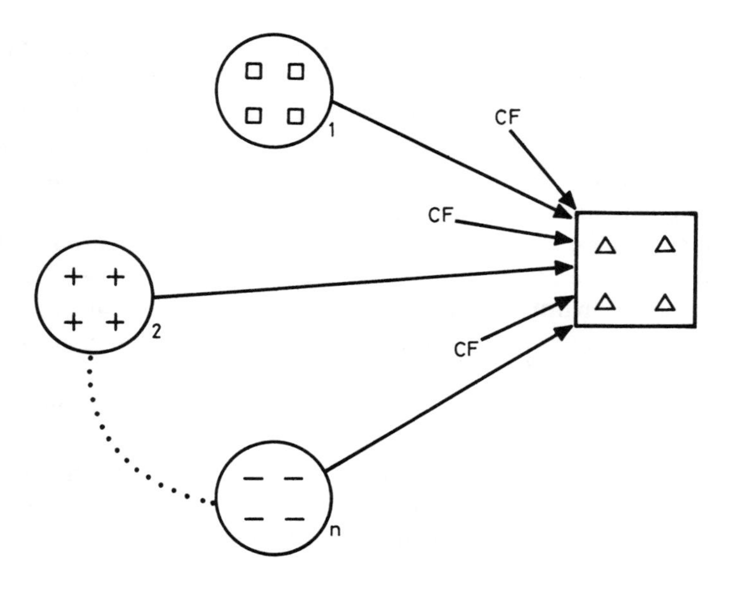

Fig. 10

For criminology it is of fundamental importance to explore mass phenomena which are in causal relation with crime, as a social mass phenomenon.

Effective prevention is possible only if the volume of mass phenomena in causal relation with crime and the intensity of their impact on crime, i.e. their causal correlation with crime, are established. We have to note that not all correlations represent causal correlations. It may happen, for example, that the numerical growth of the age-group of juveniles shows a close correlation with the growth of juvenile criminality. In spite of that the two phenomena do not show a causal relation (correlation). Empirical studies prove that the causal relations are to be found in the changes of the personality and social position of juveniles.[36]

4 Past and Future in Causal Determination

What has been said above concerns only the causal relations of criminal offences or crime committed already. Precisely for this reason, this determination is absolute in the sense that all phenomena of the past had causal relations with others. (To be

[36] Sh. Glueck and E. Glueck, "Ten Years of Unravelling Juvenile Delinquency — An Examination of Criticism", *The Journal of Criminal Law, Criminology and Police Science,* 51 (1960), pp. 283–308.

absolutely precise, they had causal relations as well as other kinds. Since we are interested only in causal relations, we are not going to discuss others.) Formulating it in a different way: all phenomena of the material universe that became reality came into existence, existed, changed or caesed to exist due to sufficient material causes.[37]

A real causal relation between the past and future does not exist, since the future for the time being is only possible phenomena, not yet having causes, and which will only have causes as time passes, when the moment, future from the aspect of the present, turns into the present first, then the past. *Causal relations exist only between cause and effect, the effect is an existing consequence, and thus it presupposes a past time.* The past is the realm of phenomena that came into existence, the future is that of possibilities and probabilities. But the future consists of real possibilities that have their roots in the past (in the present). In the possible occurrences of the future the causal laws of the past are projected forward, then, depending on circumstances, when the present future will have become the past, these determinants will become causative factors. These causative factors in the present are only in probable relation with the possibilities of the future, and consequently, in this relations there are no causes yet, there will only be, when one of the possibilities become reality, i.e. the (present) past. And in turn: the relations of the past are not probable but real, there are no possibilities in the past, by one of the possibilities turning into reality, all others cease to exist. It is in this way that the many ambiguous relations existing independent of time become in reality (in the present and the past) many unambiguous *definiteness* in causal relations.

The interpretation of the past, the present and the future frequently presents a problem for those who are not philosophers. In everyday thinking the present is identified with the near past and near future and we take the present as if it expressed a short period of time. If, however, processes are observed in their reality and not only in their reflection appearing on the surface, it has to be seen that the present has no dimension, just like a point. The present in reality is only a moment, a dividing line between the past and the future on the line of time and its position changes together with passing time. This is the reason why we mention the present only in addition to the past and in brackets, since what is the present in a given moment will belong to the realm of the past in the next.

For the aspect of causality, the interpretation of the causal relation of the future, i.e. probable relation, means that the perpetration of a criminal offence is not predestined by the causes of criminal human behaviour, such behaviour is not predetermined, the necessary causal determination does not lead to fatalism as is stated by theoreticians denying causality but reflects reality and existing, objectively real processes are expressed by it.

It is the causal, the genetic relations of the past and the knowledge of their laws

[37] Fodor, *op. cit.*, p. 224.

that make it possible for us to prepare prognoses concerning the recidivism of certain offenders, the prospective changes in crime as a statistical mass and in its sub-masses, and, on the basis of all this, to take effective, planned measures in order to prevent crime.

5 The Interpretation and Role of Necessity, Regularity and Chance

We say about causal relations that they contain necessity, i.e. the causes and conditions unavoidably bring about the effect, the criminal offence. The analysis of this relation of necessity demands the examination of the issue of whether, *if the same causes and conditions appear reoeatedly, they produce the same effect. The true Marxist conception can answer the question only in the affirmative.* If the totality and structure of the causes and conditions (in the case of human behaviour the structure of personality included) are fully identical, the effect has to be the same. With a criminological approach it may be formulated that an identical constellation of *criminogenic factors leads to the perpetration of the same criminal offence.*

However, *in reality,* precisely due to the permanent movement and changes, the constellation of causes and conditions very rarely appears repeatedly in the same form. Repetition occurs, as a rule, only on the level of similarity. This is the reason why causes seemingly the same do not always lead to the same result. To mention an example: the same criminogenic family conditions do not necessarily result in the same criminal offence, or, formulating in a general way, they do not always result in a criminal offence. Or, the other way round, favourable family conditions and circumstances at the place of work do not necessarily exclude the perpetration of criminal offences, since these circumstances constitute only a part of the causative factors participating in the determination, and their intensity and constellation as well may be different. The fundamental thesis of philosophy, according to which the totality of causes and conditions *necessarily* produces the effect, has to be supplemented with the thesis that the *relations of necessity are divided into the groups of relations of regularity and those of chance.*[38]

For criminology and, in general, for scientific studies it is precisely the establishment of what causal relations are regular and what are chance that is of primary importance, since it is regular processes that have a dominant role in the trends of development.

We cannot overemphasize that the determination of criminal behaviour is ensured by processes not of regularity but of necessity, where, in addition to regularity, chance also has a role.

[38] See Földesi, *op. cit.,* pp. 138–139.

In the case of the repetition of phenomena, of their occurrence in large numbers, some causal relations occur frequently and others occur rarely or do not occur repeatedly at all. *Material, lasting and general causal relations of necessity* which occur over and over again in the case of the repetition of phenomena, *are called relations of regularity* while causal relations occurring singly or rarely *are called chance.* It follows from this that the law (regularity) of causality compresses the material, general and permanent nature of genetic relations between phenomena.[39]

It frequently happens that philosophers and particularly natural scientists identify the relations of necessity with regularity.[40] It is due to this fact that they transfer necessity manifested in causality to the sphere of regularity (laws) and it is only a step from here to conclude that material causal relations necessarily determine the occurrence of the phenomenon or its dynamism, although material causal relations or, in other words, relations of regularity, do not define absolutely the dynamism of phenomena, they only render it probable, since relations of chance also have a role in the occurrence of phenomena. For this reason, we have to emphasize that

1. causal relations do not contain only material, regular interrelations, they contain also immaterial relations, the relations of chance;
2. in turn, laws do not contain only material causal relations, they contain also other material relations, such as structural ones.[41]

It is clear from the notion of laws, from that of the relation of regularity, that it cannot be recognized on the basis of a single causal relation producing an individual effect, it is possible only in the case of the repeated appearance of effects. Thus, e.g., the recognition of causative factors playing a role in the genesis of an individual criminal offence, producing it by necessity, does not answer our question as to what the factors participating by chance are, what factors operate as a regularity rendering probable the generation of a criminal offence in the case of others or in the future. To find the answer, a great number of criminal offences have to be examined because material and lasting relations can be distinguished from relations of chance only in this way.

According to the *Dictionary of Philosophy,* "The cognition of the law presupposes a transition from the phenomenon to its essence and it is always through abstract thinking, through the abstraction from the many, purely individual and immaterial marks of phenomena and through the many-sided (logical and empirical) checking of the abstractions created in this way, that it takes place."[42]

[39] A. Gy. Szabó, *A törvény és az ember* (Law and Man), Budapest: Kossuth Könyvkiadó, 1964, p. 121.

[40] See V. A. Fok, "Diskussiya s Nilsom Borom", *Voprosy Filosofii,* 8 (1964).

[41] Fodor, *op. cit.,* p. 227.

[42] *Filozófiai Kislexikon* (Dictionary of Philosophy), op. cit., p. 380.

The relations of chance, occurring seldom or almost never, are such only in their connection with regularity, and as has been pointed out, they are the relations of necessity of the individual determination.

We discuss only the laws of causality and their forms and the conditions of their validity in the realms of criminal offences and crime.

In criminology, the law of causality means that among the causes and conditions of criminal offences (several or all criminal offences) there are some which have a material, general and lasting connection with criminal offences, i.e. effects. If criminal offences are examined in a large number and over a longish period of the past and these causal relations are established, the presence of these causative factors will elicit the effects, i.e. criminal offences, also in the future, *as a law*. So that the notion of eliciting the effect by necessity can be clearly understood, it is advisable to survey the knowledge of the nature of laws.

6 The Laws of Causality

Instead of making an attempt to sketch the complicated debate, based frequently on conceptual differences, on the existence of dynamic and statistical laws and their relation to each other and to causality, that we find in the literature of philosophy and natural sciences[43] we quote the relevant part of the *Dictionary of Philosophy* for the sake of information. "Statistical and dynamic relations are the form of appearance of the regular causal relations of phenomena. The dynamic relation of regularity is a form of causal relations where the given state of the system completely defines all the later states, i.e. on the basis of the knowledge of the initial state the later evolution of the system can be predicted precisely. A dynamic relation prevails in all the autonomous systems dependent on external effects only to a small extent, where the number of the elements is relatively low. Such a relation defines, e.g., the nature of the movement of the planets belonging to the solar system. Statistical regularity is a form of causal relations where the given state of the system does not define the next states perfectly but only with a certain probability, which is an objective measure of the trends of change of the past. A statistical regularity prevails in all non-autonomous systems dependent on external conditions where the number of the elements is very high. In the strict sense all regularities are statistical. This follows from the fact that matter is inexhaustible and every system consists of innumerable elements. In addition, each system is actually open and is in an interaction with the environment. For this reason, all dynamic regularities are

[43] On this topic see D. Bohm, *Okság és véletlenség a modern fizikában* (Causality and Chance in Modern Physics), (in Hungarian) Budapest: Gondolat Kiadó, 1960; H. Korch, "Okság és determinizmus" (Causality and Determinism) in: *Dialektikus materializmus szakosító szemelvénygyűjtemény* (Selected Passages for the Dialectic Materialism Specialization Course), Budapest: Kossuth Könyvkiadó, 1969–70.

statistical — with a high probability of realization due to the given system, in other words, they are not influenced significantly by external effects and by the high number of relations within the system."[44]

The quotation with its logical system and contradictions represents the position of philosophy extremely well. Accordingly, the causal relation of regularity has two forms of manifestation, if we are indulgent. However, taken strictly, "all regularities are statistical", and, consequently, only one kind of causal regularity exists and it has a statistical nature, i.e. it is valid for the sphere of systems consisting of a high number of elements of the same type, for the sphere of sets.[45] Accordingly, the behaviour of the units is under the dominance of laws valid within the mass. Criminological studies appear to verify this conclusion, i.e. that only a statistical law exists. The acceptance of this thesis, however, makes necessary the interpretation of the relation between the individual, and the mass.

The general view is that the existence of the individual, in the same way as that of the system, is relative. Erdey-Grúz writes of the relation of the unit and population: "Parts and structural wholes form a hierarchical system whose every 'level' (each member) is a structural whole built of its own parts on the one hand, and is a part of the next higher level (structural element) on the other hand. Part and structural whole are relative concepts: every part is also a structural whole and every structural whole is also a part."[46]

Shifting from the purely abstract philosophical level to the specific sphere of crime, we may say that criminology deals with the field of the hierarchy of individuals and systems where criminal acts, the individual and their set, their statistical mass, form the structural whole, i.e. crime.

Quetelet already recognized in the 1830s that in the realm of human behaviour, including crime, based, seemingly, on free will, laws dominate in the same way as among natural phenomena.[47] Also in the realm of human behaviour the prevailing laws are of such a nature that the effect on the object does not produce an unambiguous result, the results have a range. Crime typically shows such laws. Objective criminogenic factors do not necessarily initiate criminal offences but make them highly probable. In other words, the factors that we call the objective causes and conditions of crime do not necessarily produce criminal behaviour in the case of every individual; if, however, we take a large number of individuals, the great majority will inevitably commit criminal offences. The essence of the law of causality is to be found in this. The existence of the causes in the past (present)

[44] *Filozófiai Kislexikon* (Dictionary of Philosophy), *op. cit.*, p. 317.

[45] Setting out from this, it appears superfluous to add the epithets "statistical" to the law of causation.

[46] T. Erdey-Grúz, *A világ anyagi szerkezete* (The Material Structure of the Universe), Budapest: Akadémiai Kiadó, 1965, pp. 40–41.

[47] Quetelet, *op. cit.*

renders the occurrence of the effect probable in the future. It is probable that a person living in criminogenic circumstances will commit a criminal offence in the future. A certain number of such persons, however, according to the empirical index of probability, will commit necessarily criminal offences, they will obey the laws of crime. Which of these persons will and will not commit criminal offences depends on relations of probability existing in the sphere of individual phenomena, i.e. on the totality of influences, regular or chance from the aspects of the dynamism of the full population.

Philosophy teaches that the law is trendlike and this trendlike character is an important trait of the laws.[48] This means that the law is not necessarily valid for every single element of the system, of the mass, for every single unit, since individual laws always exert their influence in reality through the relation of other laws and through the circumstances. Even such a natural law considered dynamic as the Galileian law of free fall is not valid in its pure form because the atmosphere, wind and other phenomena influence the speed of a body falling freely. In the same way, one might mention the law concerning the trajectory and impact of the bullet which also produces a range and is valid as a trend only. It is more so in the sphere of social phenomena, of criminal human behaviour, where the causes and conditions producing the result, occur in a large number themselves and, consequently, the constellations are innumerable. Slower or more rapid social changes occurring, by necessity do not effect every unit and every group of the population in the same way. Accordingly, social changes either strengthen or weaken the activity of certain groups of people. And where this changing activity is related to criminogenic factors crime or its particular forms increase or decrease. A structural change occurring in the sphere of causative factors affects the changes of the structure of crime and the direction of these changes defines the direction of the trends of crime.

We do not have to be criminologists to be able to predict that there will still be crime in 5 or 7 or 15 years. It is clear to everyone that if crime existed in the past year and the causes and conditions of crime have not changed materially, then crime must exist next year and in the years following it. In fact, it is the law of causality of crime that can be discovered behind this generalized everyday experience. The knowledge of the law of causality of crime permits, however, not only such general predictions, it makes possible the prognostication of crime as a whole with a relatively small tolerance (10–15 per cent) on the one hand, and on the basis of the regularities of partial masses, it is possible to estimate with a high probability (80–90 per cent) whether a person will become a criminal or a recidivist. The knowledge of the law of causality of crime makes possible the elaboration of effective crime-preventing measures to be taken, from the elimination of social causes to the decrease of technical conditions.

[48] See Földesi, *op. cit.*, p. 141.

In addition to the cognition of criminal offences, i.e. the laws of crime, the cognition of the laws of the behaviour displayed and acts (criminal and non-criminal) committed by the perpetrator of criminal offences is also needed for an effective administration of justice. The manifestations of behaviour of the perpetrator in the past also form a statistical mass, a set, and the criminal offence under study is, a unit of it. These manifestations of behaviour or their causative factors have their material, general and lasting features in the same way as criminal offences have. Consequently, in the behaviour of the perpetrator, regularity and chance also appear. In the administration of justice, the regularities appearing in the past behaviour of the perpetrator should not be disregarded from the point of view of sentencing, of employing special preventive means, since a given criminal offence may be chance or regular in this relation as well. The probability of the perpetrator's future behaviour may be established if the regularity manifested in his behaviour and acts are explored in the process of administering justice. If the studied criminal offence belongs to the regularities of behaviour, it is highly probable that under the same conditions, i.e. in the case of the same circumstances and ineffective administration of justice, the perpetrator will commit another, perhaps similar, criminal offence. And, in turn, if the given offence may be considered as chance, the perpetration of a new offence is not probable. The knowledge of the general (past) behaviour of the perpetrator and the laws of crime is the solid ground on which effective administration of criminal justice, effective sentencing and enforcement of punishment may be built.

Finally, we have to comment on the changing of laws. Laws, the laws of causality of crime among them, are not everlasting, they undergo certain changes: they come into existence, strengthen, weaken and wither away and new ones appear instead of them. The existence and intensity of laws is dependent on certain conditions. The change or conscious transformation of conditions and circumstances may influence the intensity of laws. The law of causality of crime also exists only as long as, and only with that intensity, the existence and change of causative factors permit. Consequently, one of the fundamental tasks of criminology is to explore the causative factors and their constellations and on this basis to establish the intensity of the laws of causality. The stronger, the more intensive the influence of a certain law is, the lesser the role played by chance in the genesis of the effect and the higher the probability of the prediction of the phenomenon to be expected. Thus etiology, the exploration of causal relations and of the laws of causality, are indispensable for crime control since they can form the basis of the criminal justice system and the elaboration of the proper measures.

Part Two

Factors of Causality in Criminal Offences

I Personality and Psyche

The schemes drawn in the previous chapter give us the possibility of understanding the causal mechanism of criminal human behaviour. Criminal and non-criminal behaviour do not differ from each other in this respect. The difference is manifest in the concrete factors eliciting behaviour, in the social impact of the behaviour and, accordingly, in its evaluation, in the judgement of it. The law of the causality of crime and the laws of the perpetrators' behaviour indicate, however, that generally it is one set of influences that elicit behaviour satisfying social expectations and another set that elicit behaviour declared to be criminal.

In this part we intend to answer the question of what personality, biological, social or other environmental factors participate in eliciting criminal offences, in their genesis, i.e. what concrete contents fill the abstract causal scheme formed by us. Or formulating it in a different way, under the influence of what causative factors the perpetrators have committed their criminal acts, the particular criminal offence and why they committed criminal offences at all.

For the sake of better understanding, we draw the causal scheme of the intentionally committed criminal offence again:

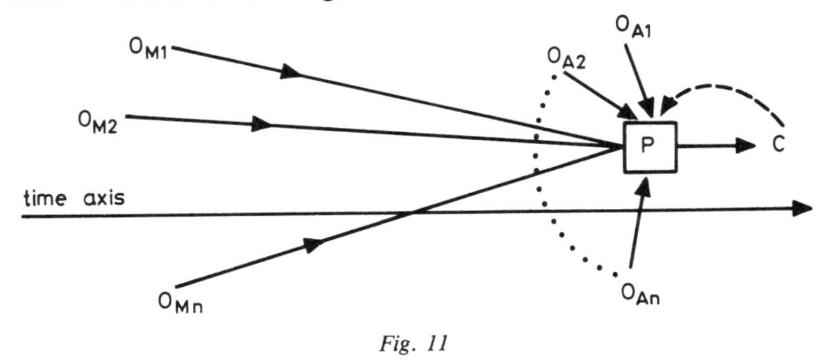

Fig. 11

In studying the scheme, it is always criminal offences or crime as an effect that we take as our starting point and we proceed backward, in the opposite direction to the actual process of causation. We do not deal with the concept and description of the criminal offence since it has been discussed in the introductory chapter. We focus our attention first on the perpetrator's personality and its material traits.

Since at the present level of science we can approach the personality only indirectly, on the basis of its manifestations, it is frequently regarded as a black box in which objective influences are restructured, combined, amplified or weakened according to the actual state of the personality and are manifested in one or other form of response, in one or other form of behaviour as the result of that process. However, we do not have an exact knowledge of the process itself.

1 The Concept of Personality

Due precisely to the inadequate information concerning the personality, even its concept appears in innumerable formulations. Medical doctors, psychiatrists and certain psychologists usually employ the concept of personality in a broader sense, i.e. in their conception the personality is the human being as the totality of somatic and psychological traits. Accordingly, the "personality is a synthetic concept which embraces all the traits of the human organization, both psyche and body, the totality of the active and acting human being from his birth to his death. The personality manifests itself in all the particular ways as someone perceives external impulses, responds to them, as his instinctive and emotional life is expressed, as he sets aims and achieves them, as he forms judgements, infers, combines, etc."[1] Böszörményi and Moussong-Kovács, referring to Gegesi Kiss, formulate a similar view in the textbook of medical psychology. The personality is "the totality and, at the same time, the unity of the individual's somatic/organizational occurrences and potential occurrences, which is individually systematized and has interrelations of a dynamic and energetic nature and which is human in general and has biological foundations specialized and fixed through the individual's predecessors and formed by general and local natural and social environmental influences."[2] This view is accepted also by Péter Popper.[3] Among the views identifying human being and personality with each other we should also mention the conception of Rubinstein, whose views are well known and generally accepted in the socialist countries. According to him, "the personality is first of all a live human being of flesh and blood who has his own needs which express his relation to the world and his dependence on it."[4]

There is another group of definitions of personality where the notion of personality focuses on the social nature of human beings. Among Hungarian authors, it is

[1] Gy. Nyirő, (ed.), *Psychiátria* (Psychiatry), Budapest: Medicina Könyvkiadó, 1971, p. 44.

[2] Z. Böszörményi and E. Moussong-Kovács, *Orvosi Pszichológia* (Medical Psychology), Budapest: Tankönyvkiadó, 1967, p. 61.

[3] P. Popper, *A kriminális személyiségzavar kialakulása* (The Development of Criminal Personality-Disorder), Budapest: Akadémiai Kiadó, 1970, p. 74.

[4] S. L. Rubinstein, *Az általános pszichológia alapjai II.* (Basic Problems of General Psychology), (in Hungarian), Budapest: Akadémiai Kiadó, 1964, p. 967.

perhaps József Lick who formulated this view most clearly in his monograph. "According to our definition based on the ideas of Marx, the individual is a single human being with the following characteristics: he is a) a biological being; b) a socially active being; c) a being separate from other individuals, from the communities of human beings and society. The individuality, consequently, is not one or other aspect "of the single human being, or a characteristic of his, but is the single human being himself together with all his characteristics and traits... This is why the notions of *specimen* (or biological individual), *individuality* and *personality,* are used. The notion of *specimen* serves the aim of stressing the biological and natural traits of the individual. Of course, a "pure" biological sphere does not exist in a human being, and consequently these traits are actually "bio-social" ones. The notion of *personality* is understood, as follows from our discussion above, as the socially active nature of the individual." Or, in more detail: "The personality expresses the socially active nature of the individual. For this reason, its development is directly defined socially, in other words, it depends on the level of development of the whole society and on the position of the individual in the social whole within that (divisions of labour, class, family relations, etc.), and on the specific conditions of life through which the effects of the whole nature of society are exerted on the personality."[5]

Similar ideas can be found in the French philosopher Lucien Séve's important work. After studying the ideas of Marx, Séve has drawn the conclusion that "relying on historical materialism, it has been discovered that a *psyche without an organic body* does exist, or more precisely, the *real limits of the psyche far exceed the limits of the living organization.*"[6] On the basis of this discovery he has concluded that the *personality is the living system of the social relations existing in the sphere of behaviour,* since "the essence of the human individual is not inherently within him but outside him, in the realm of social relations—in other words, humans are externally centered beings."[7]

Philosophers and psychologists who declare themselves Marxists usually set out from Marx's observation when they give a definition of the personality, according to which "The essence of man is no abstraction inherent in each single individual. In its reality it is the ensemble of the social relations"[8] and they build the social determination of the personality on this observation. "The personality is of social content and nature since its activities, abilities, roles and consciousness are the result

[5] J. Lick, *Személyiség és filozófia* (Personality and Philosophy), Budapest: Kossuth Könyvkiadó, 1969, pp. 174–175 and p. 178.

[6] L. Séve, *Marxizmus és személyiségelmélet* (Marxisme et théorie de la pérsonalité), (in Hungarian), Budapest: Kossuth Könyvkiadó, 1971, p. 263.

[7] Séve, *op. cit.,* p. 181.

[8] K. Marx, "Theses on Feuerbach" in: K. Marx and F. Engels, *Collected Works,* Vol. 5, Moscow, 1976, p. 7.

of interactions with the social environment; in the final analysis, they are the product of social evolution."[9]

It is also the works of the classics of Marxism that Márta Katona-Soltész refers to in her work when taking an opposite position.[10] According to her, human being, individual and personality are concepts with the same meaning. It would be possible to enumerate similar yet different definitions of personality[11] but it is superfluous, in my opinion, since my aim is not to give a detailed description or a profound examination or criticism of personality theories. I thought it desirable to present the two trends which are important from a criminological point of view. Criminology, or more precisely perhaps, criminologists need some kind of concept of personality and it is either adopted from philosophy or created as experience dictates. I, personally, accept essentially the view of Lick.

Criminological research projects known to me and my own studies have convinced me that the nature of criminal offences and crime, even of human behaviour, of human acts, in general, has a direct relationship with the degree and nature of the socialization of the human being. In other words, criminal behaviour is rooted primarily in the human being's intellectual and emotional world developed under the influence of social effects and relations, i.e. in his social and not in his biological nature. For this reason, from the point of view of the understanding and explanation of criminal behaviour and crime, a concept of personality seems to be scientifically well founded that does not identify the personality with the individual, with the human being himself, but embraces only his socialization, the system of his psychological relations with his environment and with himself, system which has evolved due to environmental, and above all, social effects on the grounds of the individual's biological endowments. This formulation expresses that it is not only social phenomena that influence the evolution of the personality, although they have the primary and decisive role, but that the nature of the pesonality depends also on biological endowments. Thus, we have to include also biological factors in factors determining the personality and they usually have the function of conditions in the causal relationship. (We shall revert later to the issue of which biological endowments and how they influence criminal behaviour.)

The concept of personality described in brief above is not only an individual view but is dominant in socialist criminology. One frequently finds similar interpreta-

[9] *Filozófiai Kislexikon* (Dictionary of Philosophy), Budapest: Kossuth Könyvkiadó, 1972.

[10] M. Katona-Soltész, A személyiség és a jog (Personality and Law), Budapest: Közgazdasági és Jogi Könyvkiadó, 1972.

[11] See H. Hiebesch and M. Vorwerg, *Bevezetés a marxista szociálpszichológiába* (Introduction to Marxist Social Psychology), (in Hungarian), Budapest: Kossuth Könyvkiadó, 1967, p. 6; I. S. Kon, *Az én a társadalomban* (The Self in Society), (in Hungarian), Budapest: Kossuth Könyvkiadó, 1969, p. 78; A. G. Kovaljev, *Személyiséglélektan* (Psychology of Personality), (in Hungarian), Budapest: Tankönyvkiadó, 1972, pp. 24–25.

tions of the personality in text-books and studies.[12] The social nature of the personality is expressed also in Kudriavtsev's opinion: "The psycho-physiological traits of the human being mean only the material foundations of the development of the personality; what the nature of a human being will be from the aspects of his social characteristics depends on the complex and lasting interaction between the individual and the environment surrounding him."[13]

Similar views are represented also by bourgeois criminologists. Manuel Lopez-Rey wrote in his report presented at the 2nd Criminological Congress of the UNO (London, 1960):

"The personality is something closely related to a specific environment which is partially reflected also by the behaviour of the person in question. As a structure the personality apparently is the result of two variables, one of them having a bio-psychologic nature and the other an external nature formed by the environment. These variables are not only in connection with each other but are interdependent to a certain extent; in short, both variables form the personality and this latter effects the two variables in various ways."[14]

Such an interpretation of the personality may appear an idealist bourgeois conception because it separates the body from the "soul" and the body plays only the role of the vehicle of the "soul" in this conception, the biological basis of the personality.

Since in this concept the personality is not identical with the individual, and it is not identical with the biological endowments of the individual either, they really are "separable" from each other to that extent. However, this separation does not mean the negation of the close relation between biological endowments and personality. It is evident that the personality cannot exist without biological endowments, without a bodily and organizational mechanism. But, in the same way, the personality cannot exist without social relations either, since it is the reflection, the reproduction of the external environment, above all social relations, that makes up the content of the personality. We have no more reason to exclude social relations from the concept of personality, or to include them in it, than to do so with biological endowments. It is true that the reflection and reproduction of the objective world are accomplished through biological endowments, primarily through the nervous system, but, without social effects, humans remain only biological beings in spite of

[12] See e.g. the Soviet textbook of criminology, *Kriminologiya,* Moscow: Yuridicheskaya Literatura, 1968, pp. 18–19, and pp. 133–134.

[13] V. N. Kudriavtsev, *Prichinnost' v Kriminologii,* Moscow: Yuridicheskaya Literatura, 1968, pp. 18–19; M. S. Leikina, *Lichnost' prestupnika i ugolovnaya otvetstvennost',* Leningrad, 1968.

[14] M. López-Rey, "The characteristic features of the activity of the UNO concerning the prevention of crime and the treatment of offenders. (Translation of the Ministry of Justice in Hungary), pp. 20–21

the potential to become humans. And criminology is primarily interested in the social nature, in the socialization of human beings, since criminal offences and crime are social categories and they are closely related to their socialization or to the lack of it.

The function of the biological mechanism of human beings could perhaps be illustrated by a comparison with computers. The nature of a computer defines its potential output but the actual output within these possibilities depends on the programme. Similarly, the expression of the personality by volition and action depends primarily not on the nature of the biological mechanism (supposing a normal, i.e. not faulty, mechanism) but on the effects that have made an impact on this mechanism, i.e. on the information that has been or is being programmed into the organism.

Naturally, the comparison of a biological and a cybernetic mechanism is rather inappropriate, the first being a living and the second a lifeless mechanism, the former having its own stimuli, impulses and needs which incite to action aimed at satisfying the needs; still, it may perhaps be suitable for illustrating the relation between the personality and biological endowments.

2 The Conscious and the Unconscious

It is apparent from the personality concept outlined by us that as far as the essence is concerned, we identify the personality with the psyche of the human being, which is, according to the most commonly accepted view, "the totality of the so-called mental phenomena; the product and means of the special interaction between the *subjective* (the individual—my italics, J. V.) and the *objective.* In the everyday sense, the psyche appears in the form of phenomena belonging to our so-called subjective world: perceptions, concepts, ideas, emotions, etc."

"The psyche is a peculiar product of the interaction between the object and the subject but, at the same time, it is the condition of this interaction in whose process functional neural systems develop that ensure the reflection of reality and are, at the same time, special regulators of the interaction between the subject and the objective world (the individual and the external world and within that, primarily the interaction of the individual and other human beings, society)."

"Making the relation between the objective world and the subject part of the consciousness is a peculiarity of the human psyche which allows the cognition of the characteristics and relations of things that belong to their essence, allows the conscious anticipation of events and purposeful planned activity. This peculiarity of the human psyche is related to the appearance and development of regular work activity and the means of social communication, speech. In the process of developing into a human being the mechanisms of neural activity are complemented and combined with the mechanisms of the second signaling system and thinking."

"In the ontogeny of the human being of our age, the essential part of the psychological development is the process in which the individual assimilates the achievements of the cultural and economic development of the preceding generations. The biologically hereditable characteristics are only the necessary conditions of this assimilation."[15]

I believe the quotations outline the concept of the psyche and its most important characteristics clearly and, although the quotations are formulated in a different way and with a different phraseology than the concept of personality, the identity of the essence and content is evident. The identification of the two concepts with each other has a particular significance from the aspects of criminology, of criminal etiology, since criminal behaviour belongs to the realm of conscious behaviour. The question to be answered here is whether the psyche, and thus the personality, represents only a realm of the conscious, or an unconscious realm, whether a system of psychological relations also exists which has come into being under the interaction between the human being and the given social environment and has been formed into its existing shape; and if the answer is in the affirmative, what connection exists between this unconscious sphere and the conscious one and, through the latter, criminal human behaviour.

It is one of the merits of the school of psychoanalysis and above all of its founder, Sigmund Freud, that the effects of unconscious or subconscious psychic processes on human behaviour receive due attention. Freud formulated it clearly that human behaviour is determined not only by conscious processes but also by processes happening in the spheres of neural activity which never come into the conscious mind. Materialist psychological and neuro-physiological research verifies the existence of subconscious psychologic processes and their effects on the conscious sphere, *but does not verify the statements* of Freud according to which the conscious and the unconscious represent two opposite poles and it is because the conscious mind is not able to keep unbridled hereditary instincts under control that human beings cannot adjust to their environment. Consequently, the criminal offence is nothing but the manifestation of various suppressed, mostly sexual, urges.

We may say without exaggeration that the views concerning unconscious psychologic phenomena are extremely heterogeneous. There are authors who distinguish several spheres in the realm of such psychologic processes. Thus they speak about the subconscious, the unconscious instincts, etc. Since it is not our aim to describe these processes, and the ideas concerning them in detail, non-conscious psychologic processes will be mentioned under the notion of the "unconscious" in the next short survey.

It has been recognized already by Pavlov that ideation is a psychological process in which incoming stimuli are transformed into an act of thinking and gain a verbal meaning, a significance in the second signaling system. The neurophysiological and

[15] *Filozófiai Kislexikon, op. cit.,* pp. 294–295.

psychological studies of our days, on the other hand, clearly prove "that human behaviour is influenced by visceral impulses, humoral and hormonal effects and proprioceptive stimuli. All this internal organic information can be regarded as the impulse source of the unconscious sphere."[16]

A characteristic concept of the unconscious psychologic phenomena has been formulated by the Georgian psychologists Uznadze and his school. According to their views, "the traditional division of mental processes into cognitive, emotional and volitional processes does not correspond to the objective situation at all. The psyche should rather be examined from the aspects of development and then the incorrectness of the position of the traditional bourgeois psychology in the analysis of mental processes becomes clear.

"If this is accepted as correct, we have to distinguish between two levels of psychologic activity: the level of attitudes where, in addition to the effective elements, we find a number of less differentiated perceptive and reproductive elements, and the level of objectivisation where we deal with certain active forms of psychologic activity—thinking and volition."[17]

Uznadze and his followers call attitude *(ustanovka)* the mental state which is not conscious "but which is determined by environmental factors through the acts of objectivation, identification and motivation. These acts as operational mechanisms lead to the conscious sphere and ensure the transition into the conscious."[18]

According to this conception, an attitude is a level of the development of the psyche preceding consciousness and comes into existence without the participation of the consciousness. "An attitude, as a psychological state, is a certain readiness of the subject to satisfy certain needs in a given situation. It is a characteristic trait of this state that it prepares definite manifestations of the consciousness or precedes or prefigures them. We may say that although this state is not conscious it represents a peculiar tendency toward certain contents of the consciousness. It would be best to call this state the attitude of the subject especially because first it is not some detailed content of the consciousness, it is not some isolated psychologic content that we contrast with, and distinguish from, or relate to, the rest of the content of the consciousness but a certain general overall state of the person; and second, this state is not simply a part of the content of the personality's psychologic life but an element of its dynamic determination. And, finally, this state is not some definite partial content of the individual but is an overall tendency toward definite activity. In short, it is more the attitude of the whole personality than an individual

[16] Gy. Ádám, *Érzékelés, tudat, emlékezés... biológus szemmel* (Perception, Consciousness, Memory... through the Eyes of a Biologist), Budapest: Medicina Könyvkiadó, 1969, p. 149.

[17] D. M. Uznadze, *Az ember beállítódása* (Attitude of Man), in: *The Psychology of Attitude,* Budapest: Akadémiai Kiadó, 1971, p. 143.

[18] I. Molnár, Előszó a *Beállítódás pszichológiájához* (Preface to the Psychology of Attitude), Budapest: Akadémiai Kiadó, 1971.

experience, but it is mostly a fundamental ancestral reaction responding to effects of the situations in which the personality sets its aims and performs its functions. This attitude appearing as an overall state provides the foundations of the fully determined psychological phenomena formed in our consciousness. It does not follow these psychological phenomena; on the contrary, it prefigures them and determines their composition and their impact."[19]

A similar position is also taken by Rubinstein. "The attitude of the personality is manifested in its relations to its aims and tasks and, furthermore, in its mobilization and readiness to act to achieve these aims. The attitude arising during the development, and being in the process of permanent transformation during the personality's activity, as the position of the personality giving rise to its actions, includes many components of various levels from elementary needs and desires to views and opinions of the level of Weltanschauung. The attitude produced by the internal interaction and interweaving of various trends expressing the tendencies of the personality, in turn, produces and defines these trends. Attitude in this sense has an extremely great significance from the point of view of the whole activity of the personality."[20]

It is worth quoting here the definition of the Great Soviet Encyclopedia: "Attitudes (in psychology) are a readiness of the human being to perform a certain activity, based on earlier experience: the purposiveness of perception, thinking, movement and action, work, etc. Depending on whether it is the readiness of perception or actuation that has a preponderance, the attitude may be sensorial or motor. An attitude is the result of the external effects forming part of the earlier experience and it is defined by the situation of the given moment. The psychological mechanism of the attitude is supplied by the system of conditional connections linked functionally to each other. An attitude develops under the effects of both direct stimuli and words through the second signaling system. The presence of an attitude hinders the development of another. An attitude is formed in the case of the repetition of external factors producing and situations defining it."[21]

From all this it follows that the personality, the psyche, consists of an unconscious and conscious sphere. The unconscious sphere is defined by "external effects forming part of the earlier experience and the situation of the given moment", in the same way as the conscious.

First of all, it is the so-called automatisms that we should mention in the unconscious sphere influencing human behaviour. A series of human habits belong to this area from walking or writing to complex activities. Forms of action may pass into the unconscious sphere which earlier could be performed only consciously but

[19] Uznadze, *op. cit.*, pp. 54–55.

[20] Rubinstein, *op. cit.*, pp. 964–965.

[21] *Bolshaya Sovietskaya Entsiklopediya* (Great Soviet Encyklopedia), 2nd. ed. Moscow, Vol. 44, pp. 402–403.

which, due to practice and repetition, have become automatisms. Such is, e.g. the series of actions on the part of a person in deep thought who takes his keys from his bag and opens the door automatically on arriving home, without being conscious of all this and without breaking his different chain of thought.[22]

An important place is taken by *emotional reactions* among the unconscious psychological functions of the human being. All environmental and biological stimuli have certain emotional features (pleasant or unpleasant etc. sensations). These emotions reach the level of consciousness only if attention is concentrated on them. Leonhard writes in connection with this: "...from the observation that our evoked emotions are frequently composed of subconscious interrelations, it can be understood that emotional processes pass off in the human being independent of intellectual cognition. If the effect ceased to exist when the notion belonging to it disappeared, we should immediately realize why we felt a certain thing at that moment. In reality, the emotions of a human being are not reflected so clearly in conscious cognition. It is not only in the case of psychopaths but also of perfectly normal people that a lot of clear emotional motives remain incomprehensible for conscious cognition."[23]

Research in neurophysiology has proved that it is in the limbic system of the brain that the control of emotional behaviour and visceral operation, at the same time, takes place. In his experiments with monkeys, Delgado was able to induce aggressivity or mildness in the animals through telemetric stimuli relayed by radio receivers planted on their collars. Although they may be significant, the results of such experiments with animals cannot be directly transferred to human behaviour, precisely because of the conscious human activity. "The non-conscious character of several factors of emotional behaviour, however, is evident also in the relations of humans" György Ádám writes in his work quoted earlier.[24]

It is a generally adopted view that the unconscious is not only the realm of mechanisms and emotions but is also the *realm of knowledge*. According to the findings of experimental psychology, the deeper and broader human cognition becomes, the more of this knowledge is stored in the unconscious sphere of the psyche. According to the actual tasks of conscious activity, various pieces of information and memory traces surface and in this way we make use of our past experience. But just as memory, the recall of old information to the conscious is needed, so it is necessary to forget, to eject parts of the memory from the consciousness. These two spheres are in contradiction but, at the same time, in balance. "The unconscious is a disposal and reserve system for the human psyche. The more we know, the more we enlarge the store of the unconscious."[25]

[22] K. Leonhard, *Biológiai pszichológia* (Biological Psychology), (in Hungarian), Budapest: Medicina Könyvkiadó, 1968, pp. 13–20.

[23] Leonhard, *op. cit.,* p. 180.

[24] Ádám, *op. cit.,* p. 156.

[25] Ádám, *op. cit.,* p. 150.

However, all this does not mean that the unconscious is only a kind of container keeping the material ready for the consciousness and that it has no independent significance. On the one hand, the unconscious has a direct relation with vegetative neural functions and, on the other hand, it is a kind of transition to the conscious sphere. There is no doubt, however, that psychologic occurrences are dominated by conscious processes because thoughts and the emotions reaching the level of the conscious are able to give rise to psychologic processes necessary for satisfying needs in a practicable way and for suppressing the opposing ones.[26] But like the conscious sphere, the unconscious contains information which has come into existence on a biological basis under the influence of external and internal effects.

The reason why I have thought it necessary to give a sketch of the unconscious is that in judging criminal human behaviour and in studying the laws of crime, criminology also has to take into consideration the existence of the unconscious and the findings of neurophysiology and psychology relevant for this sphere.

The views on the unconscious draw our attention to the fact that in the reproduction of the causal mechanism the unconscious factors must not be disregarded either. No doubt the present state of science does not yet allow the exact determination of unconscious phenomena or their measurement but the awareness of their existence and approximate inferences concerning them lead us toward a better understanding of criminal behaviour, in the same way as our knowledge of latent crime does concerning crime and offenders.

[26] P. Popper and Gy. Láng, *Általános pszichológia* (General Psychology), Budapest: BM Tanulmányi és Propaganda Csoportfőnökség, 1972, pp. 207–208.

II The Main Characteristics of the Personality of Perpetrators, Subjective Causal Factors

After giving a sketch of the notion and the structure of the personality, we may proceed with the discussion of the personality of perpetrators and with examining what main features characterize the personality of perpetrators and the contents of their consciousness and how these features are related to the perpetration of criminal offences.

It has already been mentioned, but I wish to emphasize again, that our knowledge of the personality is not exact enough and, for this reason, our observations and conclusions related to the content of the personality are of the value of probability or high probability.

1 The Content of Consciousness of the Perpetrators

In my experience gained during criminological studies, every intentional criminal offence is in a direct causal relation with an antisocial, or socially harmful, wrong view or views or attitudes of the perpetrator. (The term "antisocial" is not used to express hostility toward the political system of a society but is employed as a synonym for "harmful to society", "dangerous to society" or "socially disapprovable".)

In the volitional decision preceding the perpetration of the offence, these views are victorious in the process of the struggle of motives against motives harmonious with duties—if these were present at all. These wrong views or attitudes represent the subjective causes of criminal offences and under the necessary objective conditions, these causes manifest themselves in criminal offences.

It is almost impossible to enumerate all those views and forms of attitude that lead to a criminal volitional decision in the case of the manifestation of certain needs. It is still worth mentioning some of them as the most common ones: the outlook of selfishness, greed and living only for the moment, antisocial views or disposition of mind concerning work, family, the life and bodily integrity of others, the property of others, social coexistence. Formulating in a general way: the perpetrator does not accept social interests or their various forms as individual interests, which may find expression in several ways: 1. The perpetrator violates the norm of criminal law because he disapproves of the protected being taken as a social interest.

2. Although the perpetrator admits the necessity of social norms, conformity to them is compulsion on his part and he believes that he may deviate if he does not have to reckon with legal consequences. 3. In satisfying his needs, the perpetrator consciously sets himself against the expectations of society, accepting the possible consequences of criminal law. 4. The perpetrator has been raised in criminogenic circumstances and this is his natural way of life.

Our views and the tendencies of our consciousness have a fundamental role in controlling everyday life.

On the basis of the *tendencies of the consciousness,* of the aims, several types of people may be distinguished. There are people who take social trends and possibilities into consideration and *plan their life for long periods,* which defines the frame of their activities. As far as the contents are concerned, these programmes may be different. Where social relations are ruled by private property, the plans are based on the knowledge that the security of property, society and existence, in other words, existential security, has to be won by the individual himself. In the relations of socialism, the great majority of people know that their existential security is ensured by the relations of the state and society, the conditions of satisfying their needs are defined by the economic situation of the whole society, by the growing effectivity of the social, economic and political system. For this reason, people try to harmonize individual aims and the social goal in making their individual plans for life.

Consequently, life programmes made for the long range usually tally with social requirements, with the main tendencies of social development. Of people with such programmes only those commit criminal offences whose plan is to pursue a criminal life, a form of life conflicting with social requirements, or who are led by a strong causal inducement to satisfy their needs illegally.

There are individuals who have no *long-range life programmes* and live mostly for the present, who usually adjust themselves to the existing social framework and satisfy their needs within the limits of the given social possibilities, and do not consider social development to be expected. The behaviour of these people is influenced to a great extent by the actual objective relations (the given situation). The positive or negative nature of their behaviour depends primarily on their environment.

Finally, there are people *who pursue completely selfish goals, who disregard social interests.* This category is extremely dangerous to society because people who avoid work, habitual criminals, and the spongers of society belong to it.

In addition to aspirations and aims, Weltanschauung and moral conviction are other important constituting elements of the general tendencies of the personality. Weltanschauung and moral convictions provide the intellectual and emotional standpoint which may give guidance for behaviour if it is firm, consistent and definite enough. A materialist, Marxist Weltanschauung makes it possible to understand the connections of social relationships and, through that, to fit individual behaviour in the system of the fulfilment of social requirements.

However, we have to underline that the knowledge of interactions of social relationships and of the requirements of society alone is not enough. If a person is aware of the role of social property, he may still commit offences against it. Knowledge of Weltanschauung may become the guideline for behaviour required by society if it is accompanied by conviction, if it gains an emotional load, in other words, if the individual regards the realization of this knowledge as in his own interest. In that case, social interest appears also as individual interest and the ideas and views become the fundamental motivating forces of practical activity.

But a significant number of people have a different Weltanschauung. It is not infrequent even nowadays that in the background of the criminal offence, a Weltanschauung different from Marxism, or contrary to that, may be discovered, and this serves as a guideline for antisocial behaviour. But it is much more frequent that behind criminal behaviour one may find the right views on socialism and the awareness of the requirements, but the moral conviction of the perpetrator is lacking, and thus the satisfaction of the individual interest may come to the fore to the detriment of social interest.

However, we have to distinguish persons according to *the extent of their antisocial disposition.* There are people whose system of views is antisocial as a whole, whose aims and their relations to social requirements are dominated by negative views. In such cases we speak about an antisocial attitude of the conscious mind, which usually entails antisocial, criminal behaviour, a criminal life style. In other cases antisocial views constitute only a part of the individual's system of views, of his sphere of consciousness. In such cases the perpetration of criminal offences depends on what the character of the views that are accompanied by the actual aspirations and goals is, in other words, whether the views necessary to the realization of the actual aim include antisocial elements, or not. There are, however, cases where *the offender is not aware of his antisocial disposition, i.e. he believes that his behaviour in general* (and also in the given criminal case) is guided by social interests. It may occur that due to the lack of abilities, education or proper consideration, socialist political, economic and ethical views are distorted in the mind of the offender. In such cases, although the perpetrator is favourably disposed emotionally and he wishes to satisfy needs that he believes to be of social interest, his behaviour conflicts with social requirements and violates social relationships (e.g. abuse of authority in the "public interest").

The distinction between the socially harmful views and socially harmful attitudes of consciousness points to the degree of the perpetrator's socialization or, more precisely, to the lack of socialization, i.e. to the content of the personality. We think it necessary to distinguish between these two grades at least, because we, non-convicted people, may also, and actually do, have views that are antisocial, harmful to society. They may even surface in the struggle of motives in the process of displaying an activity suitable for satisfying the needs, but if it is the motives harmonious with our obligations that win, we do not commit criminal offences. In the case of the majority of people, the volitional decision to act in accordance with everyday duties is made in this way. But antisocial attitudes of consciousness means that a preponderance of antisocial views exists in the perpetrator's mind, they constitute a kind of system, or one or other of the antisocial views has become fixed as an aptitude, a pattern or a stereotype, which frequently wins in the struggle of motives and leads to the perpetration of a criminal offence if the conditions are suitable. It is usually the confirmed criminals who are characterized by such attitudes. We have to add, however, that even such persons may have and actually do have socially acceptable views (e.g. assisting parents, children, the weak) which may serve as a basis for transforming their consciousness.

Antisocial attitudes indicate a permanent state of the personality. They mean that the perpetrator's antisocial views have been playing an important role in his decisions of will for a long time and their manifestation in antisocial forms of behaviour have become habitual. These notions are also expressed in the expressions "confirmed criminal" or "habitual criminal".

Viewing criminal offences from the level of their subjective causes, from the level of the perpetrators's socialization, we may say in general that people commit criminal offences because they have certain antisocial, socially harmful views or attitudes and the satisfaction of a given need is linked to these and a suitable situation exists or has been created; furthermore the motives that are harmonious with the person's obligations do not even arise or lose in the struggle of motives. And, to the question why the given form of antisocial behaviour is displayed by them, the answer is that the concrete need arising "tallies" with the antisocial views or attitudes that participate in the decision of will related to the satisfaction of the need. As an example, we may mention the person who has antisocial views concerning social property and the satisfaction of his needs but recognized and respects the personal freedom of others and condemns all forms of violence applied against anyone—this person would not use force in solving his personal conflicts and would not commit criminal offences against human life and bodily integrity, but to satisfy his material needs, particularly if the conditions are favourable, he abuses social property and commits criminal offences against that.

2 Antisocial Attitudes

It seems necessary to discuss the problems of antisocial attitudes of the conscious mind in more detail since the concept of psychological attitudes is gaining ground in psychology and in the evaluation the criminological application of the concept is varied.

The concept of the antisocial attitude is well known in the socialist literature of criminology. In Soviet criminology, the concept is linked above all to Sakharov's name, who discussed his views on the topic in a monograph published in 1960.[1] The concept also appeared in Hungarian literature,[2] essentially with the same content, interpreting attitudes strictly from the aspects of consciousness, knowledge and views.

Recently in Bulgaria an attempt (in my opinion successful) was made to set up a certain kind of typology of offenders on the basis of antisocial attitudes.[3] According to Fidanov, "The antisocial attitude of the personality is regarded as the basis of *persistent* individual criminal behaviour."[4] In the case of an attitude we do not deal with single views, habits and emotions but with "the total disposition of the consciousness of the subjective, with the generalized *position* taken by the personality toward the environment, with the general "programme" of the personality to be followed in certain situations of life; consequently, we do not deal with one or other element of the socio-psychological characteristics of the personality *but with its whole organization and system.*"[5]

The concept of the personality's antisocial attitude is criticized from several aspects by Soviet criminologists. Karpets fundamentally disputes the applicability of the concept of antisocial attitudes for criminological analysis.[6] He maintains that criminology has mechanically adopted this concept of psychology, but it is the state of the unconscious sphere that the attitude indicates, and thus it cannot explain a conscious act such as a criminal offence.

Karpets is right insofar as a criminal offence is conscious human behaviour and for this reason it is connected to the motives that reach the level of awareness in the personality, in the psyche of the perpetrator. This, however, does not contradict the evaluation of the content of the unconscious sphere, since, in accordance with what has been said of the unconscious, the emotional moments, memories, fixed experience, views, and patterns of automatic action of the individual, of the perpetrator, which are not permanently present in the actual sphere of the consciousness, but may be evoked or "vibrate" together with the actual stimuli and may influence the direction of action, or its content, belong to this psychological system.[7] In other

[1] A. V. Sakharov, *O Lichnosti Prestupnika i Prichinakh prestupnosti v SSSR,* Moscow: Juridicheskaya Literatura, 1961.

[2] J. Vigh, "Kauzalitás a kriminológiában" (Causality in Criminology), *Jogtudományi Közlöny,* 11–12 (1968). The concept of antisocial attitudes may already be found, even if with a somewhat different interpretation, in the work of L. Viski, *A szándékosság és a társadalomra veszélyesség* (Intention and Danger to Society), Budapest: Közgazdasági és Jogi Könyvkiadó, 1969

[3] D. Fidanov, "Sluchainiat prestupnik", *Izvestiya na Mezhduvedomstveniya Sovet za Kriminologicheski Issledovaniya,* 2, Sofia, 1972.

[4] Fidanov, *op. cit.,* p. 69.

[5] Fidanov, *op. cit.,* p. 75., takes this position in agreement with Kudriavtsev.

[6] I. I. Karpets, *Problemy prichinnosti,* Moscow: Yuridicheskaya Literatura, 1969, pp. 82–83. See also Karpets and Ratinov in their quoted article.

[7] V. Buzov, "Za Ustanovkata i Neynoto Antiobshchestvenno Proyavlenie" in: *Izvestiya na Mezhduvedomstveniya Sovet za Kriminologicheski Issledovaniya,* 2, Sofia, 1972; L. Kardos, *Általános Pszichológia* (General Psychology), Budapest: Tankönyvkiadó, 1964, pp. 223–228.

words, conscious action depends also on what knowledge, memories, and emotional connections are accumulated in the unconscious, which of these become part of the conscious mind under the effects of internal or external stimuli, how the personality is conditioned. And if this attitude basically is an antisocial one, the method of satisfying the rising needs will usually be antisocial, too. The motives that are in harmony with the person's obligations either do not surface at all or, if they do, will lose against the intensive antisocial motives.

The negative or positive disposition of the unconscious sphere has, in my opinion, a significant role in human behaviour. Criminological studies have proved beyond doubt that the regular criminal behaviour of confirmed or habitual criminals is explicable precisely by their unfavourable, antisocial memories, impressions, views, and patterns of behaviour accumulated during their life.

So far we have usually spoken of the antisocial attitude of the *consciousness* which, no doubt, means a certain narrowed concept of the attitude, although the phenomena of the consciousness have a decisive role. Accepting that as a starting point, it seems more proper to speak of the antisocial psychological attitudes or simply antisocial attitudes of the perpetrator's personality.

An antisocial attitude, although it concerns the whole system of views, emotions and habits, may be concentrated in certain areas. Such an area may be that of attitudes antagonistic to the regime which may manifest themselves mainly in so-called political crimes, materialistic, acquisitive attitudes which are primarily the instigators of offences against property; or the attitudes of parasitic, work-avoiding persons, who are ready to commit any offence in order to maintain their parasitic life style; and we may mention also those who have violent attitudes and are characterized by roughness, lack of culture, by a disregard for the life and bodily integrity of others, by bullying, and consequently, by the perpetration of criminal offences of violence.[8]

3 The Regularity or Chance Nature of the Perpetration

The examination of antisocial views and attitudes is extremely important in the process of the administration of criminal justice, since criminal justice, if it focuses on education, can reach its aim only if the personality of the perpetrator is also taken into consideration in the sentence, in addition to the gravity of the act. We have said in connection with the causal scheme that an event occurring by necessity has factors of regularity and chance. Consequently, the causal factors that determine the perpetration of criminal offences by necessity (causes and conditions) may also be of a regular and chance nature. We have concluded that it is only on the

[8] See J. Vigh, K. Gönczöl, Gy. Kiss and Á. Szabó, *Erőszakos bűncselekmények és elkövetőik* (Violent Crimes), Budapest: Közgazdasági és Jogi Könyvkiadó, 1973.

basis of the study of a great number of units or of the full mass that the regularity can be recognized. And since the regularity manifested in phenomena is the guideline of our future actions it is a primary task of criminology to distinguish between regular and chance processes and actions.

Taking, however, a particular criminal offence as the basis, the distinction has no significance; it is enough here to establish that it has the nature of necessity. The relation of regularity or chance is a relation which manifests itself only in repetition, in mass, in the relation between the units. For this reason it is only from the behaviour of the perpetrator, from the mass of his actions, that the necessity or chance nature of a particular criminal offence can be recognized. Of course, the full mass of the perpetrator's acts cannot be subject to study, so we have to strive for the evaluation of those forms of the perpetrator's behaviour that may be known to us. These include, among others, school progress, relations with the family, with work, with fellow-workers and the forms of manifestation of these. From the totality of these acts, it is possible to establish approximately the law of the perpetrator's behaviour, i.e. whether it is views meeting social requirements or antisocial views or attitudes that dominate his actions, in other words, whether the particular criminal offence should be regarded as regular or chance. The regular or chance nature of the perpetration of criminal offences reflect one of the most important characteristics of the perpetrators. In my opinion, the grouping of offenders by these criteria is one of the basic requirements of criminology.

Such a grouping of the perpetrators raises several problems, both theoretical and practical. These categories are not alternatives, which means that it is not possible to classify every perpetrator into one of the two. Theoretically, it is not possible, because the regular or chance nature of the criminogenic behaviour is not unmistakably clear in the case of every perpetrator, since the laws operate under certain conditions, in certain circumstances. The circumstances of the perpetrator's behaviour and life style may change significantly for the better or the worse. The changes in the circumstances may weaken or strengthen the regularity of earlier forms of behaviour, or may even terminate it and create the conditions for the operation of new regularities. From the point of view of criminology, this means that in the series of acts in the case of some of the perpetrators there is no unmistakable tendency toward either the positive or the negative and the particular criminal offence cannot be put either in the category of regularity or in that of chance. For this reason, the categories of regularity and chance are only categories close to the two extreme poles. Consequently, there is a third category between the two, the so-called transitional one or the category of the non-identifiable. Formulating perhaps in a simpler way: there are perpetrators 1. whose past behaviour shows a clearly criminogenic tendency and in whose case the committed criminal offence is regular, 2. whose general behaviour shows a strong tendency toward meeting social requirements regularly, so that their criminal offence may be regarded as chance and 3. whose behaviour does not clearly show either of the two regularities.

On a continuous scale between the positive and negative poles these three categories may be illustrated in the following way:

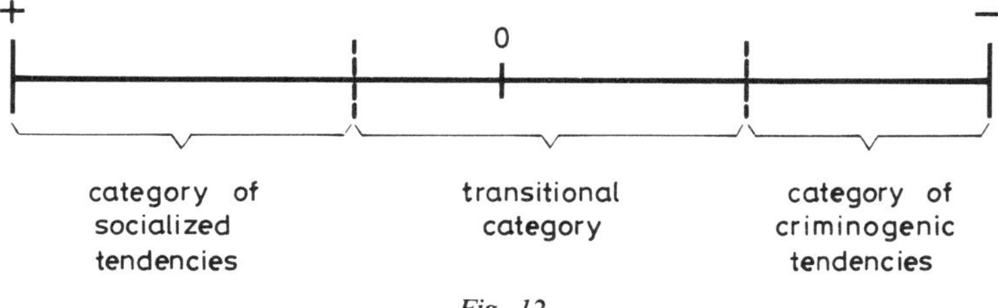

Fig. 12

Every perpetrator may be classified into one of the three categories through fixing the limit value between categories and through proper evaluation. The regularity dominating within each category renders probable the future behaviour of the perpetrator (of course, under the same conditions). The closer the regularity of the perpetrator's behaviour falls to the negative or positive pole, the higher the regularity.

These are the problems of theoretical grouping. The practical categorization represents many more difficulties. First, due to the lack of adequate information, the real regularity of the perpetrator's behaviour may not always be established clearly even if it is close to one of the poles. This produces a certain range of error and the perpetrator will not be classified in the category he actually should be. It happens very rarely that the information is incorrect to the extent that criminogenic regularity is established instead of tendencies towards socialization, or *vice versa.* The small percentage of error appears almost exclusively on the borderlines of the transitional category. This inevitable margin of error does not affect, however, the basic value of such a categorization. In practical activity the fault is never that we create something that is imperfect but that we are not aware of it or conceal it.

We have always differentiated perpetrators by their being first offenders or recidivists. This categorization is similar but it is not the same as the categorization by the regular or chance nature of the criminal offence. This is particularly true if, in addition to the criminological notion of recidivism, we take into consideration its notion in criminal law, and, furthermore, if we keep in mind that the notion of first offenders is usually limited to those who are convicted first time.

In criminology, the differentiation of casual and confirmed criminal is also known.[9] This categorization has close similarities with the categorization described by us. Criminal offences committed by confirmed criminals are the regular consequences of the degree of socialization of their personality, of their *antisocial attitude.* In the case of such perpetrators the criminal decisions of will are motivated first of all by the material features of personality, the actual objective circumstances usually play the role of conditions only. Moreover, if the conditions are unfavour-

[9] J. Földvári and J. Vigh, *Kriminológia* (Criminology), Budapest: Tankönyvkiadó, 1968.

able, the perpetrator may perform a series of preceding acts in order to create the necessary conditions for putting the criminal decision of will into effect.

The criminal offence of casual offenders is a consequence of the effects of the objective situation. We usually say that they are not proper to the personality but are situational ones, offences initiated by the favourable opportunity, by the favourable situation.

As the Soviet criminologist Leikina said: "The criminal offences mentioned do not express antisocial attitudes, they only show that the offender does not make efforts intensive enough to resist the negative circumstances and not to pass the limits set up by the law."[10]

Such criminal offences may originate from two types of personality from the point of view of socialization. The first type is on the level of socialization where it is only because of the general preventive effects of punishment that the otherwise existing antisocial views are not manifested in the perpetration of criminal offences. That the opportunity is favourable means here not only that the antisocial behaviour suitable for satisfying a need can be displayed without any particular organizational work and effort, but primarily that the probability of avoiding punishment (the establishment of criminal liability) is very high, seems to be almost certain. And since such situations are relatively rare, they are "chance", these criminal offences generally may not be regarded as regular. However, in all the cases when it is only the fear of punishment and not the recognition of the social interest as individual interest that prevents the perpetration of the criminal offence, the repeated escape from punishment may make chance perpetration regular.

Fidanov very perspicaciously remarks in connection with this in his above quoted work that "the dangerous recidivist once also used to be a more or less casual offender whose course of life led him without the proper attention and care of the socialist society. In this sense "confirmed", "incorrigible", vicious and particularly dangerous criminals represent the "tuition fee" that society pays for not taking possible and effective measures in time. The clearly marked antisocial attitude that may be observed in the case of certain criminals bears witness to the fact that a whole series of signals concerning the moral ethical development of these persons did not receive proper attention and when these people did something wrong there was no proper reaction."[11]

I fully agree with the quotation and I note only as an interpretation that the failure to take the "possible and effective" measures is regular to a certain extent, it is a necessary concomitant of the transitional socialist society. There is no doubt that the objective social potentialities for taking more effective measures to prevent crime than the present ones also exist but it would be unrealistic to expect a highly

[10] N. S. Leikina, "Vliyanie lichnostnykh osobennostei na prestupnost", *Sovetskoe Gosudarstvo i Pravo,* 1 (1967), p. 103.

[11] Fidanov, *op. cit.,* p. 93.

significant decrease in crime or its complete elimination. I only dispute that at the present level of development, the socialist state has the potentialities in general to take really more effective measures.

It is also a casual criminal offence that is perpetrated by a person who commits his offence not because of the high probability of escaping punishment but because of the extremely strong inducement of the given situation. Under everyday or usual circumstances, the decision of will aimed at the satisfying of needs is controlled by motives harmonious with obligations, by views harmonious with social requirements. Extraordinary circumstances, pressing needs and casual situations may lead, however, to an antisocial way of satisfying needs. And since these extraordinary circumstances are really very rare, such criminal offences may also be regarded as chance.

As can be seen, the classification of perpetrators by regular, or chance (and not identifiable) perpetration, since these categories reflect material traits of the socialization of the personality, provide a more reliable basis for an adequate sentence and the definition of the proper penal measures than all previous classifications, in spite of the several per cent possibility of classification error.

The classification of the offenders by the regular or chance nature of the criminal offences may be used not only in the realm of intentional criminal offences but also in the case of offences by negligence. Negligence may be characteristic, i.e. regular, and it may also be chance in the general behaviour of the perpetrator of a criminal offence of negligence, in the series of his acts. A favourable result from the point of view of special prevention may be expected of various penal measures. In the case of a perpetrator whose behaviour is characterized, as a rule, by care, due consideration, the evaluation of the possible consequences of his deeds, special prevention does not require any penal measure. In such cases only the interest of general prevention may be grounds for some "moderate" sanction, some kind of minimal legal detriment. In the case of a perpetrator whose negligence is of the nature of regularity, i.e. whose behaviour is generally characterized by continuous negligence and who has committed offences of negligence several times, or simply because of chance or the care of other persons has not committed a criminal offence yet, the continuous negligence represents a permanent danger situation of a certain probability, i.e. he is dangerous to society to a certain degree. In such cases special prevention may be served only by a measure that teaches the perpetrators to have proper care. And this may not be attained by either a fine or loss of freedom for one month or two but only through forced education or medical treatment, of proper duration.

If we accept this train of thought, it will be evident that, in addition to the basic categorization of criminal offences as offences by intention or negligence, the regular or chance nature of offences is the criterion, the characteristic of the perpetrator that should be kept in mind in sentencing and during the implementation of punishment.

4 The Perpetrator's Dangerousness to Society

The acceptance of the antisocial attitude of the personality and nature of regularity of the perpetration of the criminal offence demands that we should give expression to our views on the perpetrator's dangerousness to society.[12]

The Hungarian Criminal Code of 1961 employed the notion of the perpetrator's dangerousness to society, but the theory of criminal law, perhaps in order to avoid identification with the concept of the born dangerous criminal, linked the perpetrator's dangerousness to society to the social dangerousness of the offence, and regarded it as dependent on the latter. Kádár's and Kálmán's opinion described in their work is very clear: "The person (the subject) displaying socially dangerous behaviour is always dangerous to society at the time of the perpetration. What follows from that is that the perpetrator's dangerousness to society is dependent on the act's dangerousness to society. *There is no* such case where the act is, but the perpetrator is not, dangerous to society. For this reason the perpetrator's dangerousness to society is not an independent criterion of the criminal offence."[13]

The authors of the quotation emphasize that there is no case where the offence is dangerous to society but the perpetrator is not. This is true, but the crucial point of the issue is to be found not in this negation but in the question of whether someone can be in a state which is dangerous to society without having committed a criminal offence and whether it is true that the perpetrator's dangerousness to society exists only depending on the act's dangerousness to society.

Answering these questions, Ödön Bodnár has pointed out that a person who has not yet committed a criminal offence but has the traits in his personality and behaviour that render probable the perpetration of a criminal offence, is in a state of dangerousness to society. "The perpetrator does not become an offender overnight but as a result of the wrong development of his personality. In the process of this development the readiness (attitude) to act in a way that is a danger to society is formed. It manifests itself earlier than the criminal act, in an antisocial activity (in the so called social dangerousness whithout criminal law) which perhaps is not even perceivable (mental) or does not fall under the evaluation of criminal law."[14]

This degree of the person's dangerousness to society is, in fact, the pre-delinquent state that has been described by András Szabó in the Hungarian literature[15] and for which he has been sharply criticized.[16]

[12] Personal dangerousness to society is analyzed in the excellent dissertation of E. Bócz, *A személyi társadalomra veszélyesség a büntetőjogban* (Individual Dangerousness to Society in Criminal Law), Budapest, 1975.

[13] M. Kádár and G. Kálmán, *A büntetőjog általános tanai* (General Doctrines of Criminal Law), Budapest: Közgazdasági és Jogi Könyvkiadó, 1966, p. 400.

[14] Ö. Bodnár, "Gondolatok a személyi társadalom veszélyességről" (Thoughts on Individual Dangerousness to Society), *Magyar Jog és Külföldi Jogi Szemle,* 1972, p. 228.

[15] See: A Szabó, "A nevelő-átnevelő intézkedések és a büntető szankciók" (Educative and Re-educative Measures and Penal Sanctions), *Jogtudományi Közlöny* 11 (1966).

[16] T. Lukács, "Büntetőjogi szemléletünk alakulása" (Changes in Our View of Criminal Law), *Magyar Jog és Külföldi Jogi Szemle,* 9 (1970).

The possibility of such a dangerous state of the person without a criminal offence logically follows from our concept of causality. The admission of predelinquent state gives certain persons the idea that those who are in that state should be proceeded against with the means of criminal law, which would clearly mean a gross violation of socialist legality and would provide excellent opportunities for arbitrariness and the abuse of law.

With faulty logic it is possible to reach this and many other conclusions and no statute or theoretical opinion may provide protection against it—the possibility has existed and will exist. The right conclusion, however, may not go beyond the following: a) The existence of the predelinquent state should be proven by facts, by the tendency of the regularity manifested in the perpetrator's deeds (antisocial acts of minor importance, statements, the manifestation of his disposition toward work and fellow humans, etc). b) Adequate measures not of the nature of criminal law have to be taken in order to eliminate the dangerous state before it is manifested in the form of a criminal offence.

The other degree of the dangerous state is when the person's dangerousness to society is not eliminated by the perpetration of the criminal offence, by the establishment of criminal responsibility or by the implementation of the punishment. This is the case when we may speak of the perpetrator's dangerous state to society. In such cases the forms of the perpetrator's behaviour that may be perceived in the external world show that the situation that threatens the interests of society protected by criminal law with harm is not eliminated, and the danger of the perpetration of other offences still exists. Thus, immediately after the perpetration of the criminal act, a new danger situation has arisen.

This is what can be recognized in the case of multiple recidivists. *In such cases we may talk about the permanence of the person's (particular and in criminal law) dangerousness to society.*[17]

It is hardly possible to doubt that there are such perpetrators; on the contrary, they are recorded as "dangerous criminals", the authorities know about them and "expect" them to commit new offences and in most cases the authorities do not have to wait for long or in vain.

It is more a conceptual than a material issue whether the perpetrator's dangerousness to society is a state or a characteristic of his.[18] In my opinion, there are cases where dangerousness to society is only a condition, on the other hand, if this state has existed for years or perhaps for decades, it is not an error to speak about a characteristic, since we deal here with material and permanent traits of the perpetrator's socialization, attitude and human nature.

The conclusion to be drawn from the existence of the perpetrator's dangerousness to society, particularly if this state remains even after the implementation of the

[17] Bodnár, *op. cit.,* p. 230.

[18] See E. Bócz, "A személyiség a kriminológiában és a büntetőjogban" (The Personality in Criminology and Criminal Law), *Belügyi Szemle,* 2 (1971); Bodnár, *op. cit.*

punishment, must be the same as from the existence of the pre-delinquent state. (We shall discuss these problems in detail in subsequent parts.)

5 The Motivating Effects of Needs

According to the teaching of socialist psychology, all human activities are directed towards satisfying certain needs, wishes, desires or aspirations. Since human beings can exist only in an interaction with their environment, they need the various objects of the environment and the establishment and maintenance of a certain relation with the environment. These objects and relations represent the conditions of life for them. In other words, the basis of all human behaviour is the need, on the one hand, and the environment suitable for satisfying the need, the possibilities, the preconditions for satisfying the need, on the other hand. The history of the development of the human personality is closely linked with the history of the development of its needs. It was needs that made human beings create more and more perfect ways of satisfying them. At the same time, this activity of production created more and more manifold and sophisticated needs. As a result of this interaction, human needs are always in conformity with the level of production of the given society. For this reason, needs are inseparable from the biological and social nature of human beings, from the level of their socialization. The needs of the human being of our days are a peculiar mixture of biological and social ones. Although biological (organic) needs precede social needs in their content and intensity in general, at the present level of our social development, particularly in the case of persons living in favourable economic (material) circumstances, social needs, or the social character of satisfying needs, come to the fore. Nowadays, even the satisfaction of social needs has gained a social character. The production of material goods and social development in most countries, Hungary among them, are on a level where the fundamental organic needs of people, i.e. food, shelter providing protection against weather, and clothes, can be ensured as the result of daily work. It is the nature, the method of satisfying these needs that is in the focus of human aspirations. It is not at all indifferent what food, what clothes and what accommodation satisfy our organic needs. In the process of the development of society these ways also evolve and are in constant change. Cultural and other intellectual needs, originating from the social division of labour, are blended in the forms, the whole system, of satisfying biological needs.

The development of production and the abundance of goods make the intensification of the social nature of human beings more and more possible and the problem of satisfying social needs comes to the fore more and more.

The growth of socialization, which is manifest in the evolution of the human race (phylogenesis), can also be found in a similar form in the evolution of the individual (ontogenesis). A child is born as a biological being but has biological endowments which include potentially the operational peculiarities of the nervous system of the predecessors that evolve under the influence of social development. A child becomes a social being only in the course of his development, he learns only gradually (depending on his age and education) the knowledge that he has to use as an independent individual in the process of adaptation and co-operation. As in biological evolution, in the social development of the individual the traits of the philogenetic social development can be recognized, as with the biogenetic law of Haeckel. If this parallel development is kept in mind, it becomes evident that the biological nature of humans is only a precondition, a frame for the development toward socialization. The degree and nature of socialization can be traced back to the objective relations of society.

The most characteristic feature of human beings as social beings is that they satisfy their needs consciously, through conscious action, and not instinctively. Objective reality and its regularities are reflected in the consciousness of the human being, according to the state of the personality and depending on his knowledge. Human beings are able to recognize and take into account the hindering and assisting circumstances that have an effect on the measure and method of satisfying needs. They make their decisions concerning the satisfying of needs or social adaptation on the basis of the evaluation of these hindering and assisting factors.

Although individual needs originate mostly from the given society, they may contradict social requirements and social possibilities. Social interests, social needs, social possibilities appear to the individual in the form of various legal provisions, the provisions of criminal law among them. While legal provisions allow a broad area for satisfying individual needs according to the quantity and quality of the work done within the order of the division of labour, they express a threat of punishment for the methods of satisfying needs which violate or endanger social interests, social requirements. It is natural and regular that individuals may have needs that cannot be satisfied in a manner provided by a legal provision under the given social circumstances, since demands and needs always go beyond the possibilities. The activity of production, creative human work, is done partially in order to create the possibilities of meeting the existing but unsatisfied needs.

The main question of criminology in connection with this is why certain persons would not give up, or restrict within the provisions of criminal law, the satisfaction of those of their needs that are opposed to existing social requirements. Nowadays, under the circumstances of socialism, it rarely happens that biological needs cannot be met in a legal way, at least in their simplest forms, and that certain persons are simply compelled to commit criminal offences to ensure their living. *Criminal offences are generally committed because people want to satisfy their needs in a way different from the legal one,* in a way that represents more pleasure, a higher satisfaction to them, or because they strive for the satisfaction of needs society cannot, or perhaps does not want to satisfy. Some of the perpetrators are persons who cannot satisfy one or other of their real needs, although they have and do a regular job, and for this reason, either influenced by the opportunity and in the hope of avoiding punishment, or accepting the possibility of punishment they commit criminal offences. But there is also a narrower circle of perpetrators who could meet their needs partially or fully through work but for whom the illegal satisfaction of their needs has become a life style.

It seems from all this that tracing back the perpetration of criminal offences to the satisfaction of needs is limited to gaining material goods or other advantages connected with them, and it is difficult to find the place of offences against human life, violence against officials or rape in this picture. The perpetration of these and many other offences does not aim to satisfy needs of a material nature or needs related to material interests, indeed, but there is no doubt that they ensure the satisfaction of some kind of needs. A high percentage of crimes of violence, for example is aimed at revenge for real or imaginary injuries. The need for compensation for injuries is a rightful one but the satisfaction of this need may be attained within socially approved frames and not only through taking justice into our own hands since there are legal means for eliminating serious differences of opinion or conflicts between people, and not only physical or psychological force is available. There are, of course violent perpetrators for whom violent behaviour is itself a source of pleasure and means the satisfaction of some kind of distorted psychologic need. Psychologic needs (social success, gaining pre-eminence, certain independence, belonging to someone, etc.) play an important role in the life of humans. Satisfying these needs under socially prescribed conditions and within allowed limits may have a strongly favourable influence on the development of society. At the same time, to satisfy these needs in a way opposed to social requirements, or harmful or dangerous to society, may violate or endanger the rights of others, public order and public safety.

There are psychologists who say that people commit criminal offences because they have a law tension tolerance to lasting psychological tension coming into existence due to anger, the lack of material goods, jealousy, or sexual desire. Some people need and require short but intense tensions. A human being who is able to tolerate tensions of emotional overtones and long duration is able to adjust to social requirements, and one who is not able to do so would respond to these tensions in some way, usually through committing criminal offences.[19] According to the representatives of this view, the society of our day expects and demands that its members should live under continuous tensions and only a relatively small sphere is open for a life-style involving short but intense tensions. Regular studies, regular work, constant adaptation to various rules result by themselves in such a not very intense but lasting, continuous psychological tension. And since the personality of offenders is primitive, infantile, like children, it cannot tolerate lasting tensions but demands short tensions of high intensity, it tries to eliminate the tension that seems

[19] P. Popper, *Kriminálpszichológia* (Criminal Psychology), (College textbook), Budapest: BM Rendőrtiszti Főiskola, 1973, Chapters IV and V.

intolerable to it. This is why there are so many alcoholics, drug addicts, persons avoiding work and persons living without family or within loose family bonds, etc., among offenders.

According to this conception, the teachings of criminology have to be revised, in fact. It is not excessive drinking, a work-avoiding way of life, disorganized family relations, criminogenic factors in general that lead to the commission of criminal offences, but these criminogenic factors and crime can be traced back to a common origin, namely to the poor toleration of lasting psychologic tensions, to the satisfaction of the needs for short but intensive tensions. In a simpler and generalized formulation this means that antisocial behaviour may be traced back directly to the above-mentioned characteristic of the personality, this antisocial personality is nothing but an infantile personality whose development came to a standstill in an early phase.

We agree with the view that the personality of offenders is less than averagely developed, since it is formulated by us in our terms and phraseology that the perpetrators of crime are on a lower level of socialization on the average than so-called honest people. In this case, apart from the immaterial differences due to different phraseology, we find an identical content.

As far as the poor toleration of lasting psychological tensions is concerned, I have two remarks to make. If we accepted this opinion fully, we should establish only the causes of the perpetrators' remaining in the infantile period of personality development, whether it is biological or social causes that have a decisive role here. And for individual prognostication, for prevention, this conception would provide excellent opportunities, because it would be possible to establish through psychological, psychiatric or perhaps sociological examinations conducted in early adulthood of those people whose personality development is backward, who tolerate low level but lasting tensions poorly, or using our terms, who cannot or do not want to give up the satisfaction of certain needs, who cannot or do not want to adapt to social requirements; and these people should be subjected to special treatment, perhaps psychological or psychiatric, but at any rate, special treatment until they learn to tolerate low level but lasting tensions. Or, if it is not possible or not desirable, social relations should be reorganized so that short but intensive tensions could be dominant at least for these persons.

For my own part, I admit that a high proportion of criminals (mainly multiple recidivists) is characterized by a poor toleration level toward tensions, but I cannot accept that as the fundamental cause of all forms of antisocial behaviour. In my opinion, this concept does not provide a proper place for consciousness, knowledge, views or attitudes, which are expressed in all forms of intentional human behaviour. I also admit that the connection between criminogenic factors and crime has more than one aspect and we may rather talk of interaction, and, similarly, the various deeds of the individual have consequential effects on the development of his personality, but I find it another exaggeration to explain alcoholism, disorganized family life or avoidance of work by the same psychological causes as crime.

In my opinion, whether people adjust to social requirements or satisfy their particular needs in a way contrary to criminal law depends primarily on their views and attitudes, i.e. on the content of the consciousness, on the actual personality; in other words, how objective reality is reproduced by them, to what extent they can recognize their own interest in the social interest, to what extent they adjust their aspirations and goals to social requirements and possibilities.

In a human being, as a conscious being, if the endowments of his nervous system are normal and the hormonal functions are free of disturbances, the position that he occupies and can occupy in society, the extent to which, and the ways how, his needs may be expected to be satisfied, reach the level of the conscious mind. For this reason he conceives ideas to serve for a shorter or longer period. He forms a life plan for a shorter or longer time and acts according to that. As has been mentioned, those who form plans for long periods and follow them in life are not likely to commit criminal offences unless their plans have a criminogenic content. The perpetrators of criminal offences are mainly those who have ideas about the future years or decades but live for the present and for the satisfaction of the needs of the moment. I recall these ideas here only to point out that the method of satisfying needs, namely whether it is socially accepted or violates criminal law (and also the poor tolerance of psychological tensions), depends on what life plans people have, how much they intend to connect their individual life to social possibilities. This content of consciousness, as we shall see, depends on the objective social and other environmental and biological endowments.

6 The Rationality of the Perpetration

Criminological studies up to now have convinced us that all intentional deeds, criminal offences among them, seem rational to the perpetrator at the moment of the commission. Starting out from the fundamental thesis of psychology according to which all human deeds are directed at the satisfaction of some kind of desire, wish or need, it is easy to understand that the perpetration of a criminal offence serves the same aims. The perpetrator considers the perpetration of the criminal offence in the short or long run, directly or indirectly, suitable for satisfying the actual needs. This deed may be contrary to one or other of the perpetrator's interests, it may be unsuitable for satisfying the need serving as the basis of this interest since it is aimed at satisfying another need more important to the perpetrator. Thus, at the time of the decision of will, at the moment of the perpetration, intentional deeds are reasonable, and in fact or in the perpetrator's imagination are suitable for satisfying the actual need.

The rationality of the perpetration of criminal offences is to be found in the psychological peculiarity of human beings, that they plan and anticipate events on the basis of their repetition, in their mind. Every human being attempts to understand the world surrounding him, to foresee and plan accordingly his future actions.

People, however, differ from each other according to the state of their personality, in terms of how they create their future, of which events they are likely to anticipate or how and by what means they bring about the anticipated event. Thus, the external stimuli manifest themselves in a certain decision of will and in behaviour fitting the conditions, together with the idea of the anticipated future. The explanation of the differences in individual behaviour should be found not only in the nature and intensity of the effects of the actual objective relations but in the state of the personality that defines how the objective world is reflected and on the basis of this how the future is outlined by it.

The perpetration of the criminal offence is connected to the rational satisfaction of a need of the perpetrator in the future and this subjective reasoning is either justified or contradicted or is partially justified or contradicted by the event.

In the case of recognizing the irrationality of the criminal offence the perpetrator will refrain from committing similar acts in the future. However, as long as the criminal offence committed by the perpetrator qualifies in his consciousness as reasonable, he will find the commission of similar deeds suitable for satisfying his needs.

This value judgement concerning the relation between needs and a criminal offence on the part of the consciousness is very important also from the point of view of the administration of criminal justice. Starting from the principle of causality, we have to find, during the process of administering justice, those causal factors that produced the criminal offence by necessity, i.e. made the criminal offence rational for the perpetrator. We cannot overemphasize *that the admission and the understanding of the necessary nature of the criminal offences does not mean the approval of the act,* although these are frequently identified. The socially harmful nature of the act is independent of whether we understand or not the causal relations that have elicited the offence by necessity.

I should also like to refer to the fact here that the examination of the personality in the process of administering justice should be performed with reference to two periods. The first is the time of the perpetration of the criminal offence, when the connection between the personality and the criminal offence is examined from the point of view of causality first of all. In fact, this is the problem of exploring the chain of causality, the process of determination. The second is the time of the administration of justice, when the personality is examined also from the point of view of the effects of the time between the two periods, above all, as regards the value judgement concerning the criminal offence. The personality of the perpetrator may show significant differences, even opposed tendencies, in these two periods. It frequently occurs that the perpetrator's personality changes favourably between the two points of time. But there are also cases where the advantages gained by the perpetration have an even more distorting effect on the perpetrator's personality.

When defining the penal measures to be taken, these changes definitely have to be taken into consideration. The establishment of the chance or regular nature of the acts has to be complemented by the evaluation of the perpetrator's judgement concerning the offence at the time of the process of administering justice and by the evaluation of the other changes in the perpetrator's personality.

III The Role of Biological Factors in the Perpetration of Criminal Offences

When we speak of the *objective* factors that define the personality, we think it advisable to examine the biological endowments, first of all, since human personality develops, takes form, is in a continuous change, through biological changes, although under social influences. In fact, the evolution and development of social relations and of the socialization of the human being, the work done by humans, the set of actions, different forms of human behaviour all exist so that human beings can survive as biological and social beings and their needs (both biological and social) can be satisfied to a growing extent and in an increasingly civilized, modern way.

The personality concept used by us does not embrace the corporal organization of the human being, his body, since we regard biological endowments as objective factors from the point of view of personality. This separation of psyche and soma serves, of course, only the aims of study, the better recognition of the laws of human behaviour. In reality, the psychological and corporal endowments or peculiarities of a human being constitute a unity. But, equally, a human being can exist only together with his environment, in interaction with it, and thus he forms a unity with that, too. But for science, the human being himself is the subject matter of various disciplines, not to mention society, which occupies a number of disciplines with its complexity. For this reason, we believe that it is a justified and well-founded outlook which, in order to study human behaviour, separates the biological endowments of human beings from their psyche, from the personality; it considers biological endowments from the point of view of the formation of the personality as external objective factors having a role in shaping the personality and having an effect on the decision of will, on human behaviour.

The separation and differing evaluation of psyche and soma are justified also by the fact that the biological endowments of human beings have different roles in forming the personality. A human being has biological endowments (e.g. limbs, colour of hair, shape of skull, musculature) the size, shape and to a certain extent even the quality of which are neutral or hardly have any effect on the formation of the personality unless they show abnormality. And the nervous system, which is the organ of psychological processes and the functioning of the personality among the biological factors, has the function of the most important means in the shaping of the socialization of human beings, in human behaviour. The mechanism of the nervous system ensures the perception, fixation and combination of the objective effects and the reaction to them.

According to the present teachings of neurophysiology, the living organization as a functional system is a central/peripheral growth within which impulses circulate from the peripheries to the centres and from the centres to the peripheries. The self-regulation of the functions always happens within a regular closed system consisting of three basic chains that are interrelated, namely of the afferent, central and efferent chains. The afferent or perceptive chain conveys information arriving from the external world and from the internal changes of the organization to the centre. The central chain analyses and integrates the existing and new information according to the actual state and, in order to satisfy needs and aims, issues instructions which appear through the efferent chain, as responses.[1]

Thus, the reflection, the reproduction, of objective reality in the consciousness, and purposeful human activity linked to it, depend on what stimuli, what effects are conveyed to the central neural cells, and how these are integrated with the existing stored information (memories, knowledge). This is why the response is not in direct relation with the objective force of the stimulus. Thus, unconscious automatisms and the contents of the consciousness play a fundamental role in human behaviour.

It is an unanimous opinion of neurologists that the phenomena of human consciousness are not known well enough.

"The study of the central nervous system is still in an initial stage within biology. We do not know for sure yet how memories are stored in the brain. There is significant evidence to prove that memories are stored in the form of specially synthetized protein or nucleic acid molecules which carry the information forming memories in their structure. At the same time, it is easy enough to defend the hypothesis that remembering is some kind of permanent circuit or a series of contacts of neurons as J. C. Kenderew, Nobel prize winner biologist writes.[2]

But should any of these theories or their combination be true, or should even a completely different and, at the present time, unknown, structure be the biological (chemical or electric) form of remembering, of storing experience and knowledge, it is proven that the psychological characteristics of the personality have in some form their structural or circuit forms in the neural cells or in the nervous system. If we accept this as a fact, we have to deduce of necessity that the nervous system, the brain of human beings, the mechanism reflecting and reproducing objective reality

[1] N. Musabaeva, *Kategoriya kibernetiki i pritshinnosti,* Alma-Ata, 1965, pp. 62-67.

[2] J. C. Kendrew, *Az élet fonala. Bevezetés a molekuláris biológiába* (The Thread of Life. An Introduction to Molecular Biology, London, 1966), (in Hungarian), Budapest: Gondolat Kiadó, 1968, pp. 122. See also: Gy. Ádám, "Tanulás, motiváció, tudat." Bevezető a *Pszichofiziológia* c. tanulmánygyűjteményhez (Learning, Motivation, Consciousness. Introduction to the Collection of Studies entitled Psychophysiology), Budapest: Gondolat Kiadó, 1972, pp. 11-12.

are different according to the obtained knowledge and memories. The fact that objective reality is reflected differently in the case of children and adults and differently in the case of various adults of different knowledge is due precisely to the different "programming" of the actual biological and nervous system and this different programming is due primarily to differing social effects.

The role played by biological endowments in the formation of human consciousness and in crime is an unsolved problem of the whole history of criminology. The representatives of the schools of criminal anthropology and later biopsychology and their modern varieties profess that criminal human behaviour can be traced back primarily to hereditary biological properties. It is a fact that the reflection, the reproduction, of reality in the consciousness depends also on what the actual state of the reflecting, reproducing medium, i.e. of the brain, the nervous system, is. It is also a fact that the distorted reflection of reality, the evaluation of the relation between the individual and society differently from social expectations, in the case of actual needs and in the presence of means and conditions suitable for satisfying them, may lead to criminal offences, to antisocial behaviour.

For this reason, the question may arise in the form of what the quality of the reflection depends on, how precisely or distortedly the relation between the individual and society is reflected, or reaches the awareness, in the case of different persons, or, in other words, to what extent the personality of human beings depends on inherited or acquired biological abnormalities and to what extent on social and environmental effects.

It is generally known that, at the time of his birth, a child is only a biological being with a nervous system structure characteristic of human beings. Although a child has a nervous system, he has no consciousness or personality, has no memories, knowledge of the environment, does not have the traits that reflect or reproduce the objective reality. It follows from all this that the reflection, the consciousness of objective reality comes into existence only gradually, in the course of the ontogenetic evolution, through broadening the scope of relations and knowledge. And this evolutional process involves not only social but also biological changes and changes in the nervous system. A whole system of conditional reflexes evolves and becomes fixed in the nervous system also in some material form. Thus, the external social and environmental effects form the structure of the brain on the given biological basis of the child and this reflects and reproduces more or less precisely the objective reality in the consciousness. Now, the concrete question is to what extent inherited biological effects and to what extent external social and environmental ones influence the personality state that leads to the criminal decision of will or to the formation of a criminal personality.

Together with the development of biological sciences ever more new theories appeared to explain criminal behaviour, starting with external somatic stigmata and going on to the functional disturbances of endocrine organs and to chromosome abnormalities. It is not my intention to describe or evaluate the various schools of criminal biology and their representatives, since, apart from the newest trends, they are well known.[3] It is only two relatively new conceptions that I shall comment on since they absolutely require a statement of position, namely a) the chromosome theory and b) the so-called conditioning theory built on conditional reflexes. The position taken in connection with these theories provides the answer to be given to this whole complex of questions.

1 Chromosome and Other Abnormalities

In the early 1960s, human genetic studies attained significant achievements examining chromosome abnormalities. Various studies suggest that on excess or deficiency in the XY sex-chromosomes usual with men is accompanied by abnormal somatic and psychological traits. Such abnormalities are: in the case of the XO syndrome, feminine appearance, in the case of the XXY sydrome, mental deficiency, multiple anomalies, mongolism, or in the case of the XYY composition, tall build, unstable temperament, emotional disturbances, etc.[4] And, as happened more than once in the history of criminology, in the second half of the 1960s newly recognized biological laws again became theories explaining criminal behaviour. It was in Edinburgh, in the special security hospital for dangerously violent and criminal patients, that attempts were made for the first time to find a connection between chromosome anomalies and violation of the law, and the personality of the offenders. From that time on, XYY chromosome abnormality has been mentioned as the cause especially of violent criminal offences, acts against life and bodily integrity.[5]

Various studies discovered chromosome abnormalities among offenders in various proportions. While in a non-criminal population the surveys involving male newborn children may find such abnormalities only in tenths of a per cent, this proportion among criminals generally may be between 10 to 70 per cent.[6] P. Simor has published a graphic table concerning the XXY and XYY chromosome abnormalities in his above-mentioned work.[7]

[3] They are described in detail in the study of P. Simor, "A genetika és a kriminológia" (Genetics and Criminology) in: *Kriminalisztikai Tanulmányok VIII. ed (Studies in Criminalistics), Budapest: Közgazdasági és Jogi Könyvkiadó, 1970.*

[4] *See: P. C. Koller, Chromosomes and Genes. The Biological Basis of Heredity,* Edinburgh: Oliver and Boyd Ltd. 1968.

[5] P. A. Jacobs et al., "Aggressive Behaviour, Mental Subnormality and the XYY Male", *Nature*, 1965, p. 208.

[6] K. Stark-Ivánfi, "Bűnözés és kromoszómák" (Crime and Chromosomes), *Természet Világa* No. 1, 1969; J. Vigh, K. Gönczöl, Gy. Kiss and Á. Szabó, *Erőszakos bűncselekmények és elkövetőik* (Violent Crimes), Budapest: Közgazdasági és Jogi Könyvkiadó, 1973, Chapter 9, pp. 229-233.

[7] Simor, *op. cit.*, pp. 50-51.

Table 1
Compiled data concerning the Klinefelter (XXY) syndrome

Conductor of experiment	Number of cases with the Klinefelter syndrome	Antisocial of the previous number	per cent
Moiser	10	7	70.0
Court Brown	46	14	30.0
Nielsen	10	4	40.0
Hunter	17	11	64.0
Hambert	75	22	30.0
Total:	158	58	36.7

Table 2
Data of survey conducted by Casey and his team in groups of men taller than 180 centimeters

Type group	Number of men taller than 180 centimeters total	Number of those with XYY chromosome	per cent
Subnormal hospitalized for antisocial behaviour	50	12	24.0
Mentally ill, hospitalized for the same reason	50	4	8.0
Criminals	24	2	8.0
Mentally ill	30	—	—
Normal	30	—	—

In a Hungarian study[8] involving 10 persons convicted for homicide only one case of chromosome abnormality was discovered in the form of one excess Y chromosome.

The chromosome theory is aimed at proving the hereditary nature of crime, above all violent crime. However, the results of the studies, some of them presented here, do not prove more than that chromosome abnormalities are accompanied by various somatic features (disturbances of the nervous system, tall build, etc.).

The data of studies also suggest that the proportion of violent criminals in the group of people of such properties is higher than in other populations. According to

[8] L. Boda, A. Szabó and E. Czeizel, "A dupla Y syndroma több emberen elkövetett emberölés tettese-inél" (The double Y syndrome in the case of repeat murderers), *Orvosi Hetilap* 110, 1969, P. 1251.

our conception of causality, our interpretation of causal determination, if we want to remain consistent, we have to accept chromosome abnormalities as one of the causal factors, playing mostly the role of conditions, that manifest themselves by participating in the determination of the behaviour of the criminal offence in the case of certain perpetrators.

But the studies so far have hardly passed the point of establishing a correlation between chromosome abnormalities and criminal offences. As far as I know, no attempts have been made to work out a mechanism or scheme through which chromosome abnormalities exert their influence on the criminal decision of will. There are, of course, hypotheses and ideas, according to which these somatic abnormalities elicit psychological peculiarities or states which frequently lead to the perpetration of criminal offences, e.g. aggressivity,[9] imbalance to a high degree, irresponsibility, emotional instabilitiy, egocentricity, tendency toward arbitrariness. No doubt these psychological peculiarities have a close connection with the perpetration of various (not only violent) criminal offences. But it is not proven yet that in the case of such perpetrators the mentioned psychological characteristic are caused only by chromosome abnormalities. According to Ranschburg "modern psychological studies show that *human aggressivity is not an instinctive manifestation: social learning has an extremely significant role in its genesis.*"[10] In his opinion, emotions themselves come into existence only in a certain phase of the development of children "as an inseparable unity, an interaction of an inborn and a learned experience factor."[11]

The correlation between violent crime and chromosome abnormalities does not allow any other justified inference than that chromosome abnormalities create favourable conditions for the genesis of such psychological peculiarities. The probability of this is enhanced by the fact that similar psychological characteristics occur also in the case of criminals having no chromosome abnormalities and there are a considerable number of people even among non-criminals who have such psychological peculiarities.

The latest studies have defined the place of chromosome theory without exaggerations, formulating the real relations in the genesis of criminal human behaviour.

"An extra chromosome, should it be X or Y, cannot be alone the dominant factor in the determination of a criminal offence, it can be only if it is present accompanied by abnormality and harmful family environment," as is written in one of the British periodicals.[12]

[9] Some authors interpret all criminal offences as aggression. See J. György, *Az antiszociális személyiség* (The Antisocial Personality), Budapest: Medicina Könyvkiadó, 1967, pp. 119–121.

[10] J. Ranschburg, *Félelem, harag, agresszió* (Fear, Anger, Aggression), Budapest: Tankönyvkiadó, 1973 p. 94.

[11] Ranschburg, *op. cit.*, p. 22.

[12] M. D. Casey, C. E. Blank, T. Mobley, P. Kohn, D. L. K. Street, J. M. McDongall, J. Gooder and J. Patts, "Patients with Chromosome Abnormality in Two Special Hospitals", *Special Hospital Research Report,* No. 2, 1971.

Biological factors, if they also represent damage, an abnormality in the nervous system, may directly lead to antisocial behaviour; however it is not a criminal procedure but medical treatment that we consider as the proper measure in such case. It is valid, of course, not only in the case of chromosome abnormalities but also for all other organic abnormalities and illnesses, which have an influence on, or are accompanied by, the impairment of the nervous system (e.g. fracture of the skull, meningitis).

In addition to the extra sex-chromosome, the other factor the quotation mentions is harmful family environment. In a broad interpretation this may be identified with harmful, criminogenic social circumstances. The "double Y syndrome", e.g., which goes with a tall build and frequently with aggressivity, in its somatic manifestation (tall build) alone may not be a criminogenic factor and does not imply aggressivity of necessity either. But it is beyond doubt that particularly in childhood, when the development of the personality is initiated, tall build, a strong physique, may be significant personality forming factors in certain social (family, school) circumstances. Our survey conducted among violent offenders[13] shows that the cult of physical strength is very strong among violent, aggressive offenders, which is usually a consequence of an educational situation originating from the relations of childhood (the position occupied among brothers and sisters, friends, school-mates, appreciated superiority of strength). More than average physical strength without adequate intentional education exerting an opposite influence may easily lead to aggressivity, bad temper, emotional instability, egocentricity, etc. Similar data and observations may be found in the work of Sh. and E. Glueck. According to them:

"The most striking finding in the anthropologic analysis is the very high incidence of mesomorphic (muscular, solid) dominance in the body structure of the delinquents. Among the non-delinquents, on the other hand, there is a considerable incidence of ectomorphic (linear, thin) dominance. ... There is also less disharmony in physique among the delinquent group than the non-delinquent group, a condition which may facilitate aggressive behavior."[14]

But it is evident whithout surveys, simply through the observation of everyday life, that it is not leptosome, asthenic juveniles who commit offences against life and bodily integrity, or are hooligans, but those who, trusting in their physical strength, may attack their fellows and others in the hope of success or with certain success. It is also practical experience that human beings prefer to exercise those forms of activity that ensure success, positive experience, for them to those that are usually followed by failure and negative emotional effects.

A similar position may be taken about the effects of other somatic abnormalities. Deformities, either inherited or acquired through accident or illness, like freakish-

[13] Vigh, Gönczöl, Kiss and Szabó, *op. cit.*

[14] Sh. Glueck and E. Glueck, *Unravelling Juvenile Delinquency,* Cambridge, Mass.: Harvard University Press, 1951, pp. 273–274.

ness or impaired perception, may make difficult the satisfaction of the needs that are otherwise similar to those of normal persons. A life style differing from that of others and forced on a person by bodily infirmity or illness may prompt him to the satisfaction of needs in an illegal way. Such a person can resist strong incitement only if he has even stronger motives harmonious with his obligations, and has the right kind of consciousness.

As can be seen, biological endowments or abnormalities in the case of spontaneous development may provide fertile grounds for the genesis of negative personality traits, especially if they are accompanied by negative social effects. For this reason, it is very important in human relations during the intentional educational activity to take into consideration the biological, the somatic endowments of the individual.

The external morphological features of the perpetrator are easy to recognize, but it is very difficult, sometimes even impossible, to determine to what extent biological and social factors have each participated in the formation of the actual personality. Nevertheless, comprehensive personality and environmental studies usually make possible the approximately correct evaluation of data.

The representatives of the chromosome theory frequently raise the issue of the criminal responsibility of those who have such an abnormality. This issue has been kept on the agenda since Lombroso by the representatives of all the criminological conceptions that trace crime back primarily to hereditary biological factors. The correctness of raising the issue has to be admitted, as far as it can be proved that the perpetrator cannot adjust to the social requirements because of his biological, somatic endowments, and in such cases, it is really not the measures of criminal law but medical, perhaps medical and educational, measures that are needed. However, in those cases when somatic abnormalities have led to the perpetration of offences only in combination with the perpetrator's freakish personality traits developed under the influence of social circumstances specific to him, penal measures, possibly together with curative measures aimed at the reformation of the perpetrator's personality, at his education, may be employed. It has already been mentioned several times that the individual is in an interaction with the social environment, with social conditions of life. It follows from this interaction that it is not only the biological endowments of human beings that have an effect on the environment, on society, through the needs and the activity to satisfy them, but environmental/social effects also exert an influence through the psyche on the biological organization of human beings. "The inherited peculiarities of the organization developed under the influence of the external environment, through the assimilation to external influences during the evolutional process, and consequently, they also used to be exogenous themselves."[15]

[15] L. Keszttyüs and J. Sós, *A kórélettan tankönyve* (Textbook of Physiopathology), (Third revised edition), Budapest: Medicina Könyvkiadó, 1971, p. 43.

The effects of the environment exerted on human organization, however, may be demonstrated not only over the long distances of philogeny but also in the ontogenic evolution of human beings. The forms of social relations, relations with the family and fellow-workers, may produce illnesses of the nervous system, hormonal disturbances, illnesses in the stomach and other organs, and these can be demonstrated even histologically. *This system of interaction of the somatic, the physical and the social requires that we should determine as precisely as possible their place in human behaviour in general, and from our point of view, in the perpetration of criminal offences in particular.*

On the basis of my knowledge of the state of sciences dealing with human behaviour and on the basis of my own knowledge and experience obtained during my own research, it seems to me that the biological factors represent primarily the conditions, the mechanism, of the development of the psyche, of the personality, through which social and environmental effects exert their influence and through which the needs and the available means and conditions to satisfy them reach the level of consciousness. The nature, content and state of the personality naturally do not depend only on external social environmental effects but also on the state and nature of the organic system that mediates these external effects. In the present state of science, when human nervous functions are not known well enough, it is really difficult to determine whether unfavourable personality traits are due to environmental effects or to the faults of the organic system. Precisely for this reason, in the administration of criminal justice, special care has to be taken to recognize the faults of the "mechanism" and to distinguish them from social effects, since different preventive means are needed in each case.

2 The Conditionability of the Nervous System

The short description and evaluation of the chromosome theory has provided an opportunity for us to discuss our views in connection with various somatic factors. The second concept, the so-called conditioning theory, allows the description of the direct connection between the nervous system and psychological phenomena.

It was in 1964 that the book of the English psychologist, H. J. Eysenck, entitled *Crime and Personality,* appeared and it raised interesting and remarkable thoughts on the role of hereditary factors in the perpetration of criminal offences. Eysenck started out from the findings of research involving twins. According to him, the significant differences that may be discovered between the behaviour of identical and fraternal twins concerning criminal concordance and discordance are an indication "beyond any question, that heredity plays an important, and possibly a vital part, in predisposing a given individual to crime."[16]

[16] H. J. Eysenck, *Crime and Personality,* London: Routledge & Kegan Paul, 1964, pp. 68–69.

Eysenck in this work attempted to explore the hereditarily different mechanism that is closely connected with the psychological traits that frequently lead to the perpetration of offences. He hoped to discover this property of the nervous system. His main theory, his fundamental conclusion, may be summarized as that the human conscience, the social control of activity is simply the system of Pavlovian conditional reflexes, a psychological state formed through learning and practice, and that this forms the basis of behaviour meeting, or deviating from, social requirements. In other words, crime can be traced back to two fundamental factors: (1) an inherited peculiarity of the nervous system which defines the extent of conditionability and (2) external social circumstances which condition the individual according to the inherited peculiarities. Consequently, personality, human behaviour and criminal offences are dependent on the different values of two varying scales. Eysenck finds it proven that people differ from each other in terms of the rapidity of forming conditional reflexes, in terms of the strength and resistance of those toward extinction. On the basis of his studies he has concluded that introverted personalities are characterized by ease of conditioning and by strong conditioned links that resist modification. On the other hand, extroverts are difficult to condition, and, in situations where the conditioned connection is not reinforced, they tend to abandon them.

According to Eysenck,

"the typical extrovert is sociable, likes parties, has many friends, needs people around to talk to, and does not like reading or studying by himself. He craves excitement, takes chance, acts on the spur of the moment, and is generally an impulsive individual. He is fond of practical jokes, always has a ready answer, and generally likes change; he is carefree, easygoing, optimistic, and likes to "laugh and be merry." He prefers to keep moving and doing things, tends to be aggressive and loses his temper quickly; his feelings are not kept under tight control and he is not always a reliable person.

The typical introvert is a quiet, retiring sort of person, introspective, fond of books rather than people; he is reserved and reticent except with intimate friends. He tends to plan ahead, "looks before he leaps", and distrusts the impulse of the moment. He does not like excitement, takes matters of everyday life with proper seriousness, and likes a well-ordered mode of life. He keeps his feelings under close control, seldom behaves in an aggressive manner, and does not lose his temper easily. He is reliable, somewhat pessimistic, and places great value on ethical standards."[17]

All this means that under the same conditioning effects extroverts learn the social requirements less easily. Eysenck immediately adds that social relations mean different conditioning effects for people. From the point of view of prevention, it is the treatment of those who are difficult to condition, with drugs on the one hand,

[17] Eysenck, *op. cit.*, p. 50.

and the intensified individualization of social conditioning (education) on the other hand, that he regards as a method to be followed.

From the basic conception of Eysenck, which may perhaps be understood even from this summary description, the following considerations are self-evident to me. First of all, I approve of the aspiration to prove the role played by the biological nature of human beings in the formation of their personality and in influencing the personality, in a more exact way than all previous attempts.

Given the abundance of views, some of which are far from clear, one cannot overemphasize that the personality is the manifestation of the socialization of a human being, a system of psychological relations formed by various social effects which reflects more or less precisely objective reality, its regularities and, through them, the anticipated forms of the future. The increasingly dominant social nature of human beings, however, does not obscure the fact that human beings are not only social beings but also biological formations and the formation of their personality takes place on biological grounds, primarily as the result of the functioning of the nervous system. Thus, the nature and state of the biological mechanism and its role in the realization of social adaptation, social activity and adjustment should not be a matter of indifference.

The train of thought of Eysenck seems logical. There are people who commit criminal offences and there are others who basically adjust themselves to social requirements. These people have various views, contents of consciousness, emotions of differing intensity and various patterns of behaviour. *And Eysenck believes that these differences can be traced back to the nature of the nervous system, to conditionability, to a significant, possibly decisive, "vital" extent* in addition to social effects. Since he does not say for what category of offenders he believes his theory valid, it is presumable that his theory is generally valid for all criminals. Thus, the perpetrator of a political crime is poorly, inadequately conditioned, in the same way as a murderer, thief or one who is guilty of not reporting on offence.

In the individual being conditioned for specific offences or for crime in general, we may recognize to certain extent the mental state we call an antisocial attitude after Uznadze.

According to our views discussed earlier in connection with the various somatic traits, it seems natural to us that somatic endowments may have an effect on human behaviour. It is more evident in the case of the endowments of the nervous system. Individuals who committed their offences in a state of feeble-mindedness or mental disturbance cannot be held responsible. It is not punishment but medical treatment that is used in attempting to make such perpetrators capable of social adaptation.

The proposition among Eysenck's views that poses a problem for me is the one according to which hereditary properties play a "possibly vital" role in defining crime. It may be accepted as proven that the determining role of biological endowments may be manifested on the level of the individual but I doubt, I do not find it proven, that such cases occur in such large numbers within crime, within the mass of criminal offences, that they should have a "vital" role. Medical examinations do not show higher rates even among criminal offences against life.[18] It is true that the examinations of forensic medicine and other studies relevant to the issue have not dealt so far with the problems of conditionability but not even Eysenck himself reports data showing what percentage of people or what proportion of offenders belong to the category of the "poorly conditionable". And, since he conducted his experiments primarily with animals, his conclusions may be regarded only as hypotheses that should be verified through studies involving widely differing groups of people.

According to certain Hungarian psychologists, even those abilities do not have hereditary biological bases that are manifested in the case of children at school, in connection with their particular responsiveness to certain subjects (e.g. music or mathematics). "...In the activity of a child, before or in addition to the studies, the interiorized models representing objective content may form by chance, due to social determination taking place as a spontaneous process *by chance* into which the information, explanation or demonstration, provided by the teacher, may be built in. This is how the well known confusing phenomenon may appear, namely, that the same information provided by the teacher forms the concepts necessary for problem-solving thinking in the mind of some of the receiving children, while others appear to be unable to understand and receive the information. The phenomenon is confusing, because together with similar phenomena mentioned earlier it creates the impression that behind the varying reception of the information there are biologically inherited abilities which differ in the individuals precisely for this reason.

This false impression is particularly frequent in connection with mathematical abilities."[19]

For this reason, the most we may accept from Eysenck's view is that in the case of some of the perpetrators problems of conditionability may and do appear of necessity, from slight difficulties to the limits of impossibility. (However, those who are close to this latter limit should be regarded as ill.)

It is also included in Eysenck's concept that people who are easily conditionable, or with average difficulties, turn into criminals only if social circumstances condition them poorly, inadequately. But, of those who are difficult to condition, the ones in whose case the higher than average frequency of favourable external effects makes up for the disadvantages of the endowments of the nervous system, do not turn into criminals. We expressed this earlier as follows: "The bio-psychological endowments of human beings are manifest in a socially negative or positive form depending on the effects of the social environment. It depends on the intensity of education, on practice and on being self-conscious how far social requirements

[18] See: Vigh, Gönczöl, Kis and Szabó, *op. cit.,* Chapter 9.

[19] L. Garai, *Személyiség, dinamika és társadalmi lét* (Personality, Dynamics and Social Existence), Budapest: Akadémiai Kiadó, 1969, p. 142.

become the guidelines of the acts of individual human beings. In the case of identical environmental effects, different bio-psychological endowments produce different behaviour patterns. In turn, under the influence of different and properly differentiated social effects, differing bio-psychological endowments may find expression in identical behaviour, in behaviour that meets social requirements. The application of individualized means and methods of education is precisely one of the main aspirations of socialist pedagogy."[20] After all this, we think it very important to emphasize that children are born with different biological endowments (mainly in terms of the nervous system), which has to be taken into consideration during their education and during the process of teaching them the social skills and requirements, and the extent and method of training, conditioning, should be applied accordingly and, in this way, we may take an important step toward preventing antisocial behaviour.

Of course, it is easy to formulate requirements without elaborating the concrete methods and conditions of meeting them. At the present level of the development of neurophysiology and biological sciences in general, it is hardly possible to categorize newborn babies according to the peculiarities of their nervous system and particularly from the point of view of pedagogical requirements. Conscientious parents and experienced educators in particular are able to determine the direction of the conditioning of children, the direction of the development of their personality, after a few years, and, through proper educational methods, they can train and process the right behaviour forms and psychological responses. And, in this, we have formulated the essence of our view again, according to which criminal human behaviour, even if on biological grounds, is a consequence primarily of unfavourable external social effects, of wrong education (intentional or spontaneous) in the broadest sense of the word.

[20] Vigh, Gönczöl, Kiss és Szabó, *op. cit.*, p. 256. See also: J. Vigh, "A nevelési eszme érvényesülése a Fiatalkorúak Büntetés-végrehajtási Intézetében" (The Realization of the Educative Principle in the Penal Institute for Juveniles), *Magyar Jog és Külföldi Jogi Szemle,* No. 6, 1973.

IV Social Circumstances, Causal Factors Forming the Actual Personality

The personality of a human being develops and is in a permanent change under the influence of external environmental effects and on biological grounds. The majority of people can understand, as a result of education, intentional and spontaneous, that social norms are generally also the expression of individual interests and their observance is the most certain way to satisfy individual needs. The development of a consciousness with this content is the consequence of the chain and accumulation of stimulating and inhibiting effects. In turn, in the case of people who commit criminal offences, this socially required view and behaviour have not developed and have not become automatic. Now, after clarifying the role of the biological factors, the question for criminology may be formulated: what are the social circumstances or causal factors (causes and conditions) under the influence of which the criminal or unstable personality develops and manifests itself in a criminal offence if circumstances are suitable. This question of course could be asked in another way: what are the social circumstances that lead to the development of the adequately socialized personality. The two ways of putting the question mean essentially the same, if the aim we set is the prevention of crime. Setting out from the principle of productivity, the primary task of criminology in this respect is to determine the existing unfavourable circumstances that have led to the perpetration of criminal offences, but, at the same time, it is also its task to outline the favourable conditions by which criminogenic factors may partially or completely be replaced.

It is perhaps the connection between individual social relations and criminal offences, crime, that is the most extensively discussed in the literature of criminology. The interrelations and interactions of micro-environmental elements and crime have also been described by hundreds of studies and monographs of socialist criminologists.[1] For this reason, in the examination of the content of the scheme of

[1] Some examples from the Hungarian literature: J. Gödöny, *A társadalmi, gazdasági fejlődés és a bűnözés* (Social and Economic Development, and Crime), Budapest: Közgazdasági és Jogi Könyvkiadó, 1976; I. Diczig, *A társadalmi tulajdon elleni bűnözés kriminológiai kérdései, különös tekintettel a csoportos elkövetési formákra* (The Problems of Crime against Social Property with Consideration of the Forms of Group Perpetration), (Ph. D. Thesis), Budapest: 1975.

causality and the process of determination of criminal offences, it is not so much the detailed description of the individual social factors as their evaluation through determining their main types and the description of their place and function within the causal scheme that appears practicable. The evaluation of the social factors filling up the causal scheme reflects a theoretical and conceptional position in the same way as the definition of the place and role of the personality and the biological factors. It is only on this basis that a uniform explanatory theory of crime, as a negative social mass phenomenon, can be formed and the trends, structure and principles of an adequate system of criminal justice may be sketched.

1 The Effects of Micro-Environmental Factors

According to our scheme of causality, the personality is the subjectivization of past objective relations, i.e. the subjective effect of objective causal factors. And since personality development begins immediately after a child is born, it is advisable to follow the development of the personality of offenders from the initial phase.

a) *The effects of family circumstances.* It is generally acknowledged that the first ten years have a particular significance in human life from the point of view of personality development. Human beings are initiated into life at that age, they learn the emotions and basic knowledge (love, respect, anger, speech, reading, writing, etc.) through which they form their relations with family members, with others, with society. The fate and future of children are defined to a great extent by the family they are born in, by the nature of the emotions, views and life plans of the persons with whom they have their first contacts, who exert the first influence on them (parents, grand-parents, brothers and sisters, foster parents, etc.). For this reason, it is advisable to describe the main types of families having criminogenic influences.

1/ A *criminogenic family environment,* where the parents, brothers and sisters frequently commit criminal offences, make antisocial behaviour a natural form of behaviour for children. In such an environment, children learn antisocial views and, during the passage of years, antisocial attitudes take form in them. Psychological peculiarities developed in this way are difficult to change at school or the place of work. According to the findings of various surveys, it regularly happens that the years spent in such a family environment make their effects felt later, when the children have attained adulthood, in the form of antisocial behaviour, particularly if the children emotionally identify themselves with the family members.

2/ A significant proportion of offenders comes from families where the *parents* do not pay proper attention to the education of their children, who are educated by the environmental effects. Primarily those parents belong to this category who, as a consequence of their own education and primitive ideas, do not pursue any educational activity and regard providing food and clothes for their children as their main task. Parents who have an adequate level of intelligence but who are too busy, or attribute too much importance to their social success, or whose low income makes them work overtime, belong to this category, too. The lack of education and proper attention leads frequently to the perpetration of criminal offences in the case of children whose mothers have a job. Children living in such families usually do not develop respect or love for their parents.

In a survey involving a group of juvenile offenders in Budapest whose parents belong to the social stratum of white-collar workers, both having a job, "70 per cent of the perpetrators manifest negative emotions toward one or both of the parents (fifty per cent of them only toward the father, twenty per cent toward both parents)."[2] A typical example of this type is the Pintye family of Balassagyarmat. Both parents had, socially important positions and their children became members of criminal gangs before their eyes.

It is frequent in families where *both parents have a job* that grandparents are expected to replace parental upbringing. In a formal sense, it is perhaps a solution but in practice it means that the oldest generation with its out of date, frequently religious, views and habits ensures the education of the youngest preparing them for the future.

The lack of family upbringing shows a close correlation with the school progress of children. Such children usually are undisciplined ("cheeky") and since they are not prepared for school, they show poor progress. For this reason, they frequently have to be disciplined and punished. The permanent lack of success at school pushes them toward areas where they can be appreciated and respected. Thus, they frequently gather in juvenile gangs. And, due to the lack of close parental control, they can easily do so. It is only a short step from this point to the perpetration of criminal offences.

3/ The third major group of families to be mentioned is that where the *parents display care in the matter of the education of their children* but make serious mistakes due merely to the lack of expertise. The possibility of making such mistakes is always present with the exception perhaps of educational experts even in the case of well meaning parents. It is a frequent situation that parents approach the problems of their children incorrectly, they are too strict or too lenient. They, perhaps, do not recognize the peculiarities of the children's nervous system and attempt to restrict the agility, dynamism or relaxation of the children through incorrect means. Or the other, perhaps even more serious, mistake is, especially if the child is a single one, that parents comply with all the wishes of the child, they pamper him and do not get him accustomed to giving up certain needs, to working and to enduring fatigue.

In spite of all well-meant "education", such children will be so-called "naughty"

[2] A. Szabó, "Társadalmi, gazdasági fejlődés és a fiatal korosztályok bűnözése" (Socio-economic Development and Juvenile Delinquency), *MTA Állam- és Jogtudományi Intézetének Kiadványai,* Budapest: 1972, p. 84.

children. Perhaps, in such cases it would be more fair to speak of children badly reared, and parents and teachers badly rearing them.

In addition to the lack of intentional education or the mistakes made in the process of education in the family, it is the views, forms of behaviour concerning work, family, the evaluation of others, in general everyday life, that children have heard, observed, learned through watching, and copying that have a significant influence on the development of the children's personality. The parents' outlook on life, their life-style, their whole life have an impact on the development of children. And, if the emotional relation between a child and the parents is positive, the child will follow the parents' way of thinking and their behaviour. And if the parents are not criminals but ordinary working people, yet full of discontent and complaints about others and society, and obedient to the norms of society only because they feel compelled and fear the consequences of disobedience, nobody can expect their child to respect social requirements.

Through the favourable or unfavourable educational conditions, the development of children's personality is connected to the social situation and income of the family. Measurements of correlation show that relatively more perpetrators come from families with a low income. It is beyond doubt that needs unsatisfied for a long time may inspire the perpetration of offences if the circumstances are suitable. But in most cases, the connection is not direct but indirect. A poor financial situation exerts its unfavourable influence through the educational situation. In the circumstances of building socialism, difficult social circumstances are characteristic above all in the case of uneducated, primitive and usually alcohol consuming people. A similar indirect connection may be found between the number of children and juvenile criminality. According to the relevant criminological surveys, the proportion of perpetrators coming from families with many children is higher than the proportion of offenders coming from families with one or two children.[3] But it is not the number of children alone either that is the criminogenic factor here but generally the less favourable social and educational situation that exists in large families.

In speaking about the personality-shaping role of the family, we should mention disorganized and broken families, which can be found in all the three types of families mentioned. Frequent family conflicts, quarrels, fights, divorce, step-parents, all are factors that hinder the healthy development of the personality of children; in certain situations they may lead to criminal offences. A West-German criminological survey has found that it is juveniles who do not live in a complete family, or live with foster parents, that start their criminal behaviour at the earliest age.[4]

[3] J. Vigh, *A fiatalkori bűnözés és a társadalom* (Juvenile Criminality and Society), Budapest: Közgazdasági és Jogi Könyvkiadó, 1964, p. 189.

[4] W. Munkwitz, *Die Prognose der Frühkriminalität,* Berlin-Spandau: Hermann Luchterhand Verlag, 1967, p. 58.

Of course, the lack of family life or its faults do not necessarily lead to the development of a criminal or unstable personality. These faults can be partially or completely corrected by the education in state-run nurseries, kindergartens, and schools or by other favourable external effects (relatives, friends, institutions). Although the role of the family in the education of children is difficult to replace, in certain cases well-organized educational institutions where educators with a feeling of vocation surround the children with love, represent a more favourable educational situation than criminogenic, disorganized or broken family circumstances.

The role of the family is not limited to the formation of the personality of adults, of the married couple. Criminological research has proven that among those who live in marriage, particularly in families with children, the proportion of offenders is lower than among the divorced or those who do not live in marriage. In addition to this general positive tendency, there are certain family relations which may form the personality unfavourably. Conflicts between the married parties, serious clashes of their interests, may lead to criminal offences (causing bodily injury, homicide).

As can be seen, the family atmosphere, family relations can affect the development of the personality of children and family members unfavourably in various ways. However, these negative effects alone rarely lead directly to the perpetration of criminal offences. They manifest themselves in combination, integrated with other negative effects, in antisocial behaviour.

b) School instruction and education, learning, deepening knowledge generally, play an extremely positive role in the development of the personality of human beings, in the formation of their socialization. While children learn social requirements in the family through the views, the attitudes, the everyday and frequently uninhibited behaviour of the parents and other family members, at school they usually learn them in a *prescribed,* "authenticated" form, which perhaps is slightly coloured by the teachers.

It is a function of the school to teach children all the knowledge that makes them prepared for work to be done in one of the positions of the organization of society and to obtain further knowledge. The obtained knowledge of our narrower or broader environment, and later of the universe, makes it possible for objective reality and its laws to be reflected, reproduced by us. As the knowledge of a child grows, so his own world widens for him, he learns more and more of infinite objective reality.

From the point of view of the development of personality, one of the essential problems begins when, due to the lack or shortcomings of family education, perhaps the peculiarities of the nervous system or difficulties of conditioning children are not able to obtain knowledge even on an average level.

The system of knowledge taught by the school cannot build organically up on their knowledge if it is inadequate for their age and insufficient otherwise, too. Such children will not only evaluate school teaching differently from their school-mates but, because of the lack of a sense of achievement and appreciation and feeling the shame of negative distinction, they will leave school and form an aversion toward schools and everything represented by them. Consequently, it regularly happens that, among juvenile offenders, the proportion of those who have not completed their secondary studies in the compulsory general school is very high. In adulthood, these children can find a place only on the periphery of society since "rising" in socialist society is connected with studying, with school reports, diplomas and degrees showing the completion of various stages of education. The survey conducted among violent criminals also suggests that children failing in general school and dropping out of it represent a high proportion among offenders and persons avoiding work in adulthood.[5]

It is a frequent complaint on the part of juvenile convicts against schools (and in some of the cases it is certainly justified) that the teachers do not understand them and the other pupils who are making good progress are also alienated from them. And they seek the company of others with similar experience because they are understood and appreciated by them. Due to the unsuccessfulness in studies, their interest is turned toward spheres where they are able to perform above the average (e.g. music, sports, dance) and which are not controlled by teachers.

This is only one side of the personality-forming function of schools. The other side is "socialization", i.e. the formation of the character, emotions, correct human relations, in addition to teaching, to providing knowledge. It is a frequently voiced demand that schools should intensify their socializing activities in addition to their teaching because in our new changing society various, frequently conflicting influences affect school children. If the view formed in the family or among friends of human relations and society is different from the "official" view put forward by the school, it can and actually does happen that the pupils accept the view that is dominant in their family or among friends, instead of the views and social requirements as formulated by the school. There are, of course, cases, and they show the shortcomings of school education, when the teacher sets up the social requirements in an extreme, sterile form that nobody, including the teacher, can live up to. The high requirements set up for the children by teachers or parents (e.g. telling the truth always and under any circumstances) and the substantially different practice on the part of adults discredits pedagogy and damages the prestige of adults.

Similarly, the principle that demands the maximum in adjusting to social requirements is regarded as wrong by certain psychologists. It is a "minimum of adaptation" that they deem practicable.[6]

[5] Vigh, Gönczöl, Kiss and Szabó, *Erőszakos bűncselekmények és elkövetőik* (Violent Crimes), Budapest: Közgazdasági és Jogi Könyvkiadó, 1973, pp. 209–210.

[6] P. Popper, *Kriminálpszichológia* (Criminal Psychology), College textbook, Chapter IV, Budapest: BM Rendőrtiszti Főiskola.

It may be another significant source of mistakes in school education when educators do not set adequate requirements for their pupils. Urging the complete fulfilment of realistic obligations, the actual fulfilment of obligations and its rewards, may have an extremely favourable influence on the development of children, while leniency toward not meeting the obligations, leaving this unpunished, perhaps approving of it, lead to the underestimation of social requirements. Among factors turning personality development in the wrong direction, we should mention school discipline as a significant one. It is not an infrequent phenomenon that the means and methods of discipline are unsuitable for preventing behaviour deviating from social requirements or for breaking this type of behaviour pattern. The approach from the side of the act dominates the application of even pedagogical, disciplinary punishment, i.e. the applied detriment is according to the weight of the act. This principle is deemed right, "just", by teachers, even by pupils, while only those who are being disciplined feel it frequently unjust, and hardly any attention is paid to that in schools; for this reason, the disciplinary punishment usually is not followed by any favourable effect.

The development of the personality of children, the formation of their socialization, depends to a great extent on whether the school has a true evaluation of the endowments, of the abilities of the children, of the trend of development and its possible or probable consequences; whether the children have developed realistic ideas of the conditions and possibilities of adapting to smaller social groups or the social system; whether the children live with the illusion of great possibilities (which might come true by chance) or their ideas of the future are filled with regular, probable relations. But if all of this is provided by the school, the positive effects may be marred by other effects (family, friends, place of work).

In addition to some of the more significant mistakes of school instruction and education we could enumerate the (frequently chance) negative influences that are exerted on the pupils at school.

However, since our aim is not to demonstrate concrete interrelations but only to name the main objective relations that may play the role of causal factors in the formation of a criminal or unstable personality, we omit further discussion.

c) *School, as an organized form of micro-environment, is replaced by the place of work in the life of people.* In fact, the independence of human beings begins with their joining in the circulatory system of society by taking a job. Work not only changes man into a social being in the process of philogeny but it has an important, perhaps decisive role also in the ontogeny, in the individual development, in the socialization of the individual. It is under the influence of labour relations, of the relations of the place of work and of colleagues, that people become aware of their place in society, of their social role. It is experience gained at the place of work, among colleagues, that provides ideas about society, about the relation between individual and social interests, about the social means, and extent, of satisfying needs. It is only work that can enrich the human personality with the perception of the practice of social existence, it is only work that can lead to the understanding of the fact that individual interests, individual deeds have to be adjusted to social needs and possibilities.

Under the social conditions of the construction of socialism, the possibilities of having an income without work cease, and thus it is work that has to become the basis of life in a society. The produced goods have to be distributed according to the quality and quantity of the work done. This system of distribution inspires people to satisfy their needs by raising the quality and amount of work. The pleasure of well done work bears pure thoughts and is elevating, it advances the development of the individual and society, while idle time, loitering or poorly organized work representing only a burden, are a fertile ground for antisocial views and may easily lead to the perpetration of criminal offences.

In our present social circumstances, the estimation of work, the opinion formed of work is not always unanimously positive. For many people, work appears as the necessary evil that has to be tolerated in order to earn a living. This view can be traced back to two main factors. One of them is the adopted, learned form of consciousness, when children hear negative opinions of work in the family and among friends and adopt them as their own. Consequently, they will feel an aversion to work even before ever having a job and their own personal experience. The other factor involves objective conditions. At the present level of the means and mode of production, there are many spheres of work that are unpleasant, very tiring and hardly give any feeling of accomplishment.

It is in the nature of work that it causes tiredness. Intellectual activity involving the greatest amount of experience of success also requires a certain endurance of tiring conditions. Thus, children have to be made to like work together with its tiring nature, as with sports or games. It is part of the adequately socialized person that if necessary he should be able to give up the satisfaction of the actual needs (e.g. rest) in order to satisfy long range plans for life.

The circumstance that it is possible to earn an income legally without working has also added to the formation of the unfavourable opinions concerning work. The State Lottery, football pools, various types of raffle ticket, horse races, card games and other forms of gambling attract a significant part of the population. Certain forms of gambling are organized by the state and are widely propagated. Many people engage in these forms of gambling mostly for the sake of amusement, but the number of those whose only aim is winning is not insignificant either. With the exception of the small percentage of winners, only disappointment and vanishing hopes of winning are the reward of the majority of them. The needs that have remained unsatisfied become even stronger and not infrequently they lead to illegal ways of meeting them.

Criminological studies have proven that a wrong attitude toward work, a dislike for work have close connections with crime. People who change their place of employment frequently, who avoid work, regularly reach the point of committing criminal offences. In particular offences against property, criminal acts aimed at obtaining material goods, show a close correlation with the undervaluation of work.

The place of work may equally exert a favourable or unfavourable influence on persons who undervalue work or are averse to work. Those who do their work honestly and with devotion may form their fellow-workers favourably. They may make others like working, may teach them to respect work, may make them understand that work is the source of all goods and, in the final analysis, the satisfaction of needs can be attained through it. But where the atmosphere of the place of work is different, the aversion to work may deepen and the wrong views concerning work may become even stronger. A direct link between the place of work and crime is formed when the former becomes the influence forming the antisocial views or attitudes that lead to the perpetration of offences. At the present stage of our social development it is not an infrequent phenomenon that work discipline is lacking at the place of work, certain persons abuse their positions and, instead of honest work, it is "contacts" that are the way for succeed. A person in such circumstances cannot always resist these phenomena or fight them. It frequently happens, especially in the case of new workers, that instead of the frequently hopeless struggle for the elimination of abnormalities, the workers adapt to the circumstances, adopt the dominant attitudes and "work-style" and in this way they may easily come to the point of committing antisocial acts themselves.

An extremely dangerous and distorted tendency of personality development may be experienced with a small group of young people. One of the crucial points of the attitudes of this group is the contempt for work as a sign of their protest against welfare and against the whole social life of our times, in general. They do not want to participate in the social division of labour, only in consumption, through the income of their parents. In reality, this attitude also means the negation of the social nature of human beings through the negation of work. The consistent enforcement of the principle of distribution according to work would teach them within a short time that their attitude is wrong and they would not poison immature juveniles with their romantic fancies, would not add to the reserves of the criminal population of the future.

Among the peculiarities of work conditions influencing the development of the personality, we should also mention the consequences of the difference between physical and intellectual work. It follows from the principle of distribution according to work that there is a substantial difference in the payment for physical work not requiring skill and intellectual activity needing high qualifications. Consequently, it is a regular tendency under the conditions of building socialism that people strive to obtain various skills and training. These aspirations, however, may not be attained in many cases because the law of proportional development of society sets up certain limits. It is impossible for everyone to obtain a university degree; for the time being not all types of work require a professional qualification. There must necessarily be unskilled physical workers with low pay. However, the majority of people belonging to this category are not those who have not been admitted "for lack of room" to universities, but people who belong to this social stratum because of their abilities or family circumstances. Many of them, comparing their own circumstances with the much more comfortable life of others, cannot recognize the law of social development, the necessity of distribution according to work, in these substantially different circumstances of life. The ignorance concerning social laws, or denying them, in straitened circumstances, if the occasion arises, easily lead to the perpetration of a criminal offence. Certain criminologists believe that it is not an unfavourable financial situation and work conditions that lead to the perpetration of criminal offences but people who are incompatible with society, who have an antisocial personality, are restricted to the periphery of society and into low income categories. We have started by saying that the aversion to work formed in childhood makes it difficult to adapt to the socially defined system of work. However, we emphasize again, it is not because the lack of abilities or dislike of work have dragged them into that situation that some physical workers of low income live in such circumstances, although they could have a better life, but because at the present level of the forces of production, at the level of the development of the means of work, due to the expedient social division of labour, the possibilities of eliminating these conditions are not yet given. Of course, it does not follow from this that workers with low income commit criminal offences of necessity. However, it is a fact that the proportion of those who commit criminal offences is higher in this category than in other income categories. It is not physical work not requiring training and skill that forms the basis of the higher criminality rate but the views these people have, the educational situations, and conditions of life among which the personality of these people has been formed.

In the previous parts, we discussed mainly the work conditions fulfilling the function of causes among causal factors, that exert an influence on the formation of the antisocial, criminal or unstable personality. Favourable social changes which occur in this sphere weaken the intensity of crime at its base because they attack the roots of crime. Considering reality, i.e. that there are necessarily people undervaluing and avoiding work, there are places of work that promote the formation of an antisocial personality, intensified care has to be taken at the places of work in order to diminish the conditions that make easier or promote the realization of the criminal intent. The intensified guarding of goods and checking their handling may decrease the number of criminal offences and through that they may have a favourable effect on raising work morale.

d) Friendly relations are also social relations of the environment which play extremely important role in the life of humans, in the development of their personality. Family circumstances, the school, and frequently even the place of work, are conditions arising independently from the individual. The relation between friends, however, is much less restricted, although the formation of the contact is possible only within certain limits. The development of the circle of friends is usually a consequence of family education, an education preceding school, even in the case of school-children. Children attending school have certain personality traits, and friendly relations frequently develop among children whose personality traits are the same.

The circle of friends is usually the social community of playing, sports, amusement, of spending one's free time in general. Since it is the least restricted community formed relatively spontaneously, the desires, thinking and ideas of the members may be expressed most freely. In addition to family relations, friends have a growing role already at school age, and then the circle of friends becomes the dominant community of emotions and ideas from adolescence to the foundation of one's own family.

In the case of children, well chosen friends and amusement promote the development of the socialization of the personality. The unfavourable composition of the circle of friends, or amusement free of control, involve a lot of danger.

But it is not primarily the composition of the circle of the children's friends that deserves special attention since children can hardly be expected to follow social requirements in everything; the most serious danger is represented by the lack of adequate control. It is required from adults, parents and school society that they should organize and control the amusement of children, check how they spend their free time. Due to their necessarily incomplete and distorted ideas about society and the ways of satisfying needs, children left without supervision regularly violate social requirements. The various forms of antisocial behaviour, if they remain without pedagogical consequences, represent experience for children which will inspire them to commit similar acts. It frequently happens that adults who are supposed to educate children but fail to do so have the experience that after a period of time children will change completely and be strangers to them. The deformities of the personality are always more difficult to correct and it is a less fruitful work than to direct the wrong thinking and behaviour of children to the right course.

The organization of the free time and amusement of children is particularly difficult at the time of school vacations. This task at present belongs above all to the parents, to parents who have only 2 or 3 weeks paid vacation as compared to the two and half a month long school vacations. The lack of a positive programme, idleness, aimlessly gathered company, are all forcing grounds of instinctive, not adequately directed behaviour. Such circumstances not only represent opportunities for committing various criminal offences but, in the absence of proper guidance, are factors in the fixation and practice of incorrect ideas and emotions, of the wrong development of the personality.

In the development of the antisocial personality, harmful traditions connected with the socially accepted forms of amusement have an important role. The close connections of alcohol consumption and amusement and hospitality frequently have such an effect on the nervous system of young people that, instead of the learned cultured forms of behaviour, instinctive behaviour aimed at the direct satisfaction of needs comes to the fore. The increase of alcohol consumption can hardly be stopped in the near future, since the state is increasing production, and shopwindows full of various kinds of liquor tempt people to drink.

Parallel to that, intensified efforts are being made in the field of the obligatory treatment of alcoholics (Law-decree No. 10 of 1974.) However, no adequate measures are taken to prevent alcoholism, and consequently, alcohol consumption is increasing and the proportion of criminal offences related to alcohol consumption is also growing. Society seems to prefer carrying the burden of the increase in the number and proportion of criminal offences related to alcohol consumption, to making a serious effort against this harmful tradition.

There are, of course, other harmful traditions as well, such as the cult of physical strength and vengeance. There are circles where taking revenge in the case of personal offence is almost a moral duty. This outlook usually becomes part of the personality of children, too, in a stronger or weaker form, and it frequently leads to the antisocial forms of solving conflicts.

The unfavourable personality-forming effects of the circle of friends may be manifest in adulthood as well. A new place of work, making new friends, frequently lead to criminal behaviour. In this process, the circle of friends may not only play the role of conditions but frequently it is a cause of depravity, of the distortion of the personality and, finally, of the perpetration of criminal offences.

In connection with spending free time, we should mention the role of radio, television and the press among the factors exerting an unfavourable influence on the personality. These means of mass communication flood people with information, which significantly assists the better understanding of social and natural events taking place around them and, on this basis, perhaps a deeper anticipation of the future. Information concerning the connections between countries, nations and people, the solution of their conflicts, have a spontaneous effect on people, form their thinking and Weltanschauung. News arriving from the turbulent modern world suggests that neither individual human beings nor individual nations have inherent, intrinsic rights. The rights and obligations of individuals are defined by their parents, by the school, by the given society, by the ruling class, by the possessors of power and authority. Respect for the rights of individual nations depends on the international balance of forces, on the interests of the Great Powers. States participate in "wrongful" bombing, in overthrowing governments and political systems, as terrorist organizations or private persons participate in aeroplane hijacking or in taking hostages.

All this information provides the opportunity for more careful consideration of a better understanding of the trends of social development for a personality with socialized attitudes. Undeveloped personalities or personalities developed in the wrong way, however, may conclude that violence may be permissible to them, or instead of making long-term plans for life they may choose to live for the moment. Thus, it is usually not the programme, the quality of the information that has to be blamed but the subjective perception of the viewers, the audience, the readers, which plays the decisive role. An excellent example is the American movie, "Death's Heads". It is a good movie for someone with an adequately socialized person, it makes him averse to all forms of violence. At the same time, in young people, it may waken a craving for adventure, a disposition to follow the example given may waken aggressivity.

Although it is possible to a certain extent to make a selection for children and young people from programmes (and there is such a measure in force), this alone is not a solution. Instead, we have to accept as a fact that children and young people, sometimes even adults, do not understand the information they are bombarded with. For this reason, educators and experts have to devote much more energy to the education of young people. The basic interrelations of occurrences have to be explained. But, if adults themselves do not always understand what happens in this rapidly changing world and why, which principles are true and which are false, then what should be the measurement, what should be the basis if there is one at all? Indeed, great theories, studies on human behaviour and the laws of society are frequently difficult to understand and contradict each other, and thus they may raise doubts, particularly among laymen. There are, however, simple truths, easy to understand and free of great theoretical and scientific abstractions which reflect objective reality clearly. Such truths are e.g. that at the present level of the development of society, people are dependent on each other, due to the division of labour. In order to satisfy their needs, goods have to be produced and *everybody has to take part in this work.*

At the present level of production, goods are available only to a limited extent and for this reason, the division of goods is carried out primarily according to the quality and quantity of the work done. But as production increases it becomes possible to distribute a growing proportion according to needs (family allowance, sick pay, hospitalization, school education, etc.). We have to admit that our social system has its shortcomings and is burdened with certain types of social injustice but the correction of these, the further development of society, is possible only if people do their duties that fall on them as a consequence of the division of labour. One may put forward proposals for modifying the systems of labour division and income distribution but these proposals do not mean the better satisfaction of needs in the long run, either, unless production increases and goods are abundant.

If we could have these simple ideas better understood by those young people that live without making any socially useful efforts, only making use of the income of their parents or satisfying their needs in an illegal way, crime rates would be lower already today but particularly in the future.

2 Macro-Environment and Crime

In the above parts we have presented some, perhaps the most significant, of the micro-environmental factors influencing unfavourably the development of the personality and have attempted to point out their place and functions in the scheme of the determination of human behaviour. In addition to these factors, we should also speak about the so-called macro-environmental or macro-structural phenomena that, in the final analysis, define the direction of the development of the micro-structure and, in this way, indirectly influence the development of the personality and human behaviour.

From its beginnings criminology has always studied the effect of the basic traits and structures on crime. Criminologists with a sociological approach have demonstrated stochastic relations between crime and social phenomena like exploitation, unemployment, distribution according to capital, and their consequence, poverty.

Present day socialist criminology admits that basic social processes define the existence and trends of crime, after all.

The most important characteristics of all societies are the nature of property relations, the level of production, the degree of the development of the modes of production, and, on that basis, the general living standards of the population. Due to the economic development of the last decades, unemployment and poverty have been eliminated in the socialist countries. Nobody is compelled any more by needs to commit criminal offences against property only to ensure bare existence. Of course, it happens, even if rarely, that a low income, particularly in the case of those with a large family, inspires certain people to commit offences against property. However, criminological surveys do not show significant correlations between low income and crime. On the contrary, "in addition to the general elimination of crime born of poverty and needs, the *crime-attracting* effects of the richer spheres are stronger from the point of view of the perpetration of offences against property, because growing wealth provides more opportunity for perpetrating such offences."[7]

A materially identical situation is shown by the survey carried out among violent offenders. The data on perpetrators studied as control groups show that "the inclination to profiteering, the idea of private ownership, the passion for money-making and the satisfaction of extreme financial needs is characteristic not of the category of the most primitive, unskilled people but mainly of a certain group of persons who are usually at a higher level of financial conditions and have skill and training."[8]

Certain Western criminologists connect increasing crime precisely to economic development. According to them, welfare is manifested in a more comfortable life-style, which decreases people's ability to adapt to the rapid development of society.

[7] Szabó, *op. cit.*, p. 72.

[8] Vigh, Gönczöl, Kiss and Szabó, *op. cit.*, pp. 272–273.

This life-style increases the demand for the satisfaction of the need for luxury, and puts the satisfaction of sexual needs to the fore, since obtaining material goods necessary for existence does not demand the full energy of people.[9]

In Western countries with a highly developed economy it is certainly possible to show identical tendencies of crime and material welfare. In my opinion, however, there is no causal correlation between the two phenomena. The data on crime and economics of socialist countries prove precisely that beyond the satisfaction of basic needs, crime is no longer primarily a problem of economics but the problem of the consciousness, of the personality, which may have thousands of determinants between birth and the perpetration of the offence, from the nature of the macro-structure to the direct effects of the micro-environment. According to our experience, it is the *system of distribution* that is the most important of the structures of the macro-environment. How people will identify themselves with social requirements depends to a great extent on its just or unjust nature and on the views they form about it. It is true that even in the justest system only what has been produced by people under the given mode of production can be distributed, but as we have mentioned, in socialist countries (and in order to avoid misunderstanding, we should add, in developed capitalist countries too) production can ensure the satisfaction of the primary needs of people. Thus, it is the system of distribution that comes to the fore.

In the socialist countries, since the dominant form of property is state property, distribution is carried out according to the quality and quantity of work. According to economists, at the present level of production this is the form of distribution that exists as a regularity. It is harmonious with the structure of the economy. From the point of view of criminology, the question arises of whether this form of distribution involves social inequality, social injustice or not. On this issue I made my position clear earlier.[10] Now, I would only like to mention that the principle of distribution according to needs is better than the principle of distribution according to work. It follows from this that the principle of distribution by work involves social injustice of necessity, which may lead to the genesis of antisocial views and, through that, to the perpetration of criminal offences. However, the dominance of this principle of distribution, which involves a relatively lesser injustice than the previous one, is necessary at the present stage of social development and it may be abolished only through the increase of social production, through the growing abundance of material goods. The majority of people understand the principle of distribution according to work and see it as just at the present level of social development. In my opinion, the relatively low criminality rates in the socialist countries are due to this principle of distribution to a great extent.

[9] See: R. Grassberger, "Die Kriminalität des Wohlstandes", *Kriminalistik* 5, 1963.

[10] Vigh, *op. cit.*, Part III, Chapter 3.

However, some people cannot understand the necessity of this system and considering their limited material conditions, with their primitive intellects, they find even realistic differences in income unjust. It follows from this that even if they respect social requirements and follow the norms of criminal law, they do it only because punishment, and harm may arise from the violation of the law. And they always satisfy their needs, even illegally, if the opportunity arises and punishment seems to be avoidable. The existence of this kind of outlook is a regular phenomenon at present. The changes in objective social relations are not yet accompanied by a level of social consciousness where such ideas may have the nature of chance only. Thus the existence of crime follows as a regularity from the present level of distribution by work or the level of social consciousness, i.e. under the conditions of building socialism, the existence of crime has the nature of regularity.

The ideas discussed above are related to the *principle of distribution according to work*. The practical application of the principle may take place in various ways: it may be put into effect in a correct or in a wrong way. Wrong realization may discredit even the best principles; trust in ideas may fade away in the mind of inadequately educated people. In the history of Hungary, this was graphically demonstrated by the counter-revolution of 1956. On the basis of the failure of the distorted interpretation of the brilliant ideas of socialism and practical activity harmonious with that, it seemed to many people that the ideas of socialism cannot be put into practice, are merely grand words.

The interpretation of the principle of distribution by work and, accordingly, its implementation have undergone changes. During the first decades of building socialism, unlike the present situation, no significant difference between physical and intellectual work was seen. In terms of income, people formed a more homogeneous mass. This idea was built on the hypothesis that socialist morality would be formed in a few years and social awareness would be the main stimulus, the main incentive of work. In turn, nowadays the basic principle is that it is primarily material interests that form the basis of devoted, creative and hard work. It follows from this change in attitude that the limits of income have become broader, the population is distributed by income on an increasingly wide scale. Growing differences in income cause a certain discontent, particularly among untrained and unskilled workers. The introduction of the new system of economic management, the growing independence of the managers of economic units, have also opened better chances for various financial manipulations and abuses, which may result in more frequent violations of the principle of distribution according to work. Such and similar phenomena may increase the number of those who are not only disappointed with the practical implementation of the system of distribution but doubt that it is through more and better work that one may obtain a higher income, and from certain negative examples conclude that it is manipulations, speculation and egotistical aspirations that ensure higher living standards. People with such personalities always take into account in their everyday activity the foreseeable legal consequences, and in the perpetration of offences against property they accept the risk of punishment. The intensification of egoistical, avaricious, materialistic tendencies has clearly added to the increase in crime in recent years. Of course, it is also only one of the factors that may add to the formation of unstable or criminal personalities.

We should mention the connection between property relations and crime as one of the fundamental structures of society. It is a frequently mentioned fact that private property, exploitation, social inequality and injustice are the source of crime. In our circumstances private property is not significant, it is the socialist forms of property that are dominant, i.e. the property of the state, cooperatives or groups. No social inequality can originate from the *relations of state property,* and for this reason it is not possible to find a causal relationship between it and crime. On the contrary, we regard it as a form of property that will serve as the basis of the social system where, according to our hypotheses, crime will cease to be a *mass phenomenon* of regularity.

The evaluation of the *relations of cooperative property* is different. The experience of recent years clearly demonstrates that under the conditions of building socialism, not only individual interests may conflict with social interests but also group interests. Group interests which conflict with the interests of the whole society originate from the wish to increase the common property, from the relations of group property. This means that the relations of cooperative or group property may elicit socially harmful, antisocial views and thus, they may be in causal relations with crime. We cannot overemphasize that possible causal relations do not allow the conclusion that cooperative property should be abolished in order to prevent crime. Just as the principle of distribution according to work is deemed necessary, soo cooperative or group property is also a regular formation of social development at a certain stage of economic development. In connection with crime as being one of the causal factors only serves as an explanation for the existence of crime and, at the same time, it outlines the perspectives of the existence of criminality.

We also think it useful to mention *urbanization and the mobility* of labour among the fundamental social processes able to influence unfavourably the development of the personality. One of the aims of the socialist society is to eliminate the enormous difference that was to be seen in the life-style of city and country-dwellers. The process of development has been parallel with the industrialization of Hungary. Criminologists, particularly of the West, find both of these social processes as criminogenic factors. Various statistical data prove clearly that criminality is higher in cities, in industrialized areas, than in villages or agricultural districts. Industrialization and urbanization are necessarily accompanied by the mobility of the population, by a flow from villages to cities and by the periodical (daily, weekly and monthly) movement of labour. The effects of these factors on crime are graphically summarized by András Szabó in his work quoted earlier.

"c) the most dynamic element of economic development is industrialization, which increases the mobility of the population, and the increase of population mobility is manifested in the higher crime rate of the population *present* in the industrialized areas since the crime-attracting influence of the richer areas offering more opportunity for crime is felt also by the population present there;

d) industrialization, as the most dynamic element of economic development, influences population mobility also through the migration of the agricultural population, and since the absorbent capacity of cities does not evolve together with the transformation of the occupational structure, very large agglomerations develop around industrial centres and, due to their unorganized and temporary conditions, they are favourable to the increase of crime;

e) the extensive phase of industrial development rapidly changes the structure of the active population but the transformation of the structure of settlement is not parallel to that and, since a discrepancy exists between these two factors, the daily mobility of the active population (and the most active population also from the point of view of crime), between the place of work and home also has an effect of increasing criminality."[11]

As can be seen, the favourable structural transformation of society may entail negative phenomena, particularly if this transformation does not occur in accordance with the laws of proportional evolution, if the realization of the right principles and aims is wrong. The fundamental processes of society, the macro-structures, define the immediate conditions of life of people and these conditions form and shape the personality of people. Just as the macro-environment affects the development of the human personality through the micro-environment, so the views and attitudes of humans concerning the macro-environment are shaped through the micro-environment.

[11] Szabó, *op. cit.,* p. 73.

V The Role of the Actual Objective Conditions (Situation) in Criminal Volitional Decision

According to our scheme of causality, objective conditions, social conditions among them, participate in the determination of criminal volitional decisions, in the perpetration of criminal offences, in a double relation. We deal here with the relation when the actual objective conditions affect the given personality and manifest themselves in the form of antisocial behaviour according to the state of the personality. *In this relation it depends on the state of the personality what kind of significance the* nature, the intensity of the external objective factors have for the individual. This is the link of the chain of causality where the traits which are characteristic of the personality and actual objective conditions (naturally in a subjectivized form), play together the role of causal factors in the struggle of motives for the decision of the will.

Omitting the commonly known description of the personality we have already taken a position on certain, in our opinion, important issues concerning the personality, its state and nature. In this relation of causal relationships we regard the personality as given, namely, according to the past deeds, the series of behaviour of the individual, fundamentally socialized, fundamentally criminal or one not classifiable into either of the two categories: unstable. We use the word "fundamentally" in connection with the social or criminal personality because a purely social or purely criminal personality is not likely to exist.

The three types of personality, socialized, criminal and unstable, respond to external objective effects differently, and for this reason these external effects, situations play different roles in the displayed criminal behaviour.

That a human being with a socialized personality would not commit criminal offences even under favourable conditions, may be taken as a regularity. It may happen, however, *by chance,* that under the influence of extremely strong external influences (e.g. serious tension in the family or at the place of work) or due to some kind of disturbance of the psychological state (e.g. alcoholic intoxication) they nevertheless commit criminal offences. As we mentioned earlier, in such cases the situation has a decisive role against the personality. The decisive causal factors of the criminal offence may be found in the objective situation directly preceding the perpetration of the act.

Contrary to that, for the criminal personality, the situation usually appears only as a condition of the "habitual" antisocial satisfaction of the needs. It very frequently happens that a human being with a criminal personality creates a suitable situation for the perpetration of the offence, and if it is not given, he produces the conditions for the perpetration of the act. For this reason the situation as a motivating factor has a low value for such a person in the process of the criminal decision of will.

The situation, the actual objective conditions are important factors for people with unstable personality from the point of view of criminal behaviour. The behaviour of such people is unpredictable, they have usually no ideas about the future either. For this reason, everyday circumstances, the development of the events around them, influence their behaviour to a great extent. Even the slightest criminogenic influence may elicit the perpetration of an offence if the arising concrete need is accompanied by antisocial views on the person's part. These are the people who are controlled by circumstances. Under favourable circumstances, they follow social norms and if they live in such conditions their personality may change for the better and may be better socialized. In turn, in the opposite situation, they may easily commit criminal offences and turn into criminals. When evaluating the situation as the objective conditions directly preceding the action or the criminal decision of will, it has always to be kept in mind, of course, that such conditions are not independent of the objective conditions of the past, they are the effects of previous conditions, that is they are also points of junction of ramifying causal chains. It is characteristic of criminogenic situations, as it is of criminogenic conditions in general, that they inspire people to commit criminal offences or contain favourable opportunities for the perpetration. However, it cannot be emphasized enough that the effects of the actual objective conditions manifest themselves in human acts or criminal behaviour only depending on the actual of the personality state. Statistics have been collected by the police and by the Procurator's Office regarding the causal factors (causes, conditions) that contribute most frequently to the perpetration of criminal offences, since 1964. These factors (although they are not included in the statistics classified by the type of personality and do not include actual objective factors in a pure form but mixed with the factors of the past and mixed with the features of the actual personality) give information on the frequency of the individual factors.

The material of the complete statistical data collection for two years (1964 and 1965) was processed; the data embraced 134.215 intentional perpetrators. The frequency distribution of the individual causal factors is shown in Table 3.[1]

These data give a graphic picture of the proportion and structure of the mentioned causal factors. Alcoholic intoxication as a situational factor has a much

[1] J. Vigh, K. Gönczöl, Gy. Kiss and Á. Szabó, *Erőszakos bűncselekmények és elkövetőik* (Violent Crimes), Budapest: Közgazdasági és Jogi Könyvkiadó, 1973, p. 260.

Table 3

The frequency of the causal factors of deliberate offences

Causal factors	Per cent
Difficult financial situation	9.7
Momentary financial difficulties	9.9
Excessive drive for gain	11.0
Private property consciousness	7.6
Excessive acquisitiveness	2.5
Excessive material needs	2.5
Regular alcoholism	6.7
Alcoholic intoxication	16.4
Disturbances of family life	5.8
Depraved family environment	0.6
Bad company	5.5
Concealing another criminal offence	0.7
Hostile political attitude	0.3
Instigation	1.1
Psychiatrically established mental deficiency	0.3
Injury, real or imagined	4.6
Sudden agitation	3.5
Jealousy	3.0
Fear	0.6
Seeking adventure	1.1
Sexual urge	1.2
Other types of urge and passions	0.7
Work-avoiding life-style	2.5
Hooliganism	1.5
Other	3.3
Total:	100.0

higher proportion than the others. According to certain opinions, the connection between alcohol consumption and crime is not unidirectional: in many cases it is criminal life-style that leads to alcohol consumption. No doubt there is such a reaction. People of unstable or criminal personality are regular alcohol consumers in the majority of cases. However, from the point of view of criminology, the emphasis is shifted to cases when regular alcoholism or intoxication plays the dominant role in the commission of criminal offences, when it may be presumed that the given criminal offence would not have been committed without the influence of alcohol.

In addition to the effects of alcohol, causal factors of a pecuniary character are also prominent, partially as momentary or lasting financial difficulties and partially as the inclination to profiteering and greed. It appears from the data that crime may be traced back primarily to the effects of alcohol and financial causes. Considering,

Table 4

The distribution of offenders of violence and offenders against property by causal factors, in percentage

Factors	Violent offenders	Offenders against property
Difficult financial situation	0.3	11.8
Momentary financial difficulties	1.8	0.7
Excessive drive for gain	—	12.7
Private property consciousness	1.5	7.5
Excessive acquisitiveness	—	4.4
Excessive material needs	0.7	4.4
Regular alcoholism	4.2	9.5
Alcoholic intoxication	39.6	9.6
Disturbances of family life	6.0	2.2
Depraved family environment	0.7	1.1
Bad company	0.3	1.0
Concealing another criminal offence	0.7	—
Hostile political attitude	—	—
Instigation	—	0.4
Psychiatrically established mental deficiency	3.0	—
Injury, real or imagined	11.3	—
Sudden agitation	9.4	0.4
Jealousy	1.5	0.7
Fear	0.7	—
Seeking adventure	—	0.4
Sexual urge	11.3	—
Other types of urges and passions	0.3	0.4
Work-avoiding life-style	1.2	5.4
Hooliganism	3.7	—
Other	1.8	6.7
Total:	100.0	100.0

however, that crime is a rather heterogeneous mass, criminal offences, as forms of behaviour with greatly varying content, have only one common trait, namely that they are all dangerous to society and they are declared by the law to be criminal. For this reason, the circumstances giving rise to their perpetration appear more clearly if relatively homogeneous groups of offences are studied. The group of offences violating property relations and the group of offences committed in the sphere of relations between people are two relatively homogeneous partial masses. The proportion of these offences within the structure of crime as a whole also defines the frequency of causal factors. The pecuniary element among the causal factors of crime as a whole is predominant because about two-thirds of all criminal offences are committed against property.

Causal factors show quite different proportions if violent offences against persons and offences against property are examined together. It was the investigation of violent crime that made the comparison possible.[2] (See Table 4)

It may be clearly seen from the data that the high proportion of the factors of a pecuniary nature is characteristic only of the perpetrators of criminal offences against property and these factors represent only an insignificant ratio among perpetrators of violence. However, alcoholic intoxication plays a prominent role with violent perpetrators above all. In this category, it is such factors as real or imagined injuries, sexual desire or sudden agitation and psychiatrically established mental deficiency that replace financial factors. It would be possible to analyse the data further since regular alcoholism and a work-avoiding way of life are significant factors among property offenders, while in the case of offenders of violence the disturbances of family life or hooliganism are significant, from which the perpetration of the offences regularly follows. Such strong differences in the causal relations

Table 5

Factors	Percentage
Violation of security measures	1.9
The lack of basic security devices	2.9
Participation in the offence of a person responsible for supervision	2.3
Lack of control	14.6
Careless supervision	5.1
Lack of supervision	12.4
Non-carrying-out of instructions from superiors	1.3
Wrong organizational or administrative instruction	0.5
Lack of prescribed guarding	2.1
Criminal record of person handling money or material	0.8
Shortcomings of storing	3.0
Negligence of person responsible for handling	5.3
Alcoholic intoxication of person responsible for handling	0.2
Inexpert supervision	0.5
Lack of organizational or administrative instruction	0.4
Assignment of untrained person	0.4
Desolation of the area	19.6
Lack of illumination of the area	6.5
Disobeying administrative instruction	1.9
Unlocked premises	3.3
Vehicle left unlocked	1.0
Carelessness of the injured party	4.7
Other	9.3
Total:	100.0

[2] *Op. cit.*, p. 263.

Table 6

The frequency distribution of secondary

Primary factors \ Secondary factors	Acquisitive-ness	Influence of alcohol	Momentary financial difficulty	Difficult financial situation	Disturbed family situation	Bad company
Acquisitiveness	×	24.8	1.1	0.6	16.9	21.5
Influence of alcohol	0.6	×	0.4	0,2	22.9	10.3
Momentary financial difficulty	18.5	28.5	×	0.4	21.2	12.5
Difficult financial situation	12.1	13.3	14.1	×	27.8	4.6
Disturbed family situation	1.1	3.4	0.9	1.2	×	18.6
Bad company	2.0	1.5	0.7	0.2	2.1	×
Injury, real or imagined	0.6	6.6	—	0.3	1.2	0.3
Sudden agitation	1.2	15.0	—	—	2.2	—
Sexual urge	0.5	20.1	0.5	—	10.9	9.0
Excessive urge and passion	1.9	2.6	0.9	1.4	8.8	15.6
Work-avoiding life-style	1.5	19.8	6.0	12.8	20.8	11.5
Hooliganism	1.1	51.9	—	—	2.8	18.2
Mental deficiency	—	—	0.7	—	2.8	0.7
Other	10.5	11.5	1.0	2.1	7.7	9.8

justify the conclusion that people with one kind of personality belong to the one group and people with a different kind of personality belong to the other, and the different groups of criminal offences come into existence under the influence of different situations. This typification may be uniformly found in the case of multiple recidivists.

Criminal statistics take into consideration the actual objective conditions like the neglected state of an area, the lack of illumination, the lack of guarding or checking, under the title "causes and circumstances promoting the perpetration of criminal offences." It is not purely situational factors that we deal with here, either; however, the effects of the actual objective relationships playing usually the role of conditions in the perpetration of criminal offences may be felt. The official bodies compiling criminal statistics process these data only for certain types of offences against property. For this reason, we present the frequency distribution of the factors only as an example.[3] (Table 5)

It can be seen from the data that the desolation of the area and the lack of checking are those of the objective factors that play a prominent role in the perpetration of offences.

However, the data of statistics do not provide any chance to study what personality has been affected by the actual objective conditions, so the role of the situation

[3] The data refer to cases of theft, burglary, robbery, embezzlement, malicious mismanagement and causing damage to customers, recorded in 1970.

factors accompanying primary ones

Injury real or imagined	Sudden agitation	Sexual urge	Excessive urge and passion	Work-avoiding life style	Hooli-ganism	Mental deficiency	Other	Total
6.7	2.0	0.3	5.1	9.4	2.4	0.5	9.3	100
12.3	10.9	4.6	2.1	11.9	18.5	0.8	4.5	100
1.0	0.5	0.1	0.9	21.6	0.5	0.3	3.2	100
9.0	9.9	4.6	8.6	28.3	3.3	1.0	10.1	100
3.9	1.9	5.2	26.3	20.9	22.7	1.1	11.6	100
×	66.6	0.2	2.9	1.4	10.1	0.4	9.4	100
19.0	×	0.5	3.2	1.5	28.3	0.8	28.3	100
—	—	×	4.0	14.5	34.5	2.5	3.5	100
2.2	0.5	7.3	×	22.6	20.1	0.5	15.6	100
0.5	—	1.0	1.5	×	19.0	0.7	5.1	100
9.9	1.7	5.0	0.5	2.8	×	1.2	4.9	100
27.4	19.7	18.3	9.9	7.8	2.1	×	10.6	100
18.9	10.3	2.1	11.5	5.1	6.6	2.9	×	100

cannot be evaluated in this respect. On the other hand, police and procuratorial criminal statistics have made it possible for the first time in Hungary to establish, in the process of surveying the causal factors, not only a single, the dominant one of those that determine the criminal decision of will, but also others which are secondary to the main factor in their effects and intensity. These so-called secondary factors show extremely interesting interrelations, although they could only be established in about two-thirds of the whole surveyed mass of perpetrators in 1964 and 1965 (31.767 perpetrators). The low frequency of the occurrence of these factors demanded a certain grouping for analysis.[4]

The connection between primary and secondary factors is shown by Table 6.[5]

If we take the primary factors included in Table 6 and examine what secondary factors accompany them and in what proportion, we may have a general picture of the actual personality of the perpetrator and the situation initiating the perpetration of the criminal offence. This interrelation of the factors allows the conclusion that

[4] The grouped factors are given after the new titles in italics: *acquisitiveness;* excessive drive for gain private property consciousness, passion for making money, satisfaction of exaggerated needs; *disturbed family situation:* disturbances of family life, depraved family environment; *influence of alcohol:* habitual alcoholism, alcoholic intoxication; *excessive urge and passion:* seeking adventure, other types of urges and passions; *other:* concealing another criminal offence, hostile political attitude, instigation, fear, other.

[5] Vigh, Gönczöl, Kiss and Szabó, *op. cit.*, p. 266.

Table 7

Distribution of secondary factors accompanying primary factors occurring with the highest frequency in the perpetration of certain offences of violence

Primary factors / Secondary factors	Influence of alcohol	Disturbed family situation	Bad company	Injury, real or imagined	Sudden agitation	Jealousy	Fear	Sexual urge	Hooli-ganism	Other	Total
Influence of alcohol	×	3.9	3.8	28.0	28.0	0.6	—	9.7	17.7	8.3	100
Injury, real or imagined	7.6	—	—	×	74.0	2.6	3.5	—	7.7	4.6	100
Disturbed family situation	0.5	×	1.6	16.6	37.7	16.8	12.3	11.5	2.1	11.0	100
Sudden agitation	15.0	—	—	16.2	×	12.8	13.8	0.8	19.8	21.6	100
Sexual urge	22.6	9.4	9.4	—	—	—	—	×	45.2	13.2	100
Hooliganism	51.2	2.4	2.4	17.0	—	—	—	17.0	×	7.6	100

the *perpetration of a criminal offence,* beyond the fact that it occurs because of the joint effects of several factors, *accompanies a certain constellation of the factors.* For example, where the primary, the dominant factor is a difficult financial situation, a disturbed family situation, work-avoiding life-style and the influence of alcohol are accompanying phenomena. Or, if we take a disturbed family situation, the accompanying factors are a work-avoiding life-style and bad company above all. Perhaps work-avoiding life-style also deserves special mention as a primary factor; it is accompanied by the factors of a disturbed family situation, the influence of alcohol and hooliganism.

Even closer interrelations may be discovered if the relations of factors are not studied on the level of total crime within a more homogeneous mass, e.g. among the perpetrators of criminal offences of violence.[6] (See Table 7)

Injury, real or imagined, as a primary factor has close connections with the factors of sudden agitation, with the influence of alcohol and hooliganism. The causal factor of hooliganism is accompanied most frequently by the secondary factors of the influence of alcohol, real or imagined injury and sexual desire.

On the basis of the findings of investigations of homogeneous groups of criminal offences, it is possible to deduce the nature of the offence from the constellation of causal factors.

It can also be seen from the Tables that in principle, primary factors are followed by several secondary factors; according to concrete statistical data, the number of these secondary factors having high proportions is three or four. On the basis of this relationship, we may put forward the hypothesis that a constellation of several defined causal factors implies a strict (highly predictable) regularity that may be confidently used as a basis for prognostication. It was the analysis of Hungarian criminal statistical data that led me to this realization while other criminologists came to similar conclusions in the process of their studies concerning prognostication.[7]

[6] *Op. cit.,* p. 267. The criminal offences studied are: homicide, rape, grievous harm, violence against an authority.

[7] See Sh. Glueck and E. Glueck: *Unravelling Juvenile Delinquency,* Cambridge, Mass.: Harvard University Press, 1950.

VI The Causal Factors of Criminal Offences Committed through Negligence

In analysing the mechanism of causality, we have also presented the causal scheme of offences through negligence, noting that these offences belong to the universal system of causality in the same way as offences by intention. However, as can be seen, the schemes show structural differences, offences committed through negligence being determined in a different way than the ones committed intentionally.

Crime by negligence as a part of total crime, as a mass phenomenon, raises a number of questions and as a result, criminologists are paying more and more attention to studying criminal offences committed by negligence. This follows from the recognition that:

1. Criminal offences of negligence cause significant harm and injury to society. According to the findings of Soviet studies, for example, in 62.4 per cent of criminal offences resulting in the death of the victim, the result was due to negligence. Only 6 per cent of fire cases (forest fires excluded) were arson. The great majority were the consequence of negligent human behaviour.[1]

From such and similar data, certain authors conclude that crimes of negligence in their total mass do not cause less harm to society than deliberate crime.

2. Statistical data clearly prove that the proportion of crimes of negligence is increasing within total crime. However, this increase can be found not only in the realm of traffic crime or in the sphere of negligence displayed in one's occupation but also in the realm of such offences as homicide where the proportion of homicide through negligence is also increasing. Here we may also refer to a Soviet author. It can be read in one of the studies by Serebryakova that the proportion of homicide through negligence was 11 per cent in 1962, 12.2 per cent in 1963 and 14.5 per cent in 1964.[2]

3. During the process of building the communist society, the decrease of inten-

[1] P. S. Dagel, "Pritshiny neostorozhnykh prestuplenii v SSSR", *Sovetskoe Gosudarstvo i Pravo,* No. 3 (1973), pp. 67-68.

[2] V. A. Serebryakova, "Izuchenie prichin neostorozhnykh prestuplenii protiv lichnosti", *Sovietskoe Gosudarstvo i Pravo* No. 7, 1967, p. 76.

tional criminal offences is more possible than that of offences by negligence. In all probability, negligence is more difficult to eliminate from the behaviour of people than intentional confrontation with society.

The growing significance of crimes of negligence is also reflected by the fact that in recent years in Hungary three monographs have been written on negligence in order to obtain academic degrees for the authors; one of them deals with the problems of negligence in general,[3] while the other two treat the problems of traffic criminal law and traffic criminology, respectively.[4]

The latter of the two takes the firm position that the responsibility for the considerable damage caused by offences of negligence has to be established under criminal law, in other words, such types of human behaviour have to be qualified as criminal acts, although it admits that such cases are antisocial to a lower degree. I also believe, that some of the forms of behaviour that are not intentional but still harmful to society have to be declared criminal offences; I immediately add, however, that here we are dealing with forms of behaviour which require a special procedure for establishing responsibility, and special evaluation (legal consequences) due precisely to their being antisocial in a different way, so that, in the future, they may be separated from offences of intention in terms of the system of establishing responsibility.

Even nowadays, keeping the two forms of criminal offence (deliberate or of negligence) together has more formal than material elements. Their main common trait is the violation of penal norms. Setting out from that, I. Békés has written correctly: "...in a *formal sense,* the conduct is not different in the case of a deliberate offence or an offence by negligence. Offences of negligence and of intention cannot be separated from each other through the separation of the notion of conduct.

Similarly, the way in which offences through both intention and negligence take place is also identical and, accordingly, the same causality characterizes the two categories."[5]

While I agree with emphasizing the formal identity, I consider the identity in terms of causality to be disputable. It is quite clear from the preceding parts that there is a difference, a material difference, between the way in which the two types of offences take place from the point of view of causality. Naturally, offences of negligence are also causally determined, as intentional ones are, but not in the same way and usually not by the same causal factors either. And from the point of view of criminology, this is the important thing.

[3] See I. Békés, *A gondatlanság a büntetőjogban* (Negligence in Penal Law), Budapest: Közgazdasági és Jogi Könyvkiadó, 1974.

[4] L. Viski, *Road Traffic Offenders and Crime Policy,* Budapest: Akadémiai Kiadó, 1982; F. Irk, *Közlekedési balesetek kriminológiai vetületei* (Criminological Aspects of Traffic Accidents), (doctoral thesis), Budapest, 1976.

[5] Békés, *op. cit.,* pp. 421-422.

It is a generally accepted idea that the basis of an offence of negligence is faulty behaviour which has not been aimed at the violation of a norm of penal law, but, together with other factors, has led to a harmful consequence that could have been avoided by more careful consideration, by displaying the care that may be expected socially. In the opinion of the Soviet professor Dagel, for the establishment of an offence committed through negligence, it is necessary that

1/ the situation or the means of the act, in other words, the external objective conditions, should provide information indicating the possibility of causing damage or producing a dangerous situation:

2/ the situation or the means should provide an objective possibility for the subject to avoid the harm;

3/ the person himself, due, to his individual qualities, should be able to perceive and understand the information and on this basis, to make the right decision and, through the correct implementation of the decision, to avoid the harm.[6]

It follows from the above that we may speak of a criminal offence if the person did not make use of the possibility provided by the situation, if his individual qualities did not satisfy the requirements of care because

1/ the objective situation was incorrectly reflected in the perpetrator,

2/ in spite of the correct reflection, the perpetrator drew an incorrect conclusion (made an incorrect decision),

3/ the perpetrator could not adequately implement the correct decision which would have been needed to avert the harmful consequence.

It is evident that from the point of view of the expected care the perpetrator has a faulty, unsatisfactory state of personality. These shortcomings of the personality represent the subjective causes of criminal offences committed through negligence. Proceeding along the chain of causality, the objective factors producing these subjective causes as their effects should be searched for.

It is advisable, however, to examine first the perpetrator's personality, the subjective causes, in the cases of offences of negligence, just as has been done in connection with deliberate offences.

We have said of deliberate offences that it is the antisocial, socially harmful views, habits or attitudes of the perpetrator that manifest themselves in the offence —in other words, criminal offences have a direct relation to these subjective causes; and the elements of the consciousness have a decisive role in the perpetration of the criminal act.

Psychological defects leading to the perpetration of criminal offences of negligence are also rooted in the intellectual or volitional or emotional sphere of the perpetrator. The most frequent forms of the manifestation of the defects are carelessness, recklessness, lack of discipline, absent-mindedness, panicking, underrating the rules of precaution, lack of concentration on the work to be done, weak will, etc.

[6] Dagel, *op. cit.*, p. 68.

L. Viski wrote correctly in his book published in 1959: "Carelessness, recklessness, neglect and indifference concerning the interests and good of the community are also the survival of the past in the consciousness, they are harmful attitudes, although naturally there are great differences in degree between these attitudes and those of the consciously hostile injurer. This is the basis of extending the realm of socialist criminal law not only to consciously immoral and dangerous acts but also to those that originate from rashness and neglect, thereby promoting the education of the socialist type of person, the strengthening of communist moral."[7]

As can be seen, harmful, wrong views play a less important role in the case of offences of negligence. A mental defect frequently finds expression in the unconscious state or characteristics of the personality.

The question arises here too whether an antisocial attitude may be characteristic of the perpetrator or not. Dagel answers the question correctly, in my opinion, in the same vein as Viski, when he takes the position that two degrees of antisocial attitudes have to be distinguished. One of them is having *antisocial* attitudes (attitudes built on antisocial views, principles and habits) which may be characteristic of intentional perpetrators above all; the other degree is that of *asocial* attitudes (the lack of the necessary positive views or the distortion of the scale of social values) which may be found primarily among negligent offenders.[8]

It is advisable to note that offences of negligence cannot be traced back only to antisocial attitudes, in any of the degrees; it is possible to commit offences of negligence without attitudes, under the influence of antisocial or asocial views, as has been mentioned in the discussion of intentional criminal offences.

Negligent perpetrators can also be classified like intentional ones according to whether the offence committed, relative to the mass of the perpetrator's other deeds, has the nature of chance or regularity. In accordance with the ideas discussed earlier, the offence of negligence may be deemed chance if its perpetrator is generally careful, performs his everyday activities with due care and consideration. In the case of such a way of life, views, and personality state, if carelessness or other personality disturbances and, as a consequence, a criminal offence occur, this behaviour qualifies from the point of view of the perpetrator as chance. However, proceeding toward the other pole of the continuous line, we see that there are people whose behaviour is generally characterized by the mental defects mentioned above. In their case, mental defects are not the manifestation of a momentary or temporary state but are the lasting characteristics of the personality. The personality is disposed to indisciplined, careless behaviour, omitting the expected caution. If this permanently careless behaviour and the situational factors in their joint effects result in the perpetration of a criminal offence, we may regard that offence of negligence as having the nature of regularity. The fact that continuous carelessness

[7] L. Viski, *Szándékosság és társadalomra veszélyesség* (Intention and Dangerousness to Society), Budapest: Közgazdasági és Jogi Könyvkiadó, 1959, p. 66.

[8] Dagel, *op. cit.*, p. 74.

does not produce a criminal offence over a long period of time is frequently the consequence of the caution displayed by others or of the fortunate coincidence of events.

This group of offences of negligence is not so neutral from the point of view of society as it would appear at first glance. Although not owing to a conscious opposition to society, as a consequence of permanent negligence the danger of violating social interests also protected by criminal law exists. And since it is a lasting personality defect, a personality inadequacy, its correction is only possible through long education.

In the examination of the personality of the perpetrator of a criminal offence of negligence, the most important question from the point of view of causality is on what depends the lack of the recognition of the foreseeable consequences of the act, the inadequate reflection of the situation, the lack of proper attention or concentration, the weakness of will, or, under a collective term, the absence of the expected care. As in the case of intentional offenders, the causes here are also to be found in criminogenic social conditions, and in biological endowments hindering normal co-operation. This basically double division may also be recognized in the dissertation of Viski, who defines the causes of accident groups originating most frequently from human faults as follows:

1. Causes in the area of psycho-physical abilities
2. Causes to be found in the structure of the character
3. Causes deriving from social attitudes
4. Somatic disorders
5. Mental or neurotic illness
6. Short-comings of the education
7. Causes preconditioned by the situation.[9]

As far as the role of biological factors is concerned, we note only that they have a more important role here than in the case of intentional offences. Automatized conditional reflexes and the conditionability of the nervous system serving as the basis for them are extremely important from the point of view of the generation or cessation of inattention, the lack of concentration, absent-mindedness, etc. Nevertheless, it is the objective conditions of society that have the decisive role in forming the subjective causes of criminal offences of negligence. In my opinion, the psychological disturbances mentioned are social factors in most of the cases: they are the consequences of conditions of work, of the way of life, of educational mistakes, of wrong traditions. Negligence shows that the proper positive relation to social interests has not developed in the human being in one or other sphere of social life. People are affected daily by a great amount of information and they select from it according to their needs, disposition and value system. What is significant to a person and what is not, what is how he will select, depends on his social position,

[9] Viski, *op. cit.*, see Note 4.

family situation, political and moral views to a great extent. Negligence displayed in a certain field also shows that the violated social interest is not important enough to the perpetrator. To prove that, we may mention that usually an intentional violation of a lower level statute or moral norm, i.e. intentional administrative infraction, disciplinary offence or other type of antisocial behaviour, can be found behind criminal offences of negligence. Traffic accidents are the best example. "Most traffic accidents may be traced back to the violation of the most elementary rules of traffic", Viski has written in his work quoted.[10]

However, criminal offences of negligence show a correlation not only with the violation of norms of a lower level but also with the violation of penal norms. In several Western countries surveys have been conducted in order to clarify the interrelations of traffic and other common, mostly violent, criminal offences. The question usually arises in the form of whether those who cause traffic accidents are honest people or criminals. Terence Willett had studied the data of two years in one of the English home counties. He found that 20 per cent of 653 persons causing traffic accidents had been convicted earlier for non-motoring offences. A further 15 per cent had no criminal record but were "known to the police" as notoriously quarrelsome persons and troublemakers. Similar results were found in another survey carried out in Canada by W. A. Tillmann and G. E. Hobbs. They compared a group of drivers who had caused traffic accidents repeatedly with two other groups consisting of drivers who had never caused accidents. 43 per cent of the accident repeaters had been before adult courts; of the accident-free group only 1 per cent. 17 per cent of the repeaters had been before juvenile courts; of the other groups only 1.2 per cent.[11]

Graphic data have been published by Klette about the conditions in Sweden. He surveyed 4000 drunken drivers in 1966. 30 per cent of them had committed a serious criminal offence in the previous year, 40 per cent had been convicted for traffic criminal offences, and 20 per cent for drunken driving.[12]

We could enumerate the experience of other surveys, too, but the data presented clearly prove that a significant part of the perpetrators of criminal offences of negligence violate the norms of human behaviour, penal norms among them, not only through negligence but also deliberately.

In spite of the fact that a significant overlapping exists between intentional perpetrators and negligent ones, i.e. they cannot be completely separated, the causal factors of criminal offences of negligence have a structure differing from that of intentional offences. Unfortunately, I do not have statistical data as I have concerning intentional perpetrators, but the statement may also be verified deductively. As we have seen, intentional perpetrators come in significant proportions from the

[10] *Op. cit.*, p. 392.

[11] Both surveys are described by Eysenck in his work *Crime and Personality*, London, 1964, Chapter I.; Irk published similar data in his work mentioned earlier.

[12] See *Belügyi Szemle Tájékoztatója* No. 9, p. 57.

lumpen elements of the population. The main body of known intentional perpetrators is accounted for by unskilled, work-avoiding persons, by those who change their place of employment frequently, by uncultured, primitive, heavily drinking people. On the other hand, the group of negligent perpetrators is not linked so significantly to the mentioned stratum but is approximately equally distributed among all strata of society. Of course, it also adds to this situation that those who belong to the mentioned stratum can commit, for example, traffic offences to a lesser extent at the present time, due to their social situation.

But beyond that, Soviet experience also proves that there is no essential difference, e.g. in terms of education, between the general population and the perpetrators of offences of negligence.[13] It is particularly chance offences of negligence that can occur in any layer of society or with any member of society. Theoretically it is possible, of course, to assert that the number of criminal offences committed by negligence is higher in occupations where there are more risks, more situation involving danger. This is true, but the possibility of displaying negligent behaviour and so the possibility of committing a criminal offence through negligence, is present in the case of every human being.

It logically follows from our discussion concerning the causes of offences of negligence that people have to be taught, educated for carefulness, for weighing the possible consequences of their deeds. It must not be allowed that the intensity of the striving for these aims should be decreased by a relation that seems to be a regularity, namely that human negligence may only be decreased below a certain level but may never be eliminated completely. For this reason, the means to be used against it should be selected with extreme care and perpetrators committing criminal offences of negligence by chance or regularity, or those who have committed other offences as well, have to be strongly differentiated.

By presenting the most important causal factors in the causal scheme, I may perhaps have succeeded in demonstrating the process of causal determination on the level of crime and partially of the level of certain types of criminal offences as well. The generalization formed or that can be formed on the basis of many individual phenomena renders possible the recognition and realistic evaluation of the causal mechanism of concrete criminal offences. The exploration of the perpetrator's personality traits, of the past objective conditions forming them, and the exploration of the objective conditions affecting the actual personality make understandable for us the nature of necessity of the perpetration of the criminal offence and, within that, the nature of regularity or chance of the perpetration. From the causal constellations of a similar type, we can infer with high probability (if the conditions are unchanged) the future behaviour of the perpetrator. The admission and recognition of the existence of the laws of causality and causal determination represent the outlook which may serve as a compass for evaluating criminal human behaviour, for creating the system of the administration of justice.

[13] Serebryakova, *op. cit.*

VII The Constellation Theory of the Causality of Crime

The aim of the brief presentation of the main personality traits and objective external conditions was to demonstrate the action mechanism of causal factors playing a role in the occurrence of criminal offences. The relations of primary and secondary causal factors prove clearly that the causal factors participating in the genesis of criminal offences: 1. are of varying composition, depending on the character of the particular groups of criminal offences or individual offences; 2. are of varying intensity; 3. are of varying structure; and, within that, the combination of varying intensity creates a particular constellation of the factors.

It follows from this that for the understanding of the perpetration of an offence and for the recognition of the process of determination of the nature of necessity it is not enough to establish their material causal factors, it is very important to establish the limits of their intensity and, on that basis, to define the constellation of the factors, too. The causal constellation may have, of course, innumerable varieties but, depending on the peculiarities of criminal offences and offenders, they show similarities. To put it in a more concrete form, as we have seen, the structure, and through that, the constellation of factors is different for offences against life, against property or for traffic offences.

It is the similarity of constellations that makes it possible for us to formulate the particular types of constellation for particular types of offence (the constellation occurring frequently with the type of offence). In this way we may arrive at the typology of causality, at the form studying the causality of crime, where maintaining the study of causality of the individual offence and crime as a whole, we focus our attention on the system, types, and constellation of the causal factors of particular offence-types.

The theory explaining crime on the basis of constellation-types is similar in more than one respect to the theory of mono-causality presented by Kudriavtsev in his monograph in 1976, which may best be demonstrated by the following quotation: "If we approach the questions of causality of crime as a system, i.e. we view causes and effects as the elements of a system, with the assistance of the Marxist method, we may recognize the fundamental, definitive link of the interaction of causes and effects. That is, it is the totality of interactions itself that has to be considered as the cause. This ensures a monistical, mono-causal answer to the question."[1]

The constellation theory, im my judgement, beyond expressing the "totality of interactions", indicates the differences in the systems of the causes and interactions and also the various constellations issuing from their combinations.

The constellation theory is only an idea at present which has to be verified in matters of detail and needs elaboration. The development of the theory requires an empirical study first of all, in which the causal factors are examined in a classification according to the scheme of causality presented earlier, i.e. by personality features, actual objective situations and past objective situations. Furthermore, it is necessary to make possible the evaluation of the intensity of material causal factors by means of some scale. The number of theoretically approved "material" factors has to be defined on the basis of their practical occurrence. It is almost inconceivable to do all this through surveying the full mass, therefore it is through an adequate representative sample that the survey of the relations and combinations of primary, secondary, tertiary, perhaps even quartiary factors is practicable. It is only in this way that the multi-factorial constellations, as situations which, depending on the state of the personality, lead most frequently to the perpetration of criminal offences, can be determined, on the one hand, and, on the other hand, it is through the same method that the educational situations can be defined that lead to the formation of a criminal or unstable personality with a high probability.

From a different aspect, those educational situations that are best for ensuring the socialization or resocialization of the personality could be demonstrated for pedagogical aims.

As a matter of fact, it is the elaboration of causal constellation-types that creates the scientific basis for individual prognostication: for the prognostication of turning into a criminal, becoming a recidivist.

Thus, the constellation theory as an explanatory theory of crime would not only allow its better understanding but could provide effective assistance in crime prevention in practice, too.

Naturally, certain doubts could also be raised in connection with the elaboration of the causal constellations. The basic one, perhaps, would be whether it is possible to survey the causal factors with adequate exactness, whether we can know well enough their mechanism of operation, considering that we also want to establish what the limits of their intensity are. We have to admit that even the recognition of the factors may be difficult in certain cases, e.g. the biological endowments of the perpetrator that may disturb the "normal" mediation of social effects are not always brought to light. However, if the number of the studied cases is high enough, chance effects and the errors of the survey will be equalized or will fade away, the relations of regularity will be more prominent and easy to recognize. It is an

[1] V. N. Kudriavtsev, *Pritshiny pravonarushenii,* Moscow: Yuridicheskaya Literatura, 1976, p. 67.

empirical fact that similar situations, constellations, result in similar effects, independent of whether we know precisely the process, the mechanism, through which the influence is exerted. The inexact recognition of constellations is a source of certain errors and it definitely decreases the probability of the exact definition and evaluation of the effect during practical activity. In criminology, as in any other discipline, if we do not want to err, beyond theoretical exactness we have to be content with high probability in practice.

It may happen that, the first surveys show a high percentage of errors. This does not mean that we cannot advance on the road of the practical application of theory through the improvement of our methods and it does not mean that the constellation theory cannot serve in practice.

Part Three

The Interpretation of Determinism Existing in Human Behaviour

I The Determinism of Behaviour

After the investigation of the main theoretical issues of causality, since we usually started from the effect and so it was basically the real relations of the past that we subjected to examination within this topic, it is advisable to expand our studies to the future, to the possible relations as well. It is in this way that the role of causality in the process of determination, which embraces the past and the future and has universal validity, becomes clear.

In the socialist countries, and we can say without exaggeration above all in Hungary, the interpretation of determinism has been heatedly discussed. The differences of opinion concerning the determinacy of will, of human deeds, are particularly significant. In this particular area, we have to admit that for the time being no uniform or predominant view exists which could be adopted, which could be uniformly interpreted and applied by disciplines dealing with human behaviour. Some of those engaged in criminal sciences, and in legal sciences in general, attribute a prominent role to the determinism of human behaviour because the laying of the theoretical foundations of responsibility demands the scientific materialistic definition or description of the determinism and nature of human behaviour. It is particularly the process of establishing criminal liability that cannot do without the clear definition of positions, since the fate, the future of the hundreds of thousands of offenders depends on the adopted solution to the problems. The frequently voiced (but never written) view which underrates the significance of theory, and according to which it makes no difference to the criminal whether he is convicted and sentenced on the basis of a determinist outlook or an indeterminist one, is false.

The kind of punishment, its content and the methods, the regime of the execution of punishment are defined essentially by the theoretical foundations. The system of punishment follows the aims of punishment as they are set up: either they are defined as retribution or as prevention with the purposes of education, or, perhaps, both.

The cognition of the laws of human behaviour is not less important for us than to know the laws of natural phenomena. To use an analogy, the determinist view of human behaviour leads precisely to consequences of the same magnitude as the acceptance of the heliocentric world concept instead of the geocentric. The Ptolemaic system also allowed a certain orientation according to the position of stars, allowed the approximate definition of the length of the year, but it could not explain many of the universe's phenomena. It would have been possible to ask, and perhaps it was asked, after the introduction of Copernicus' ideas why the rejection of the geocentric concept and the acceptance of the fact that the earth revolves around the sun would be beneficial for mankind. Today, however, it is clear, that precisely on the basis of the Copernican laws, satellites orbit in space and human beings can visit other celestial bodies. In my judgement, the acceptance of the determinism of human behaviour and the consistent adherence to this recognition are sooner or later going to produce revolutionary results in the education of people. And that will be the time when Marxism, the materialistic Weltanschauung, will be dominant in their fullness and will be characteristic of a social era, of a social formation containing qualitatively new human relations.

For this reason, taking a position in connection with the determinism of criminal human behaviour exceeds in its significance the limits of the administration of justice, serves as a guide-line for the establishment of responsibility for acts dangerous to society to a smaller extent only and also affects the general judgement on human behaviour.

In Hungary, the re-interpretation of the determinist conception and the attempts to adapt it to the sphere of legal responsibility started in the 1960s, on the basis of Marxist philosophy. Excellent works were published[1] whose authors formulated a consistent determinist conception and developed their own conception of responsibility according to that.

Nowadays, due to the idea of sentences of indeterminate loss of freedom, the discussion concerning the determinism of human behaviour is stronger again. The debate helps the crystallization of the view of criminology and has a fertilizing effect on other branches of criminal sciences as well, for it strengthens the materialist approach. Although the debate appears as a debate on the interpretation of determinism, in my judgement, it is materialism, determinism, that is fighting its battle against idealist, indeterminist views or their vestiges, in this debate. The debate takes the form of interpretation because everybody admits the prevalence of determinism in the flow of phenomena and everybody professes to be a materialist but there are differences of opinion concerning the extent and way of determinism. For this reason, it is not the description of the determinist conception that I regard as my task; I wish to discuss my position concerning only a few concepts and certain basic disputed issues.

[1] T. Földesi, *Az akaratszabadság problémája* (The Problem of Free Will), Budapest: Gondolat Kiadó, 1960; Gy. Eörsi, *A jogi felelősség alapproblémái. A polgári jogi felelősség* (The Basic Problems of Legal Responsibility. Responsibility under Civil Law), Budapest: Akadémiai Kiadó, 1961; A. Szabó, *A fiatalkorúak és a büntetőjog* (Juveniles and Criminal Law), Budapest: Közgazdasági és Jogi Könyvkiadó, 1961.

1 The Concept of Determinism

Through my own experience, I see H. Korch's statement verified: "Saying yes to the principle of causality directly leads to determinism."[2] It was through studying the causality of crime that I arrived at the study and understanding of the principle of determinism. The investigation of the causes of criminal human behaviour and crime, the investigation of the laws of crime, necessarily involve the clarification of problems belonging to the conception of determinism. And determinism is inseparably related to some essential theses of Marxism, e.g. the principle of the material unity of the world, the exclusion of any supernatural, the infinity and motion of the material world, the nature-forming potentials of conscious human activity.

Approaching determinism from the side of causality necessarily raises the issue of clarifying the relation between the two concepts. I have discussed my position concerning causality in detail in the preceding parts, and its essence is that *all effects,* criminal offences among them, are determined by causes and conditions. And determinism, according to the most general formulation of philosophy, is a notion formed on the universal determinacy of natural, social and psychological phenomena. Or, putting it in a different way, "the term 'determinism' is the denomination of the trends and doctrines of philosophy that admit the existence of the regularity of the order of the world, its determinacy as a result of interrelations and interactions."[3]

Textbooks of philosophy or monographs usually put the concepts of causality, interaction, law, necessity, chance, probability, possibility, reality, and the concepts of content and form in the notional sphere of determinism. Nevertheless, the discussion of determinacy is commonly restricted to the examination of causality and regularity and to the examination of the relations of necessity, chance, probability, and possibility which are needed, as has been mentioned in the discussion of the problems of causality, for the understanding of the first two owing to the fact they are the most material relations of determinacy.

In the examination of causality, we have taken the position that causality belongs to the sphere of the past, the relations of cause and effect belong to the sphere of the phenomena that have already occurred and the regularity (law) manifested in them is projected into the future and renders probable the occurrence of the phenomena in the future. In the present, causal factors have only a relation of probability with the potentialities of the future. The possible causal relation may be regarded as a relation of probability and in this relation there are no effects yet, they will only

[2] H. Korch, "Okság és determinizmus" (Causality and Determinism), *in: Dialektikus materializmus.* Szemelvénygyűjtemény a filozófia szakosító hallgatói részére (Dialectic Materialism. Selected passages for the students of the specialization course in philosophy), Budapest: Kossuth Kiadó, 1969=70, p. 168.

[3] J. Fodor, *A determinizmus koncepció és kapcsolatai a kvantummechanikával* (The Concept of Determinism and its Connections with Quantum Mechanics), Budapest: Akadémiai Kiadó, 1972, p. 143.

exist when one of the possibilities becomes reality, i.e. it passes into the sphere of the (present) past. And, in turn, the relations of the past are no longer probable, there are no possibilities in the past. By the materialization of one of them, the others cease to exist as possibilities. This is the way in which an ambiguous relation existing independently of time becomes in reality an unambiguous determinacy in the (present) past, in the causal relation.

As can be seen, in the interpretation of the causal relation, an extremely important role is attributed to the time factor, the separation of the past and the future. On the other hand, determinism as the principle of universal determinacy is equally valid for the occurrences of the future and the past, independently of the passage of time. The relations of the future, possible and probable relations, belong to determinacy in the same way as the relations of the past. For this reason, in my opinion, the most important elements of determinacy are the relations of causality, regularity, chance, possibility and probability. On the basis of all this, the essence of determinism may be defined as follows; phenomena which have already occurred have been determined by necessity through regular and chance causal relations, while future phenomena (representing one of the possibilities) will be determined at the time of their realization in the same way.

On the elements of this definition I consider it important to sketch repeatedly the notion of necessity. We cannot emphasize enough what a great importance the correct interpretation of the notions of necessity, regularity and chance has in criminology, in the understanding of the problems of crime.

For my own part, as I have already pointed out, I accept the opinion of Földesi who divides the abstract notion of necessity into the concepts of regularity and chance. I find this division verified also in the sphere of crime. According to Földesi, all phenomena have occurred and will occur by necessity, but some of them are regular and some are chance, from a certain point of view. Thus, the chance should not be contrasted with the necessary but with the regular which is also necessary. In a given relation, chance and regular are notions excluding each other. In the same system, a particular phenomenon may be either only regular or only chance. It follows from this that the notion of determinacy is linked first of all to the notion of necessity. Phenomena have occurred by necessity and will occur as the result of causes and conditions, also in the future when the future has turned into the present. However, within this necessity, there are phenomena which are the effects of causal relations of regularity and there are chance phenomena. Regular phenomena can be recognized from the frequency of the causal constellations or factors.

Of the possibilities of the future, primarily those occur, those find an expression in human behaviour, that are probable under the laws ruling the given realm. The phenomena that occurred in the past according to rigid regularity will occur with high probability in the future also. Laws, however, according to their essence, will be valid in the future only as tendencies. Chance has a stronger or weaker effect on their influence. The cumulation, the increasing repetition of chance phenomena weakens the validity of the law, and beyond a certain limit, the law ceases to exist and gives way to a new regularity prevailing in phenomena which used to be only chance earlier.

In connection with the concept of determinism we should mention one more problem. There is a question of whether we need to qualify the word determinism. This question arises from different aspects. It arises, first of all, in connection with the problem of whether it is advisable to use the attribute "dialectic" in order to separate the so-called mechanical deterministic trend which evolved during history. As a similar problem of differentiation, the use of the attribute "materialist" arises in connection with the negation of free will when divine determinacy has to be separated from our notion. In my opinion, qualifying the noun in this way be justified in certain cases, but I do not find it generally necessary because we seldom speak of determinism without mentioning material contents that make clear what kind of determinism we have in mind. To use an attribute seems more advisable when it is not dialectic and materialist determinism we speak or write about.

However, the use of the attribute arises also in connection with showing the extent of determinacy. One frequently hears expressions like relative determinacy or consistent determinacy. Since only one kind of determinacy exists, in my opinion, and we either accept it or not, it is unnecessary to use either of these attributes. The difference between the two attributes is that "consistent" does not change the essence of determinacy, while "relative" means indeterminism, since full determinacy, or simply, determinacy has no degrees. This is formulated with particular clarity by E. Farkas: "Marxist philosophy, analysing the facts of reality and using the attainments of various disciplines, accepts the dialectic determinist thesis according to which all objects, phenomena and processes of the material world, and each of these separately, are determined directly or indirectly by material factors. There is no exception to this determinacy, it is equally valid for the organic and inorganic world, in the same way as for social and psychological processes. Consequently there is no mystical factor either in the material world or in human nature which could exert an influence on itself or on the material world through self-induction. Thus, consistent determinism directly follows from consistent materialist monism, and the other way round: consistent determinism leads to materialism. Contrary to that, even slight indeterminism leads eventually to a mystical factor, and, in this way, to idealism, and idealism leads somehow to indeterminism. Consistent materialist dialectic determinism applied to human acts is the refutation of the mystical notion of indetermined free will."[4]

[4] E. Farkas, *Szabadság és egyéniség* (Freedom and Individuality), Budapest: Kossuth Kiadó, 1968, pp. 58-59.

2 The Possibility of Free Choice

This is actually an issue of the freedom of will or free will. The opposing or different opinions conflict sharply here. The dispute concerns mostly the possibility of choosing or the freedom of choice.

In connection with the freedom of choice, the question is usually put in the form of whether human beings can choose from various ways of action, or whether such a possibility of choosing exists if human behaviour is determined. For our part, after analysing causality, we may consider our opinion concerning phenomena belonging to the sphere of the past and having already occurred, as one formed with finality by asserting that past phenomena as effects have been determined completely by causes and conditions. Thus, logically, only this question remains: what causes and conditions, what causal constellation, produce the phenomenon, the human behaviour, what laws participate in the formation of the behaviour. There are authors who ask the question whether the human being could have displayed different, say, non-criminal, behaviour. The answer is very simple: yes, if other types of causal factors, another causal constellation, had participated in the formation of the behaviour. But since precisely these and no other causal factors and causal constellation had a role, the human being displayed the particular behaviour. In other words, *the displayed behaviour could occur only in one way and only in the way it did.*

The determinacy of phenomena already materialized is hardly disputed, although the law of the determinism of future events directly follows from it. Past forms of human behaviour once had a place on the line of time as possibilities, as relations of probability and, at the moment of their materialization, became determined. For this reason the laws regulating their causal determinacy provide a guide-line for the determinacy of future human behaviour forms as well. The principle of determinism may be considered as universal precisely because it derives the determinacy of future phenomena from the determinacy of the phenomena of the past. The answer to the question asked, consequently, is provided by the analysis of causality and by the study of probable relations.

The opinions of experts are divided as far as the freedom of choice is concerned. There are authors who support so-called consistent determinism. Of those, I first mention Gy. Eörsi, who denies freedom of choice, setting out precisely from the material origin of consciousness and from causal determinacy, in his excellent work on legal responsibility. "The formation of the consciousness is the operation of the brain. The brain has a material nature, and consequently it is subjected to the most general laws of the motion of matter. Thus, the operation of the consciousness is also subjected to these general laws of motion; the highest order motion of material nature has specific laws, valid for it only, but even with these, it cannot be free from the influence of the laws that are valid for all material motions. One of the laws is determinacy; all motion of matter has causes and effects. The totality of the causal factors fully determine the effect; if it were not so, an element without a cause would remain. And, it follows from this, all types of human behaviour are determined by their causes, i.e. by the totality of factors eliciting them. And, in a different formulation, it means that *human behaviour is completely determined, there is not possibility of choice.*"[5] A similar position is taken by T. Földesi with one difference, namely that he admits the possibility of making a choice in a certain situation but he deems the choice determined completely by internal and external determinants.[6] Á. Heller supports freedom of choice without any restriction: "The relative autonomy of people is essentially nothing else but relative freedom of choice. It means that a human being can choose from certain goals, acts and means and thereby he can choose himself as a moral being, in the final analysis. And he can choose not only in the sense that he decides for one or other of several possibilities—this would not of necessity be a manifestation of autonomy—but in the sense that he could have made a different decision from the one he actually did. Thus, he can choose in the sense of true, real choice."[7] Similarly, I. Békés, an advocate of freedom of choice, that is, of incomplete, "moderate" determinism, has written in the university textbook of criminal law: "Determinism is a part of the Marxist—Leninist Weltanschauung and part of the scientific world and human concept of our age. The position of those engaged in natural sciences studying human beings' genetics and psychology above all and the opinion of materialist philosophers, however, are not uniform concerning the degree of the determinacy of the personality of human beings."

"The position of the representatives of various sciences is homogeneous to the extent that the *personality* of a human being necessarily determines the action in a given situation. This means that a human being cannot act in a situation differently from the nature of his personality; that is he cannot step outside himself and cannot act independently from himself, from his intellect, temperament, emotions and character."

"a) Many people, following the rules of logic, have concluded from the previous statement that life is simply the flow of situations following each other; consequently, the behaviour of a human being is determined in every situation. Accordingly, a human being cannot act differently in his whole life than he always does. And, if the

[5] Eörsi, *op. cit.,* p. 84.

[6] T. Földesi, "Miért olyan amilyen?" (Why is it such as it is), *Magyar Filozófiai Szemle* No. 6, 1967. In recent years more and more jurists demand that the principle of determinism should be made to prevail in the administration of justice. e.g. L. Viski, *Road Traffic Offences and Crime Policy,* Budapest: Akadémiai Kiadó, 1982; G. Tokaji, *Adalékok a bűncselekmény-fogalom felépítéséhez* (Contributions to the Formulation of the Concept of Criminal Offence), (Ph. D. Thesis), 1972; P. Szilágyi, "A jogi felelősség fogalma és alapjai" (The Concept and Basis of Legal Responsibility, *Jogtudományi Közlöny,* No. 6, 1974.

[7] Á. Heller, *A szándéktól a következményig. Előadások az általános etikáról* (From the Intention to the Consequence. Lectures on General Ethics), Budapest: Magvető Kiadó, 1970, p. 77.

behaviour of a human being is determined in every situation and every moment of his life, the *development of his personality* is necessarily defined."

"b) Others profess, contrary to a), that the person also has the power of *self-determination,* is able to educate, to develop oneself. The self-determining role of the personality is ensured by the 'will'. Accordingly, the will, which is under the control of the intellect, has a *retrospective effect* on the personality; it is able to restrain the temperament (impulses, emotions), to reject bad habits, to develop the character, to lead the intellect to serve right aims. The significance of the will controlled by the intellect is to be found in the fact that in a certain sphere—within the limits defined by inherited properties and social effects—it opens a door for the self-regulation of human life according to correctness, reasonableness, the norms of social coexistence, and moral values."[8]

The Soviet criminologist Kudriavtsev interprets the principle of determinism in a characteristic way. He formulates the question in the form of whether the perpetration of criminal offences ("output") is unavoidably determined by their causes ("inputs") or whether chance also has a place in this process.[9] He answers the question as follows: "Marxism unconditionally admits the determinacy of all acts of a human being and, at the same time, it emphasizes its complicated character. But this determinism is not identical with the Laplacean mechanical, plain dependence. The physiological, psychological and philosophical studies of our age provide rich factual data to explore the physical nature and character of causal relations existing in nature and society. A number of disciplines studying human beings and human activities point rather strongly to the statistical character of the relations between causes and effects manifest in the sphere of human behaviour including antisocial behaviour.

"The statistical approach does not contradict determinism, it is one of its varieties. We have to distinguish between dynamic and statistical relations and regularities but both presuppose an explanation of causality and both are completely embraced by determinism in its Marxist sense."[10]

Essentially, Kudriavtsev here identifies the causal relation, determinacy, with the regularity manifested in phenomena, and in this way he leaves room for chance of necessity, and from this he derives the thesis of the relative independence of human behaviour. This is perfectly clear from his statement that a plain and strict relation between causes and effects is lacking in human behaviour. "...It means that negative influences affecting the human being even regularly would not unconditionally elicit the violation of law on his part."[11] Kudriavtsev's opinion is criticized

[8] I. Békés, *Büntetőjog. Általános rész* I. kötet. (Criminal Law. General Part, Vol. I), series ed. J. Pintér, Budapest: Tankönyvkiadó, 1973, Chapter I, p. 23.

[9] V. N. Kudriavtsev, *Pritshinnost v Kriminologii,* Moscow: Yuridicheskaya Literatura, 1968, p. 118.

[10] *Op. cit.,* pp. 120=122.

[11] *Op. cit.,* p. 124.

in the Soviet Union, too. According to one author, Kudriavtsev's conception originates in the "wrong, or at least incorrect" interpretation of the dialectic relation between necessity and chance.[12]

One could quote further similar opinions but I consider it unnecessary because the opinion of the authors quoted show the types of the various positions and I, myself, do not wish to dispute so much the ideas mentioned as to state clearly my position.

The problems of the possibility of choice, of the determinacy of future behaviour, have to be approached from conscious human behaviour as a point of departure. We have pointed out in the discussion of causality that human behaviour is a behaviour which is aimed at the satisfaction of needs, built on the possibilities, and is purposeful. Human consciousness has the quality that it reflects objective reality more or less precisely and within that a person's own existence, activity, and social values become part of his awareness. In connection with this, A. Szabó has written correctly: "The determinacy of human behaviour means the determinacy of human awareness above all and the determinacy of the behaviour is accomplished through the effects of various behaviour-determining factors exerted on the consciousness."[13] As we have shown in our causal schemes, the determinacy of the consciousness also includes the anticipated images of the possible phenomena and of their foreseeable consequences. These participate in the determinacy of the behaviour in the form af aim-causes. When needs arise in human beings and reach the level of awareness, the objects, relations, means, and elements of objective reality that are suitable for satisfying the needs appear in the consciousness and there also appears the way in which they may be used. The satisfaction of needs is possible in more than one way and through several means which are not equivalent in terms of the energy and method used in order to obtain the elements which can satisfy the needs. They are not equivalent from the point of view of social judgement either. There exist socially accepted and approved methods and means of satisfying needs, and there are also forms which are not allowed, legally prohibited and punished under criminal law. Thus, the satisfaction of a need is attainable in different ways. Society offers various possibilities to individuals. For example, after finishing secondary school, in objective terms a number of universities, a number of possibilities are open for everyone to study for a degree; or, a fairly wide selection of ways is open to satisfy the needs for food or clothing. Naturally, it may happen that in a given situation the possibilities of satisfying needs are not of a wide variety and there are only two alternative choices, or perhaps only one way, or even none exists. The variety of possibilities exists in this sense externally, on the part of society, it is an objective reality. In Heller's words: "This would not of necessity be a manifestation of autonomy". This is so. Philosophers and those who are

[12] See D. B. Vozhenkin, "Deterministicheskaya kontseptsiya prestupnogo povedeniya", *Sovietskoe Gosudarstvo i Pravo* No. 2, 1971.

[13] Szabó, *op. cit.,* p. 167.

interested in the problems of free will do not dispute this side of the possibility of choice, they dispute the other side, i.e. whether the individual is free to choose from the various objectively existing possibilities. Can we say and, if we say it, can we say correctly that human beings choose from the possibilities or is all this a fiction and is the volitional decision of a human being concerning the choice of a possibility determined?

It is a fact that the behaviour of a human being is the realization of one of the various possibilities. However, the behaviour is preceded by the setting of the behaviour as an aim, i.e. the acceptance of one of the possibilities and thinking out the ways of implementing it. This decision of will, i.e. defining the purposeful action, is the direct result of subjective causes, of the struggle of motives; in other words, it is determined by the motives. And the fact of what needs, what possibilities, what means and what methods of implementation arise in the consciousness of which person, i.e. reach the level of awareness in the form of motives, depends on the state of the actual personality and the joint effects of the actual objective factors. It depends on the state of the personality what influence is exerted on it by the external objective reality, what is perceived of that according to its disposition, its attitude. And the state of the personality has been determined by the objective factors of the past. Consequently, the fact of what motives arose prior to the setting of the aim is also determined. The chain of causality, as can be seen, means the process of determination as well. *The process of the determining of a future human act already starts in the past (in the present) and proceeds parallel to the passage of time and lasts until the realization of the phenomenon, i.e. until the phenomenon becomes an effect.* Thus, determinism is fully valid also for the sphere of human behaviour; no mystical force exists which could participate in the determination of behaviour in addition to the causal chain. But if we want to use the word choice for human aim-setting psychological activity, the volitional decision accepting one of the possibilities and planning the implementation, this does not raise any difficulty, it is a question merely of convention; we have to know, however, that this choice is determined in the same way as all other natural or social phenomena[14] and has nothing to do with the content attributed by indeterminism to the concept of free choice.

It frequently happens in the dispute concerning the principle of determinism that it is incorrectly interpreted, certain incorrect conclusions are drawn from it and, by refuting these wrong conclusions, the principle of determinism is regarded as refuted. For example, according to Kudriavtsev, the acceptance of mechanical determinism would lead to fatalism in criminology. "In reality, if certain causes always elicited the same effects without exception, the individual educated in a negative environment would inevitably become a criminal and there is no need for the unnecessary waste of time and to put society in danger by waiting for the perpetration of his illegal act."[15] In fact, Kudriavtsev is fighting predestination here, which is right.

[14] See Földesi, *op. cit.*.

[15] Kudriavtsev, *op. cit.* p. 119.

But predestination does not follow from the thesis that completely identical causes and conditions always produce identical conclusions. We have to pay attention here to the fact that in reality, even if the environment of a person is extremely criminogenic, he is affected not only by such influences but also by positive ones. In other words, the so-called criminogenic environment does not include all the causes and conditions that may play a role in the formation of the personality, and then in the actual behaviour of the individual living in such circumstances. For this reason, the perpetration of a criminal offence does not follow inevitably even from such a situation. It means only that a part of the causal factors, even the overwhelming part, cannot determine the phenomenon; only the totality of the factors, their constellation, can do so, i.e. the thesis that the totality of the causes completely determines the effect is not refuted. A criminogenic environment, consequently, does not predetermine the perpetration of the offence, but only makes it regular, i.e. renders it probable. But regular and chance effects together determine human behaviour, including criminal behaviour.

II The Problem of Relative Free Will

1 Autonomy of Action

One of the crucial points of the interpretation of the determinist conception is the problem of the autonomy of action or relatively free will. There are authors in whose interpretation the autonomy of action means that the human will is not completely determined, and human beings are free to decide within certain limits. In other words, they may decide independently of objective influences, even contrary to them, their will is not influenced by anything. We do not discuss this evidently indeterminist conception any further, since we have made our position clear in the previous parts.

There are, however, those who interpret the autonomy of action or relatively free will as the relative freedom of the personality, of the individual, against the actual external factors participating in the determination.

One of the most prominent representatives of this conception is E. Farkas, who finds it necessary to admit the existence of the autonomy of action within the general domain of the principle of determinism.

"As far as human activity is concerned, the special form of manifestation of dialectic materialism can be explored only within human actions, through the examination of the relation between external and internal forces. For this reason, within the issue of so-called free will, it is not full determinacy but the autonomy of action expressing the relation between external and internal forces, the relative freedom of action, that is the central problem." After some remarks, irrelevant for us, E. Farkas goes on: "Human actions, as we have demonstrated in the previous parts, come into existence on the basis of the mutual determinacy of the external and internal forces. And, if this dialectic is examined from the point of view of internal forces, we may say that the external forces do not determine the action in one way only; without the internal factors the flow of events, the 'circuit', would not even be closed. It is precisely in this that the relative independence of the personality against the external environment finds an expression. Consequently, the autonomy of human action expresses precisely the fact that human action is not determined only by the internal but also by the external forces of those exerting an influence on it in the given moment, and the internal factors themselves play a very important role in their generation (as internal causes and internal activity)."[1]

Materially we can fully accept the ideas formulated in this way. Autonomy of action which asserts the relative independence of the personality measured by the actual objective influences does not contradict the principle of determinism.

For science, the acceptance of the autonomy of action within determinism is self-evident. But it is also important for people educated in the atmosphere of indeterminism and still professing such views, because it promotes the understanding and acceptance of the principle of determinism. For this reason, emphasizing that the personality has relative independence with regard to the effects of external factors, i.e. they do not elicit the response mechanically, is justified, because it expresses unambiguously that materialism does not identify determinism prevailing in the sphere of human behaviour with the principle of mechanical determinism.

We have given expression to this in the causal scheme by evaluating the objective factors which, as the objective factors of the past, determine the actual personality as a separate relation, and, by accepting the anticipated image of the future behaviour, as an aim-cause. As we have mentioned, the actual personality screens the external effects and transforms and adapts them to the disposition, the attitude of the personality. But the way in which the personality screens and perceives the external factors is also determined by the time at which it happens. In other words, the autonomy of action is also determined, or is being determined. Precisely for this reason, we must not identify the relative independence of the actual personality, measured against the external objective world, with the concept of relatively free will. Relatively free will means that the decision of will cannot be traced back completely to the causes eliciting it, which are material causes in the final analysis, but that, independently of those, "something" manoeuvres within the limits of objective possibilities.

But the term relatively free will is also incorrect notionally, since it is not the will but the actual personality prior to the decision of will that has a relative independence, a relative freedom, relatively to the actual objective (biological, social) effects. Or, formulating in a different way, the decision of will is not an adequate reflection of the nature and intensity of the actual objective influences; but these influences find expression in the decision of will (in the volition) and, under suitable circumstances, in criminal behaviour only in compliance with the state of the personality. We should mention that the relative independence of the actual personality is not the same with every human being. In the case of children it is less markedly expressed than with adults, and a similar difference may be found in the case of simple people of low intelligence as compared with highly socialized, experienced persons who are well aware of the regularities.

[1] E. Farkas, *Szabadság és egyéniség* (Freedom and Individuality), Budapest: Kossuth Könyvkiadó, 1968, pp. 66–67; See also H. Hiebsch and M. Vorwerg, *Bevezetés a marxista szociálpszichológiába* (Introduction to Marxist Social Psychology), (in Hungarian), Budapest: Kossuth Könyvkiadó, 1967, p. 59.

2 Self-Determinism

Autonomy of action has close connections with the problem of self-determinism. Views concerning the self-determinism of behaviour may be found in the literature of almost all disciplines, of philosophy, psychology and law. As far as the literature of the last fifteen years is concerned, the idea of self-determinism of the subjective mind reflects the influence of the Soviet psychologist Rubinstein's works. The authors refer to him almost without exception.

Let us see what interpretation of the self-determining role of the subjective mind is given by Rubinstein: "The genesis of will is preconditioned by the change in the interrelationship between the individual and his environment, the external world, which also generates an internal change. The starting point of the genesis of will is constituted by the desires (and also by the effective components of the desires, the elementary experiences that make something desirable, attractive or repulsive for us. However, as long as the acts of the individual are subjected to the desires, as long as they are directly determined by organizational, natural properties, the individual has no will in the specific sense of the word. In fact, the will comes into existence when a person becomes able to reflect upon his desires, so that he can pass a judgement on them. In order to do so, the individual has to overcome his desires and independent of his desires he has to be aware of himself as an ego, who may have desires but is not submerged either in a single desire of his or in their totality, but rises above them and can select them. As a result, his actions would not be directly determined by his desires, as natural forces, but by himself. The generation of the will, as a part, or component, is linked inseparably to the genesis of the individual, as a *self-determining* consciousness, who himself defines his behaviour freely—*arbitrarily*—and is responsible for it. A human becomes a conscious being who has the capacity of self-determination, through the ideation of the relations between him and other human beings, relations which are objectivized in moral and legal norms."[2]

Rubinstein's words are not in accord with the phraseology of determinism. His scientific activities do not reflect a clear-cut position either. The overwhelming majority of his statements express unmistakably the principle of determinism. In addition to those, however, perhaps due precisely to his striving to separate his ideas from predeterminism, views similar to the above may be found in his works. T. Földesi, for example sharply criticized Rubinstein for his theories on the determination of the will, which are easy to misunderstand.[3]

Due to lack of a clear, unambiguous formulation of Rubinstein's position, the

[2] S. L. Rubinstein, *Az általános pszichológia alapjai II.* (The Basis of General Psychology), Vol. 2, Budapest: Akadémiai Kiadó, 1964, pp. 791–792.

[3] T. Földesi, *Az akaratszabadság problémája* (The Problem of Free Will), Budapest: Gondolat Kiadó, 1960, pp. 289–291.

views of his followers are not free of contradictions either. I refer, again, to a quotation from the work of Farkas, as an example. Speaking of the role of aim-causes playing a role in the process of determinism, he correctly notes: "There is no mystical indeterminism, self-generating free will anywhere in this process, neither in the struggle of motives nor in the formation of the purpose, nor in the volition of thought; on the contrary, it is consistent determinism that prevails.

"This complete determinacy, however, does not mean a fatalistic predestination. Everything in the life of a human being is determined but nothing is predestined, since the determinacy of human action is also conditioned by the self-determinacy of the subjective mind. This self-determinacy, as we have seen, takes place in two forms: through the operation of the internal causes and of internal conditions."[4]

The reference in the quotation in the phrase "as we have seen" concerns the interlinking of the psychological occurrences between the inducement to action and the performance of the action: in the struggle of motives between the two, "the internal forces have the role of determining factors",[5] if I understand the previous discussion correctly. Farkas quotes Rubinstein to verify his own assertion: "This self-determinacy of the subjective mind is a necessary link of the chain of the determinacy of the action. As long as it does not take place, the conditions determining the action are not all present, and consequently, the action is not determined either. If we supposed that the action is determined earlier and the freedom of the human being were excluded, we would replace determinism by predestination."[6] On this basis Farkas has drawn the conclusion: "Summarizing the answer to the first group of problems of free will, i.e. to the question of determinism or indeterminism, we may state that as with all other phenomena of the material world there is no mystical, indetermined phenomenon in the human psyche. Human activity (or using the traditional terminology, human will) is determined and self-determined in the process of determinism by the totality of the internal and external forces, which may be expressed by the simplified formula $K \rightleftarrows B = A$. (K means external conditions and circumstances, B means the internal causes and conditions and A means the will [activity]). This teaching denies the doctrines of indeterminism concerning free will and those of fatalism concerning predestination, and replaces mystical self-generating free will by complete determinism which also includes human self-determinism."[7]

No doubt, Farkas is an adherent of determinism, but his discussion of self-determinacy is not clear, it is rather ambiguous: the difference between "mystical self-

[4] Farkas, *op. cit.*, p. 62.
[5] *Op. cit.*, p. 61.
[6] *Op. cit.*, pp. 62—63.
[7] *Op. cit.*, p. 64.

generation" and "self-determinacy" is not clear, so that humans seem to be above the process of determinacy, they are not subjected to it, but control it. Such a theoretical conception of purposeful human activity has led to the result that certain authors express their acceptance of determinism in ambiguous formulations. J. Földvári, for example, believes that the theory that "the individual may influence the development, the formation of his personality",[8] i.e., that the individual is above his personality, belongs to those that concern the determination of will. Then he defines the basic question from the point of view of responsibility as follows: *"To what extent does the way in which the personality is formed depend on the individual?* Do the external circumstances alone determine the formation of the personality; or is it controlled by the inborn, inherited endowments of the human being; or do these two perhaps act together; or can a person who has an intellect, and has the ability to make an evaluation and to choose, determine the direction of the development of his personality perhaps against the influence of the external circumstances and inherited endowments?"[9] M. Ficsor correctly notes in connection with Földvári's views: "The essence of a human being is his personality; mentioning the individual as something that exists outside the personality and is able to influence it... may cover a hidden duplication of the human being."[10]

We may jusitifiably ask the question: with what concepts may the personality be described if "the person who has an intellect, and has the ability to make an evaluation and to choose" is above the personality? Földvári, referring to Rubinstein eventually concludes that "either we admit the ability of human beings to transform their character and personality, and in this case we also have to admit the possibility that a person can make more than one decision, or we deny the possibility of self-education, of the transformation of the personality, and in this case we may also regard the will as unambiguous and predetermined... We believe in the full determination of the will by the material factors, but, together with Endre Farkas, we also admit the possibility of choice between various activities.

The external and internal factors completely determine the will of human beings but they also leave room for more than one kind of activity. Denying that would be equal to fatalism, which is characteristic of mechanistic and not of dialectic materialism."[11]

In my judgement certain contradictions may be discovered here. If the external and internal factors determine the will completely, then in a given situation, at a certain time, only a certain kind of behaviour can be displayed by a person.

[8] J. Földvári, *A büntetés tana* (The Doctrine of Punishment), Budapest: Közgazdasági és Jogi Könyvkiadó, 1970, p. 69.

[9] *Op. cit.,* p. 72.

[10] M. Ficsor, "A determinizmus szerepe a büntetési célok megvalósításánál" (The Role of Determinism in the Attainment of the Aims of Punishment), *Jogtudományi Közlöny,* No. 1, (1973).

[11] J. Földvári, *op. cit.,* pp. 73–74.

Evidently, in a concrete case, the causal factors do not allow any other kind of action. The reference to the opinion of Farkas shows that, due to the formulation which is not easy to understand, Földvári misunderstood the essence of Farkas' autonomy of action, his self-determinism.

In my opinion, the "self-determining function of the subjective mind" only makes it more difficult to understand the principle of determinism. The main question here is how human behaviour, the deed, is determined. Although the determination of the will, of the volitional decision, is the most important part of the process of determination, the personality determines the act, the deed, only together with the external conditions. And the volitional decision, the intention, is not identical with the deed either, it becomes a deed only if the right conditions are given.

A characteristic interpretation of the determinacy, of the self-determinacy of human behaviour, is given by M. Bihari,[12] who, in my opinion, exaggerates the relative independence of human consciousness. He wrote at the end of one of his studies, almost as a summary: "Thus, as it is true that a human being is born 'into' objectively existing and ready circumstances and lives within their objective limits, and thus far he is 'made' by his environment, it is also important at least to the same extent, and for our topic it is an element of vital importance, that a human is a being created by himself: he is a self-determined being."[13] Accordingly, it is not the objective, the material influences that have a decisive role, directly or indirectly, in human activity but self-determinacy, which is not in causal relation with material conditions.

This outlook is a logical consequence of Bihari's basic conception, according to which it is not the causal relations that are the main form of determinacy in human behaviour, but *"work teleology* and the corresponding *selective/evaluating choice."* In his own words: "It is not the causal 'sets' that form human aim-setting and will in the framework of some kind of mechanical determination, but the human being setting, and in his choices willing, his aims that makes use of causal (and other) relations in reaching his aims."[14]

According to Bihari, causal relations are "the overwhelming elements" of determinism only in the world of lifeless nature. For this reason, those who regard causal relations as the main relations of determinism also in the sphere of society, are reductionists, predeterminists.

In his study, beyond the fact that he identifies causal relations in general with the

[12] See the study of M. Bihari, published in two parts, "A teljes determinista felelősség-felfogás filozófiai kritikája" (Philosophical Critique of the Total Determinist Conception of Responsibility), *Jogtudományi Közlöny,* No. 12, (1976), (Bihari 1.); "A teljes determinizmus ember- és társadalomfelfogása" (The Conception of Total Determinism with regard to Human Beings and Society), *Jogtudományi Közlöny,* No. 1, (1977), (Bihari 2.).

[13] Bihari 2, *op. cit.,* p. 17.

[14] Bihari 1, *op. cit.,* p. 682.

causal relations that prevail in lifeless nature, Bihari regards causal relations as secondary elements in the social sphere and does not believe it impossible to prove a form of existence, unknown before, where causality is not valid at all.[15]

Phenomena which cannot be traced back to antecedents, to causes, do not exist in our world, in the world having material origins and known to us, where in the existence and change of phenomena, the relations of cause and effect dominate, where material determinacy rules.

Bihari's study does not deal with the question to what antecedents human will may be traced back according to the form of determination which he calls "selective/evaluating choice" and puts in the place of causal relations, or whether human will has antecedents (causes) from which it follows by necessity. A deterministic view of phenomena, of human behaviour, which does not make it possible to trace back phenomena directly or indirectly to material relations, to the effects of such, cannot be materialist determinism in my opinion. All scientific achievements up to now, including the achievements of social sciences, originate from viewing phenomena as the consequences of previous phenomena, and the phenomena of the present also participate in the genesis of new phenomena originating in the nature and laws of the former. The basic task of science is precisely to explore the mechanism of the genesis and generation, and, on the basis of that, to discover the regularities, because this makes it possible to eliminate or decrease undesirable phenomena and to maintain the desirable ones and to develop them. And human will, conscious human activity, cannot be exempt from this causal determinacy either, as is clearly proved by pedagogy and psychology, since the types of influence (causes) that lead to forms of behaviour and are judged as positive or negative in social terms are commonly known. Bihari is right, of course, to the extent that this mechanism is different in lifeless and living nature and it is different, more complex, in conscious human activity than in mechanics. But the opposite of this has never been stated, even by authors who are called vulgar materialists by Bihari or whom he calls by other derogatory names; some of them even have emphasized the difference.[16]

[15] Bihari 1,*op. cit.*, p. 679.

[16] J. Vigh, "A determináció egyes problémái és a bűnös emberi magatartás" (Certain Problems of Determinacy and Criminal Human Behaviour), *Jogtudományi Közlöny,* No. 3. (1976). "It is a fundamental mistake to presume that the principle of determinism operates in the same way in the realm of natural phenomena, e.g. mechanics, as in the realm of social phenomena, e.g. in crime. The way of operation always shows the specificity of the phenomenon. Mechanical determinism is not incorrect in itself; what is incorrect is the attempt to transplant determinacy manifest in mechanics, in the motion of solid bodies, to the realm of human behaviour. Human behaviour is a different form of motion, and consequently, the scheme of determinacy and the regularities are different. The specificity in this respect is the personality, consciousness and purposeful activity of human beings." See also "A bűncselekmények oksága és törvényszerűsége" (The Causality of Criminal Offences), *Acta Facultatis Politico-Iuridicae Universitatis Scientiarum Budapestiensis de Rolando Eötvös Nominatae,* Vol. XVII, 1975.

To my knowledge, none of the authors calling themselves Marxists deny that the personality of a human being, the actual personality, has a certain independence from the external environment or inner needs. The essence of purposeful activity is precisely the fact that the actual personality, according to its orientation to its attitude, screens the external stimuli, selects the measure and order of satisfying the needs and considers the possibilities. As a result of this psychological process, the decision of will is made to display one of the possible activities in a manner which appears as the most suitable and rational for meeting the needs of the individual. But we cannot consider this psychological process as self-determinacy because it does not mean that a human being or even only the personality, is above determinacy, and can determine itself, it means that *the actual personality and the effects of the external and internal objective conditions generate the will together.*

The question of whether a human being can educate himself, can form his own personality, is, of course, justified. Marx himself claimed that human beings not only transformed and humanized the external world but changed themselves at the same time.[17] The basis of this change is the interaction between human beings and the external world. Human nature and society-forming human acts not only result in external changes but they in turn have effect upon the acting human being. A. Szabó, too, speaks in this sense, of the self-determining element of the personality. "Marxist sociology, while admitting that human beings are also a part of the causal chain which determines social reality, emphasizes the total determinism of human actions, but the *self-determining element* of the personality also belongs to this total determinism. Without admitting the self-determining element of the personality, we would deny the human ability to realize possibilities, we would deny its role in the perpetration of occurrences."[18]

In connection with causality, we have mentioned that our own acts have particularly significant effects on us, for we have the most direct connections with them. If our acts prove to be suitable for satisfying our needs according to our ideas, or even beyond them, they motivate us to similar actions, and vice versa.

Owing to their consciousness, human beings are able to recognize the laws that can ensure the satisfaction of their needs in the long run, i.e. these laws may be reflected by them. Thus, they may consciously perform deeds (getting a university degree, for example) which enable them to do things they were unable to do earlier. Or they can recognize the fact that knowledge means better understanding of social relations and this is useful for individuals, serves their interests, and, for this reason they try to obtain knowledge. We may regard this as self-education, as the conscious forming of our own personality. All this, however, does not contradict the principle of determinism at all, because the will to display this activity and the actual activity

[17] K. Marx, "Thesis on Feuerbach" in: Marx—Engels: *Collected Works,* Vol. 5, Moscow: 1976, p. 7.

[18] A. Szabó, "A kriminológiai alapkutatások elvi kérdései" (The Problems of Principle of Basic Criminological Research), *Állam- és Jogtudomány,* No. 3. Vol. VI, (1963), p. 332.

are implemented through the process of determinacy, in the same way as any other phenomenon.

The adherents of determinism also do not deny the reality of self-education, purposeful activity displayed or to be displayed in order to obtain the ability needed for adaptation, in order to satisfy the needs to a greater extent; on the contrary, they attribute a great significance to it.[19]

Tokaji has written correctly: "Since the changes of the personality are also determined, in our opinion (at least by the preceding personality development), we believe that no kind of minimal freedom of will opening the 'closed system' of determinants may be smuggled back even through a reference to the 'self-determination' of human beings acting consciously".[20]

Consequently, "self-determinacy" may be accepted only if it is understood to mean that the consciousness of the individual reflects, reproduces objective reality and its law more or less precisely and his will acts according to that, and the activity of the individual, as objective reality, exerts a certain reaction on the formation of his personality and plays the role of a new determinant in the process of being determined.

[19] See Eörsi, *op. cit.*, p. 96.

[20] G. Tokaji, "Adalékok a bűncselekmény-fogalom felépítéséhez" (Contributions to Creating the Notion of Criminal Offence), *Iuridica et Politica* Vol. XIX, (1972), p. 31.

III The Illusion of Free Choice. The "Dialectic" Interpretation of Determinism

1 The Illusion of Free Choice

From the preceding discussion, it may be seen clearly that causal determinacy prevails in the formation of will in the same way as in the genesis of any other phenomenon, and consequently free will which is independent from material relations does not exist. It frequently happens that this opinion is confronted with the fact that human beings feel they decide freely and they can choose any of the possibilities. In a deterministic conception, the subjective experience of free choice is a fiction, the erroneous reflection of reality. The prominent psychiatrist Gy. Nyirő has written in connection with this: "Idealist philosophers are indeterminists and they presume the existence of a special human ability, independent of matter and having a spiritual nature, in the 'will'. According to their views, human beings freely decide what they will do. They try to prove the truth of their assertion through the teachings of religion and by subjective experience, according to which when we do something we have the feeling we have done it freely and we could also have done the opposite. Materialist medical science cannot accept this idea and does not regard the will as free, as an independent psychological occurrence rising above the psychological whole. We do not feel that our decision is determined because our will is dependent on the organization of external influences and internal happenings..." "The subjective experience, that we make our decisions freely, is an illusion, self-deception. It originates in the fact that human beings in possession of the second signaling system have far more possibilities of connection than any other beings. Humans reflect the world doubly: not only in perception but also in words. By the ability to translate the content of the first signaling system into another signaling system, i.e. into the world of words, and by the fact that in their physiological effects words represent, even if abortively, the stimuli they symbolize by their name, it seems to be proved that the 'process of will' is not even a psychological projection of some psychological event, it is only a consequence which will occur depending on the conditions. — Animals are able to make connections only simultaneously, stimuli can produce previous memories in their mind which are similar to the stimuli and this memory will control their kinetic behaviour. Humans who have the second signaling system, also have the possibility of successive connection and masses of ideas arise in them under the influence of an external stimulus, the trace of all the knowledge that has been stored and transformed into dynamic stereotypes in the process of learning about the world, through studying, under the influence of fashion, under various types of social influence, through social inheritance and through relating."[1]

The German psychiatrist Bleuler takes an identical position. According to him, psychological happenings and complexes may lead to a result in the ego which we experience as our own will, due to identification. Aspirations, desires, aims may become part of the consciousness only as our own will. The force of willing originates at the level of the instincts, the feelings; and this level is determined causally and to the same extent, through ancient experience, as any other biological occurrences. It is a specific delusion that human beings feel they could have acted in a different way, but this would be possible only if the motives or inborn instincts and inclinations were different.[2]

Delusions similar to freedom of will may be experienced in other realms of everyday life as well. For example, a straight object appearing bent in water as a consequence of the refraction of light, the relations of the size of objects near and far because of the distance, or the appearance that the sun turns around the Earth, are all phenomena where perception differs from reality. We only know reality, we imagine it, as a perception, an experience; it is the distorted reflection that remains. And as long as knowledge and experience do not turn a person's attention to the processes of objective reality, he has an erroneous outlook, he accepts false appearances as truth.

Human knowledge has by now gone far beyond the limits of direct perception. Through indirect methods and deductions, laws may be recognized whose existence may be proved beyond doubt. I only mention the discovery of Copernicus or the periodic system of Mendeleev, where deduction led to the discovery of certain missing elements.

According to psychiatrists and neurophysiologists, medical science and biology provide undeniable proof of the causal determination of human behaviour. It is proved that the consciousness is the product of the brain. It is also known where the ability of understanding speech, for example, is located in the brain.[3] What biology and medical science cannot prove at present is not the determinacy of the will but the exact neurophysiological process of being determined. It is particularly among the representatives of social sciences that the determinacy of human behaviour is not considered adequately proven. A typical example is the view of I. Békés: "*The question of whether... the conception of mechanical determinism or moderate*

[1] Gy. Nyirő, (ed.), *Psychiátria* (Psychiatry), Budapest: Medicina Könyvkiadó, 1971, pp. 65–66.

[2] Quoted by A. Szobor in: *Affektív és voluntáris magatartásmódok elmekórtani értékelése* (Psychiatric Evaluation of Affective and Voluntary Modes of Behaviour), Budapest: Medicina Könyvkiadó, 1971, p. 164.

[3] See Gy. Ádám, *Érzékelés, tudat, emlékezés ... biológus szemmel* (Perception, Consciousness, Memory—through the Eyes of a Biologist), Budapest: Medicina Könyvkiadó, 1969.

determinism is correct cannot be decided for the time being, because neither of the two can be proved by natural sciences. Both of them are only theories at present."[4]

Even the way itself of putting the question is incorrect, since the question in reality is not whether mechanical determinism or moderate determinism is correct; it is first whether determinism is valid for human behaviour, criminal human behaviour included, and, second, if the answer is in the affirmative, how determinism operates there, in what form and through what mechanism. The first question formulated in this way was answered unambiguously in the affirmative by science a long time ago and the answer to the second one is becoming more and more exact, as science develops.

The history of ideas and trends of thought clearly proves that ideas also come into existence through determined causes and conditions and they yield their place to new or more exact ideas because the conditions change. The existence of the ideas of indeterminism, too, is closely related to a certain level of cognition, of science. Technology, biology and social sciences have already proved that causality as the relation between cause and effect exists in all forms of phenomena. The principle of determinism in this realm also follows from the principle of causal relations of human behaviour. This outlook may be said to be generally accepted nowadays; there are only a few defenders of indeterminism. Thus, it is hardly possible scientifically to take the position that we should maintain indeterminism, or its limited form, "moderate" determinism, simply because the physiological processes of the determinacy of human will are not known in full detail. The fact that the principle of determinism is not in harmony with a number of theories concerning human behaviour (e.g. retribution as the aim of punishment) must not lead to the denial of determinism; on the contrary, our earlier views conceived on the grounds of indeterminism should be changed according to the requirements of determinism.

Many of the opposers of the conception of determinism refuse to accept it because they believe it entails the denial of the notion of freedom. These two notions, however, do not exclude each other; on the contrary, they are preconditioned by each other. The content of freedom was expressed clearly already by Engels:

"Freedom does not consist in any dreamt-of independence from natural laws, but in the knowledge of these laws, and in the possibility this gives of systematically making them work towards definite ends. This holds good in relation both to the laws of external nature and to those which govern the bodily and mental existence of men themselves—two classes of laws which we can separate from each other at most only in thought but not in reality. Freedom of the will therefore means nothing but the capacity to make decisions with knowledge of the subject. Therefore the freer a man's judgement is in relation to a definite question, the greater is the necessity with

[4] *Büntetőjog. Általános rész I.* (General Part of Criminal Law), ed. J. Pintér, Budapest: Tankönyvkiadó, 1973, p. 23.

which the content of this judgement will be determined; while the uncertainty, founded on ignorance, which seems to make an arbitrary choice among many different and conflicting possible decisions, shows precisely by this that it is not free, that it is controlled by the very object it should itself control. Freedom therefore consists in the control over ourselves and over external nature, a control founded on knowledge of natural necessity; it is therefore necessarily a product of historical development."[5]

Thus, we may speak of free will only as far as the will follows the laws manifest in the phenomena, if it coincides with them. On the other hand, all decisions that do not consider the dominating laws are arbitrary. (For the detailed discussion of the concept of freedom see E. Farkas, op. cit.)

Szabó transplants the ideas of Engels into the sphere of criminal human behaviour quite descriptively: "Can we speak of freedom of will, if the behaviour in a particular case does not meet the requirement set up by legal norms, if the behaviour does not reflect the legal obligatons? Only someone who acts in a socially correct way (the content of his will and his behaviour are in accordance with the law that is objective/external from the point of view of the subjective mind) acts freely, all other acts are arbitrary and only have the semblance of freedom, since a criminal offence is a willed act: the implementation of the anticipated aims of the offender. However, we have seen that willed activity means a form of higher order of an act of the will if it corresponds with the objective conditions in its content."[6] We have to emphasize that all this is true only if the norms of law, of criminal law, reflect social laws correctly.

Such an interpretation of freedom of will, of freedom, is compatible, as we shall see, with the interest of decreasing crime and with the correctly interpreted socialist establishment of criminal responsibility.

2 The "Dialectic" Interpretation of Determinism

My last remark in connection with the principle of determinism concerns its *"dialectic"* interpretation. It happens, particularly in the literature of philosophy, that in order to "dissolve" contradictions, usually the contradictions of the author's formulation or views, and actually in order to disguise them, formulations which are contradictory are called dialectic. In his debate with A. G. Szabó, T. Földesi has proved with great wit that a phenomenon cannot be determined and indetermined at the same time. According to Földesi, this type of argumentation has as much to do

[5] F. Engels, *Anti-Dühring,* Moscow: Progress Publishers, (Fourth Printing), 1962, pp. 140–141.

[6] A. Szabó, *A fiatalkorúak és a büntetőjog* (Juveniles and Criminal Law), Budapest: Közgazdasági és Jogi Könyvkiadó, 1961, p. 245.

with dialectics as if we asserted "the universe is *essentially material*—the universe is *essentially spiritual.*"[7]

Such a formulation is that of J. Fodor, but in her case only the formulation may be criticized, her position being clearly a deterministic one. In examining the problems of the "one ambiguous" and the "many unambiguous" in determinacy, she has drawn the conclusion: "The contradiction may be dissolved with a turn not at all alien to dialectics, by showing that a thing could come into existence only in the way it actually has and at the same time it could have come into existence in another way, determined and undetermined simultaneously, inasmuch as in the process of formation it turns into determined from undetermined."[8]

The expressions "at the same time" and "simultaneously" mean simultaneity to me. In that case, the statement cannot be true and Földesi's observation is valid for it. But if it is not simultaneity, as may be inferred from the last part of the sentence, a clear explanation instead of the "dialectic" one would have been much better from a scientific point of view.

This outlook has encouraged me to demonstrate the untenability of the position of "being both". Taking houses, there are houses which are built, in the process of being built and to be built in the future. Can we say, as an analogy of Fodor's definition, that a house is simultaneously finished, being built, and also unfinished? Or can we say of a finished house that it has been built in the only way it could be built or not? No special expertise is needed to decide this question. And, in the second sentence, only part is true: it has been built in the only way it could be because if it had been built in a different way it would not be the same house. Houses, of course, can be and actually are, built in various ways but to build a particular house is possible in only one way, the way it actually has been built. And every house which will be built in the future can be built in only one way, the way determined by the design and construction. It is the same in the realm of human behaviour. A particular act in the future, any particular act, and thus, any human behaviour, may happen only in a single way, as it is determined by the subjective and objective factors. Naturally, if we speak of houses, human behaviour, or phenomena in a general sense, the words have different meanings. In a general sense, there are determined phenomena (houses already built, already displayed human behaviour) and there may be and are phenomena in the process of being determined (not yet determined; houses under construction or to be built in the future, criminal offences just being committed or to be committed, etc.). These thoughts, however, must not be compressed into one sentence which asserts that phenomena are determined and also not determined, as it is nonsense to say of a house that it is built and not built at the same time.

[7] T. Földesi, "Miért olyan amilyen?" (Why is it such as it is), *Magyar Filozófiai Szemle,* No. 6, (1967).

[8] J. Fodor, *A determinizmus koncepció fejlődése és kapcsolata a kvantummechanikával* (The Development of the Concept of Determinism and its Connection with Quantum-Mechanics), Budapest: Akadémiai Kiadó, 1972, pp. 174–175.

Part Four

The Role of Prognostication in Criminal Behaviour

1 On Prognostication in General

As we have seen in the previous chapters, causality belongs to the sphere of the past and the future is the province of possibilities, of probabilities. Determinacy has been understood as a principle of universal validity; the phenomena of the past are determined, were determined, came into existence of necessity, and the events of the future will be determined at the moment of their occurrence. Prognostication, as a science, has the task of finding the limits of future events, to define the probability of their occurrence and to forecast them.

The primary task of all the sciences is to discover the interrelations in the sphere of the phenomena studied and to make use of them in the service of mankind. Those who are engaged in various sciences have been making efforts for a long time to determine the future formation of the studied phenomena, at least approximately, to prognosticate these phenomena on the basis of the discovered regularities. It is particularly so in the case of natural sciences. But for more than a hundred years there have also been scientifically sound prognostications in social sciences, even if not as exact as in natural sciences. In the recent literature of prognostication[1] one can frequently read that the works of the classics of Marxism, especially of Marx, have given a prognosis of social evolution in certain respects. However, the beginnings of prognostication, as a system of knowledge, may not be reckoned from that time; it is the quickening social development of our age that has made necessary the elaboration of its theoretical basis and its increasing practical application. The increasingly complex organization of society in our times demands that the planned control of society should be based on appropriate scientific prognostication. Prediction of the kind of crime to be expected and of the future behaviour of offenders is also necessary in the realm of the administration of justice, in the sphere of crime control.

Scientific forecasting is a creative process, like any other form of scientific cognition, and it changes together with reality and the knowledge of that. The theory of the cognition of the future, or more correctly, the theory of its cognoscibility is

[1] L. Lavellée, *A marxista prognosztikáért* (Towards Marxist Prognostication), (in Hungarian), Budapest: Kossuth Könyvkiadó, 1972; I. Korán, *Jövőkutatás és gazdasági előrejelzés* (Futurology and Economic Prognostication), Budapest: Közgazdasági és Jogi Könyvkiadó, 1972, pp. 11-12.

founded on the philosophical view reflecting reality which holds that it is laws that dominate the objective world, social relations included, and the regularities link the occurrence of the past, present and future together. From this it follows that some of the determinants of some future events, and phenomena are already in existence in the present, while other determinants will appear only immediately before the occurrence of the phenomena. It follows from this process of determinacy that we can prognosticate future events to the extent that the phenomenon studied has its determinants already in the present and to the extent that we recognize them or to the extent that we may establish the probability of the future events from them.

The future that is not linked to the present by anything is not the subject of prognostication. Prognostication is the system of scientific information and inferences concerning the past, the present and the future. If we do not keep it in this way we move necessarily into the world of utopias.

In prognostication, it has to be kept in mind that the future is not a simple repetition of the past and the present. From the fact that phenomenon was frequent in the past it does not follow that it will have the same frequency in the future as well. The real value and reliability of a prognosis depends on its reflecting the intensity of phenomena forming the future, their tendencies to increase or to decrease.

Truly scientific prognostication is built on the laws of dialectics. In the prognostication of social phenomena, the knowledge of reality, and of the views and value judgements concerning it, have a very important role. It is not only, and frequently not primarily, the effects of the actual objective conditions that dominate human will, behaviour and activity, but the effects of the past objective conditions which are sometimes difficult to determine or to recognize at the time of the act and which exert their influence in a subjectivized form, as the features of the personality. The methodology of prognostication is characterized primarily by quantitative techniques. Prognostication today is inconceivable without the use of the methods of mathematical statistics. Moreover, the abundant data needed for reliable prognostication can be processed by computers. All this, however, does not mean, or should not mean, that qualitative analysis may be committed. The analysis of qualitative changes to be expected has a very important role particularly in making medium and long range prognoses.

Since the ideas on the causality and determinacy of criminal human behaviour were disseminated at the end of the last century by the schools of criminal-anthropology and criminal-sociology and their varieties, the possibility of foreseeing the future on the basis of the knowledge of the past and the present has been examined in more and more areas. The theoretical possibility, due to the accumulation of information collected by the criminological surveys of the last decades, has become a practical one. Criminological prognostication, however, is not only a possibility but also a need, since an effective and planned struggle against crime is conceivable only if not only the past and present of crime, of criminal behaviour, are known to us but their future formation can also be taken into consideration. Nowadays, the demand for criminological prognostication on the basis of the preconditions mentioned is spreading and is strengthening to the same extent as the conception of causality is gaining acceptance in the realm of the administration of justice.

In the socialist countries criminological views concerning prognostication were hesitant or hostile at first. At the present time, however, the possibility of prognostication is accepted in theory[2] to the extent that teaching material about prognostication has been prepared and criminological prognostication is considered as an organic part of the subject of criminology.[3] In criminology, two main fields of prognostication are distinguished, namely:

a) the prognostication of the dynamics and structure of crime and

b) the prognostication of recidivism, i.e. prognoses concerning the convicts' behaviour to be expected and the prognoses of becoming a criminal or, under a collective name: individual prognostication.

2 The Prognostication of the Dynamics and Structure of Crime

According to socialist criminology, crime is a social mass phenomenon and it has all the traits that are characteristic of mass phenomena in general: it has dynamics and structure and it has stochastic relations with other phenomena. From this, it follows that the law of the formation of crime is a law of tendency, which means that the formation of crime is also influenced by random factors in addition to regularities. The better the trends are known to us the more exactly the significant relations can be taken into account and the more realistically the possible random factors can be considered.

Crime is one of the social phenomena on which we have had the most important data for long decades, so that the fundamental precondition of prognostication is ensured. On the other hand, particular care is required because of a special factor which makes measuring the volume of crime more difficult as a consequence of the specific nature of the phenomenon. The data of criminal statistics do not measure precisely the extent, dynamics and structure of crime. Criminal statistics consider only discovered criminal offences and their known perpetrators. Statutes, the opera-

[2] See e.g. R. A. Safarov, "Prognozirovanie i yuridicheskaya nauka", *Sovietskoe Gosudarstvo i Pravo* No. 3, (1969); P. Zakrzewski, *Zagadnienie prognozy kriminologiczsej* (The Problem of Criminological Prognostication), Warsaw: 1964; E. Buchholcz, R. Hartmann and J. Lekschas, *Sozialistische Kriminologie. Versuch einer Theoretischen Grundlage,* Berlin: Staatsverlag der DDR, 1966; A. Szabó, "A bűnözés alakulásának előrejelzése. Prognózis" (The Prognostication of the Formation of Crime), *Gazdaság és Jogtudomány,* Nos 3-4, Vol. V, (1971).

[3] G. A. Avanesov, *Osnovy kriminologicheskogo prognozirovaniya* (Uchebnoe posobie odobreno sovietom vysshei shkoly MVD SSSR), Moscow, 1970; *Fejezetek a szakkriminológia köréből* (Chapters on Specialized Criminology), ed. J. Vigh, Budapest: Tankönyvkiadó, 1973.

tional standards of the organs of crime control and administration of justice, and other "formal" factors, may significantly influence a change in statistical data without a change in the dimensions of crime or alternatively, statistical data might change only to a small extent while the number of antisocial acts grows or diminishes. Precisely for this reason, criminological prognostication has to work with a time sequence from which the effects of formal factors are screened as far as possible; and even the estimation of the dimensions of latent crime is desirable, both of crime as a whole and of individual groups of offences. All this uncertainty existing of necessity does not exclude, however, the prognostication of the formation of crime as a whole or of its particular parts, with the proper methods. We can assert with certainty, without prognosticative examinations, that there will be crime next year or even in ten years' time, but its volume and structure can be told only by correct prognostication.

The prognostication of the formation of crime is not new, particularly not in certain capitalist countries.[4]

However, research on prognostication shows the marks of the difficulties of the beginning. The methodology is not elaborated adequately and the theoretical bases also have varieties. In spite of all this, it is clearly proven that it is possible to prognosticate crime, and a prognosis prepared with an adequately restricted tolerance (if the prognosis is good, of course), may be a very useful guideline for state bodies dealing with crime and for the administration of justice. At present, prognostications are made in a number of socialist states. In Hungary, too, the experts of the competent authorities are working on the prognostication of the formation of crime.[5]

Experience so far shows it is the trends of crime in the past that have to be taken into consideration, first of all, for forecasting the trends of crime. In the short run even the mechanical extension of the line of tendency may show the predictable formation of the future. In the case of medium range (5–10 years) and long range (10–15 years) prognoses, however, the study of the changes, or possible changes of causal factors, is indispensable.

Since crime is a mass phenomenon determined first of all by socio-economic conditions, the establishment of the dynamic tendencies of these conditions and the estimation of their effects are indispensable for its prognostication. According to international experience available up to now, the method that appears the best is the one which attempts to express the connection between causal factors and crime in a numerical form (usually computing correlation; or factor analysis). The prognosis

[4] See e.g. D. A. Ward, "Inmate Rights and Prison Reform in Sweden and Denmark", *The Journal of Criminal Law. Criminology and Police Science* 63, (1972), p. 242.

[5] See P. Déri, "A bűnözés, különösen a helyszínes bűncselekmények várható alakulása és a bűnüldözés távlati tervezése" (Foreseeable Formation of Crime with Special Respect to Offences with a Location of Perpetration and the Long Range Planning of Crime Control), *Belügyi Szemle,* No. 11 (1973).

of crime as a whole may be best founded if it is prepared by synthetizing such partial or factor prognoses.

In addition to the establishment of the future tendencies of total crime, the separate prognostication of particular spheres of crime is also very important. Thus, prognoses concerning recidivists, juvenile offenders, or certain types of criminal offence, may be needed.

The formation of the population distribution by age has an effect on the formation and structure of crime through the age-specific criminality rates. The exceptionally high birth-rates in the "Ratkó era" (when abortion was banned—the editor) caused problems not only in connection with the room in schools and school admission but increased significantly the number of juvenile offenders and, thereby, the number of those who served a term in penal institutions. The effects of this kind of demographic change or its opposite may be felt in the number of offenders or offences without any change in the actual causes of crime.

The research carried out in the sphere of violent crime demonstrated that different types of offences may be traced back to different causes. The views, attitudes, social circumstances, the relation to work are quite different in the case of violent offenders than in the case of the perpetrators of offences against property. Consequently, in preparing prognoses, the causal factors have to be taken into consideration on the level of types as well, since the future formation of a certain group or type of offence depends on causal factors differing from the ones playing a role with another group.

The proportion of recidivists and first-time offenders, or, to be more precise, the proportion of the perpetrators of offences of chance or regular character is one of the basic indices of the structure of crime, of the dangerousness of crime to society. It is evident that a prognosis indicating an unfavourable formation of that ratio is very important for all the agencies dealing with offenders. Such changes in ratio and the shifts in the ratios of similar areas of crime express the structural changes to be expected.

Although it seems a simple question, it is actually difficult to answer what period of crime prognostication is optimal under the present circumstances.

Considering our social development which involves major changes and rapid and easily perceivable shifts, long range prognostication of the formation of crime does not seem practicable, since exactness can be ensured only with difficulty or not at all. Medium range prognoses are conceivable, but it is desirable that the time of their beginning should match the starting point of new periods of social development. The preparation of short range (maximum 5 years) prognoses seems the most realistic. The necessary data for these are available and the trends of social development are also clearly definable. Legislative practice also supports short range prognostication. The change in statutory provisions within long and medium range prognostication periods may introduce significant changes to the system of establishing criminal responsibility which render the preparation of exact prognoses difficult or even impossible.

3 The Prognostication of Becoming a Recidivist or Offender

The attempts at prognosticating the future behaviour of offenders with the help of the so-called prognostic tabulation method have been considered as unscientific by the socialist literature of criminal law for a long time. The essence of this prognostication may be summarized by saying that from the data concerning the history of the perpetrator, his social and family circumstances, it is possible to forecast with high probability whether a convict will become a recidivist, the perpetrator of a new offence, or not.

Nowadays even in the literature of socialist countries, it is becoming a generally accepted opinion that the prognostication of recidivism may be considered as theoretically verified and its application under proper conditions is acceptable. In the capitalist countries many criminologists have attempted to prepare individual prognostications.[6] The so-called scoring method has become the most widely used; its essence is that in addition to the enumeration of factors determining and rendering the future behaviour probable, their intensity is also evaluated and the differences are scored by points. The best prognostications so far show 80-90 per cent validity, i.e. this proportion of the prognostications come true. In spite of these facts, the question is still voiced, even if less frequently, of whether it is possible to find a theoretical basis for the prognostication of human behaviour and criminal behaviour within that.

In my judgement, the answer to be given depends on how we view human behaviour. If we consider human behaviour as dependent on free will, any prognostication is senseless: in this sphere it is only a pastime of doubtful value, a game with numbers. If, however, human behaviour is viewed as belonging to the universal system of causality, as something determined by the objective conditions through the consciousness, then the prognostication of human behaviour has its *raison d'être,* the prognosis is dependent on the recognition of the regularities. It follows from the existence of causality that the future, particularly the near future, originates in the conditions of the past and the present. And this is so because the future does not float rootless before us but is a consequence of the past and the present, according to the regularities. From this point of view, prognostication is no more than an approximately precise, or precise, determinacy of a future link of the chain of causality.

[6] Quoted by W. Munkwitz, *Die Prognose der Frühkriminalität,* Berlin—Spandau: Luchterhand, 1967; S. B. Warner, "Facts Determining Parole from the Massachusetts Reformatory", *Journal of Criminal Law and Criminology,* Vol. XIV. 1923; E. W. Burgess, "Factors Determining Success or Failure on Parole" in: H. Bruce and E. W. Burgess, "Parole and the Indeterminate Sentence", *Journal of Criminal Law and Criminology,* Vol. XIX, 1928; Sh. and E. Glueck, *Five Hundred Criminal Careers,* New York, 1930; Sh. and E. Glueck, *Unravelling Juvenile Delinquency,* Cambridge, Mass.: Harvard University Press, 1950; K. Schmid, *Ergebnisse psychiatrisch-kriminologischer Prognosen,* Stuttgart, 1964.

Of course, we must not forget that the recognition of factors and their interactions needed for the prognostication of human behaviour is possible only approximately and for this reason a prognosis can express only a probability. The measure of probability, the occurrence, or the lack of occurrence of the named event, depends on how far the recognition and evaluation of the material factors has succeeded. In preparing prognostications it is absolutely necessary to view the past, the present and the future as a continuous flow, i.e. to have the dialectic view of the permanent changes and motion. It is a frequent phenomenon that certain investigators take exclusively or primarily the features of the past and the present into consideration and regard the future formation of the circumstances as unchanging, although these also change, or may change, and may significantly influence the value of prognoses.

F. Simon has correctly noted in his monograph[7] that the forty methods of prognostication examined by him deal primarily with the past of the perpetrator and with the conditions during the implementation of the punishment, and they do not, or not properly, consider the objective factors after the "treatment" (family and work conditions, friends, etc.).

It is a frequently voiced criticism of the prognostication of recidivism, particularly score-prognostication, that it considers the personality and human consciousness as uniform, although every individual is single and irreproducible. However, the fact that human beings are not the same, that one individual differs from others, and various persons act in various ways under the influence of the same external causes, does not exclude the possibility of prognostication. Prognostication is not based on the absolute identity of individuals, it is based on the common traits discoverable in various individuals. Criminological research has proved that the various groups of offenders have traits of action, views, and environment, which may be found in the majority of offenders belonging to the same group. On this basis, we speak of typical ways of perpetration, offender- and environment- types.

The basis of individual prognostication is the recognition that human behaviour is dominated by regularities too, i.e. *persons having similar psychological traits, attitudes, under similar conditions, respond to similar effects in a similar way.* This regularity is valid, of course, only for a certain group, for a certain mass of people, of criminals, and always only with a certain probability. Precisely for this reason the question frequently arises of whether the prognostic tabulations valid for groups, may be used in the case of an individual offender. It may happen that the factors appearing in the tabulations and rendering recidivism probable are present in the case of a certain offender, but other factors also exist which render social adaptation more probable. Of course, judges or officials in the implementation of punishment always pass decisions in the individual cases of individual persons, and it may

[7] F.H. Simon, *Prediction Method in Criminology: Including a Study of Young Men on Probation,* London: H.M.S.O., 1971.

happen in such cases that the categories of the prognostic tabulation and the circumstances of the case do not tally. We would like to make two remarks in connection with this. The first is that the value of prognostication can not really be measured by one or two cases, it can be done only by examining a high number of units. For example the 95 per cent probability of a prognosis, which is relatively high, does not mean that a person of whom it is predicted that he will become a criminal will of necessity commit an offence; it only means that 95 out of 100 of such persons will become offenders, if the prognostication is reliable. The second remark is, and it should be strongly emphasized, that the *predicting tables alone must never be the basis of a decision, they can only be means, which pass on the essential experience of never identical but strongly similar cases for individual consideration.*

The fact of prognostication being theoretically well founded does not of necessity mean the success of a particular prognosis. Successful prognostication depends on a number of factors. The success of the prognostication of recidivism is dependent primarily on the criminological conception of causality. The representatives of theories tracing criminal behaviour back to bio-psychological or social causes necessarily attribute a fundamental role either to bio-psychological or to social factors in future behaviour as well. It depends on the theory of causality whether bio-psychological or social factors come to the fore in prognostication, or what their proportions or ranking are. However, a prognosis can only be successful, really good, if it is built on the real causes, on the criminogenic factors that are really significant under the circumstances for criminal behaviour. Consequently, if the applied technique is right, prognostication also means the test of the conception of causality. In the case of success, prognostication may enforce our view of causality, while its failure is an incentive for its revision. It is not a coincidence that it is the theories of causality of Western criminologists whose relatively effective prognostic tabulations are the most successful that are the closest to causality theories of dialectic materialist content, to the concept of causality of Marxism.

The issue of the theoretical basis of the establishment of criminal responsibility must also be mentioned among the theoretical problems of criminological prognostication. The prognostications of recidivism at present go by the system of criminal law, by the system of punishment, which is built on the principle of retribution proportional to the act. Consequently, for prognostication at the time of conditional or final release from prison, the establishment of the criminogenic or socialized nature of the released prisoner's personality is attempted on the basis of behaviour before and during the implementation of the punishment. Circumstances after the discharge, and their changes, are commonly not considered, because it is said the future behaviour of the discharged person depends above all on the state of his personality. This view is fairly realistic, since in the case of a system of punishment, or of a kind of punishment, where neither the law nor the judicial decision expects of the implementation of punishment the re-education of prisoners, and only the application of a legal detriment in proportion to the gravity of the act is expected, the most important question is what views, what intentions, the discharged person has. Prognostic tabulations of a quite different structure are needed (or were needed) in the case of a system of punishment or kind of punishment where the correction of prisoners, i.e. that prisoners should have the subjective preconditions of social adjustment at the time of their discharge, is also expected from the implementation of punishment. In this case prognostication should be built primarily on the conditions after the release (employment, family, friends, etc.), in addition to the socialization of the personality, since recidivism is dependent on them above all.

The value of prognostication depends to a significant extent also on the expertise of the person preparing the prognosis. In the case of intuitive prognostication, the basis of prognoses is individual knowledge. With the technique of social scoring, it is a person with legal, sociological, or pedagogical qualifications able to prognosticate adequately. For the preparation of so-called clinical prognoses or social prognosis tabulations combined with bio-psychological factors, a person with psychiatric expertise is needed. All this knowledge, however, produces success only if it is accompanied by an adequate statistical approach. To prepare a prognosis it is not enough to explore the causes and conditions of the individual criminal offence; the exploration of individual causality, and the understanding of the perpetration of the crime, the knowledge of the causality of mass phenomena (statistical causality), are also needed. It must also be known under what circumstances and due to what causes that type of criminal offence is perpetrated, and what criminal measure is usually the most effective in the case of perpetrators of similar attitudes. In my opinion, the prognoses of recidivism should be prepared, if possible, by a team of people with different kinds of expertise.

The prognostication of recidivism may be used in principle in the case of any kind of punishment. But it is used most frequently after the implementation of imprisonment, partly for conditionally released persons with the aim of making a sounder decision on the release, and partly in the case of final discharge with the aim of establishing, or at least estimating, the effectivity of imprisonment of a determinate term.

There are also prognostications of recidivism which are to be used in the case of offenders on probation or whose sentence is suspended. This type of prognostication, in fact, is intended to assist the court in defining the kind of punishment to be imposed. These prognostic tabulations indicate with a close approximation, whether it is justified to put the offender on probation or to suspend his sentence, or whether it is advisable to employ another punishment accompanied by expert education (imprisonment). In fact, it is the examination of the effectivity of punishment not in general or in respect of particular kinds of punishment, but by certain groups, types of perpetrators, which provides an adequate device for judicial individualization.

It may be clear from the above that we consider the prognostication of recidivism as theoretically sound and practically appropriate for use under the conditions of a socialist society, and so in our country, too. Its widespread use, of course, is practicable only if we accept previously and develop properly, through tests of adequate dimensions, the techniques usable under our conditions.

As a matter of fact, decisions based on probability, based on prognostication, may be found in our system of establishing responsibility.[8] According to our present penal law, after a defined period of time, the court may conditionally discharge an offender from prison if it may reasonably be presumed that the aims of punishment may be attained without further deprivation of liberty (Art. 47, of the Penal Code). Obligatory psychiatric treatment may be ordered by the court if there is a danger of the perpetration of another criminal act by the mentally ill perpetrator (Art. 74 of P. C.). The implementation of the sentence may be suspended if the aims of punishment may be attained, considering the personal circumstances of the perpetrator, without the implementation of the sentence. Or, let us take a provision of procedural law: the court may impose a fine without a trial if the aims of punishment may be attained without the trial (Art. 351 of the Code of Criminal Procedure). As can be seen, our law provides a possibility for the judge in certain cases to form a probabilistic, prognostic, judgement concerning the future behaviour of the offender. Similar provisions may be found in the criminal law of other socialist countries, too.

Thus, the question is not whether prognostication may be used in the process of administering justice, it is more correct to ask whether we should remain on the level of intuitive and frequently not even conscious prognostication or whether we should develop various scientifically sound techniques of prognostication and render the struggle against crime more effective through their application. The answer is indisputable. In my opinion, the level of sciences studying man, and computerized data processing, render possible the preparation of usable prognoses[9] and we may be witnesses to the process of development as a result of which the prognostication of recidivism in general may be on the agenda, even in the not-too-distant future.

The tabulations of prognostication could be well used in Hungary, too, in the process of decision-making when considering conditional discharge from corrective institutes of juvenile offenders, and from preventive detention of adults.

However, from the point of view of the future, it is in sentencing that prognostication built on the effectiveness of particular kinds of punishment imposed on various offender types would provide considerable assistance. In my opinion, research on prognostication should be closely connected to studies concerning the effectiveness of punishment. And since effectiveness studies are demanded and are carried

[8] This problem is discussed by T. Király, *Criminal Procedure—Truth and Probability,* Budapest: Akadémiai Kiadó, 1979.

[9] See e.g. M. Veverka, "Replication of Glueck Table in Czechoslovakia" in: *Sample of Young Adult Offenders Leading to Follow-up by the Glueck Method,* New York Intercontinental Medical Book Corporation, 1972.

out in broad areas, research on prognostication is going to expand as a regular process.

As we have mentioned, individual prognostication is employed in two main fields in Western countries. One of them is the prognostication of the behaviour of persons who have already committed criminal offences, i.e. forecasting recidivism; the second is forecasting the behaviour of non-criminal persons, mainly of those belonging to the age-group attending school, from the point of view of becoming offenders.

Theoretically it is also an acceptable idea that the family circumstances and bio-psychological traits of children of school age should be examined with scientifically sound methods and, according to the findings, preventive measures should be taken. But here, we have to emphasize that the widespread application of examinations of this type may be feasible only if the methods of examination are exact enough.

Empirical studies carried out up to now warn us to be cereful. Independently of the reliability of the method applied, prognostication itself affects the subjects, particularly juveniles. According to certain bourgeois authors, merely giving information about the prognosis "makes the good better and the bad worse"; it labels the "bad" as a "criminal" before committing any criminal offence. This danger is real, indeed, but it may be avoided if adequate care and pedagogic experience is used in the examination and in the application of measures taken on that basis.

It belongs to the essence of prognostication that it shows only a probability, even if the best method is used, although this probability is very close to certainty in certain cases, and, for this reason, we always have to take into consideration the possibility of error. In other words, we have to take the risk of a small percentage of wrongly taken measures and their consequences. For this reason, measures to be taken on the basis of prognostication require intensified care. In the administration of justice, measures without prognostication are usually taken in good faith that they are useful for society. Errors and mistakes are discovered only later. And the proportion of these random errors and mistakes is usually higher than of those that would be committed consciously, on the basis of prognostication. The future, as a rule, does not appear in our perspective without prognostication, or it appears only in the form of vague varieties, while the aim of measures taken on the basis of prognostication is precisely to render possible the prevention of a negative, regressive prognosis coming true, to allow us to take measures which influence "the natural flow" of the given relations, according to the interests of society. For society, and also for the individual, it is favourable if negative prognoses never, or only very seldom, come true. But even in the case of positive prognoses measures frequently have to be taken to ensure that the prognoses come true. Consequently, individual prognostication makes sense, and may be used, only if it is followed by the taking appropriate measures, if the persons examined receive the necessary assistance, the "external determinants", that ensure or promote behaviour meeting social requirements.

Part Five

Putting the Principle of Determinism into Effect in the Establishment of Criminal Responsibility

I Conceptual and Theoretical Foundations

1 Determinism and the Establishment of Responsibility

The acceptance of causality is also valid for human behaviour and the acceptance of the principle of determinism defines fundamentally the contents of responsibility to be established for conduct violating penal law. These basic theses of Marxist philosophy may represent, at the same time, the theoretical foundations of our administration of justice. That is they could do so, but actually do not, because the theoretical foundations of our administration of justice are not in harmony in all respects with the principle of determinism. The specialists of criminal law are worried about the consistent putting into effect of the principle of determinism in the administration of justice either because they adhere to indeterminism (this is the less frequent case) or because they interpret determinism incorrectly (this is common) and usually identify it with mechanical determinism. In reality the question still arises in the form of whether the establishment of criminal responsibility makes sense at all if the principle of determinism is consistently put into effect whether the denial of free will, the assertion of the nature of necessity of the criminal offence committed does not eliminate the principled basis of responsibility and acquit the perpetrator. Before answering the question in detail, it seems advisable to remind ourselves what it would theoreticaly mean for crime control and for the administration of criminal justice if we started out from the principle of indeterminism or from the conception of limited free will, at least.

1 Etiology, and together with it criminology as a whole, would be superfluous. What sense does etiology make if we profess that the perpetration of offences is not fully determined by the causes; that "human free will" also has a role in their occurrence, in addition to the causes? With such a conception, can we expect that the process of building socialism would educate people to meet social expectations since people will display behaviour also in the future as they choose, can educate themselves to be the sort of persons they want to be? Or, if we like, the number of the criminal offences perpetrated might increase "by chance", dependent on relatively free will, even under the conditions of complete communism.

2 It also follows from the conception of relatively free will, and not only from that of free will, that there are no laws in the sphere of human behaviour which connect the past with the future, and consequently prognostication has no sense either. Prognostication has no raison d'être either in the sphere of the formation of

crime or in that of the behaviour of the individual human being. But it is impossible to recognize the direction of development, too, and consequently it is impossible to answer the question of why crime shows a tendency to rise under the conditions of capitalism and not under the conditions of socialism. Why do a higher proportion of people commit criminal offences e.g. in the USA than in Hungary?

3 If we do not admit the validity of the principle of determinism for human behaviour, we have to deny the possibility of crime prevention, too. For the measures to be taken by us cannot ensure prevention even in optimal cases, since the will of people is independent, or does not depend fully on the phenomena of the material world. Punishment, too, is significant above all from the point of view of vengeance, retribution, i.e. only if the effects of punishment are of no interest for the administration of justice.

However, if we admit the existence of determinism in criminal human behaviour, etiology, prevention, and prognostication have their raison d'être. They may contribute to the reduction of crime, may render possible the recognition of regularities prevailing at the given time and may contribute to the improvement of the system of the administration of justice.

Thus, the striving to put into effect the principle of determinism originates in a social necessity. The representatives of criminological views demanded as early as at the turn of the century, during the reform movement mentioned earlier, that the establishment of responsibility should be put on new theoretical foundations. However, the battle of determinism and indeterminism came to an end in a compromise. This is clearly formulated by the departmental Motivations of the Act on the First Amendment of the Penal Code (1908): "As far as the battle between determinism and indeterminism is concerned, the Bill accepts free will, but admits a limitation, namely that the existing social environment *(milieu social)* and the physical, mental, and moral development of the offender act as determining factors in the process of forming the volitional decision. From this the Bill concludes that by changing these factors, public power can influence not only the external behaviour of individuals but also the formation of their moral life."[1]

This formulation of relatively free will, or incomplete determinism, may be regarded as the one most commonly accepted by the specialists of criminal law.

It is not my aim to describe the history of the struggle between these contradicting views in the bourgeois states let alone in the administration of justice of capitalist Hungary, for in countries where religion and idealism are raised to the rank of state institutions the materialist outlook necessarily can not be dominant in the administration of justice either. For this reason, I shall write of the trends that appeared after the liberation, in the era when Marxist, materialist ideas could be put into practice.

The possibility of, and the demand for, putting into effect the determinist concep-

[1] *Collection of the Laws of Hungary,* 1908, p. 835.

tion in the sphere of responsibility, and in a narrow sense of the word, in the sphere of criminal responsibility, was first formulated in a generally perceivable form in the early 1960s. As has already been mentioned, monographs were published in various fields (philosophy, civil law, penal law) which professed the determinism of human behaviour, of human will, and made an attempt to elaborate the theoretical foundations of establishing criminal responsibility.[2] Even if the authors did not discuss their views in the same way, it was a common trait of their works that they regarded the putting into effect of the determinist conception as possible and necessary in the sphere of establishing criminal responsibility.

The ensuing debates and the latest views[3] allow the conclusion that a general acceptance of the principle of determinism will happen sooner or later. One of the important issues of the struggle for reforms gaining new strength nowadays is the modification of the theoretical basis of the establishment of criminal responsibility which may, of course, be entailed by modifications in the details. Only a few people profess what I. Békés has formulated in his above quoted work as follows: "Through the movement of one of the pillars of the dogmatic construction, the whole system will be shaken and the restoration of the balance may demand the restructing of the whole system."[4] No doubt the consistent putting into effect of the principle of determinism would require a considerable reconstruction of the system of the administration of justice. But we always have to make a distinction between the acceptance, approval, formulation as a principle, of a theory, and putting it into effect or the extent to which it is put into effect. Practical experience proves that theories frequently serve only as guidelines for practice, as long as the necessary conditions for putting them into effect are not given. And these conditions, as a rule, do not come into existence or can not be created overnight, but only step by step, as a result of scientific, social, or technological advances. Similarly, a system of establishing responsibility which is based on different, modified theoretical foundations can be built up only gradually. But to accept or declare principles as official ones is possible through making a new law. A new Penal Code may include theoretical requirements, the fulfilment of which is intended only gradually, depending on the conditions. Viski has written correctly in his above quoted dissertation, that penal law, too, may be given a scientific foundation only through

[2] T. Földvári, *Az akaratszabadság problémája* (The Problem of Free Will), Budapest: Gondolat Kiadó, 1960; Gy. Eörsi, *A jogi felelősség alapproblémái. A polgári jogi felelősség* (The Basic Problems of Legal Responsibility. Civil Responsibility), Budapest: Akadémiai Kiadó, 1961; A. Szabó, *A fiatalkorúak és a büntetőjog* (Juveniles and Criminal Law), Budapest: Közgazdasági és Jogi Könyvkiadó, 1961.

[3] G. Tokaji, "Adalékok a bűncselekmény-fogalom felépítéséhez" (Contributions to the Notion of Criminal Offence), *Acta Iuridica et Politica,* Vol. XIX (1972); L. Viski, *Road Traffic Offenders and Crime Policy,* Budapest: Akadémiai Kiadó, 1982; P. Szilágyi "A jogi felelősség fogalma és alapja" (The Notion and Basis of Legal Responsibility), *Jogtudományi Közlöny,* No. 6 (1974).

[4] I. Békés, *Gondatlanság a büntetőjogban* (Negligence in Penal Law), Budapest: Közgazdasági és Jogi Könyvkiadó, 1974.

the acceptance of the deterministic conception. In this assertion, another assertion is also included in a negative formulation, namely, that the institutions of penal law that are not based on the determinist conception are not adequately sound scientifically and their modification or reform is needed.

Of the earlier works that of Eörsi's is the most quoted, approved of and criticized. This may be explained partially by the fact that the central issue of the monograph is responsibility, and, for this reason, the issue is discussed in its complexity and the analysis is extremely thorough, and partially by the fact that it is founded on the grounds of the "most consistent" determinism. That monograph, and other works with similar content, also discuss the fundamental problems of reprehensibility and punishment, i.e. the basic issues of responsibility, from the point of view of the determinist conception. But the principle of determinism can be put into effect not only in fundamental theoretical issues but also in areas like the system of punishment, sentencing, the effectiveness of punishment, and aftercare. In this part I shall attempt to sketch the possibilities of putting into effect the principle of determinism in these areas.

2 The Distinction between Responsibility and the Establishment of Responsibility

Criminal responsibility may be regarded as one of the forms of responsibility in general. The clarification of the general notion of responsibility promotes the better understanding of criminal responsibility, of the content of the establishment of responsibility.

The notion of responsibility is used in everyday language in various senses. We often speak of work performed with responsibility, we mention "responsible" positions. However, in the most general meaning of the word, we regard responsibility as an obligation on the basis of which someone is responsible for someone or something.[5]

A peculiar definition of the notion of responsibility is given by E. Bócz. In his opinion, responsibility is the relation of a group having an interest in the action of the acting individual. *Responsibility is an objective category, independent of the individual,* its basis is the fact that the individual belongs to the social collective. The fact of belonging to a community originates from the social nature of human beings, from the fact that the activity of human beings is not isolate but is the element of co-operation with others, and as such, it is related to, and is in interaction with, the activity of others, in terms of its aims, causes, reason and results, and owing to that, it influences the conditions and results of the existence and activity of others (the members of the community.)

[5] *Magyar Értelmező Kéziszótár* (Dictionary of the Hungarian Language), Budapest: Akadémiai Kiadó, 1972, p. 374.

"Nevertheless, the awareness of responsibility is not a precondition of responsibility but the result of the putting into effect of responsibility. Thus, responsibility is neither a moral nor a legal category by itself, it is a relation on the part of the community toward its members which originates in the basic objective property of human existence, the necessity of co-operation."[6] Bócz has written correctly that responsibility expresses the relation between the community and the individual, but in my opinion, he has overemphasized the side of the community, and the reciprocity in the relations is obscured. It is true that the expectations of the community, of society, appear in various norms and this is independent of the acting individual, but these norms are elements of the external environment and thus they are the determinants of behaviour, of the relations of the individual toward the community, and the awareness of responsibility, the conscious relation to the norms of the community comes into existence in the individual. Thus, responsibility is a general relation from the side of the individual as well, which may find an expression both in a negative or positive form. In the case of positive behaviour satisfying social requirements, we may speak of responsible behaviour[7] while in the case of negative behaviour, i.e. one deviating from the norms, or contradicting them, we speak of irresponsible behaviour.

In society, especially in contemporary society with its complex organization, we find a whole system of norms expressing social requirements. There are norms whose violation entails only the disapproval of the members of the community. Such are above all, moral norms. But even among them, we find grades. There are, however, norms the violation of which entails graver consequences.

Primarily the norms of law, of various kinds—the norms of labour law, civil law, criminal law, etc.—belong to this group. Thus, we may speak of moral, social and legal responsibility or of its various forms (responsibility under civil law, criminal law, etc.) and in the case of a violation of law the establishment of responsibility is divided accordingly.

The community, society, however, prescribes not only norms, behaviour to be displayed, for the individuals, but holds out, on the one hand, various sanctions for the violations of norms and, on the other hand, rewards, bonuses, medals, distinctions for outstanding performances in meeting these requirements.

The content of responsibility, consequently, is made up, on the one hand, of social requirements appearing in the various norms, and, on the other hand, of the relation of the individual toward these norms, which may be manifested in positive,

[6] E. Bócz, *Személyiség és felelősség* (Personality and Responsibility); manuscript of a lecture delivered at a session of October 1974, of the Criminological Work Group. He expressed an identical view in his dissertation, *Személyi társadalomra veszélyesség a büntetőjogban* (Individual Social Dangerousness in Criminal Law), Budapest, 1975, pp. 271-282.

[7] See Á. Heller, *Szándéktól a következményig* (From Intention to the Consequence), Budapest: Magvető Kiadó, 1970, pp. 105-107.

i.e. responsible, or norm-following, behaviour or in negative, i.e. responsible, or norm-violating behaviour.[8]

It is clear from the above that the notion of responsibility has to be distinguished from the notion of the process of establishing responsibility or from the possibility of such a process, whose basis is precisely a violation of a norm, i.e. it happens in the case of irresponsible behaviour. Thus, the violation of a norm does not entail the establishment of responsibility, it entails the possibility of the initiation of the process of establishing the responsibility.

It is a generally accepted concept in the legal literature that it is in the case of a failure to fulfil a legal obligation that legal responsibility is engendered and the violator of a norm has the obligation to suffer the sanction prescribed for the violation. I mention only as an example Leikina's opinion which represents the views of the majority of Soviet criminal jurists in this respect. "Responsibility is an obligation of people to subject themselves to measures taken by the state against the violation of the order of society."[9]

A similar interpretation of responsibility can be found in the Hungarian professional literature, too. For example according to Eörsi, "Legal responsibility means the prescription of the use of a repressive legal sanction in the case of blameworthy breaches of obligations."[10] But it is even more clearly formulated in the next sentence: "The group of unlawful acts that may or do generate responsibility we call neglect of obligations."[11]

But the difference between responsibility and the process of establishing responsibility is obscured in the same way in Földvári's views, according to which: "Responsibility essentially is simply bearing the consequences of the value-judgement formed on types of behaviour."[12] P. Szilágyi notes correctly in connection with the views mentioned that responsibility can not be dependent on the initiation of the process of establishing it, responsibility exists independently of the process and it is not a consequence of a value judgement, even less is it bearing the consequences of value judgements; it is a relation, a normative relation, involving a value judgement, too.[13] However, Szilágyi also connects the existence of responsibility to the violation of a norm and it is only from the fact of establishing it that responsibility is independent, in his opinion. In his own words: "If, however, legal responsibility has been generated in any way, later procedural obstacles cannot

[8] A similar view may be found with Soviet authors, e.g. V. P. Tugarinov, *Lichnost'i obshchestvo,* Moscow, 1965; G. Smirnov, "Svoboda i otvetstvennost' lichnosti", *Kommunist,* No. 4, 1966.

[9] N. S. Leikina, *Lichnost' prestupnika i ugolovnaya otvetstvennost,* Leningrad, 1965, p. 25.

[10] Eörsi, *op. cit.,* p. 67.

[11] Eörsi, *loc. cit.*

[12] J. Földvári, *A büntetés tana* (The Doctrine of Punishment), Budapest: Közgazdasági és Jogi Könyvkiadó, 1970, p. 62.

[13] Szilágyi, *op. cit.,* p. 281.

eliminate it. The consequence of responsibility, a sanction, however, does not follow in every case. This, however, does not mean the lack of responsibility, it means only the lack of the possibility of calling someone to account, either in a legal or in a physical sense (the lack of private complaint or the flight of the defendant, respectively)"[14]

The words of A. Szabó are also of interest here: "In criminal law, responsibility is always the same as the process of establishing responsibility."[15]

Szabó declares openly that responsibility and calling to account are synonyms in criminal law. It is true that this usage (i.e. in our terms, replacing the establishment of responsibility by the notion of responsibility) has a history of many decades. It does not seem to cause any problem to the experts, for commonly they understand each other's expressions, but if we want to make the principled issues and theses of law understandable to the whole population, and this is a particularly important requirement in the case of criminal law, we have to pay due attention to the use of notions, too. If we identified responsibility with the process of establishing responsibility, people would not owe responsibility as long as they have not violated a norm. People would declare the existence of nonexistent things when signing various declarations admitting they accept the consequences in full awareness of their criminal responsibility. It is evident that criminal responsibility exists not only when a false declaration is made but also in the case of a true declaration. The false declaration creates the possibility of the initiation of the process of establishing responsibility and it is not responsibility that it calls to life.

Consequently, all human beings who become aware of the existence of the norms of criminal law together with the sanctions attached to them, and the possibility of the initiation of the establishment of responsibility as a consequence of the violation of the norms have criminal responsibility. If it were different, i.e. responsibility could be established only in the case of norm-violators, citizens respecting norms or following the law would have no responsibility. It can hardly be said that the majority of people live and work with no responsibility. On the contrary, it is precisely this overwhelming majority of the population that act in a responsible way, and the activity of the smaller part, of norm-violators, is irresponsible, and this is exactly the reason why the establishment of responsibility in a pejorative sense, i.e. the taking of a measure involving some sort of sanction *(malum),* is needed.

In principle, it would be possible to understand the requiring of the rendering of an account of socially useful activity doing this together with the measure expressing its appreciation, approval and reward, as establishing responsibility. However, in common usage, the establishment of responsibility always is a consequence of norm-violating behaviour. For this reason, the establishment of criminal responsibil-

[14] Szilágyi, *op. cit.,* p. 282.

[15] Szabó, *op. cit.,* pp. 246–247.

ity may be understood as taking measures to clarify how responsibility has been put into effect in a particular form of behaviour, whether a particular human activity really has violated a penal norm and, if it has, the application of one or other of the possible sanctions.

And now our task is to sketch the connection between establishing responsibility in criminal law and the theory of determinism.

3 The Theoretical Bases for Establishing Criminal Responsibility

Criminological studies up to now, the recognition of the regularities that find an expression in crime, allow the conclusion that the types of human behaviour that cause grave harm and danger to society occur for the time being and, within the foreseeable future, will continue to occur by necessity. We still have to take into consideration for a long time to come that criminal offences will be committed since the formation of crime is determined by the causes and conditions, like any other phenomenon, and the existence of criminogenic factors will result in the perpetration of criminal offences in the future as well, in the same way as it did in the past. The acceptance of the determinism of criminal human behaviour of necessity raises the issue of the reconsideration of the essence, of the aims of the establishment of criminal responsibility, and the possible modification of theories accepted up to now or their new formulation.

The attempt on the part of Földesi, Eörsi and Szabó to explain the reason and aim of the establishment of criminal responsibility in the spirit of the determinist conception and to prove that the administration of justice may be given scientific foundations only in this way, has started a favourable course in legal thinking. Nowadays, even the specialists of criminal law in a growing number take the position of denying free will and try to fit the establishment of responsibility to the conception of fully determined criminal behaviour.[16]

The conception of determinism, of course, has its own reaction. There are authors who criticize it and call it mechanical determinism or predeterminism and through the refutation of those they believe dialectic materialist determinism refuted. It is L. Bólya Jr. who has directed the strongest attack against the transplantation of the principle of determinism to the spheres of the establishment of criminal responsibility. According to him determinism eliminates the bases of responsibility, and renders punishment unrealistic, if the perpetrator could not act any other way than he did, if he committed the offence by necessity.[17]

[16] See Viski, *op. cit.;* Tokaji, *op. cit.*

[17] L. Bólya, Jr., "Büntetőjogi felelősség alapjának kérdései" (Questions of the Theoretical Foundations of Criminal Responsibility), *Jogtudományi Közlöny,* No. 12, 1966.

Eörsi's determinist conception is called predeterminism and held unfit to provide the foundations of the establishment of responsibility by G. Ádám (the philosopher and not the neuro-physiologist quoted earlier).[18] There is also uneasiness that may be felt in the words of Békés concerning the linking of the establishment of responsibility and the principle of determinism. "Man is part of the scientific world concept of our age, but the concept of man still has a relative independence from the world concept. The concept of man is a social concept which embraces the social relations and social task of man.

"According to our world concept, a human being takes nourishment, in our concept of man, he eats lunch and dinner; according to our world concept he consumes protein and carbohydrates, in our concept of man he eats meat and cake. Both concepts are true but both have different functions."

The task of jurists is not to take apart the individual but to maintain him even if the scientific world concept of it is unconditionally true, i.e. even if the personality and all its manifestations are determined. "However, the question of whether a human being is only a puppet in the hands of fate and all his external and internal manifestations are causal consequences of the inherited personality structure and the decisions built on that continuously and in a sequence, under the influence of external stimuli—i.e. whether a human being is regularly determined from the moment of his birth to his last decision, for the time being may be answered in reality according to the principles of faith and not of knowledge. Mechanical materialism absolutizes causality in the same way as the idea of determinism absolutizes the determining effects of God's (pre-)cognition."[19] Békés does not deny the possibility of the determinacy of criminal human behaviour but he considers the old model of man having at least relatively free will and not the new scientific world concepts as one to be followed by jurists and, of course, legal institutions, including the establishment of responsibility, should be shaped accordingly. This is even clearer from the next quotation: "Every socialist criminal jurist with a scientific knowledge accepts the philosophical thesis of the determinacy of human thinking and regards it as psychologically explained. In spite of that, the doctrines of socialist criminal law even in our times protect (although the freedom of the will is not accepted) the concept built on the fiction of the freedom of the will."[20] Békés is not alone in viewing the establishment of responsibility as built on the fiction of the freedom of will. Such views are also voiced by G. Tokaji, although he professes consistent determinist ideas. Describing and evaluating the various theories of responsibility Tokaji has concluded: "Responsibility can not be derived from the determinacy of already displayed behaviour, which in reality excludes the freedom

[18] Gy. Ádám, "Determinist Concept—Indeterminate Imprisonment", *Jogtudományi Közlöny,* Nos 1-2, p. 10.

[19] Békés, *op. cit.,* pp. 496-497.

[20] *Loc. cit.*

of choice completely. What requires more attention is the fact that the complete determinacy of the act in the past is inadequately reflected by both social and individual consciousness and it is the illusion of free choice, influenced to a certain extent but not excluded by the determinants, that lives in the consciousness of people. And, as the distorted reflection of one or other trait of reality has not always proved to be socially harmful in its indirect effects, the illusion of relative freedom of choice reflecting full determinacy inadequately will, presumably, be playing a useful role for a long time yet, since the awareness of responsibility is built on that. And, should it be built on a reflection inadequate to any extent, it is the awakening of the awareness of responsibility which provides the grounds in the personality on which the preventive function of the correctly imposed and implemented criminal sanction is optimally fulfilled."[21]

The illusion of the free choice is also given a role by Viski in laying the foundations of the establishment of responsibility, but he does not consider it as the basis of the establishment of responsibility. "...psychologically the illusion of free choice is closer to reality than to mere delusion."[22] He finds an explanation for that in the fact that, according to our present knowledge, the totality of the causes may not be known to us, we cannot follow the causal chain to its end. The too distant, indirect factors of determinism, in turn, have a role in every action, and, for this reason, the decision is not a groundless illusion but due to the necessarily determined limits of the capacity of the operations of the brain it is a psycho-physiological reality and it is an illusion as far as human action is not viewed on the level of the practice of life but of a metaphysical abstraction.

"On the other hand, and this is the essential point, we do not have to stop on the level of the illusion of freedom of choice in order to save the concept of responsibility. We have no reason not to look behind the illusion and we do not have to deny that we hold the acting human being responsible in the evaluation of a particular human action not because he did something different than he should have done but because he had to act the way he did, i.e. because of being himself. Society evaluates a human being according to what he is like and what he means to society."[23]

I am in complete agreement with Viski, there really is no need for illusions to depend on, instead of reality. It is precisely the recognition of reality that provides the real significance of the establishment of responsibility. Nothing but the deed itself and the human being behind it, the way he is, can be the basis of the establishment of responsibility. The measures that are to determine (partially determine) the future behaviour of the perpetrator in a favourable way also have to go by these. But it is also the same (and it is right that it is so) on the reverse of the medal, in the

[21] Tokaji, *op. cit.*, p. 33.

[22] Viski, *op. cit.*, p. 165.

[23] *Loc. cit.*

sphere of responsible behaviour. Through the appreciation and rewarding of behaviour useful to society and also determined and also necessarily displayed, society strives to make this type of behaviour more frequent and continuous.

But let us see some basic arguments against admitting the principle of determinism in the sphere of establishing criminal responsibility. The dominant view was expressed most graphically by T. Lukács in his study when he voiced his doubts over the theoretical correctness of indeterminate confinement sentences. "The basis of this idea—which sets aside all our principles concerning criminal offences and punishment—is found in the determinism of human behaviour and our present system of punishment is built on the ideas of freedom of action, on the ideas of free will. We should note that our present system of punishment pays due attention to the ideas of Marxism, only it takes the position of relative freedom of will. This is why the institution of the obstacles to punishability is elaborated in it."[24]

The system of punishment and the establishment of responsibility are built, according to Lukács, on the principle of "relative freedom of will", although the ideas of Marxism are also taken into consideration, but the determinism of behaviour is alien to it, it is contrary to the principles of socialist criminal law.

L. Bólya Jr. has a similar view on the incompatibility of the establishment of responsibility and the principle of determinism. "...we do not find the foundations of responsibility in determinism. In proving this, we do not attempt to refute the theory of determinism since it is an issue of philosophy, on the one hand, and we do not want to fight it, on the other hand; we only assert that *determinism and responsibility are the phenomena of two different realms and the one cannot be derived from the other*." ... "Accepting determinism we regard it as universal, a law valid everywhere, which is necessary like air, present but unnoticeable; it is an objective fact but it does not manifest itself in institutions and it does not serve the purpose of deriving theories from it."[25]

It is clear from Bólya's study, even from the quotations, that the principle of determinism as a philosophical thesis may be true but it cannot be put into effect in the realm of the establishment of responsibility, in spite of its being "a law valid everywhere". In his opinion, these two concepts have nothing to do with each other. "They can be bound on different levels of the structural system and just as determinism does not define responsibility, so responsibility does not define determinism."[26]

According to Bólya, we should let determinism remain a philosophical theory but we should not try to put it into practice through institutions or to use it to derive further theories from and, concretely, to apply it in the establishment of criminal

[24] T. Lukács, "Büntetőjogi szemléletünk alakulása" (The Formation of Our Views on Criminal Law), *Magyar Jog és Külföldi Jogi Szemle,* No. 9, 1970, p. 657.

[25] Bólya, *op. cit.,* pp. 656-657.

[26] *Loc. cit.,* p. 656.

responsibility, or responsibility in general, for if we do so we necessarily have to give up either responsibility or determinism.[27]

The main charge against the establishment of responsibility on the basis of the principle of determinism is that it does not—cannot—take into consideration the subjective elements, for the genesis of the act is indifferent from the point of view of determinism, "since it is determined"; the important thing is the occurrence of the harmful result. And the punishment is not applied because the perpetrator is guilty, but only with the purpose of prevention in the future.

It is here, in my opinion, that the distorted interpretation of determinism is the most striking. We have seen in the discussion of the causal scheme that criminal human behaviour is the result of the struggle of conflicting motives, it is a manifestation of the perpetrator's wrong, harmful views, his emotions, perhaps of his psychological attitudes. To evaluate behaviour violating a norm of criminal law, from the point of view of the establishment of responsibility, the fact of the violation of the norm cannot be enough, precisely because of the purpose of prevention. On that basis it is not possible to define the correct measures, to define the determinants that are to have a favourable effect in the future. To find them it is absolutely necessary to clarify the ways of becoming determined, to answer the question of "how", as demanded by Bólya and others. The *subjective* and *objective* causes that elicited criminal behaviour as a regularity have to be explored. It is precisely on the basis of evaluating the features of the perpetrator's subjective mind, the psychological process of forming the will, the anticipated ideas related to behaviour displayed, that it is possible to decide whether we can influence favourably the personality of the perpetrator and the members of society or whether other means are better suited for this aim.

The establishment of responsibility cannot take place without clarifying how the behaviour violating the penal norm was reflected in the perpetrator's consciousness or whether it was reflected by it at all, whether it was a purposeful action of the perpetrator, or a faulty performance on his part which elicited together with other causal factors the socially harmful consequence. The examination of the perpetrator's awareness of responsibility is also indispensable. We agree with Tokaji that "it is the awakening of the awareness of responsibility which provides the grounds in the personality on which the preventive function of the correctly imposed and implemented criminal sanction is optimally fulfilled" but we do not share the opinion that the awareness of responsibility is built on the illusion of freedom of choice reflecting full determinism inadequately. In my judgement, the awareness of responsibility may be derived precisely from the correct or less correct reflection of reality surrounding us. The awareness of responsibility means that the existence of social norms and the evaluation of the relation toward them—i.e. that the observation of norms is rewarded by appreciation, and the violation of norms is

[27] *Loc. cit.*, p. 664.

followed by a sanction—becomes conscious in the individual. This obligation to account for one's actions forms the psycho-social basis of the awareness of responsibility.

The awareness or feeling of responsibility, of course, is not an inherited property, contrary to the assertion of certain Western authors.[28] It is in the process of ontogenic evolution that the awareness of responsibility of people evolves as a result of the environmental influences. The norms of law, of criminal law, together with their consequences, are reflected as a part of the objective universe in the human consciousness and the awareness of legal responsibility, developing in this way, becomes a part of the human personality, of the human consciousness.

The process of a human being's becoming a social being, a subject of social obligations and rights, begins in the first moment of his individual life. He obtains a certain knowledge already in childhood, and learns in an organized way the norms that prevail in the community, in the society surrounding him. His behaviour is subjected to evolution from the point of view of moral responsibility. It is in this way that his awareness of moral responsibility, which becomes a trait of his personality, is formed.

The awareness of moral responsibility, however, is gradually accompanied by the awareness of legal responsibility, since direct and indirect information indicates the existence of norms whose violation may entail grave consequences, by legal detriment.

Keeping in mind the achievements of pedagogy and other disciplines studying man, Hungarian legislation has determined the fourteenth year of age as the time of human development by which the awareness of criminal responsibility is formed and may be an active factor in the formulation of further behaviour.

The awareness of criminal responsibility is built in various ways in the personality of people. There are people in whom due respect toward the norms of criminal law is never formed or who form a negative value judgement. If, depending on the environmental influences, on the conditions, such persons violate the norms of criminal law, the establishment of criminal responsibility has the function of creating or awakening the awareness of responsibility in them at least to the extent that in the struggle of motives the duty-bound ones should win against the criminogenic ones and thus a decision to display law-abiding behaviour should be formed by them. We emphasize repeatedly that the establishment of criminal responsibility may have a favourable effect not only on the violator's personality but may create, or reinforce, the awareness of criminal responsibility in other members of society, as well, and in this way, it may serve as a determinant for law-abiding behaviour. Thus, the establishment of criminal responsibility, owing to its consciousness-forming effects, is suitable for promoting the observance of norms reflecting the interests of the ruling class of society.

[28] M. Ancel, *La Défense Sociale Nouvelle,* Paris: Edition Cujas, 1966, p. 312.

Although the process of establishing criminal responsibility has its effects on the consciousness, on the personality, as a whole, it is primarily the traits of the personality that have manifested themselves in criminal behaviour that are examined in the process. The establishment of responsibility has to correct these negative personality elements first of all. One kind of preventive measure is needed if the perpetrator has committed his act purposefully, and a different one if it is only a breach of the duty of displaying care that has led to the criminal offence. And, again, one kind of measure has to be taken if the perpetrated offence is a causal, chance, non-habitual manifestation of the personality, and another kind if we are dealing with a confirmed, hardened criminal.

Thus the accusation that the establishment of responsibility which is based on a deterministic conception omits the consideration of the perpetrator's subjective characteristics and thereby creates a system of strict liability is unfounded.

Viski has correctly written that the determinist conception does not compel us to give up the concepts of criminal responsibility, blameworthiness, culpability; on the contrary, it is the only one that is suitable to explain these concepts scientifically.[29] It is true, of course, that these concepts have a somewhat different meaning if we bring them into harmony with the principle of determinism instead of free will. Thus, someone's conduct violating a penal norm qualifies as a criminal offence not because he had freedom of will in displaying law-abiding or norm-violating behaviour and he chose the latter, and consequently he is guilty, but because, owing to his subjective traits, it is from the application of a penal sanction for the antisocial behaviour displayed as dictated by determinism that the attainment of the preventive aims may be expected.

Actually, it is the linking of the past and the future in the establishment of responsibility that is the criterion of the superiority of the administration of justice, over that based on the establishment of responsibility where only the past is taken into consideration, and the punishment is imposed only according to the "seriousness of the act" and the "degree of culpability", independently of the aims of prevention. A scientifically sound system of establishing responsibility can not be content with sentencing the perpetrator according to the customs of decades or centuries, not caring what the perpetrator's fate will be, whether the imposed sanction is suitable for forming the perpetrator's consciousness favourably or not. The opponents of determinist responsibility recognize this as an issue of linking the past and the future, i.e. that etiology and prognostication have a fundamental role here, and they object to that. According to our views, however, this is not a shortcoming but a great merit of the establishment of responsibility based on the principle of determinism. Prognostication making use of the achievements of etiology provides the method through which the preventive aim of punishment may be attained.

[29] Viski, *op. cit.*, p. 169.

The consistent putting into effect of the principle of determinism in the sphere of the establishment of criminal responsibility is opposed by certain authors, because they feel it endangers the moral basis of the establishment of responsibility. For example, according to Földvári, if behaviour were unequivocally determined, the moral foundations of responsibility would be denied. In this case we should regard punishment as a simple determining factor and not as a means for society to express its disapproval of the perpetrator.[30] It seems impossible to understand why we could not morally disapprove of the criminal offence, of behaviour harmful to society to a significant extent, if the perpetrator has committed it determined by his personality and the objective factors and not according to his own free will. For it is precisely the disapproval of types of behaviour harmful or dangerous to the ruling class or society that is the basis of both penal norms and penal sanctions. Moral norms contain social requirements, expectations in the same way as penal norms, only the level is different. It is a sanction (disapproval, censure) that is applied against the violators of moral norms, in the same way as it is against the violators of penal norms, only these sanctions are of a different kind. There are, of course, differences, because moral norms may be different even within one country, but penal norms, as a rule, are the same for everyone. A penal norm may not be approved by a significant part of the population, but in such cases no kind of punishment is approved by this part of the population whether it is imposed either with a retributive or preventive aim. Thus, the moral approval of a punishment depends primarily on the approval of the penal norm. The observance and approval of the prevailing moral norms of a society of necessity also means the observance and approval of the overwhelming majority of the penal norms, since the violations of penal norms represent much greater harm and danger to society than the violations of moral norms. The principle of determinism prevails in the case of the violators of moral norms in the same way as in the case of offenders. The establishment of moral responsibility has preventive aims in the same way as the establishment of criminal or any other form of responsibility. Moral condemnation also cannot merely have the aim of stigmatization, vengeance, the restoration of "moral justice." To put the establishment of criminal responsibility on a moral basis requires "only" that the prevailing moral norms and the norms of penal law should be in harmony, that penal norms should express the interests of society, and the members of society should recognize that content of these norms.

In connection with the moral foundations of punishment of the establishment of criminal responsibility, we should mention Földesi's view presented in his monograph quoted many times earlier. Answering Heller's question of whether it is meet and just to establish the criminal responsibility of persons if their will is fully determined, he has stated: "From the point of view of the teachings on the full determinism of the will, penal law is unjust to a certain extent, when it punishes

[30] Földvári, *op. cit.*, p. 73.

those who have committed offences intentionally or through negligence, since their will has been fully determined, too, and they could have not acted in the given case in another way than they have."[31] Földesi believes this injustice to be as necessary in the present phase of our social development as the system of distribution according to work. "While in the case of distribution according to work, equal law applied to unequals results in inequality, here inequality is created by the application of unequal laws (some are punished, others are not) to equals (everyone's will is determined)."[32]

In my opinion, Földesi has missed the difference of levels here, since punishment or reward are not the consequence of the determinacy of the behaviour, they are of the nature of determinism. Productive work performed with dedication is determined in the same way as robbery committed by a recidivist. The process of the establishment of criminal responsibilitv may be initiated if the determinacy of the behaviour has been manifested in a negative, harmful result. Thus we cannot speak of even a "certain injustice", because what is employed in the interests of the overwhelming majority, for the protection of society, cannot be unjust. A particular norm of penal law, a particular judgement or a certain way of implementing a sentence may involve injustice, but the institution of the establishment of responsibility itself is socially useful and just, it is one of the basic means of social coexistence and of forming social consciousness.

While, on the one hand, the system of establishing responsibility that is built on the determinist conception is accused of being the system of strict liability, unlimited "subjectiveness" is attributed to the representatives of this conception. Bólya claims that the acceptance of the aims of education may lead penal law into the quagmire of the school of social defense, for "the basis of responsibility is the necessary punishment, the aim of which is to change the perpetrator. This aim determines the means and this aim provides the basis of responsibility. Thus, everything is subordinated to the attainment of this aim. And since in this conception *responsibility cannot fulfil its functions* in every case, as we have demonstrated, other means are needed.

Culpability is expelled from criminal responsibility, and it is followed by discarding criminal law because if it cannot attain the aim, it is not needed."[33]

It is true that the advocates of the determinist establishment of responsibility do not want to consider only culpability (intention, negligence) on the perpetrator's part, they want to take into consideration blameworthiness, which has a much broader scope,[34] or, as a recent development, psychological attitudes.[35] But nobody

[31] Földesi, *op. cit.,* pp. 308-309.

[32] *Loc. cit.,* p. 310.

[33] Bólya, *op. cit.,* p. 662.

[34] See: Eörsi, *op. cit.;* Tokaji, *op. cit.*

[35] P. Szilágyi, "A jogi felelősség társadalmi érvényesülése és feltételei" (The Social Putting into Effect of Legal Responsibility and its Conditions), *Jogtudományi Közlöny,* No. 9, 1974.

wants to discard criminal law, only to modernize it, to adapt it to the newly recognized regularities. The leading idea of our age and society is dialectic and historical materialism. The materialist outlook is increasingly penetrating criminal sciences, the theory of the establishment of criminal responsibility, and driving out the remains of idealistic bourgeois views and institutions.

As can be seen, the determinist conception attributes a great significance in the establishment of criminal responsibility to the subjective mind of the perpetrator, to his psychological attitude to penal norms, to the socially harmful or dangerous consequences of his act. The imposition of a sentence is possible only if the punishment is able to determine the perpetrator's future behaviour favourably. It follows logically from this that not all the violations of penal norms entail punishment, penal measures, only those the prevention of which seems practicable solely through the application of punishment. The differentiation, deciding what kind of sanction should be imposed for a violation of a norm, may be done primarily according to the state of mind of the perpetrator, the content of his consciousness, in addition to the nature of the violation. There are kinds of behaviour for which the establishment of responsibility is not done by means of a criminal procedure, such as a child's behaviour violating a norm of criminal law. There are cases where no sanction is applied, but on the contrary, medals, distinctions are awarded, e.g. in certain cases of emergency, when significant harm is averted through the causing of minor harm. Cases when behaviour violating a norm does not qualify as a criminal offence, i.e. when the establishment of criminal responsibility or, more precisely, the imposition of punishment is excluded, are enumerated by the Hungarian Penal Code under the title "causes excluding punishability."

II The Aims and Principles of Punishment

1 The Aims of Punishment

As we have seen, the establishment of responsibility is carried out in order to protect society. Its basis is the recognition of the fact that the prevention of human behaviour particularly dangerous or harmful to society may be promoted through the establishment of responsibility and through the application of some compelling measure, punishment. For this reason, the establishment of responsibility, and punishment within that, are useful and expedient measures for society to exert a favourable influence on the consciousness of people.

The view that punishment should be applied in order to prevent crime became commonly known at the end of the last century, at the time when criminology came into existence. The debate still going on about the definition of the aim of punishment was started by propounding the regular nature and the determinism of crime. It is the determinism of the criminological outlook and the indeterminist classical outlook of criminal law and penal codes built on the latter that are confronted here. It is not my aim to provide a detailed historical survey of the debate and the ideas expressed in it (ranging from vengeance to education). All this may be found in most monographs dealing with the topic.[1] I shall only attempt to set out the present state of the debate, together, of course, with my own views.

a) *Retribution and prevention.* It is a fundamental trait of the penal laws of the socialist countries that their function is to protect the socialist order of society and their theoretical basis is Marxism—Leninism. This is usually manifested in the formulation of the aims of punishment, although the wording of the various penal codes is different.

In terms of the definition of the aims of punishment, the penal codes of the socialist countries may be divided into two groups. Some codes define the aim exclusively as prevention, the re-education of the perpetrators and general prevention, while others mention also retribution, in addition to prevention, as an aim of punishment. As examples of the first group, we may mention the Penal

[1] See M. D. Shargorodsky, *Nakazanie, ego tseli i effectivnosti* (Punishment, its Aims and Effectiveness), Leningrad: Izdatelstvo Leningradskogo Universiteta, 1973; J. Földvári, *A büntetés tana* (The Doctrine of Punishment), Budapest: Közgazdasági és Jogi Könyvkiadó, 1970.

Codes of Bulgaria and the GDR.[2] For the second group, the Soviet[3] and the 1961 Hungarian Codes may be mentioned. The new Hungarian Code of 1979, however, defines the purpose of punishment as prevention. In the Soviet literature and in the practice of the Supreme Court of the Soviet Union, at present, however, it is an unambiguously expressed view that the aim of punishment may only be prevention not retribution.[4]

Considering Hungarian conditions, differences could be found in the interpretation of the aims of punishment, particularly before the new Penal Code (which came into force July 1, 1979). As a result of the broad discussion going on during its preparation the new Code defines clearly and correctly the aims of punishment as the protection of society and prevention. It is very instructive, however, to survey the material of the debate in connection with the previous Penal Code, in force from 1962. According to Art. 34. of that Code: "The aim of punishment is: in order to protect society, to apply a legal detriment for the crime, to correct the perpetrator and to deter the members of society from crime."[5]

The text of the provision was not interpreted uniformly by the experts, although the general Preamble of the Code do not leave any doubt concerning legislative intentions. "This means (criminal punishment,—J. V.) should be used by the socialist state in such a manner that the punishment should not only ensure the effectivity and power of retribution but should fulfil, at the same time, the educational task and meet the requirements of socialist humanism." Or, at another place: "If the main task of punishment is also correction in addition to retribution..."[6] On

[2] According to the Bulgarian Penal Code of 1968: "The aim of punishment is the correction and re-education of the offender and the exertion of a preventive/educative effect on other members of the society. The punishment is not an act of retribution which is aimed at the stigmatization and humiliation of the perpetrators of criminal offences. The punishment and other educative measures have the aim of educating the offender through state and social influence and preparing him for socially useful, honest work." *Sotsialisticheskо Pravo,* No. 4 (1968), p. 6. The Penal Code of 1968 of the GDR declares that the aim of punishment is "the protection of the socialist social order of the citizens and their rights against criminal acts, the prevention of criminal offences and the effective education of the offenders in the spirit of the observance of state discipline and consciously responsible behaviour to be displayed in all spheres of social life." (§ 2, (1)).

[3] According to the Soviet Penal Code of 1958, "the punishment is not only retribution for the committed criminal offence but also has the aim of correcting and re-educating the offender in the spirit of honest relation to work, precise observance of the law, the rules of socialist coexistence, to prevent the perpetration of new offences either by the offender or by others." (§ 20.) In the Hungarian Code of 1979 the aim of punishment is set as follows: "A punishment is a prejudice defined by law, to be applied for the perpetration of an offence. The purpose of punishment is prevention with a view to the protection of society from the commission of offences by the perpetrator or any other person." (Section 37.)

[4] See M. D. Shargorodsky, *Nakazanie, ego tseli i effektivnost,* Leningrad: Izdatelstvo Leningradskogo Universiteta, 1973.

[5] *The Penal Code of the Hungarian People's Republic,* Budapest: Közgazdasági és Jogi Könyvkiadó, 1962.

[6] *Loc. cit.,* p. 22.

the other hand, the Preamble on the Penal Code does not regard the application of legal detriments as an aim of punishment and deems this interpretation self-evident saying that the representatives of socialist legal sciences agree with it almost without exception.[7]

In my interpretation—agreeing with the Preamble the 1961 Code defined a double aim of punishment: the application of a legal detriment, i.e. retribution, and prevention, i.e. restraining the perpetrator and other citizens from committing criminal offences. And this text cannot be regarded as an inaccurate formulation; on the contrary, it is a precise reflection of the ideas of the experts, of the lawmakers, at that time.

As we shall see, there are authors who approved of the definition in the Code and also considered retribution an aim of punishment, in addition to prevention; and there are others who accepted only prevention as the aim, and demanded the modification of the text of the law and the omission of retribution from the aims. Thus, we have to examine whether the formulation of the aims of punishment in the Code and all the measures taken on the basis of the Code to attain these aims were in harmony with the determinist conception accepted in words by everyone.

Experts professing so-called consistent determinism regard punishment, naturally, as a measure to be taken for past behaviour, for criminal behaviour, which is suitable for reforming the personality, the consciousness of the perpetrator and other persons, and thus for preventing criminal offences. Hence, naming prevention as the aim of punishment is a direct consequence of the determinist conception, while retribution is of necessity attached to indeterminism, to the conception of free will. Historical development, too, proves that the idea of prevention comes to the fore and is given a legal formulation in parallel with the acceptance of the determinist conception. The idea of retribution is in complete harmony with faith in God. Pope Pius XII, for example emphasized the retributive and expiatory function of criminal punishment in his address to the participants of the Rome Congress of 1953 of the International Association of Penal Law (AIDP).[8]

The text of the Penal Code of 1961 is a reflection of relatively free will, i.e., in addition to the idea of prevention, of education, retribution also may have a place here, since in this conception human behaviour is only moderately, partially determined, and not fully so.

Kádár und Kálmán attribute a double function to punishment: repression and education. They identify the repressive function with the repressive aim which they evaluate as follows: "The repressive aim of punishment is given expression above all in the case of more serious offences. It consists of the offender's isolation from

[7] *A Büntető Törvénykönyv Kommentárja* (Preamble of the Penal Code), Vol. I, Budapest, 1968, p. 198.

[8] See K. Györgyi, "Büntetési elméletek a német burzsoá jogban" (Theories of Punishment in German Bourgeois Criminal Law), *Acta Facultatis Politico-Iuridicae Scientiarum de Rolando Eötvös Nominatae,* Vol. XV, Budapest: ELTE Állam- és Jogtudományi Kar, 1973.

society for a shorter or longer period of time, and his influences on society which may become harmful are limited in this way. At the same time, the element of general prevention is also present, beyond doubt, in such penalties to the extent that the imposed sanction restrains others, by its gravity, from the perpetration of similar acts.

This means that the penalties prescribed and imposed for grave offences should be suitable for attaining the repressive aims. For this reason, it is long-term loss of freedom penalties that are available in the system of punishment to serve this aim. Repression is a necessary and indispensable element of punishment, but it does not have a dominant function."[9]

According to the authors, the repressive aim of punishment prevails in the case of the perpetrators of more serious offences, mainly because the prisoners cannot carry on their criminal activities due to the imposition of a long-term loss of freedom sentence. It may also be understood as removing dangerous criminals from society for a certain period, in order to prevent the perpetration of their foreseeable criminal offences during this time. But no word is said of the re-education of these perpetrators. "The special preventive element of punishment comes to the fore particularly in the case of short-term or suspended sentences, reformatory and educational work, and fines. Of course, it does not mean that long-term imprisonment serving first of all repressive aims would not put into effect the special preventive aims of punishment in the long run."[10]

It appears from this that repression, retribution, may be applied against the perpetrators of more serious offences while education should be applied in the case of the perpetrators of lesser ones and mainly to first offenders. A similar principle, or the retributive nature of punishment, finds expression in the categorization of sanctions applicable against juvenile offenders into the group of measures and penalties. According to the 1961 Code, a penalty may be applied in the case of juvenile offenders only if the educational measure would not succeed. Such a contrasting of educational measures and punishments unmistakably underlines the repressive character of punishment. (We shall be discussing this in detail in later parts.)

But we do not have to infer for ourselves the existence of views professing the retributive character of punishment, we can find them in an unambiguous formulation, too: "The fundamental thesis, i.e. that punishment has a double aim, is inarguably correct. On the one hand, it is the application of a legal detriment, i.e. retribution, on the other hand, but not in the second place, it is education, general and special prevention," D. Bagi wrote in one of his papers.[11]

[9] M. Kádár and Gy. Kálmán, *A büntetőjog általános tanai* (General Doctrines of Criminal Law), Budapest: Közgazdasági és Jogi Könyvkiadó, 1966, p. 667.

[10] *Loc. cit.*, p. 668.

[11] D. Bagi, "Büntetési rendszerünk és a büntetéskiszabás egyes kérdéseiről" (On Some Problems of Our System of Punishment and Sentencing), *Magyar Jog és Külföldi Jogi Szemle,* No. 6 (1968), p. 328.

J. Földvári took an inconsistent position in connection with the retributive aim of punishment. He denies and admits the retributive character of punishment at the same time. "However, while we exclude retribution from the aims to be attained by punishment, we admit that the application of a punishment means retribution in a sense and perpetrators—and the other members of society, too,—understand it as such. A punishment is retribution in the sense that it is applied on account of a criminal offence perpetrated previously. It is on account of the perpetration of the offence that the offender has to suffer a lesser or greater detriment, and in keeping with this the retributive character of punishment is also stronger or weaker. We should only deny the retributive character of measures imposed not because of a previously committed criminal offence but e.g. on account of behaviour to be expected in the future. Such a measure, however, could not be regarded as a criminal punishment, since it belongs to the essence of punishment as we shall see, that it is imposed because of a previously committed criminal offence. The retributive character is, hence, to be found in the fact that it is the perpetration of a criminal offence that is followed by the imposition of a punishment, the detriment caused by the perpetrator is repaid by the state with a detriment.

Thus, retribution in this sense belongs to criminal punishment. However, it is not an aim, not even in this sense. But it is an aim of the state that punishment should follow the perpetration of offences in every case, that no criminal offence should remain unpunished, without retribution. This is necessary because of the demand on the part of members of a society, if for nothing else. The perpetration of any criminal offence elicits shock, disapproval, perhaps outrage, in a smaller or greater part of the population. Punishment is necessary also to appease these feelings, and one of the aims of applying punishment is precisely this. By linking what has been said, we may say that the state may set as an aim the retribution of the perpetration of all criminal offences, through the imposition of a punishment, in order to satisfy the demand on the part of society for that."[12]

Here, Földvári regards retribution above all as the essence of punishment, and the retributive character is expressed, in his opinion, by the measure or severity of the punishment. In other words, he identifies retribution with the detriment, which is a necessary element (means) of punishment. But eventually, taking into consideration the demand for retribution on the part of the members of society, he sets the retribution of the perpetration of all criminal offences, through the imposition of a punishment, as an aim. Since the establishment of responsibility is a measure taken by the state, retribution has here the role of the aim of the establishment of responsibility realized in the punishment. Földvári's ideas are also remarkable when he asserts that "we should only deny the retributive character of measures imposed not because of a previously committed criminal offence but e.g. on account of behaviour to be expected in the future." But Földvári does not make a connection

[12] Földvári, *op. cit.*, pp. 45–47.

between the punishment and the perpetrator's future behaviour: in his opinion the punishment is applied only on account of a criminal offence committed in the past. In my opinion, this is precisely the essential point. It is an erroneous assumption that we cannot deny the retributive character of punishment unless it is imposed on account of behaviour to be expected in the future and not because of a criminal offence perpetrated previously. Földvári correctly recognizes the connection between punishment without retribution and *future behaviour,* but incorrectly denies the connection between punishment without retribution and a criminal offence committed *in the past.* According to the determinist conception, punishment not involving retribution is applied on account of past behaviour in order to prevent future criminal behaviour. This is the rational, useful aim for the attainment of which the establishment of responsibility is initiated against the perpetrators of offences. *Viewing only the past* or *only the future* in connection with the punishment cannot be identified with the determinist conception.

The connection of the punishment with the past and the future is also put into words by. A. Szabó in his work quoted earlier. "The social function of criminal responsibility is not retribution, but prevention. If the means—causing a detriment—is considered to be an aim, if the element of compulsion is examined in isolation, then punishment is really only retribution and as such looks towards the past. Owing to that, we could speak of an educational role as a role looking towards the future. The aim of punishments is defined by the social function of criminal responsibility and it is prevention, the future determination of behaviour according to the requirements of criminal law."[13]

Keeping in mind the general public's demand for retribution, Viski also finds it necessary to recognize retribution as an aim of punishment. "At present we may say that the view that prevention does not have a retributive function is already more commonly accepted. However, it is beyond doubt that the recognition of retribution as an aim of punishment also has certain advantages." These advantages are manifested in the fact that punishment has to serve the restoration of public peace, the satisfaction of the existing demand of society for punishment in a way that "this historically preconditioned demand should change toward the right direction", at the same time.[14]

It is a fact that the notion of justness is still linked with punishing in proportion to the deed, approximately with the principle of *talio,* in the consciousness of people. This is natural, since the majority of experts participating in the administration of criminal justice day by day do not know or do not accept the views concerning the determinism of behaviour and their necessary consequences. *In my opinion, however, the legal definition of the aim of punishment must follow the recognized regularities and not the wrong views of the masses.* A punishment applied with the

[13] Szabó, *op. cit.,* p. 261.

[14] Viski, *op. cit.,* 1982, pp. 95.

aim of prevention can satisfy the general public's demand for punishment just as well as, or even better than one with a retributive aim, if people learn the fundamental laws of human behaviour. M. Ficsor has written correctly in one of his studies discussing the aims of punishment: "It is not at all the same thing to explore the views which are right in principle while taking into consideration the obstacles existing over a shorter or longer period, or, on pragmatic grounds, to accept the situation existing because of the practical obstacles as right also in principle. In the first case we can strive for the elimination of the obstacles, and, after this is done, for the solution which is right in principle; in the latter case this perspective is lost."[15]

It is not only putting reality into words that is demanded of legislation but also that it should point out the future perspective. A statute with its theses and system of requirements sets the course of human behaviour. And if it is possible anywhere, it is particularly possible in the sphere of formulating the aims, since an accepted aim is necessarily an anticipated form of the future satisfaction of a present need, and is thus the guideline of action. This is the way in which the preventive aim of punishment becomes the inspirer of socially useful activities, whereas retribution is a settling of the account, a requital, without the perspective of expedient future effects. Shargorodsky has correctly written in his monograph published recently: "Retribution, in the final analysis, is but the modernized form of primitive vengeance. As long as any form of vengeance can be found in the punishment, we cannot reasonably govern the administration of criminal justice."[16]

One could frequently read in the works of authors representing socialist penal law that the aim of punishment is just compensation.[17] But the punishment compensates nobody, neither society nor the victim. This is so not only because compensation is frequently objectively impossible (e.g. homicide) but because the kinds of punishment are not suitable for that, even in cases when the nature of the injury caused would allow it. The present system is based on confinement and consequently it is unsuitable for compensation, but even fines do not serve the aims of compensation.

It is a similar conception where the restoration of the violated order of law is named, or is also named, as the aim of punishment. One finds such views in the Hungarian literature of law, too. According to Viski, for example, "we may not leave out of consideration, in addition to general and special prevention, the aim of the application of punishment that it should restore the violated legal order, it should provide retribution for the attack against the legal order."[18] Or, let us take the views of J. Székely: "Retribution is a category originating from the age of

[15] M. Ficsor, "A determinizmus szerepe a büntetési célok meghatározásánál" (The Role of Determinism is Setting the Aims of Punishment), *Jogtudományi Közlöny,* No. 12, 1972, p. 673.

[16] Shargorodsky, *op. cit.,* p. 28.

[17] Reported by Shargorodsky in *op. cit.*

[18] Viski, *op. cit.,* p. 95.

private vengeance. In Sicily, etc. it can still be found in its ancient form, in the form of the blood feud. However, in the system of the state monopoly of punishment the retributive role of punishment has undergone modifications, on the one hand, and, on the other hand, it has had to share its former monopolistic position among the aims of punishment with other aims: with general and special prevention and the correction of the perpetrator.

"The element of compensating the victim has faded away in retribution by now. It is more the satisfaction of society's hurt sense of justice and the balancing of the loss of state prestige caused by the violation of the prohibition of penal law (in the case of offences by intention) that colours punishment with the element of retribution in our age. However, this—seemingly autotelic—protection of prestige has its strictly rational foundations."[19]

Such and similar opinion reflect a law-centred conception i.e. there is legal order, the good, the true, the inviolable, and if someone violates it, we impose a punishment on him, we retaliate for the attack against the order of law. This formulation reflects the views of legal positivism dominant at the turn of the century. I quote the words of K. Edvi Illés of the end of the last century, just as one example: "From the point of view of positive law, punishment is the external evil that is prescribed by the laws for the perpetrators of an act to be punished, in order to ensure the just retaliation for the act, in the interest of the legal order of the state. The precondition of punishment is, accordingly, *the act to be punished* (nulla poena sine crimine), its bases are the law and the *judicial decision* passed according to the law, its *purposes are* just retribution and the *restoration* of the violated *legal order.*"[20]

b) *The means of prevention.* If we take the position that punishment can have only preventive aims, or, formulating in a broader sense, retribution cannot be the aim of punishment, which follows logically and clearly from the principle of determinism, in my opinion,—our further task is to examine what means can ensure the attainment of the aim.

Prevention as the aim of punishment embraces both general prevention, i.e. restraining the public from the perpetration of criminal offences, and special prevention i.e. restraining the perpetrator from new offences. These two requirements define the means to be used, the choice of means.

The preventive aim of punishment can be ensured through the use of means suitable for restraining people from behaviour that is harmful or dangerous to society and serves the satisfaction of a need of the individual. Evidently, to teach

[19] More up-to-date and effective treatment of multiple recidivists. A session of the Criminological Work Group, ELTE Állam- és Jogtudományi Kara, February 26, 1971. Proceedings, Budapest, 1972, p. 32.

[20] K. Edvi Illés, *A Büntető Törvénykönyv Magyarázata* (Preamble of the Penal Code), Budapest: Révai Testvérek kiadása, 1894, Vol. I, pp. 78–79.

people the observance of social requirements, social norms, to form their law-abiding behaviour, is not the task of criminal law, in the first place, but of education in the broadest sense of the word; the educational influence of the family, school, the place of work, the circle of friends, the mass media. The establishment of criminal responsibility may have a role from the point of view of special prevention if the mentioned educational means are not able to ensure the observance of social norms manifested in the norms of penal law. The general preventive effects of the punishment may restrain morally unstable individuals from the violation of social requirements if such behaviour on their part entails detrimental consequences, limiting the satisfaction of their needs in a way that could not be compensated for by the satisfaction that might be ensured through the violation of the norms of penal law. Hence, the general preventive effects may be expected of the consequences that represent a detriment *(malum).* For this reason, the *malum* is a necessary element of any punishment, it belongs to its essence.

Restraining is the essence of special prevention as well, but as far as the means are concerned, in addition to the legal detriment, other means not involving a detriment to the perpetrator may have a significant, in certain cases vital, role. The causing of a detriment and the negative memory formed by it, which ensures general prevention, can provide a significant assistance in restraining the perpetrator from the commission of a new offence. However, according to criminological experience, considerably more favourable results are produced by the positive formation of the consciousness, by making the perpetrator understand that the observance of social norms is in his own interest, too, and the observance of the norms of penal law is a more certain way, in the long run, to satisfy the individual needs. The recognition of this has led to the consequence that the special education, the correction of the perpetrator is also given a place among the means of punishment in most penal codes, particularly in connection with juveniles.

In this chain of thought, education does not appear as the aim of punishment but as a means of prevention. On this point, I fully agree with Shargorodsky, in whose opinion education can be a means, a secondary aim at most, of the fundamental and single aim of punishment i.e. prevention.[21] Shargorodsky is sharply criticized by Karpets in whose opinion punishment may have more than one aim, such as the protection of society, education retribution, etc.[22]

Keeping in mind the dialectic relation between aims and means, namely that every aim is the means of another aim and every means is the aim of an activity, we can conclude that the establishment of responsibility, and its essence, the application of a sanction, are to serve the protection of society, it is a means to this end (like other means e.g. the army). And the aim of this is the prevention of criminal offences

[21] Shargorodsky, *op. cit.,* p. 31.

[22] I. I. Karpets, *Nakazanie, Sotsialnye Pravovye Kriminologicheskie Problemy,* Moscow: Yuridicheskaya Literatura, 1973.

which can be achieved through the application of a legal detriment or the education of the perpetrator, as appropriate means. Education as a fundamental, as a specific aim appears as that of the implementation of punishment. And the aims of education are achieved through the means, measures applied in the process of the implementation of punishment (work, training, various activities).

As we do not feel education to be the specific aim of punishment, so the legal detriment can not be an aim. In the hierarchy of aims and means it is prevention as an aim that is on the same level as punishment, because prevention is the most comprehensive, hence, the most specific task for the establishment of criminal responsibility. It is similar to the causal chain described in the discussion of causality. In the long sequence of causes and effects linked in a chain, we examine the section where the criminal offence is an effect and try to find the factors that have produced this effect as causes and conditions. We have to proceed in the same way also in the case of punishment. It is neither from the position of the protection of society, nor of the implementation of punishment, but from the position of the penal measures that we examine the aims that we wish to achieve, and, in my opinion, it can only be the prevention of criminal offences.

When the aim of punishment is examined, the question frequently arises of what the mutual relation of deterrence, restraining, and education, general and special prevention, is. First of all, I should like to point out that it is two different, although closely related, questions that are asked here.

Over the last hundred years torture, corporal punishment, the use of methods causing corporal pain and suffering to the prisoner, have been gradually excluded from the penalties. Thus, restraining effects of punishment have been limited mainly to the social censure entailed by the punishment, to the loss of freedom and to causing financial and existential detriments. One can find data in the international literature according to which it is not so much the punishment itself, the nature of the punishment, as the certainty of the establishment of responsibility, the disapproval of the discovered norm-violating act by the state and society, that have a general restraining effect.

The noted criminologist, Nigel Walker, reports data[23] according to which 49 per cent of the interviewed juveniles pointed out the opinion of the family, 22 per cent losing their job, 12 per cent the embarrassment of standing before the court and 10 per cent the punishment to be imposed, as the factor they feared most in the case of getting caught. Marc Ancel has put into words in his book quoted earlier an opinion which is in harmony with these data.[24] In his opinion, too, it is the possibility of initiating the process of prosecution or its automatic initiation which represents the fundamental restraining force. We could also refer to Lenin's statement on the same

[23] N. Walker, *Sentencing in a Rational Society,* London: The Penguin Press, 1966, Chapter 4, § 3, p. 66.

[24] M. Ancel, *op. cit.,* p. 345.

theme, or to our own experience. We may draw the conclusion from all this that the evolution from cruel penalties toward penalties with a pedagogical content may be considered right, is in harmony with the laws of human behaviour, with the formation of social consciousness. It is not a red-hot iron and similar penalties that are needed but punishments which have, in addition to the detriment, consciousness-forming effects, i.e. urge the recognition of the relations of penal norms, society and individuals.

However, *malum* as a means of preventing criminal offences, of restraining people from them also has a significance from the point of view of special prevention and not only from that of general prevention. The legal detriment applied as a punishment, the limitation of the satisfaction of needs, may encourage the perpetrator to law-abiding behaviour. But if general prevention does not require the application of punishments which cause physical pain or violate human dignity, so much the less is it required by special prevention. Changing the perpetrator into a law-abiding citizen is possible through the use of pedagogical means corresponding to his personality state. There are offenders in whose case a warning, making them more deeply aware of the socially harmful effects of this behaviour, is enough, and there are others who need long-term rehabilitation. It may happen that at the time of the establishment of responsibility special prevention no longer requires any preventive measure, the application of any legal detriment, because the necessary change in the perpetrator's personality has already taken place. In such cases the interests of special and general prevention "clash". The opinion of specialists is different concerning which of the preventive interests should be preferred. Viski, for example, claims that the considerations of general prevention should be limited by the interests of special prevention. This view is right as far as special prevention may limit the interests of general prevention, but the basic point, in my opinion, is still general prevention, the establishment of responsibility and the imposition of a legal detriment (even if a minimal one) because this is the basis of forming and maintaining the awareness of criminal responsibility. Owing to that, it might happen that a punishment is imposed for the purposes of general prevention, but it is impossible to apply a punishment with an aim of special prevention only. It is clear from this opinion that the perpetrator may not be viewed alone but only as a member of society, of a certain community, and the process of establishing his responsibility is set in motion on account of his negative relation to this community.

It is a further question whether legal detriment applied as a punishment may be judged as a means of education. If we set out from the principles of general pedagogy, the answer is yes. For among the means of pedagogy, in addition to the recognition, crediting and rewarding of good behaviour or useful performance, one finds chastisement, the causing of detriment for undesirable behaviour, i.e. the means of pedagogical punishment. The aim of these pedagogical measures is to form the consciousness, the personality of the young generation correctly. In adulthood, when intentional educational activity fades away or comes to an end, pedagogy is replaced by the system of recognition, rewards, existential advancement on the positive side, and by the systems of establishing responsibility under various rules and by the system of sanctions, on the negative side. Thus, the aim of criminal punishment in the case of adults is analogous with the pedagogical punishment of "naughty" children. *Hence, the establishment of criminal responsibility may be properly regarded as a special pedagogical, a criminal-pedagogical process, in terms of its content.* Punishment and the establishment of responsibility with a criminological approach has gained a broadening acceptance not only in theory but also in practice, in the implementation of punishment. In Hungary, for example, attempts are made to regulate the implementation of the confinement punishment according to the guiding principles of education that are built on the recent achievements of criminal pedagogy. (The principles of the education of prisoners were worked out years ago by the National Headquarters of the Implementation of Punishment.)

The last question concerning this topic is whether the punishment can attain its aim. The answer is yes in the sense that it can, and if the proper means are used, actually does assist in the prevention of criminal offences. Many people are restrained from the perpetration of criminal offences even nowadays by the establishment of responsibility, by punishment. Punishment produces favourable effects with a significant ratio of prisoners. In spite of that, there is still crime and it is to be expected that there will be for a long time to come. Under the present social conditions and at the present level of the development of consciousness, the general preventive effects of punishment are not able to restrain a small percentage of people from the perpetration of criminal offences. Similarly, in the case of some prisoners, punishment is ineffectual, it does not attain its preventive aim. The causes spring primarily from two sources. The first is the inadequate or unsatisfactory means of punishment, the second, and the more important, are the existing social conditions and the level of consciousness. The improvement of the system of establishing criminal responsibility may promote the process of decreasing crime but cannot eliminate it, for other social trends may have a counter-acting influence or may lose their criminogenic influence only gradually. Thus, the aim of punishment is an aim which may be attained in the case of many people but we cannot attain it completely even if the system of punishment and establishing responsibility is theoretically perfect. But this does not mean that prevention as the aim of punishment is wrong. On the contrary, it is in the nature of an aim that we can attain it only through a sequence of activity and we cannot always attain it perfectly.

One finds opinions in the literature according to which the aims of punishment are not definable in general, but can be defined only by the structuralization of perpetrators. Considering the heterogenity of criminal offences and their perpetrators, T. Horváth wrote: "a) the aims of punishment that can be set realistically depend to a considerable extent on the characteristics of the various perpetrator types; b) general or special prevention as the general aims of punishment can be attained through education aimed at the formation of a positive personality in the case of certain offender types, and through isolation of a deterrent nature in the case of others; c) various offender types require different treatment during the implementation of punishment; d) the different aims of punishment and the different methods of treatment require different types of penal institution."[25]

A basic requirement of pedagogy is given a clear formulation here, namely that people with different personalities can be educated for the same aim only if differentiated means are used. The author's ideas show that the preventive aims can be achieved only through a differentiated system of penalties and individualized punishment. But what the author formulated under item a), i.e. that the aims of punishment that can be set realistically are dependent on the characteristics of offender types, does not follow from all this. I hold that the aims are identical in the case of all kinds of punishment, it is only the means, the methods by which we wish to achieve the results, that may vary.

G. Ádám also considered it necessary to distinguish the aims of punishment by offenders. In his opinion, educational aims are proper in the case of juveniles but retribution must come to the fore in the case of adults. He refers to the fact that the personality of children, of juveniles, is immature, it still needs education, but adults have independence, and hence they should accept responsibility for their deeds according to the gravity of their acts, as follows from proportionality. Ádám doubts that punishment with an educational aim can have a place at all in the case of adults.[26] In my opinion, it is a fundamental mistake to restrict education to childhood. The process of education is continuous during the whole of human life. It is true, of course, that the forms of education change. Society sets the requirements for children and adults differently. Similarly, the form of judging, rewarding, or calling to account, is different, too. It is also a fact that intentional education comes to an end at the time of becoming independent, as a rule, but, in my opinion, if it is needed, it has to be resorted to not only in the case of juvenile offenders but also with adults. What has not been done by the intentional education provided in childhood, or has been perverted by the environment of adulthood, has to be supplied or corrected by organized education even in adulthood.

Since intentional education may be understood also as relaying accumulated human experience concerning human behaviour and the prevailing ideology in a condensed form it is worth subjecting adults also to such a process so that they should become law-abiding citizens as soon as possible. It is in the interest of both the society and the individual.

[25] T. Horváth, "Gondolatok büntetéstani problémáinkhoz" (Thoughts on Our Problems of Penal Doctrines), *Magyar Jog és Külföldi Jogi Szemle,* No. 5, 1971.

[26] Gy. Ádám, "Visszaeső bűnözők — visszaeső büntetőjog" (Recidivist Criminals — Recidivist Criminal Law), *Magyar Jog és Külföldi Jogi Szemle,* No. 9, 1973.

It may be seen clearly from the above that we find the aim of punishment in prevention. But it is also unambiguously stated that punishment cannot attain alone the prevention of crime since crime has a social origin above all, and hence crime prevention is not dependent only on the effectiveness of punishment, but also on other state and social measures. Thus, prevention is not a specific aim of punishment, since it is not punishment exclusively (and primarily) that has to prevent crime. For this reason, even if we are right in defining the aim of punishment as prevention, we have to realize that punishment, with its means, only has the function of promoting or advancing crime prevention. It has become evident as a result of effectivity studies that neither recidivism nor crime in general can be traced back to the ineffectiveness of punishment alone, since other factors also have a significant (sometimes vital) role in the formation of things.[27]

Setting out from this, a more precise formulation of the aim of punishment is to advance crime prevention with its means in the field of both general and special prevention.

2 Principles of Punishment

The principles of punishment are usually not formulated or collected in one group in the penal codes.

This is easy to understand in eras when the principle of *talio,* the principle of punishment proportional to the deed, can be considered predominant and the aim of punishment is defined mainly as retribution. But in our times, when the aim of prevention becomes predominant, when criminal human behaviour is deemed determined, the principles of punishment go far beyond the principle of proportionality. Even if we do not agree in everything with the school of social defense or with the trend of the new social defense, their theses concerning the principles of punishment, like the results of modern criminological studies, should not be left out of consideration. From the preventive aims of punishment certain principles of punishment logically follow, the elaboration of whose material elements and forms is still partly a task of the future. In the preparation of the 1979 Penal Code the matter was more to try to screen out those of the existing punishments that were incompatible with the principles of punishment with a preventive aim.

1. The requirement of prevention necessarily excludes all the principles or systems of punishment that are concerned only with settling the account for the past and do not consider the future, are not aimed at the right determination of future human behaviour. Punishment with preventive aims is applied in order to resocialize or socialize the perpetrator and other members of the public. It follows from the principle of determinism that theoretically 1. every biologically normal human being

[27] See J. Vigh and I. Tauber, "A szabadságvesztés büntetés hatékonyságának főbb jellemzői" (The Main Characteristics of the Effectiveness of Imprisonment), *Jogtudományi Közlöny* No. 11, 1976.

can be socialized or resocialized, dependent on 2. the time and 3. adequate environmental determinants. In reality, however, we frequently come across prisoners in whose case the measures applied have not produced the expected favourable effects. But the failure must not be explained by the uneducability of such people; the causes have to be found in the lack or inadequacy of one of the three conditions mentioned. The acceptance of this view has the promise of a positive result for the administration of justice, namely that instead of accepting failures it urges the exploration of their causes and conditions, the elimination of those, and the improvement of the system of the administration of justice and through that of society.

2. It follows from the preventive aim of punishment that it cannot have elements which are tormenting and violate human dignity because they encourage defiant opposition to the administration of justice and social norms, and hinder, or even cause the failure of, the process of resocialization.

If we admit the importance of resocialization, the requirements of special prevention exclude, as a matter of course, every form of punishment which renders special prevention impossible, such as the death penalty, or a fine and confiscation of property which reduce the offender to destitution, or a prison sentence which eliminates all the contacts of the prisoner with free society for a long time. We have already mentioned that the interests of general prevention may limit the measures that appear to be best from the point of view of special prevention. The negative requirements mentioned here, however, are not linked with the demands of general prevention either.

3. The application of the means of coercion, deprivation of freedom included, is the right of every society, because no society can be maintained without them. But it is a requirement that civil rights should be limited only in cases of absolute necessity, if the favourable effects could not be expected from any other means. And deprivation of freedom can be justified even in such cases only by the socially dangerous act of the perpetrator and by the necessity of a forced education from which the reformation of the perpetrator's consciousness can be expected.

4. The aim of prevention can not be reconciled with a system of punishment, with principles of punishment, which make an outcast of offenders and lead to their permanent stigmatization, or might do so. An offender is a human being, too, who may become a useful member of society with the assistance of society itself. The fact that offenders are regarded even after the implementation of their punishment with the same contempt as at the time of the perpetration of the act, can be traced back to the retributive aim and system of punishment, when it is not expected of the punishment that it should correct the perpetrator and make him a law-abiding citizen. It is not yet a basic task of the court, and the administration of justice in general, to see what the results of the punishment are.

A criminal record as a negative label is attached to the perpetrators of offences for a long time after the implementation of their punishment. For the application of the legal detriment does not end when the punishment is actually executed. Or, to put it in a different, perhaps more precise way, the punishment lasts until the moment of rehabilitation, the moment of exoneration from the consequences of having a criminal record.

Legal rehabilitation, however, does not mean rehabilitation also by fellow employees, by the micro-environment. For this reason, in addition to thé effective system of punishment, it is also necessary to change the views of the public, so that they should accept discharged prisoners with understanding and a readiness to help them.

5. The principle of proportionality is perhaps the most discussed of the principles of punishment. The predominant view of the time was aptly expressed in the work of Kádár and Kálmán: "In order to impose a right and just punishment, the court has to apply the punishment within the legal minimum and maximum limits in such a way that it should correspond with the concrete characteristics of the perpetrator and the act. A criminal offence primarily is an act which is dangerous to society. Dangerousness to society is not only a fundamental trait of a criminal offence but it is also the basis for punishing the perpetrator. It is the danger to society that is the standard for deciding what the gravity of the act is. The punishment has to be in proportion to the act's dangerousness to society. It must never be more serious than that, and it may be less serious only if circumstances related to the perpetrator's person justify is. It is in this that the requirement of the proportionality of act and punishment is expressed in socialist law; the requirement that was first put into words as a progressive idea against feudalistic law in the realm of criminal law by the bourgeoisie striving to rise."[28] The quotation contains two basic ideas. First: apart from exceptional cases, the punishment has to be in proportion to the gravity of the act, and secondly: it is a fundamental socialist principle although it was first proclaimed by the progressive bourgeoisie.

The system of proportional punishment was criticized from several sides. Some Hungarian authors[29] wished to attribute an increased significance to the personality of the offender in sentencing. In turn, other authors believed it is only punishment in proportion to the deed that is right. For example, G. Ádám[30] justified punishment in proportion to the deed with the requirement of proportionality to be found in every sphere of society. (E.g. wages in proportion to work-performance.) In my opinion, however, it is not with the problem of proportionality in general that we are dealing here but with the proportionality of the harm or injury caused by the deed. In theory, the punishment may be proportional to the socialization of the personality in the same way as to the gravity of the act. Arguing for proportionality

[28] Kádár and Kálmán, *op. cit.*, p. 783.

[29] See e.g. G. Gárdai and J. Vigh, "Észrevételek büntetési rendszerünk problémáihoz" (Remarks Concerning the Problems of our Penal System), *Magyar Jog és Külföldi Jogi Szemle,* No. 10, 1969.

[30] Ádám, *op. cit.*, see Note 26.

is not enough in itself, the less so since I have never seen the general requirement of proportionality denied in the literature. The crucial point of the issue is to what the punishment, or even the distribution of income, should be in proportion. The differentiation of proportionality is predominant in most spheres of social life. Contrary to Ádám's assertion, not even material goods are distributed according to work only i.e., already at the period of building socialism, not only "equal standards" are applied, not only work counts. Socialist principles are more just than that, and owing to social advancement, they will be more and more so, because a significant part of the national income is already distributed according to needs, in proportion to them (family allowance, social insurance, etc.). Hence, socialist society is not the executor "of inequality in a bourgeois sense"; it is the gradual accomplishment of its own equality "in a proletarian sense." This is why we cannot agree with Ádám's views on the interpretation of the tasks of law under the conditions of socialism. "In the final analysis, socialism does not, and cannot, have any other real achievement in the realm of law than the accomplishment of what was declared by the bourgeoisie in its progressive era! *In law,* the socialist basis is never anything else but the consistent, material, real putting into effect of principles formulated (but never realized) by the progressive bourgeoisie."[31] It is a fact that during the process of building socialism a number of principles declared by the rising bourgeoisie are put into practice. But to reduce the goals and tasks of law to that would lead under our present conditions to the preservation and revival of the remains of capitalism, instead of the development of the achievements of socialism. In the establishment of responsibility, it would mean that we would protect the indeterminism of the classical views of criminal law against materialist, determinist conceptions, the Marxist ideas would be replaced by bourgeois views. The rising bourgeoisie built the establishment of responsibility on the grounds of indeterminism, of idealism, and for this reason it applied retributive punishment in proportion with the deed, on account of the past only, on account of the perpetrated offence. It is my firm belief that socialist criminal law, the socialist administration of justice, has higher aims. Taking into consideration the discovered laws of human behaviour, what follows from the principle of determinism is not that punishment in proportion with the deed should be replaced by the system of punishment corresponding to the personality, but that in addition to the gravity of the harm or injury caused, the state and resocializability of the perpetrator's personality also has to be evaluated and, with a view to special prevention, the kind and measure of the punishment has to be determined accordingly.

No doubt there is some correlation between the gravity of acts and the degree of the perpetrator's dangerousness to society, the extent to which they are antisocial. Owing to that, it may happen that in certain cases there will be a correlation between the gravity of the acts and punishments, even if we renounce the rule of punishment

[31] *Loc. cit.*, p. 549.

proportional to the deed. To avoid misapprehension, I emphasize again that the deed may never be left out of consideration in the process of sentencing, since the establishment of responsibility sets out from the deed and it is on account of the deed that we apply a measure or penalty against its perpetrator. But our decision as to what the applied punishment should be may not be consequent only on the gravity of the act, but the personality, socialization and the conditions of the resocialization of the perpetrator have to be taken into consideration with equal, occasionally with even more, weight. Or, if we prefer, the punishment should be in proportion not only to the events of the past but also to the requirements of a favourable determinacy in the future.

Certain authors justified the necessity of maintaining the principle of punishing in proportion to the deed by stating that it satisfies the sense of justice of the public, i.e. it is just in the opinion of the members of society. Apart from progressive specialists, the sence of justice of the public goes by the principle of punishing according to the gravity of the act. This became evident when "the deserved" punishment was demanded in thousands of letters sent to the authorities, in certain serious criminal cases (i.e. a death for a death). This is natural since people have been reading and hearing all their lives that a just punishment corresponds to the gravity of the act. Even more, the perpetrator has a right to be able to count the consequences of his deed, to be able to foresee the consequences of the act (reckoned, perhaps, in days or money).

It does not follow from this, however, that if we recognize a new principle, better and more effective than that of punishing in proportion with the deed, we still have to maintain the old one because it is considered just by the general public. On the contrary, the public has to be enlightened about this deeper truth, has to be taught the laws of human behaviour, the role of rewards and punishments, the essence of these, and then the sense of justice of the public will change. Putting into effect the new principles of punishment gradually makes it possible that people will not be antagonistic toward them. It may happen, however, that the introduction of the new principles is not a smooth, unhindered process. We always have to be prepared for that because the struggle between the old and the new is still a struggle, even if it takes the mildest form. And, in my opinion, this struggle causes more trouble among specialists than among the general public since these principles serve as guidelines for the everyday activities of the specialists.

A further requirement is that the interests of the perpetrator should be considered in the punishment also through the interests of the smallest community that the perpetrator belongs to, if such a community exists at all. For the punishment as a rule, represents a detriment also to the family and, perhaps, to the place of work of the perpetrator and not only to him. It is not likely that it is possible to develop a system of punishment which is not detrimental to the family of the perpetrator, particularly not if he is a parent. The lost income, the lack of parental care and control, the shame accompanying the conviction of the parent of a child, the contempt, are all detriments which have their effects also on innocent persons in most of the cases. Here the question is really justified of whether this kind of sentence, this kind of punishment, is just or not. No doubt a criminal punishment frequently has detrimental effects on the position of the offender's family members, even on their chances in the future. However, in my opinion, this is not the problem of punishment but a problem of official and general social judgement on an offender and his family. Relatives are frequently subjected to unjust moral contempt and to isolation, the severance of previous relations, accompanying the first, as a rule. It is inherent in social co-existence that a human being is not responsible only for his own acts but has to answer to a certain measure also for the community he belongs to. The moral condemnation, hence, is justified to the extent of these obligations, but only to that extent. However, under our present conditions, this requirement of proportionality is neither clarified adequately nor is made part of the consciousness yet. Thus, the punishment brings about consequences unjust to the perpetrator's relatives. Young children, for example can hardly be held responsible for the behaviour of their parents. For this reason, society has to do everything so that the negative behaviour of parents should not be a handicap for their children. In my opinion, it is through changing social prejudices and people's way of thinking, through taking stronger social measures, that an advancement could be made in this sphere. But it is precisely the awareness of the unjust disadvantage burdening the family and the community, that might strengthen the adaptation to social requirements and the feeling of responsibility for each other within the family or community.

Some of the mentioned principles of punishment may also be found in the representatives of progressive bourgeois views under the slogan of humanism.[32] In my opinion, however, deriving the principles of punishment from the principle of humanism is not scientifically sound. In its original meaning, humanism expresses and protects the rights, interests and dignity of individuals. The principle of socialism accompanied by materialism means much more than that because it emphasizes the collective, the interests of the collective, in addition to individual interests. Hence, it becomes clear that "inborn, fundamental human rights" proclaimed by the progressive bourgeoisie are not inherited traits but are determined by the interests of the collective. The rights and obligations of a single human being, of the individual, are dependent on the given social system, social organization, the dominating political principles. Hence, in our society, the rights and obligations of people derive from the principles of socialism, materialism, determinism, and, in the final analysis, from social reality, from the laws of development. Consequently, those concrete forms of punishment may be considered right that form the perpetrators according to the interests of the majority identifying themselves with social development and that are suitable for generating the awareness of responsibility, or maintaining it, in the case of law-abiding citizens.

[32] See M. Ancel, *op. cit.*

III The System of Punishment

When examining the theoretical basis of the establishment of criminal responsibility we have seen that the establishment of responsibility is only one of the means of protecting society and crime prevention. The reduction of crime is dependent primarily on the favourable change in social relations and on people's growing awareness. The aim of the means of penal law is to promote the formation of, and to maintain, the awareness of responsibility in people, to change norm-violators into law-abiding citizens, i.e. to ensure to the greatest possible extent the prevention of crime.

The first fundamental question from the point of view of determinism raised by theory is how suitable the present means of penal law are for attaining the aims of the establishment of responsibility.

During the process of building socialism we have already modified several times the penal laws inherited from capitalist Hungary, we have been trying to make them fit the existing social requirements. The means themselves and the ways of their application, however, have changed less, essentially they reflect the reforms of criminal law that took place at the turn of the century. It is only now that we have come to the point in the process of our socialist development where we can put on the agenda the examination of the state of our whole administration of justice, the reconsideration of our system of establishing responsibility, as reflected by the real materialist Weltanschauung, by consistent determinism. At the present time it is not on the basis of theory only but also on the basis of practical experience that the question may be justifiably raised of whether or not a system of punishment is right where more than half of the offenders are sentenced to loss of liberty, where retribution as an aim of punishment has a position equal to prevention, and where the idea of education is put into practice mainly in the penal law of juveniles and there is an unwillingness to extend it to adults.

It is possible that the answer to one or other of these or similar questions may be a partial or definite yes. But in order to enable ourselves to answer these questions with responsibility, we have to put them under scrutiny and have to demonstrate that the means of penal law employed by us do not exist only because we have inherited them, because they existed fifty or a hundred years ago (and have remained valid even after such a long time), but because they are in harmony with the spirit of Marxism, the present state of science, the requirements and possibilities given in the process of building socialism; or we have to say what areas of our penal law have to be modified.

1 Ways of Establishing Responsibility without Criminal Procedure

According to the laws valid at present, the responsibility of the perpetrator of an offence of minor significance may be established in disciplinary proceedings in lieu of criminal procedure. Before 1976, for about 15 years, social tribunals were also empowered to proceed in criminal cases of minor significance. These forms of establishing responsibility were intended to serve the aspirations of criminal policy aimed at the gradual socialization and democratization of the administration of justice. These aims, which were formed in the early fifties, are theoretically sound and their realization is an extremely important requirement of building socialism.

Similarly to other socialist countries the gradual socialization and democratization of the administration of justice was given momentum in the middle of the fifties in Hungary as well. Law decree No. 11 of 1956 permitted the heads of state enterprises or institutions to initiate the proceedings of establishing the responsibility of the perpetrator of minor offences against social property in a disciplinary procedure. Later statutes extended this authority over other minor offences violating different legal interests.[1] The statutory provisions concerning the organization and operation of social tribunals, Law decree No. 24 of 1962 in particular, permitted, in addition to cases related to labour relationships and minor civil disputes between the employees of the same employer, such offences as the minor varieties of theft, causing bodily injury, libel and slander, etc. to be tried and decided by the social tribunal, if a penal authority relegated the case to them.

However, due to incorrect legal regulation and insufficient central control, these forms of establishing the responsibility for criminal offences, which express broad democratism and an intensified responsibility for the affairs of fellow-employees, started declining. It has become a more and more generally accepted view in the literature that the preconditions of this type of administration of justice do not exist in

[1] The whole of the following argument was originally written before the introduction of the new Penal Code in 1979; indeed, the chapter was intended as a contribution to the discussion carried on during the preparation of the new Code, and had the definite aim of influencing the decisions of those responsible for drawing it up. The new Code has certainly moved closer to the ideas expounded here (see, for example, the definition of the aims of punishment quoted in Note 3 to Chapter II of Part Five); but one reason for leaving the argument here as it stands is that even the new Code does not fully embody a rigorous application of the determinist point of view—the movement toward this is still going on, in the minds of experts and the public, at the present.

Hungary at the present phase of our social development; the reinforcement of the administration of justice by the state is required.[2]

The declining trends of these forms of establishing the responsibility for criminal offences are well demonstrated by the data in Table 8.

Table 8

The distribution of defendants by the mode of establishing responsibility

	1968	1969	1970	1971	1972	1974	1975	1976
Proffering accusation before court	55 203	63 364	61 145	70 315	71 708	78 021	82 203	91 110
Termination of proceedings — relegated to social tribunals	1.307	480	271	235	118	166	218	—
— relegated to disciplinary authorities	2.174	1.179	785	1.042	741	1.497	1.312	1.164

According to the data, the number of defendants whose case was relegated to social tribunals in 1968 was still more than one thousand and in 1975 this number was only 218. The reduction in the number of offenders subjected to disciplinary proceedings for the offence is not so unambiguous.

Law-decree No. 24 of 1975, effective from January 1, 1976, was aimed at putting into effect the principle that responsibility for a criminal offence may be established only by a criminal court, and, for this reason, it prohibited the proceedings of social tribunals in criminal matters independently of the unimportant character of the dangerousness of the act or the perpetrator to society.

In my opinion, in spite of the statutory provisions, it is not a definitely decided problem of principle whether the type of criminal proceedings conducted at the place of employment and which calls for the broad participation of fellow-employees should be completely abolished or whether the operation of social tribunals should be allowed within an appropriate legal framework in certain minor criminal cases.

If prevention, and the resocialization or socialization of the perpetrator within that, is accepted as the aim of the establishment of responsibility for criminal

[2] A. Horváth, *A társadalmi tulajdont sértő cselekmények bíróságon kívüli elbírálása az egyes európai szocialista országokban* (Adjudication of Acts Violating Social Property, Outside the Court, in European Socialist Countries), Budapest: MTA Állam- és Jogtudományi Intézet Jogösszehasonlító Osztályának Kiadványai, 1969.

offences, under identical conditions those forms of establishing responsibility that allow a more direct putting into effect of democratism, social education and self-management, should necessarily be preferred, in principle. To be called to account for our deeds in the presence of our fellow-employees has stronger educational and preventive effects than the same proceeding before officials and strangers. Experience also shows that it is offenders and potential offenders, i.e. people who think minor violations of norms permissible for themselves, who object mostly to the operation of the social tribunal for fear of the disapproval of fellow employees, of the familiar public, and for fear of their immoral, law-violating behaviour becoming known. The interests of socialist society require an atmosphere, the creation of organizational frames, where minor criminal offences entail serious moral condemnation, due precisely to publicity.

It is an unarguable fact that social tribunals represent a much greater restraining force, much more significant preventive effects, than separate state courts. The strongest proof of the social usefulness of this form of establishing responsibility is precisely the fact that morally unstable people like the operation of social tribunals less than that of the official courts, i.e. they are less ashamed of their socially harmful acts before the courts of the state. In my opinion, the essence of the operation of the social tribunal is not to be found in the circumstance that lay elements pass a judgement instead of specialists of law, but in the fact that the process of establishing responsibility takes place in the presence of the fellow-employees at the place of work and the representatives of the fellow-employees can participate in the process of judging. And legal correctness demands that the proceedings should be conducted with the participation or under the supervision of jurists, and should have adequate procedural rules.

In the Soviet Union and in the socialist countries in general, this form of establishing responsibility for antisocial behaviour is attributed a considerable importance.[3] The progressive criminologists of capitalist countries see an example of the administration of justice to be followed in the social tribunals of the socialist countries.[4] On the other hand, in our country, their operation has gradually stopped. My opinion is that this is so not because the preconditions of such a socialization of the administration of justice do not exist in Hungary, but because legislation has not created the necessary legal framework for their operation. T. Szabó correctly noted in her recently published book:

"Antagonism against the operation of social tribunals would have never risen to the present degree, even in the literature of procedural law, had the legislator had in

[3] See e.g. P. Wierzbicki's lecture given at the regional seminar of Central European countries; *Przegląd Penitencjarny i Kriminologiczny* (Warsaw), No. 4, 1972.

[4] G. Rudas, "Az ENSZ-nek a bűnözés megelőzésével és a bűnözőkkel való bánásmóddal foglalkozó IV. kongresszusáról" (On the Fourth Congress of the UN on Crime Prevention and the Treatment of Offenders), *Belügyi Szemle* No. 12, 1970.

view the fundamental object of the establishment of social tribunals, namely the gradual socialization and democratization of the administration of justice and not in the first place the relief of the organs of the public administration of justice of procedure in criminal offences of little importance."[5]

Therefore the realization of a good initiation has become a provisional assuring of certain administrative aims.

It is a well-known fact that it is difficult to revive discredited principles and institutions. This is so also in the case of the socialization of the administration of criminal justice. In my judgement, however, the democratization and socialization of the administration of criminal justice and, together with them, the increase of its effectiveness, grow out of the essence of socialism, and, for this reason, the forms of establishing responsibility that will be an organic part of our system of administering criminal justice in addition to the courts of the state, are going to come into existence sooner or later, of necessity.

2 The System of Penal Measures

At the present stage of our social development, as we have seen, the establishment of responsibility for criminal offences is done primarily through the operation of the courts of the state. It is our courts that have the function of passing judgements within the limits prescribed by the penal laws on the perpetrators of criminal offences.

It is a long accepted view that the essence of the administration of justice is defined by the system of punishment. Of course, procedural rules and the methods of establishing responsibility are also very important, yet the most important thing is what the consequences of socially harmful acts are. It is above all by the system of sanctions defined by the penal codes, by its practical application, by the way of enforcing the sanctions, that can be measured what principles are followed in the administration of justice and whether it satisfies social requirements, or not.

The data finished in 1978, because a new Code came into force in 1979. The tendency of the most recent years is not yet quantifiable. At present we can only say that there is not a very significant difference as compared to the earlier one.

For the examination of the system of punishment from the point of view of the determinist establishment of responsibility, of the principle of punishment with preventive aims, the best way is to set out from statistical data. (See Tables 9, 10, 11 and 12)

Reading the Tables what we see at a first glance is that up to 1972 confinement was dominant in our system of punishment. In 1973 the rate of prison sentences

[5] T. Szabó, *The Unification and Differentiation in Socialist Administration of Criminal Justice,* Budapest: Akadémiai Kiadó, 1978, p. 78.

Table 9

The distribution of adult offenders subject to public prosecution by the kinds of punishment

	1968	1969	1970	1971	1972	1973	1974	1975	1976	1977	1978
Death sentence	5	4	6	3	6	3	4	3	1	1	1
Imprisonment	29 804	29 386	26 876	32 439	33 695	28 521	27 054	52 210	29 054	28 688	26 934
— suspended, of that	12 964	11 831	8 611	12 843	14 736	12 512	11 866	10 645	12 367	12 508	12 144
Corrective educative labour	7 367	6 744	5 451	7 711	7 337	4 667	3 584	3 623	4 023	4 058	4 007
Fine	9 889	10 743	9 055	12 092	17 578	26 550	28 674	25 247	27 269	28 025	30 360
— suspended, of that	311	308	225	346	469	573	560	341	336	318	384
Total	47 065	46 877	41 388	52 245	58 616	59 741	59 321	54 083	60 347	60 772	61 302

Table 10

The distribution of adult offenders subject to public prosecution by kinds of punishment (percentages)

	1968	1969	1970	1971	1972	1973	1974	1975	1976	1977	1978
Death sentence	0.0	0.0	0.0	0.0	0.0	0.0	0.0	0.0	0.0	0.0	0.0
Imprisonment	63.3	62.6	64.9	62.0	57.4	47.7	45.6	46.6	48.1	47.2	43.9
— suspended, of that	43.5	40.2	32.0	39.5	43.7	43.9	43.9	42.2	42.6	43.6	45.1
Corrective-educative labour	15.6	14.4	13.2	14.8	12.5	7.8	6.1	6.7	6.7	6.7	6.5
Fine	21.0	22.9	21.8	23.1	30.0	44.5	48.3	46.7	45.2	46.1	49.5
— suspended, of that	3.2	3.1	2.5	2.9	2.7	2.1	1.9	1.3	1.2	1.1	1.2
Total	100.0	100.0	100.0	100.0	100.0	100.0	100.0	100.0	100.0	100.0	100.0

Table 11

The distribution of juvenile offenders subject to public prosecution by the kinds of punishment and measure

	1968	1969	1970	1971	1972	1973	1974	1975	1976	1977	1978
Imprisonment	1881	2091	2249	3451	3698	2986	2476	2129	2334	2171	1926
— suspended, of that	1030	1012	926	1602	1826	1546	1351	1119	1239	1156	1011
Corrective-educative labour	475	444	301	581	659	547	381	388	454	384	399
Fine	264	291	202	354	512	825	786	717	731	687	752
— suspended, of that	14	14	11	11	22	32	19	16	19	15	15
Judicial reprimand	300	304	318	407	488	456	301	226	280	245	300
Probation	1108	1095	1179	1377	1249	1153	1194	1250	1503	1505	1547
Education in a corrective institute	427	375	486	454	378	359	376	439	420	400	436
Medical treatment	98	100	160	177	187	180	229	190	209	163	152
Total	4553	4700	4942	6801	7171	6506	5725	5339	5931	5555	5512

Table 12

The distribution of juvenile offenders subject to public prosecution by the kinds of punishment and measure (percentage)

	1968	1969	1970	1971	1972	1973	1974	1975	1976	1977	1978
Imprisonment	41.3	44.4	45.4	50.7	51.5	45.9	43.2	39.9	39.4	39.1	34.9
— suspended, of that	54.7	48.3	41.2	46.4	49.3	51.8	54.6	52.6	53.1	53.2	52.5
Corrective-educative labour	10.4	9.4	6.1	8.5	9.2	8.4	6.7	7.3	7.7	6.9	7.2
Fine	5.8	6.2	4.1	5.2	7.1	12.7	13.4	13.4	12.3	12.4	13.6
— suspended, of that	5.3	4.8	5.4	3.1	4.2	3.9	2.5	2.2	2.6	2.2	2.0
Judicial reprimand	6.6	6.4	6.4	6.0	6.8	7.0	5.2	4.2	4.7	4.4	5.4
Probation	24.3	23.2	22.4	20.2	17.4	17.7	20.9	23.4	25.3	27.1	28.2
Education in a corrective institute	9.4	8.0	9.8	6.7	5.3	5.5	6.6	8.2	7.1	7.2	7.9
Medical treatment	2.1	2.2	3.2	2.6	2.6	2.8	4.0	3.6	3.5	2.9	2.8
Total	100.0	100.0	100.0	100.0	100.0	100.0	100.0	100.0	100.0	100.0	100.0

decreased by about 10 per cent, which can be explained by Resolution No. 14 of 1973 of the Presidential Council of the People's Republic of Hungary of the guiding principles of legal policy of the application of law. For the Resolution took the position that in the case of first offenders whose earlier behaviour had been blameless, if criminal proceedings are necessary, a punishment not involving confinement should be imposed (fine, correctional-educative work or suspended prison sentence).

Earlier, before the resolution, criminologists and certain specialists of criminal law had been criticizing the confinement-centred system of punishment which they thought unnecessary. In their opinion, the dominant role of imprisonment necessarily followed from the provisions of the 1961 Penal Code, since 172, 91 per cent, out of the 188 kinds of conduct were to be punished with confinement; in 9 cases, 5 per cent, confinement could be imposed as an alternative to corrective-educative work and the Code prescribed fine or corrective-educative work exclusively for only 7 kinds of offences, i.e. 4 per cent.

If we consider the provisions concerning mitigation, attempt and accessories, (Art. 68.) we see that the imposition of confinement was mandatory for 25 per cent of criminal offences. In the other cases (not counting the seven mentioned) the imposition of a fine or correctional-educative work was possible, depending on various conditions. In fact, this possibility was being realized in such a way that many more than half of the offenders were sentenced to confinement before 1973, and after 1973 almost half of the offenders were being sentenced to that punishment. Of these, in the case of adults about 40 per cent, in the case of juveniles 50 per cent, were given suspended sentences. Thus, confinement to be implemented concerned one fourth of adult and one fifth of juvenile convicts. Even so, it still represented a high rate among punishments. (The new Code, 1976, authorizes loss of freedom as the punishment for "only" 68 per cent of the criminal offences; for 28 per cent either loss of freedom of under one year, reformatory educative labour or a fine may be imposed; and for 4 per cent of the offences the Code excludes the imposition of loss of freedom.)

Although the data of other socialist countries are not available to me in such detail, in my opinion, the differences are not very significant. In Bulgaria, for example, 64 per cent of offenders were sentenced to confinement in 1970. The proportion of prison sentences to be carried out was 33 per cent.[6] Significantly differing data may be found, on the other hand, in certain Western countries, such as The Netherlands, Sweden and England, where actual imprisonment accounts for 10—20 per cent of the cases. These countries have changed their system of punishment in accordance with the criminological studies which show that imprisonment-centred systems of punishment do not meet the requirements of prevention. According to these views, repressive, retribution-oriented penal

[6] The Bulgarian criminologist P. Spasov's contribution at the Central European regional seminar: *Przeglad Penitenjarny i Kriminologiczny* (Warsaw), No. 4, 1972, pp. 29-30.

measures should be replaced by penalties, or to be precise by penal measures, which have an educational content and promote the social adaptation of offenders.

In the years before the introduction of the new Code the question frequently arose in Hungary and in other socialist countries of whether the existing system of punishment, which was built primarily on measures of repression, in addition to the use of educational means, was in accordance, or not, with the principles of materialism, determinism, and whether it satisfied, or not, the requirements and conditions of socialism.

At present, the majority even of specialists of criminal law are of the opinion that the imprisonment-centred system of punishment and penal law has to undergo fundamental changes. This idea is unmistakable, e.g. in the resolutions of the Varna preparatory colloquium of the XI. Congress of the AIDP

1. The sanction system, based on *repression,* does not satisfy the present requirements any more.

2. At the present stage of development, criminal punishment is indispensable; but it is measures (security and other) and not penalties that should have a central position among sanctions.

3. Imprisonment, as a kind of punishment, has to be an exceptional means, the *ultima ratio;* the sphere where it is employed should be more and more limited.

4. Imprisonment should be replaced by other institutions, more adequate from the point of view of the educational aims of penal law. A new system of social reaction to criminal offences should be created which would gradually fulfil its function of replacing the classical sanctions of penal law. In this sphere, special attention has to be paid—particularly *in the socialist countries*—to means already existing (relegation of the case from criminal procedure to social tribunals, or to disciplinary proceedings; bringing penalties of a monetary nature into prominence; warning; the limitation of rights; compensation; various other means and methods of influence and discipline).

5. The principles of *decriminalization* and/or *penalization* should be elaborated, in the process of which the effects of scientific and technological developments on crime, crime control, and the scope of penal law, should be examined.

6. The features of the *"crisis" of penal law* of our times should be explored, and their nature should be precisely determined.[7]

Some of the new principles appearing in the administration of justice are also accepted in the Hungarian system of establishing criminal responsibility. The above-mentioned Resolution of the Presidential Council (No. 14 of 1973) on the principles of legal policy of the application of law was aimed at restricting imprisonment and demanded the more frequent application of fines. The introduction of the relatively

[7] E. Cséka, "A Nemzetközi Büntetőjogi Társaság budapesti kongresszusának várnai és freiburgi előkészítő kollokviuma" (The Varna and Freiburg Preparatory Colloquia of the Budapest Congress of the International Association of Penal Law), *Jogtudományi Közlöny* No. 4, 1974, p. 172.

indeterminate confinement sentence in the case of recidivists can be evaluated in the same way (Law-decree No. 9 of 1974), and so can the work-therapeutical treatment and crime (Law-decree No. 10 of 1974). All this, however, was no more than taking one or two steps enforced on us by our social development and by practical needs. The need for the transformation of our whole system of administration of justice, for reflection upon the possible and actual use of the new principle, for the elaboration of a theoretically more sound system of establishing responsibility, still existed.

However, it is a fact that it is much easier to repudiate principles and institutions appearing obsolete than to work out new ones to replace them and to put the new ones into practice. The difficulties appearing here warn all specialists that to put into practice theoretically correct new principles is possible only as far as the preconditions are present or can be created.

3 Replacement of the Prison Sentence

(The analysis which can be found here contains the situation before the new Penal Code 1979.)

In the examination of the issue, it is advisable to set out from the data of statistics. In addition to confinement, fines, correctional-educative work and the death penalty exist as penalties applicable in the case of adults (Tables 9 and 10). If we disregard the rarely imposed death penalty and accept the view according to which corrective-educative work under the present conditions is essentially a fine to be paid in instalments, we can say that our system of punishment consists of two categories as far as principal punishments are concerned: imprisonment and fines, or their suspended forms.

In addition to principal punishments, supplementary punishments have a relatively wide scale (interdiction from public affairs, local banishment, interdiction from practicing an occupation, expulsion from the country, confiscation of property, supplementary fine). Within the system of sanctions we find also measures to be sharply distinguished from punishments, according to the dominant opinion. (Warning, forced psychiatric treatment, forced de-intoxification, confiscation.)

The system of punishments and measures applicable in the cases of juveniles is different from that of adults, above all in terms of the proportion and content of the *measures*. The Code itself states that an important role is attributed to education in the resocialization of juveniles and education is the function of measures above all. The kinds of punishment for juveniles are the same as for adults, with the exception of the death penalty. However, the measures, which embrace four categories, i.e. probation, education in a corrective institute, judicial reprimand and measures of cure, show marked differences. The measures of education here serve as substitutes for punishments since they are imposed in a sentence for the perpetration of criminal offences, frequently grave ones.

The inclusion of the educational measures in the Code is partly the result of the right aspiration that the requirements of pedagogy should be given a place in the penal law of juveniles and partly of the wrong idea which wants to satisfy the requirements of pedagogy by permitting the application of measures of education instead of retributive punishment in the case of those who commit minor offences or in whose case it seems justified. According to the data of statistics, judicial practice finds the imposition of a punishment necessary in the majority of the cases. (See Tables 11 and 12)

In the light of the principle of punishments with preventive aims it is evident that such a separation or, perhaps more precisely, contrasting of punishments and educational measures is incorrect, theoretically unsound, for imprisonment should be employed with a preventive aim and as a means of education, of consciousness-forming in the broadest sense of the word, in the same way as a judicial reprimand or probation. Which is used in the case of the one and which in the case of the other perpetrator is dependent, in theory, on the offence committed, on the offender's personality, endowments and social circumstances. Sanctions with preventive aims have a homogeneous theoretical basis and since they are applied on account of the perpetration of criminal offences, they may be uniformly named penal measures.

The variety of penal measures applicable already at present in the case of juveniles render it possible for a penal measure individualized to the personality of the perpetrator to be applied instead of an unnecessary prison sentence. It does not exclude, of course, the introduction of other forms of penal measure (such as weekend supervision, similar to the institution of weekend custody in England, or placing someone under the supervision of the workers' brigade that can be found in the Soviet Union). While the present selection of penal measures provides relatively good possibilities for individualization in the case of juveniles, the system of penalties for adults appears to be in need of significant extension.

Penal measures cannot be properly individualized through the application of fines or imprisonment, not even if the variations are increased, but new forms have to be found. It seems natural that we should consider the applicability of the educational measures proven useful in the case of juveniles with the aim of adapting them to the penal system of adults.

Certain authors, as we have mentioned while discussing the aims of punishment, object to this idea, saying it is incorrect to take pedagogical measures in the case of adults whose personality has already been formed. One type of punishment is needed in the case of adults (retributive), and another in the case of juveniles. We can certainly accept part of this opinion, that different concrete means of education may indeed be necessary in the case of adults and with juveniles. But I consider the measures of an educational character as important for adults as for juveniles. Precisely for this reason, the kinds of punishment may be identical, since the sort of punishment primarily defines its framework which may be filled with various contents. An excellent example is loss of freedom punishment which may be equally applied at present in the case of adults and juveniles. The way of implementation, the regime, however, is significantly different. Thus, the argument that the kinds of punishment applicable for juveniles cannot be adapted to the penal system of adults in principle is refuted.

For my own part, I would consider the introduction of probation particularly expedient (in the new Penal Code, probation for adults finds its place together with other proposed measures). In the case of criminal offences of negligence and also in the case of intentional but chance offences, this form of penal measure could replace the short-term imprisonment of offenders. Probation does not bring about a break, a change, in the family, work, and other social relationships of the offenders, it may only result in changes in the offender's consciousness if the conditions are favourable. According to experience accumulated in prison studies, there are also adult offenders in whose case any legal detriment is needless, the judicial process, the deepened awareness of the antisocial nature of their offences and the perspective that the detriment prescribed by law may or may not occur, depending on their behaviour, being enough.

Probation can be organized in various ways. The control of the probationer may be ensured through professional probation officers, or it is possible to ask for the help of the social organs of the place of work, in order to attain the aims of the penal measure.

The use of judicial reprimand as a penal measure should be considered, in my opinion, also in the case of adults. We have a similar measure at present, namely, warning; the difference is that, although it is applied on account of a criminal offence mostly by the police, it is not considered a punishment, a penal measure. This "warning" could be much more effective if the court could use it as a penal measure, as a punishment, at the end of the process of establishing responsibility. It could be particularly effective in the case of perpetrators in whose offence the situation had a decisive role. (It is also included in the new Penal Code.)

According to the guiding principles of legal policy, the more frequent application of fines is aimed at restricting prison sentences. From the point of view of the future, of ensuring the aims of prevention to a greater extent, a transformation of correctional-educative work, which would eliminate its character of fines paid in instalments and would change it into corrective-educative work in the real sense of the word, could be particularly effective. In my view offenders sentenced to corrective-educative work should be concentrated in certain factories where they could work all the week under proper supervision and on weekends they could go home to their families if they had a family. In this way deprivation of liberty can be avoided but the proper supervision could be ensured. Hundreds of thousands of non-criminal persons work under similar conditions if their place of work is far from their home. Programmes organized after work, group and individual education, the relatively tight daily schedule of the hostels reserved only for such offenders, could ensure the necessary educational influence.

Such corrective-educative work should be imposed primarily on offenders who frequently change their place of employment, who do not like working, lead an undisciplined, disorderly life and who committed the offences as a consequence, in part or completely, of this way of life. In practice it would mean the realization of the right theory in a new form, according to which penal measures would go by the various types of perpetrators. The typology of offenders provides the scientific basis, according to causes and possibilities of prevention, on which the effective penal system can be built.[8] It follows that a wide selection of punishments not involving deprivation of liberty should be created so that the courts could individualize the sentences more extensively.

As far as suspended imprisonment is concerned, practice has proved that it is a form of punishment which serves the aims of prevention well. Our administration of justice uses it adequately, for about 40 per cent of the prison sentences of less than a year term are suspended. On the other hand, suspended fines are restricted to merely a few per cent. (See Tables 6 and 7.) It seems to me that the prospect of a concrete financial detriment may be suitable for restraining people from the perpetration of new offences. Consequently, the more frequent suspension of sentences of a considerable fine, perhaps for a longer period than at present, would mean another form of individualization in our penal system.

A further enrichment of the sanctions of penal law, and thereby a further possibility of individualization, could be ensured by applying the supplementary penalties of e.g. interdiction from an occupation, or confiscation of property, as principal punishments (or also as principal punishments). I believe one does not have to explain in detail how effective a means of prevention, interdiction from the occupation could be in the case of the endangering of life committed in the sphere of one's occupation, or how the protection of property, particulary, social property, could be intensified against offences through the partial confiscation of the offender's property (land, summer house). The elimination of luxury, or comfortable circumstances, is much more effective in the case of avaricious people, or those who damage social property, than short-term imprisonment, or even fines. In the new Penal Code there is the possibility of applying some supplementary penalties as principal punishments.

The restriction of prison sentences to cases when long educational activity is needed serves economic interests too, although it is desirable for the intensified realization of demands for prevention above all. The maintenance of penal institutions is a particularly expensive form of the implementation of punishment, especially in the case of short-term imprisonment. According to international data, the costs of guarding one prisoner are higher than the yearly pay of a professional probation officer. Financial resources made available in this way could be used in other fields of the realization of the aims of punishments.

[8] See K. Gönczöl, "A tipológia szerepe a kriminológia továbbfejlődésében" (The Role of Typology in the Development of Criminology), *Jogtudományi Közlöny* No. 11, 1974.

4 The Application of Imprisonment
Indeterminate Imprisonment

The second fundamental problem raised by the reform of our system of punishment is the determination of the method of application and the application and the duration of the Confinement.

It is worth having a glance at the rates of offenders sentenced to imprisonment in various European countries.[9]

Table 13

Country	Population January 1, 1971	Number of persons in prison	Persons in prison per 100.000 inhabitants
Holland	13 199 000	2 919	22.4
Belgium	9 660 151	5 815	60.2
Denmark	4 800 000	3 350	69.8
England and Wales	55 534 000	40 178	72.4
France	51 004 000	29 533	59.9
Luxemburg	343 300	218	64.1
West Germany	61 194 600	31 175	83.6
Sweden	8 092 693	4 977	61.4
Norway	3 866 468	1 432	37.1

These low rates of imprisonment in countries where criminality is much higher than in Hungary show that imprisonment as a punishment is applied in these countries only to a strongly limited extent. (Hungarian data are not available, but specialists knowing the number of prisoners and the average length of the imposed prison terms can easily make an estimate.)

During the last half century, various opinions have appeared concerning the duration of the term of imprisonment.

In the last twenty years, it has become a predominant view in criminology that short-term confinement sentences, particularly those shorter than six months, are not suitable for attaining the pedagogical aims of punishment. For this reason, in several countries (e.g. England, West Germany) the application of short-term imprisonment has been abolished or limited. In 1960, on the suggestion of the II. Criminological Congress, the UN proposed that the member nations should decrease short-term imprisonment sentences to the minimum possible. In spite of that, according to certain estimates, the number of offenders in prison in 1972 was

[9] Kriminal varden 1972. Sveriges Officiella Statistik, Stockholm, 1973, p. 11.

between 1 500 000 and 2 000 000, political prisoners excluded. Of that, 1 300 000 persons, i.e. about 70 per cent, were sentenced to less than six months.[10]

Confinement sentences are distributed in Hungary by duration as shown in Tables 14–17.

Comparing these data with the data of other socialist countries, we see similar proportions. For example, in Bulgaria in 1970, prison sentences for less than six months accounted for 47 per cent of all prison sentences, between 6 months and 1 year for 26 per cent, between 1 and 3 years for 16 per cent, between 3 and 5 years for 6 per cent and more than 5 years for 4 per cent.[11] Almost identical data can be found in Yugoslavia.[12] In Poland, the rate of confinement sentence for less than 6 months is somewhat lower. This rate in 1968 was 19.5 per cent without suspended sentences, in 1970 only 10.5 per cent.[13]

Viewing Hungarian data, we can see that the rate of short-term prison sentences is high and only a small decrease may be seen in the period studied. In this respect, our penal system has not shown significant changes for a long time. The theoretical assertions that a serious restriction of short-term prison sentences is justified do not appear either in statutes or in the practice of the courts. It is perhaps the latest guiding principles of criminal policy, aiming at the general reduction of loss of freedom sentences, that will also result in the decrease of short-term imprisonment sentences.

The conclusions formed on the basis of criminological studies do not completely oppose the application of short-term prison sentences, they only propose to decrease their number significantly. According to a study carried out in Yugoslavia, short-term sentences are least effective among recidivists, particularly special recidivists, among property offenders and among juveniles.[14] For this reason, the authors do not consider the application of this form of punishment useful to the mentioned categories. On the other hand, they consider it acceptable in the case of first offenders, offenders over 30 years of age and particularly those who commit offences of impulse, where this form of punishment may be effective.

Recently there have been defenders of short-term imprisonment, whose ideas are closely related to the denial of the preventive effects of punishment, or to its underrating. This is particularly evident in the works of Dutch, Danish and Swedish criminologists. In these countries, one can frequently hear opinions that the significant changes that have occurred in the penal system during the last fifty years have had no particular effect on crime.

[10] M. López—Rey, "Crime and Penal System", *Australian and New Zealand Journal of Criminology,* March (1971), pp. 1=6.

[11] Spasov, *op. cit.*

[12] D. Davidovič, J. Spadijev, D. and B. Vukadinovič, *Efikasnost kratkich hazni lisenja slobode* (The Effectiveness of Short-Term Prison Sentence), Belgrade, 1965.

[13] Wierzbicki, *op. cit.,* p. 10.

[14] Davidovič et al, *op. cit.*

Professor van Bemmelen has written in one of his studies: "We have to draw the conclusion that although we have been successful in humanizing our penal system without any loss to society, we have seen no profit from that in the struggle against grave criminality."[15]

In Holland, for example, on April 12, 1974, 2446 convicts were in prison and the overwhelming majority had been sentenced to a short term. The number of those who had been sentenced to more than two years was not more than 50. The Danish professor, Karl O. Christiansen, has also mentioned that, according to criminological surveys, the various kinds of punishment have almost the same effects on the convicts.[16] And, since the humanization of the penal system is a very important task, in his opinion, short-term imprisonment may be given preference over long-term sentences. The fundamental considerations in choosing the appropriate punishment may be humanism, economy and the protection of society.

We, socialist criminologists, hold that the means of criminal law are neither the exclusive nor the most important means of preventing crime. Crime as a social phenomenon is rooted deeply in social relations, the personality and the consciousness of people. The establishment of criminal responsibility, however, has its role in the prevention of crime. In addition to the uncontested general preventive effects, the well-chosen punishment necessarily has to have also special preventive effects. Discussing the theories of causality, we have said that phenomena in direct relation with human beings exert a particularly strong influence on their subjective mind. And punishment is such a causal factor exerting a direct influence, a determinant which determines, together with other factors, the future behaviour of the perpetrator. The question here is only whether we have found or are able to find at the present level of the development of sciences the penal measures that exert a *favourable* influence on the perpetrator, and whether this favourable influence is enough to ensure that the perpetrator will not commit another criminal offence in spite of the negative external effects.

As far as the first half of the question is concerned, it is precisely with this aim that reforms of penal law are carried out. It is precisely with this aim that we try to transform our system of punishment, leaving out the forms of punishment that are proved to be not able to serve adequately the aims of prevention and introducing new penal measures we expect to exert a favourable influence on perpetrators. But when this favourable influence is sufficient in a particular external situation and when it is not is a question not primarily of the system of punishment but that of after-care, that of society as a whole, whose interests demand the reasonable

[15] J. M. Van Bemmelen, "A bűnözés és a társadalmi fejlődés, különös tekintettel Hollandiára" (Crime and Social Development, with Particular Reference to Holland), *Belügyi Szemle Tájékoztatója,* No. 17. p. 71.

[16] K. O. Christiansen's contribution at the Central European regional seminar, *Przeglad Penitencjarny i Kriminologiczny* (Warsaw), No. 4, 1974, p. 89.

elimination of the social conditions and human relations that inspire the perpetration of offences.

My experience has led me to form the conclusion that the imposition of a prison sentence is expedient in principle if it is prognosticated that the perpetrator may be educated to be a law-abiding citizen only under strict control and over a long period of time. Such perpetrators are recidivists in the first place or those who are first-time offenders, but whose way of life and personality renders long-term forced education necessary, or perhaps whose criminal intentions are evident or highly probable at the time of passing the sentence so that the protection of society justifies it. In any other case, the imposition of a sentence other than imprisonment is expedient.

Theoretically, this could be formulated, perhaps, by saying that the punishment of confinement should be or may be imposed if the perpetrator's dangerousness to society does not cease to exist by the time of passing the sentence, if a certain probability remains that the convict would commit another offence unless he is put under strict control. Thus, the examination of the perpetrator's dangerousness to society and of his objective circumstances is a task for the courts that must not be neglected. It is true, of course, that the exact determination of the perpetrator's dangerousness to society is not possible in every case, even if experts (psychologists, educators, psychiatrists, etc.) are employed to establish it. For this reason, it may be determined as a general guide-line for the practice of sentencing that the imposition of a prison sentence is unnecessary if the offender will probably not commit another offence in the near future, while the imposition of prison sentence is indispensable if the perpetrator's dangerousness to society can be determined with a high probability. And in the cases when the prognostication does not show a high probability either in the negative or in the positive direction, which is a significant proportion of the cases, the kind of punishment should be selected by the court on the basis of the measure of probability.

This principle, appearing correct from the theoretical point of view, could hardly, however, be put into practice at present, since the sense of justice of the general public, and of a significant proportion of the specialists, goes by punishing in proportion with the deed, which is seen to be accomplishable in the determining of the length of the term of imprisonment. For instance in a case of homicide committed in a sudden emotional agitation, when the perpetrator has repented of and condemned his deed, it is highly probable he would not commit another offence. Theoretically there is no need for imprisonment here. I do not believe, however, that the judicial practice could be changed in this way overnight. But we could mention other examples and examples of the opposite case, too. This should not mean, however, that we do not have to transform gradually our system of establishing responsibility so that we could approximate as closely as possible to the theoretically correct requirements.

It appears from the above that the application of the punishment of confinement is justified only if longer (more than a few months) forced education is necessary.

Table 14

The distribution of adult offenders subject to public prosecution sentenced to imprisonment by the length of term

	1968	1969	1970	1971	1972	1973	1974	1975	1976	1977	1978
30 days–6 months	17 564	16 809	13 812	17 326	18 107	14 119	13 179	12 321	13 855	13 556	12 867
6–12 months	7 779	7 796	7 335	8 949	9 316	8 562	8 475	5 682	6 686	8 970	8 786
1–2 years	2 788	2 913	3 555	3 721	3 814	3 597	3 432	4 431	5 116	3 800	3 307
2–5 years,	1 482	1 621	1 917	2 198	2 205	2 009	1 748	2 552	3 120	2 070	1 740
more than 5 years	191	247	257	245	154	231	214	219	269	262	220
life sentence	—	—	—	—	—	3	6	5	8	10	14
Total	29 804	29 386	26 876	32 439	33 695	28 521	27 054	25 210	29 054	28 686	26 934

Table 15

The distribution of adult offenders subject to public prosecution sentenced to imprisonment by the length of term (percentage)

	1968	1969	1970	1971	1972	1973	1974	1975	1976	1977	1978
30 days–6 months	58.9	57.2	51.3	53.4	53.7	49.5	48.7	48.7	47.7	47.3	47.8
6–12 months	26.0	26.5	27.3	27.6	27.6	30.0	31.3	22.6	23.0	31.3	32.6
1–2 years	9.3	9.9	13.2	11.5	11.3	12.6	12.7	17.6	17.6	13.3	12.3
2–5 years	5.0	5.5	7.1	6.7	6.5	7.1	6.5	10.2	10.7	7.2	6.5
more than 5 years	0.6	0.8	0.9	0.7	0.7	0.8	0.8	0.9	0.9	0.9	0.8
life sentence	0.0	0.0	0.0	0.0	0.0	0.0	0.0	0.0	0.0	0.0	0.0
Total	100.0	100.0	100.0	100.0	100.0	100.0	100.0	100.0	100.0	100.0	100.0

Table 16

The distribution of juvenile offenders subject to public prosecution sentenced to imprisonment by the length of the term

	1968	1969	1970	1971	1972	1973	1974	1975	1976	1977	1978
30 days–6 months	1314	1321	1221	1938	2122	1679	1459	1124	1277	1200	1063
6–12 months	393	514	570	953	1053	850	683	639	608	624	532
1–2 years	140	191	366	373	401	342	263	277	311		
2–5 years	27	58	126	176	116	104	64	83	70	338	322
more than 5 years	7	7	11	11	6	11	7	6	8	9	9
Total	1881	2091	2294	3451	3698	2986	2476	2129	2334	2171	1926

Table 17

The distribution of juvenile offenders subject to public prosecution sentenced to imprisonment by the length of the term (percentages)

	1968	1969	1970	1971	1972	1973	1974	1975	1976	1977	1978
30 days–6 months	69.8	63.1	53.2	56.1	57.3	56.2	58.8	52.8	54.7	55.3	55.2
6–12 months	20.9	24.6	24.8	27.6	28.4	28.5	27.8	30.0	28.6	28.7	27.6
1–2 years	7.4	9.1	15.9	10.8	10.8	11.6	10.6	13.0	13.3		
2–5 years	1.4	2.7	5.5	5.1	3.1	2.3	2.6	2.9	3.1	15.6	16.7
more than 5 years	0.4	0.3	0.5	0.3	0.2	0.4	0.2	0.3	0.3	0.7	0.5
Total	100.0	100.0	100.0	100.0	100.0	100.0	100.0	100.0	100.0	100.0	100.0

Consequently, this is a way of decreasing short-term imprisonment to the minimum and of replacing it by other penal measures that should be followed, in my opinion.

The other great problem is the issue of *longer duration.*

If we accept the education-centred system of punishment, the length of the term of imprisonment should be considered first of all as dependent on the perpetrator's personality and on the applied means of education.

The formation of the subjective condition (i.e. the intention to adjust) of social adjustment, the length of the process, may significantly vary, depending on the socialization of the perpetrator's personality. According to the experience of prison studies, given the present regimes of prisons, the reversal of the system of views or attitudes justifying the perpetration of offences, and the formation of a Weltanschauung affirming social requirements, are a long or impossible process. It is conceivable, however, that the educational methods necessary for increasing the pace of this process are going to be found as a result of criminal-pedagogical studies. Thus, the length of the term of forced education may become significantly shorter. The average necessary length of the term of imprisonment, hence, may decrease. In a certain period, however, we have to reckon with a certain level of the means of education and we have to determine the length of the forced education of the perpetrators, the term of imprisonment, which depends on the widely differing personalities of perpetrators. Taking into consideration the state of the regime of prisons at present and in the near future, and also the attitude of perpetrators, adequate special preventive effects cannot be expected of imprisonment terms only a few months long. Criminological studies usually define the lowest limit of imprisonment as six months. And the upper limit of the term, where imprisonment may still be effective, is between 10 and 15 years. It is a fairly widely accepted opinion that imprisonment for more than 10 years has negative effects in the majority of cases, and for this reason such a punishment is applicable only exceptionally (e.g. instead of the death penalty). One can also find opinions in the Soviet literature according to which the upper limit of reasonable imprisonment is 9—10 years.[17]

There is a further question: how can be judged the length of a term that is minimally or optimally necessary to form the intention in the perpetrator to adjust to society, given the methods of criminal-pedagogy? The logical answer can only be that the length of the necessary forced education cannot be determined precisely in advance, it can be determined only approximately, with a relatively high possibility of error. For this reason, the definition of the term in days, i.e. forced education of a predetermined term, appears to be feasible mainly in cases where the viewpoint of general prevention prevails, where special preventive effects are not primarily to be expected of the length of the term.

[17] G. A. Avanesov and V. H. Rutgajzer, "Matematikai statisztikai módszerek a kriminológiai kutatásokban" (Mathematical Statistical Methods in Criminological Studies), *Magyar Jog és Külföldi Jogi Szemle,* No. 2, 1971, p. 112.

In the case of perpetrators when we expect their correction and that they cease to be dangerous to society with the help of educative measures applied during the implementation of punishment, however, it is more reasonable if the term is not defined in days but only relatively (between lower and upper limits), and the perpetrator is discharged within the term depending on his behaviour, on the transformation of his personality, and on the effectiveness of the applied means.

Relatively indeterminate prison sentences appeared on the agenda historically as penal measures to be applied against dangerous criminals, multiple recidivists, most frequently as security measures. Such security measures were always justified and legalized by the interest of the intensified protection of society. According to the prevailing principle of criminal policy in the given era, the measure gave expression to intensified retribution and to deterring severity. However, since prevention came to the fore among the aims of punishment, or became the single one in certain legal systems, indeterminate imprisonment has gained a new meaning. It is the intensified use of pedagogical methods, the preparation for social adaptation, that have become predominant in it, instead of retribution, the mere incarceration and making the prisoners work for profit.

At present, relatively indeterminate imprisonment is applied in several capitalist countries.[18] Of the socialist countries, Poland and the GDR introduced it several years ago. Law-decree No. 9 of 1974 permitted the imposition of relatively indeterminate sentences also on adult multiple recidivists in Hungary as well.

The antecedents of the Hungarian legislation reflect truly the theoretical debates and practical considerations that are still not definitely finished. And since I consider relatively indeterminate sentences as the fundamental form of imprisonment in the future, I consider it necessary to discuss the issue in more detail.

Indeterminate prison sentence was introduced into Hungarian penal law by Act XXI of 1913 for people avoiding work, representing a danger to the public, under the name of "labour camps". According to thist Act, a person could be sent to a labour camp:

"—in the case of the misdemeanours of avoiding work, prohibited gambling, or being kept by a prostitute, if the court deemed it necessary 'for educating to work and a decent way of life' (otherwise these offences were punishable with jail), "—in the case of misdemeanours against life, bodily integrity, decency, or property, if the perpetrator was sentenced to loss of freedom to be served in prison or to at least three months confinement in jail and the court determined that he had committed his act in connection with his work-avoiding way of life."

Incarceration in the labour camp was imposed as an indeterminate term but it had to be at least one year and not more than five years. The Act prescribed that the

[18] See in detail: T. Würtenberger, *Kriminalpolitik im Sozialen Rechtsstaat,* Stuttgart, 1970, pp. 78-105.

offender had to be occupied with work and had to be made used to an orderly way of life. A supervisory board was organized in every labour camp, with 5—10 members. The members were appointed by the Minister of Justice, from the officials of the courts, prosecutorial offices, the police, and other appropriate people.

The supervisory board could release the offender conditionally if he had spent at least one year in the labour camp, had been displaying good behaviour and proper diligence and, owing to the transformation of his character, had given reason to hope that he would lead a decent, honest way of life in the case of his release. After five years, the offender had to be discharged independent of the conditions.

The conditionally released person had to stay at a locality determined by the board, to lead an orderly life and to work. The observance of the prescriptions was checked by the police.

The period of conditional release was one year. If the offender followed the prescribed rules during this period, his conditional release became final. On the other hand, if he led an immoral, drunken or work-avoiding way of life or gravely violated the prescribed rules in any other way, the court having jurisdiction sent him back to the labour camp.

The more severe version of this institution, the hard labour camp, was introduced by Act X. of 1928 on the regulation of some issues of the administration of justice. According to the explanation given by the committee of the House of Representatives, this institution was intended to be used against habitual criminals, numbering about 800—1000 persons. The views serving as the basis for the introduction of the institutions are well characterized by the following part of the Motivations: "There is no other defense against them but to render them harmless, while leaving the hope of being set free in the form of conditional release. This is doubtless a security measure, but it is also a punishment deserved through the previous criminal offences. Rendering harmless means a security incarceration until they correct their ways, if they ever do. The intention of correction on the part of these malefactors is improbable and society is protected against them only when they are locked up."

It was "confirmed criminals" who could be sent to a hard labour camp. A confirmed criminal was a person, who — "passed his 21st year of age by the time of sentencing, — after having passed his 18th year of age, committed at least three different offences in different times and independently of each other, against life, decency, or property, in such a way that—the perpetration of the last offence and the one before that occurred within the last five years and—he committed the offences as a line of business or showed a permanent inclination to commit criminal offences."

In the determination of whether a person was or was not a confirmed criminal, his character, his way of life, life circumstances and the nature of the perpetrated offence had to be taken into consideration.

The shortest duration of the term of hard labour camp was determined by the court, within the sentence. This term, however, *could not be shorter than 3 years.* According to the Motivations for the Bill, the shortest duration of the term had to be determined according to how long a term of confinement was in proportion to the objective gravity of the act and the subjective guilt of the perpetrator. According to the view expressed by the Motivations, this shortest term was the actual punishment and the excess period was to be counted as a security measure.

After serving the minimum term, the offender could apply to the Minister of Justice and request his conditional release. The request could be repeated yearly.

A three-member supervisory authority operated at every hard labour camp. Its chairman and one of the members were appointed by the president of the court of appeal in the jurisdiction of which the hard labour camp operated, while the other member was appointed from the members of the judiciary or prosecutors by the chief prosecutor.

The Minister of Justice handed out his decision on the conditional release after hearing the opinion of the supervisory authority.

The period of conditional release was three years. If the conditionally released person worked regularly and led a proper way of life during this period, the conditional release became final. However, if he pursued an immoral, drunken, or work-avoiding life or gravely violated the rules of conditional release in any other way, *the court* that had sent him to the hard labour camp could order his return to the institution. For this purpose, a trial had to be held where the offender and the prosecutor had to appear. An offender sent back in this way could be conditionally released again only after five years at least.

The theory of socialist penal law developing after the Liberation has condemned the institution of the hard labour camp with sharp words. The written material prepared for university students,[19] for example discusses security incarceration together with the so-called "school of perpetrator penal law" and connects its application with the inhuman policy of fascist states. This evaluation can be explained primarily by the fact that during the rule of fascism legality was trampled underfoot, the creation of concentration camps resulted in the killing of thousands of people and in the mockery of human dignity. Thus, after the liberation, the hated epithet "fascist" was added to all the forms of security measures. Although in the process of building socialism, particularly after breaking the rule of the cult of the person, certain phenomena of the past became understood differently, evaluated more realistically, and the emphasis shifted from the form and slogans to the content, the appearance of the idea of imprisonment for an indeterminate term with pedagogical content[20] elicited an outcry, particularly among the specialists in criminal law.

[19] J. Békés, Z. Bodgál, K. Györgyi, E. Károly, J. Molnár, J. Pintér and L. Szűk, *Büntetőjog* (Penal Law), General Part, Vol. I, Budapest: Tankönyvkiadó, 1973, pp. 27-29.

[20] G. Gárdai and J. Vigh, "Észrevételek a büntetési rendszer problémáihoz" (Notes on the Problems of the Penal System), *Magyar Jog és Külföldi Jogi Szemle,* No. 10, 1969.

The idea of indeterminate prison sentences had not been raised with the aim of rehabilitating the past, restoring concentration camps, nor the institution of the hard labour camp of the Horthy era, but with the aim of throwing the light of materialism and consistent determinism on punishment with preventive aims and with a pedagogical content, setting out from the social demand for more effective penal measures against multiple recidivists.

From the camp of the opposition, certain opinions have appeared in writing, too, from which it may be seen that the authors have raised their voice not only against indeterminate prison sentences but also in order to defend the principle of guilt built on the concept of free will, to defend the prison-centred proportional system of punishment, and, in general, to defend criminal law actually in force, i.e. "socialist criminal law".[21]

The idea of the applicability of indeterminate sentences has arisen not only in Hungary but also in other socialist countries. T. Horváth has written correctly in one of his studies: "It cannot be considered a coincidence that the issue appeared in the practice of several socialist countries about the same time."[22] It seems, indeed, it is in the present phase of building socialism that we have arrived at the level of advancement where vigorous efforts for the reform of the system of administering criminal justice demand the admission of the aims of prevention, the intensified use of penal measures of pedagogical content, and, not less, the creation of more favourable conditions for the resocialization of the offenders.

The main argument of the opposers of indeterminate prison sentences has been that this form of punishment leads to the abolition of legal guarantees, and provides favourable grounds for subjectivism. On the one hand, the argument is senseless because nobody wants the elimination of the legal framework. This penalty can be surrounded by legal regulations as any other kind of punishment can. The guarantees of legality can exist here in the same way as in any field of law. On the other hand, as far as legality is concerned, history has proved that the inhumane, lawless criminal policy of a state is independent of the valid laws of the given country. On the contrary, the valid laws, or legislation, are always dependent on criminal or general policy. Ruling classes or groups never shape their interests according to the valid laws; on the contrary, they form the laws according to their interests. The argument, hence, is refuted on the plane of theory. It may be taken into consideration only in the elaboration of the modes of implementation.

It is also a frequently voiced argument that offenders have a fundamental human

[21] T. Lukács, "Büntetőjogi szemléletünk alakulása" (The Formation of Our Views on Criminal Law), *Magyar Jog és Külföldi Jogi Szemle, No. 9, 1970; I. Gáll,* "Büntetési rendszerünk problémái II" *(The Problems of our Penal System II), Magyar Jog és Külföldi Jogi Szemle* No. 3, 1971; Gy. Ádám, "Determinista koncepció — indeterminált szabadságvesztés?" (Determinist Conception—Indeterminate Imprisonment?), *Jogtudományi Közlöny* No. 1=2, 1972.

[22] T. Horváth, "Gondolatok büntetéstani problémákhoz" (Ideas Concerning the Problems of Penology), *Magyar Jog és Külföldi Jogi Szemle* No. 5, 1971, p. 260.

right to know when they are going to be free. This argument deserves special consideration under socialist conditions. Is it really an innate right of human beings, of perpetrators, that the term of their punishment should be determined in days in advance, or is it a right approved by an international forum and recognized by every state? I believe we cannot speak of either. It is true that the International Convention on Civil and Political Rights exists but the duration of the term of imprisonment is not even mentioned in it. Art. 7 declares only: "—No one shall be subjected to torture or to cruel, inhuman or degrading treatment or punishment. In particular, no one shall be subjected without his free consent to medical or scientific experimentation."

(Annex to GA Res. 2200 (XXI) of 16 December 1966, New York)

It is also proven by historical facts that since society came into existence, individuals have rights only of the degree and kind that the concrete conditions of social coexistence, classes or groups exercising power (or, formulating generally, the given society) ensure. Among inalienable civil rights formulated as a result of the bourgeois revolutions, the right to private property, e.g. occupies a central position. But socialist constitutions declare other rights to be basic human rights, e.g. the right to work, sharing material goods according to the quantity and quality of work, etc.

The fundamental interests of the working class and the peasantry, i.e. of the masses of society, are expressed at the present phase of social development in the principles of socialism. And the simplest way of putting this, perhaps, is to say that the interests of the community, of society, define the rights and obligations of the individuals. Hence the decision on what rights offenders have, or can have, cannot be made without taking into consideration social interests, the protection of society, the maximum possible satisfaction of human needs. To ensure public order and public peace is an interest of our society, too, and to achieve that, society has the right to apply measures of forced education, from which preventive effects may be expected, against the regular violators of public order and the laws. One of the fundamental tasks of socialist society is to educate people to respect the interests of the collective, of society. Among the means of education, various sanctions, those of penal law included, are employed of necessity.

Punishment with preventive and educational aims excludes retribution, mere isolation and the causing of unnecessary detriment and suffering. The issue here, therefore, is not that of basic human rights; what has to be examined is whether the present system of determinate sentencing that is more suitable for attaining the aims of prevention in the case of recidivists, or relatively indeterminate sentences, or perhaps a third variety. It is here that arguments for or against are possible.

The manifest aversion to relatively indeterminate sentences is a consequence of the incorrect association which links the name to the old measures representing primarily retribution and which disregards the preventive aims and pedagogical content. If we consider the punishments existing at present by their content and not only by names, we have to admit that our present system of punishment also has relatively indeterminate prison sentence with a pedagogical content, applied against juveniles and called education in a correctional institution. This fact is admitted even by certain specialists of criminal law.[23] This measure involves deprivation of liberty, its lower limit is one year, and its upper limit is passing the 18th year of age. After the one year it is not a court but the Council of the Institution that decides the question of conditional release. This measure is usually mentioned as a remarkable example of "socialist humanism." But introducing a similar measure in the case of adults has the appearance in the eyes of many people of violating the law, represents the abandonment of "guarantees", of fundamental principles of penal law, the renewal of the infamous school of doer penal law.

This illogical distinction can be explained partially by the fact that according to the Code, and on its basis, in public opinion, penal measures applicable against juveniles do not qualify as punishments, but educational measures. But practice shows that the regime used in the case of juveniles serving their confinement *punishment* does not differ in terms of pedagogical content from the educational systems used in the case of juveniles who are under *forced education* in correctional institutions. It follows from the name chosen by the Code for education in a correctional institution (i.e. for indeterminate prison sentence), that its application usually precedes the application of imprisonment of a determinate term. For the Code prescribes: "Against a juvenile, an educational measure shall be applied, as a rule. A punishment shall be imposed on the juvenile if the educational measure does not appear expedient or the juvenile has passed his 18th year of age by the time of judging the offence." (Art. 87 of the Penal Code)

We have seen above (Table 8, and 9) that the demand of the Code that above all education measures (i.e. punishments enumerated under this title) should be applied against juveniles is only theoretical, since the greater part of offenders are sentenced to punishments. It seems that educational measures do not appear expedient in a large number of cases and the courts are forced to impose punishments containing "retribution" or involving retribution as well. According to the Code, education in a correctional institute may be used mainly in the case of first offenders who appear to be educable, i.e. in the case of uncorrupted juveniles, for whom punishment seems to be too severe or unnecessary. Imprisonment may be imposed to punish the perpetrators of more serious offences, or recidivists, whose re-education and correction would need a longer time, hardly possible to determine in advance. Such application of legal consequences leads to the result that due to the shortness of the term (and perhaps its being determinate), the implementation of the punishment remains ineffectual, does not attain the aim of special prevention, in a significant proportion of prison sentences. And, similarly, education in the corrective institution also remains ineffectual, or even has negative effects, when the indeterminate term of imprisonment is unnecessary for eliminating the juvenile's dangerousness to society and it is on account not so much of the personality of the offender as of taking him

[23] *Loc. cit.*

out of his unfavourable environment that this kind of punishment has been imposed. Presumably, the high number of escapes from corrective institutions is not explicable only by the shortcomings of the applied means and methods of education but also by the fact that the educational situation worked out for the institution is not suitable for offenders sent there.

I judge such offenders to be rather heterogeneous as a group in terms of dangerousness to society, in terms of the personality of the offenders, and this would require the use of quite different educational systems. Corrective institutions, in fact, are a peculiar mixture of student hostels and open prisons, operating under the supervision of the Ministry of Education. At present, it has become a generally accepted opinion that results in the sphere of the enforcement of punishment may be attained through adequately differentiated means following homogeneous principles of criminal policy and individualized criminal-pedagogical methods.

It is clear even from a sketchy comparison that it is wrong to divide legal consequences applicable to juvenile offenders into educational measures and punishment. We cannot emphasize enough that we expect the re-education of convicts from the so-called punishments in the same way as from educational measures. And if we set up grades, then, in theory, determinate and short-term loss of freedom has to be applied before relatively indeterminate sentences. The use of relatively indeterminate imprisonment appears to be most expedient in the case of perpetrators for whom the use of other kinds of punishment has proved ineffectual, who are multiple recidivists or have the characteristics of hardened criminals.

This train of thought also demonstrates that it is best to include all legal consequences that may be imposed for criminal offences in the collective term "penal measures or penal sanctions". The term shows clearly that those measures of pedagogical content are meant here that are most suitable for serving the aims of criminal justice and are applied to the perpetrators of criminal offences in criminal proceedings. The name "penal measure" shows that it is applied as a sanction for a criminal offence and is well distinguishable from other measures of penal law or criminal procedural law. But, ultimately, the sanctions of penal law may be called punishments as well; the important matter is that we should work with a homogeneous concept embracing every sanction.

The aspiration of the legislation to introduce the idea of education or give a broader scope to it in the implementation of punishment is right and should be appreciated. Nevertheless, our present criminological knowledge makes it clear that modifications are needed as far as the putting into practice is concerned, from the point of view of both taxonomy and the use of more effective educational means.

It is also clear that not only juvenile offenders can and should be educated to be law-abiding citizens, but adults as well. And if we approve of relatively indeterminate imprisonment, or, under a different name, of forced education, why should it be impossible to introduce a similar institution for adults? It is not by chance that relatively indeterminate loss of freedom may be found primarily in the penal law of juveniles, where the idea of education, prevention is clearly accepted, where criminal behaviour is traced back to the influence of the causal factors and not to the manifestation of free will. Such a distinction between juveniles and adults is contrary to the principle of the universal law of causality, determinism. Penal law must not lose sight of the thesis of socialist pedagogy concerning the educability of human beings, including adults, either.

The opponents of relatively indeterminate loss of freedom sentences frequently voice the argument that the present prison conditions, and prisons in general, are unsuitable for promoting social adaptation, particularly in the case of those who have been leading a criminal way of life for a long time. One may find a good deal of truth in this argument. It is really difficult to form an awareness of responsibility going by the requirements of free life, to teach the offenders to plan their own future independently, to form the model of right behaviour in everyday situations, under the conditions of isolation. For this reason, the idea of setting up semi-free types of prisons or work camps (it sounds better) and the idea of gradualism arise necessarily.

The semi-free form of control, approaching a free life, can be considered in this case as the last phase of prison education (forced education) before release. Offender should go through various grades of restriction and liberty, from the most restricted form to the one allowing the most freedom. This gradualism, joined to the institution of conditional release, might be able to ensure the effectiveness of forced education.

In connection with indeterminate sentencing, we have to touch on the problem of *duration*. The opponents of the institution frequently refer to the indeterminacy of the upper limit as an argument, and disapproving of that they reject the institution as a whole. Experience shows that in countries where this kind of punishment is employed it is mainly the relatively indeterminate form that is dominant, i.e. there is an absolute upper limit beyond which even hardened criminals may not be kept in prison. This is, as a matter of fact, the relatively indeterminate form, or, if we prefer, the relatively determinate one. And, taking into consideration that criminological studies determine the period of time within which imprisonment, forced education, can be effective as between 10 and 12 years, this form is becoming generally used.

The adherents of relatively indeterminate prison sentences do not claim that between the minimum and maximum time limit every perpetrator can be formed into a law-abiding citizen, without exception. There are necessarily some offenders of whom we cannot say, even after the maximum time, that they are highly likely to have formed the intention of social adjustment. It is possible that punishment will remain ineffectual in their case; still, the relatively indeterminate term has the advantage of creating the possibility of the intensive use of the means of criminal pedagogy; state and society have done everything possible at the given level of development and science, and, parallel to that, the chances for the offender to commit new offences are limited at least for that period. Of course, it is also a conceivable solution that after the maximum term has passed, in exceptional cases, the court would decide on the prolongation of the term, if the convict is still dangerous to society, i.e. the perpetration of a new offence, perhaps of a grave one, is to be expected.

In several countries, Hungary among them, relatively indeterminate imprisonment is not regarded as a penalty but as a security (protective) measure, internment, an institution of re-adaptation, or, as it is called in Hungary, "custody of intensified severity", and frequently it is not employed as an independent penal measure, but as a subsidiary deprivation of liberty in addition to the determinate term. One of the main reasons for this organizational solution is that such classical principles of penal law as the determinate system of punishment, punishment in proportion with the gravity of the act, guilt based on free will, cannot be given up.

The signs of this view of adhering to the past can be discovered in the Hungarian legislation, too. Custody of intensified severity, introduced some years ago, with the lower and upper limits of 2 to 5 years, respectively, is applicable under certain conditions against recidivists who are sentenced for the offence in question to at least one year's confinement (Art. 1., item A of Law decree No. 9, of 1974). That is, formulating it more clearly, a multiple recidivist is first sentenced to a determinate term in proportion to the gravity of the act (to more than one year). This he deserves according to the words and spirit of the Penal Code in force. And, according to Law decree No. 9 of 1974, it has to be supplemented by relatively indeterminate custody of intensified severity of between 2 and 5 years, which is not a punishment but only an "effective step" taken for the intensified protection of society against criminals particularly dangerous to public order and public security.

In reality, however, it means that a recidivist who would otherwise be sentenced to one year's imprisonment now has to serve at least three years in the most severe regime of confinement, in a prison. Custody of intensified severity, hence, is merely the prolongation of the punishment by at least two, at most five, years. The Law decree does not emphasize the possibility or importance of the re-education of such offenders, it mentions only the restraining of the offenders from crime; it is rather the touch of retribution that can be felt from its provisions. Setting out from the fact that "the relatively long term of imprisonment could not restrain them from the perpetration of new offences" the motivations of the Law decree finds that custody of increased severity is more suitable for that aim in the case of recidivists.

From the point of view of measures with a pedagogical content, I consider the proposals of the Varna preparatory conference for the XI. Congress of the International Association of Penal Law, and the General Report prepared on that basis, very significant. The Report clearly states that the traditional system of penal law, based on repression and having a retributive character, is no longer effective and it is not in harmony with the generally accepted humanist criminal policy, and, at the same time, this system is increasingly attacked from other points as well.[24]

[24] T. Király, "Progress of the Means and Methods of Penal Law", Lecture given at the International Symposium of Penal Law, Budapest, September 9-15, 1974.

IV The Effectiveness of Punishment

1 Measuring the Effectiveness of Punishment

The effectiveness of punishment appears more and more frequently as a topic in the literature of criminal sciences and the makers of criminal policy also urge such studies. All this seems natural, since the preventive aim of punishment may be attained only if effective measures are taken against the perpetrators of criminal offences. But we are less aware of the fact that we may speak of the effectiveness of punishment only if we find the aim of punishment in prevention, in resocialization of the offenders. Where the aim of punishment is retribution, the examination of the effectiveness of special prevention cannot even arise since the aim of punishment is automatically attained as soon as the implementation of punishment is completed. Thus, the intensification of studies concerning the effectiveness of punishment also shows that retribution, repression, are driven out more and more from among the means of crime control, and criminal-pedagogical means ensuring the forming of the consciousness, persuasion, are becoming predominant.

As can be seen, the problems of the effectiveness of punishment have a close connection with the definition of the aim of punishment. According to certain specialists setting out from this, punishment may be considered as effective if it attains its aim, if it results in the prevention of crime.[1] The noted Soviet scholar Shargorodsky regards the dynamics of crime as the criterion of the effectiveness of punishment. He studied the general preventive effects in the dynamism of crime as a whole, and the general preventive effects in the dynamism of recidivism. In his opinion, punishment can be effective only if the right conditions are given, for no system of punishment can lead to the desired results if the objective requirements ensuring the effectiveness of punishment are unsatisfied. Shargorodsky mentions as such requirements: 1. The harmony between the prohibitions of criminal law and the objective laws of society; 2. the observance of the principles of socialist criminal law; 3. the inevitability of punishment; 4. the stability of criminal policy; 5. the harmony between criminal policy and the sense of justice of society.[2]

[1] I. M. Galperin, "Rol'nakazaniya pri sotsialnykh izmeneniyakh", *Sovietskoe Gosudarstvo i Pravo* No. 3, 1972.

[2] M. D. Shargorodsky, *Nakazanie, ego tslei i effektivnost'*, Leningrad: Izdatel'stvo Leningradskogo Universiteta, 1973.

Without approving of, or criticizing, this formulation or grouping of the criteria of effectiveness, we may say that phenomena can exert their influence only if the conditions allow it. It is very important to realize this also in the effectiveness studies of punishments.

a) *Special prevention.* When the effectiveness of punishment is discussed in the literature of criminal sciences, it is usually understood as the attainment of the special preventive aim of punishment. For this reason, the measure of effectiveness is defined in various ratios of recidivism. Such a viewing of effectiveness is, admittedly or unadmittedly, the consequence of the theoretical position according to which punishment may be considered effective if it can restrain offenders from the perpetration of new offences under any circumstances of life.[3] In this case it is expected from punishment that it should render offenders resistant to criminogenic external influences and should reinforce their intention to adapt themselves to social requirements (the law) to the same extent as can be seen with the highly socialized part of the population. If we accept this view completely, the effectiveness of punishment can in fact be measured through the indices of recidivism. Criminological studies in this sphere usually accept this conception.[4]

There is, however, another view, according to which the effectiveness of punishment in terms of special prevention can be measured by the indices of recidivism only indirectly and with certain corrections, since it is only the formation of the intention of social adaptation on the perpetrator's part that can be required of punishment, particularly of imprisonment.[5] If this subjective condition of social adaptation has been formed, the punishment has attained its aim, exerted a favourable influence. The objective conditions, on the other hand, should be considered as in the case of any other human being who does not intend to commit a criminal offence, i.e. it depends on future effects, on the constellation of objective and subjective causal factors, whether he will commit a new offence or not.

That a certain proportion of people commit criminal offences follows regularly from the level of social development (objective conditions, the level of consciousness). At present, there are still circumstances which determine the behaviour of certain people toward the perpetration of criminal offences. And if this is true, it also has to be true that a certain percentage of offenders will commit criminal offences again following the regularities, even if the punishment has produced in them the intention of social adaptation. From this it follows logically that if we measure

[3] See A. E. Natashev and N. A. Struchkov, *Teoreticheskaya osnova ispravit'elnotrudovogo prava,* Moscow: Yuridicheskaya Literatura, 1967.

[4] See P. Uusitalo, "After fall i brott after frigivning öppna reszpektive slutna anstalter", in: *Collected Studies in Criminological Research,* Vol. I, Council of Europe, 1968; D. Davidovič et al., *Efikasnost kratkihkazni lisenja slobode* (The Effectiveness of Short-Term Prison Sentence), Belgrade, 1965.

[5] J. Vigh and K. Gönczöl, "A fiatalkorú bűnelkövetők redukciója az utógondozás során" (The Reduction of Juvenile Offenders During Aftercare), *Jogtudományi Közlöny* No. 8, 1972.

b) *General prevention.* In the preceding parts we have discussed some of the main theoretical issues of the special preventive effectiveness of punishment and we may say that the measurement of the effectiveness has not been worked out adequately yet, a number of theoretical questions and problems of counting are still not decided. This is even truer in connection with the evaluation of the general preventive effects of punishments. There are authors who believe that special prevention has a primary importance, i.e. the content of the various penalties should go by its requirements, while others believe the same of general prevention. By now it has become clear that the general preventive effect of a punishment is to promote the formation of the correct social consciousness, the observance of social requirements, i.e. to restrain people from violations of the law through prescribing and applying a detriment, a *malum,* for such acts. And this is so even in cases where the application of special preventive measures would not be necessary because the return effect of the deed and the accompanying circumstances have exerted a sufficient preventive influence. In such cases the application of a punishment is justified only by the interests of general prevention.

As far as the effectiveness of general prevention is concerned, the most common opinion is that punishments have a general preventive effect mostly on the morally unstable elements of society, that it is these elements that punishments restrain from the perpetration of criminal offences.[14] Certain authors believe this preventive effect to operate only in a narrow scope,[15] whereas others presume it to be felt in relatively broad strata of the population.[16] In my opinion, independently of how large a proportion of the population we consider unstable, the general preventive effect of punishment can not be given such a limited interpretation.

It is a generally accepted thesis that the various forms of establishing responsibility have an important function in the adjustment to social requirements, in the formation of the awareness of responsibility. Hence, the establishment of criminal responsibility and its indispensable part, taking a punitive measure, have their effects on the formation of the consciousness of the whole population, albeit the majority of law-abiding citizens are restrained from the perpetration of criminal offences not by the fear of punishment but by the awareness that adaptation to social requirements, i.e. recognizing social interests as the interests of the individual, is the most certain way of satisfying needs in the long run. Realizing this, however, necessarily implies the knowledge of the life of offenders, criminals, the social value judgement concerning them. The general preventive effect of punishment, consequently, is regarded as one of the components forming the awareness of responsibility.

The criminological examination of the general preventive effect of punishment is

[14] See Shmarov, *op. cit.*

[15] N. A. Belyaev, *Tseli nakaznija i sredstva ikh dostizhenjiya v ispravitel'nykh trudovykh uchrezhdeniya,* Leningrad, 1963.

[16] A. V. Sakharov, *O lichnosti prestupnika i prichinakh prestupnosti v SSSR,* Moscow, 1961.

particularly difficult, because in the broad masses of those who do not commit criminal offences it is difficult to determine what proportion of the factors forming law-abiding behaviour is represented by the effect of punishment. We can say no more with certainty than that the effects vary from person to person. There are people in whose case behaviour satisfying social requirements has become a stereotype form due to their consistent practice, and such people would not satisfy their needs in an illegal way even in situations ensuring the certainty of the failure of the establishment of responsibility. Or, even if the satisfaction of the need in an illegal way arises in the struggle of motives, motives harmonious with the obligations win easily, without negative emotional effects, due to the socialized attitude. And there are people who are restrained from satisfying their needs through the perpetration of offences by the legal detriment manifested in the punishment and even more by the social condemnation (by the family, friends, work-collective) entailed by the establishment of criminal responsibility. In such cases, the struggle of motives takes the form of a conflict and usually involves negative emotional effects.

At present, it is far from being a settled question what kinds of punishment ensure the best preventive effects. It has been a predominant view for a long time that it is severe punishments, causing grave detriments (suffering, corporal pain and mental anguish), perhaps the death penalty terminating even biological existence, that have the most deterring effects, and through that, restrain people from committing criminal offences. By now, practice has proved that the lack of the so-called severe kinds of punishment does not entail the increase, or at least a significant increase, of crime. There is no need for the death penalty or a punishment causing extreme suffering to ensure that duty-bound motives should win in the struggle of motives; making the case public, the loss of a position, property, perhaps freedom, will suffice.

In the case of individuals with whom these penalties do not have a role as motivating factors, extreme suffering or even death have not the same significance as for people in general. Such persons usually do not have adequate social connections, and for this reason the opinion of the collective is not significant to them, they do not have a social position, they do not have anything to lose, they have no property, they cannot be deprived of anything, and finally, due to the above traits, prison means only a form of life to them. Such people do not usually fear danger or death or, if they do, they do it in a way different from the majority of people. For this reason, severe punishments are not respected precisely by those they should affect the most, against whom they are applied primarily. It is only social advancement, obtaining a certain skill in a trade, building certain social connections, in a word resocialization, that can help these people. They can hardly be changed by retribution, by deterrence.[17]

[17] See the findings of the research program concerning homicide, conducted by the Research Group of Criminal Pedagogy of the National Headquarters of the Implementation of Punishments. (The library of the Headquarters)

Marx wrote a hundred years ago in his article on the death penalty:

"Statistics prove with the most complete evidence that since Cain the world has neither been intimidated nor ameliorated by punishment. Quite the contrary."[18]

This Marxian thesis is becoming generally accepted in our days. Lenin's frequently quoted observation that the general prevention effect of the punishment is to be found not as much in its severity as in its inevitability, is becoming more and more verified. A number of surveys prove, e.g. that long-term prison sentences of retributive character do not deter even prisoners from the perpetration of new offences.[19]

In measuring the effectiveness of punishment, it has also to be taken into consideration what observance of statutory provisions is intended to be ensured through the punishment. If a certain penal norm is contrary to, or not in accordance with, the development of society, the punishment applicable for its violation can hardly be effective.

Effectiveness indices used in the literature (recidivism, etc.) in reality do not measure the favourable effects of punishment but precisely its ineffectualness. This observation may seem formal at first glance since the lack of something within a system (in the sense of philosophy) is preconditioned by the presence of its opposite. Thus, the index of the ineffectualness of the punishment shows, at the same time, the ratio of the favourable effects, and vice versa. Using an example: if punishment proved to be effective in 75 per cent of the cases in a group of offenders, the ratio of ineffectual punishment is 25 per cent; in other words, if we know the index of effectiveness we also know that of ineffectualness. If we stay on this plane, it is really only a formality whether we speak of effectiveness or its lack. But we immediately find a material difference if we examine, e.g. the causes of effectiveness. On this plane we cannot infer unambiguously the causes of ineffectualness from the causes of effectiveness since the studied result is to be traced back to different causes, to different constellations of causes.[20] For the establishment of criminal responsibility it means that it is not enough merely to eliminate the negative, criminogenic factors in developing preventive measures, but the nature of the positive factors should also be determined.

These ideas have to be kept in mind particularly if we do not want to change our accepted phraseology and we speak consistently of the indices of effectiveness even if we deal, in fact, with the lack of effectiveness.

[18] K. Marx, "Capital Punishment" in: K. Marx and F. Engels, *Collected Works,* Vol. 11, Moscow, 1979, p. 496.

[19] W. H. Hammond and E. Chayen, *Persistent Criminals,* London: Tavistock Publication, 1963.

[20] On the constellation theory of causality see J. Vigh, K. Gönczöl, Gy. Kiss és Á. Szabó, *Erőszakos bűncselekmények és elkövetőik* (Violent Crimes), Budapest: Közgazdasági és Jogi Könyvkiadó, 1973.

2 The Achievements of Investigations into the Effectiveness of Punishment

Investigations into the effectiveness of punishment up to now, as we have mentioned, have studied primarily the special preventive effect of punishment and considered recidivism, re-conviction, as the criterion of effectiveness. On the basis of these investigations, a number of authors have come to the conclusion that the various penalties do not differ materially from each other in terms of effectiveness. The Danish criminologist Christiansen, for example, has written in one of his studies: "If we analyse the findings of the great number of studies concerning the effectiveness of the means of punishment, we have to admit that their great majority show little or no difference of various means of punishment in terms of effectiveness. These findings are sometimes called negative, which is a mistake, in my opinion, since the demonstration that the two (or more) compared educational methods are equally good means, we can choose either of them at our convenience. Consequently, we may think which means are the cheapest, which means are the most effective, which ones serve the recognized social aims the best, which ones ensure the maximum protection to society."[21]

A similar view is given expression in the work of Shoham and Sandberg. They compared suspended loss of freedom sentences with executable ones and draw the conclusion that the effectiveness of the punishments is more closely connected with the personality of the offenders than with the various kinds of punishment. They found the age and record of the offenders very significant among the personal traits.[22]

a) *Punishments not involving imprisonment.* Measuring effectiveness by the indices of recidivism, the majority of investigators believe that a material difference may be demonstrated between punishments not involving imprisonment and punishments involving "institutionalization", in favour of the former.

In one of the publications of the British Home Office, comparative data have been reported on the effectiveness of various penal measures grouped by the distribution of the age and previous record of the offenders.

According to the data, fines proved to be the most ranking even before probation.[23] One can read in the literature also of the GDR that the faith of the administration of justice in fines has increased and this may be explained by the high effectiveness indices of fines applied in cases when no deep conflict exists between the offender and society, i.e. in traffic and property misdemeanour cases.[24]

21 Karl. O. Christiansen's contribution at the Warsaw regional seminar; *Przeglad Penitencjarny i Kriminologiczny* (Warsaw), No. 4, 1972, p. 89.

22 S. Shoham and M. Sandberg, "Suspended sentences in Israel", *Crime and Delinquency,* January 1974.

23 Home Office (1964), "The Sentence of the Court", p. 40.

24 H. Wolf, "Zum Character und zur Anwendung der Geldstrafe", *Neue Justiz* No. 6, 1973.

According to the author of the paper, fines directly concern the monetary interests of the perpetrator and affect his future behaviour through that. On the basis of investigations carried out in Poland, Wasik also reports favourable results concerning the effects of fines. The proportion of recidivists of offenders sentenced to this penalty is only 11.2 per cent.[25]

A number of studies deal with the effectiveness of *probation*. W. Middendorf has written in his Report prepared for the VI. International Congress of Criminology:

"The hundred year's experience of probation in England and in America has proved the value of this institution. Probation is particularly suitable for replacing the punishment of Confinement since it makes it possible to avoid the harmful effects and high expenses concomitant with imprisonment."[26]

A favourable evaluation is given to the effectiveness of punishments not involving imprisonment (institutionalization) by other investigators as well. According to the studies of prognostication by Börjeson, of Sweden, educational methods applied to juveniles without penal institutions proved to be significantly more effective than criminal-pedagogical methods employed within penal institutions.[27]

However, in connection with the favourable effectiveness, indices of punishments not involving loss of freedom, we have to emphasize that according to the valid laws and the present judicial practice, they are usually employed in the case of less antisocial offenders, who are in conflict with society to a lesser extent than those sentenced to imprisonment. Thus, the ratios of recidivism have necessarily to be also more favourable. However, it is possible, even probable, that these more favourable ratios are accounted for in a fairly large percentage of the cases by this kind of punishment, in addition to the differences of the perpetrators.

b) *The effectiveness of imprisonment.* The most significant area of effectiveness studies is the punishment of imprisonment. Although it is true that the effectiveness of confinement cannot be fully evaluated without the other kinds of punishment, the comparison of the various forms of imprisonment, also provides a good opportunity for studies. In addition, these are the forms of punishment that are supposed to generate in their own process the intention of social adaptation on the part of the offenders' to shape the offenders, awareness of responsibility for the better.

Some confinement sentences are executed at present under prison conditions where restrictions, guarding, and work dominate without intensive pedagogical influencing and where retribution is above all the aim to be ensured. The other group of offenders sentenced to confinement serve their sentences in penal institutions where the prescribed form is an educational regime; these are mainly the institutions

[25] J. Wasik's contribution at the Warsaw regional seminar, Przeglad Penitencjarny i Kriminologiczny (Warsaw), No. 4, 1972.

[26] W. Middendorf, "Studies Concerning the Effectiveness of Probation", Section I, Informs. No. 4, p. 20.

[27] B. Börjeson, *Om Paföljders Verkningar,* Stockholm: Almquist and Wiksell, 1966.

for juveniles or the open, semi-free, and similar institution, where less restrictive conditions, approaching those of free life, dominate.

The examination of the effectiveness of *closed* and *open* or semi-free institutions has not substantiated the assumption that open institutions are much more effective. In the evaluation, however, it must be kept in mind here, too, that it was not identical or not completely identical groups of offenders that were compared. Usitalo from Finland, examining the effectiveness of closed prisons and open work-colonies has found only a minimal difference in favour of open institutions and has drawn the conclusion; "The more severe prison sentence did not prove to be more effective in preventing recidivism than the less severe punishment of the work-colonies."[28] Mannheim and Wilkins compared the recidivism rate of boys discharged from borstal institutions, and formed the opinion that those who assume the higher effectiveness of open institutes will be disappointed.[29]

Similarly, criminological investigations do not show materially significant differences between *long-term* and *short-term* prison sentences. Applying the method of Mannheim and Wilkins, Benson compared the recidivism rates of juveniles sentenced to 4 months imprisonment on the average, with those of juveniles sent to borstal institutions for one and a half years. According to his findings, the difference was negligible.[30] The same results were obtained by Weeks in the USA.[31]

Different data have been found by Soviet investigators. Avanesov and Rutgaizer using mathematical methods have concluded that, in the case of first offenders, the longer the term of the punishment served the higher the rate of those who do not commit a new offence. This positive correlation may be demonstrated for up to 6–7 year-long terms, and for this reason, in the authors' opinion, "the expedient upper limit of the punishment, from the point of view of restraining persons sent to correctional work-colonies of regular system for criminal offences of lower significance, may be conditionally accepted as 6 or 7 years."[32] Similar investigations were carried out involving first offenders convicted for grave intentional criminal offences. It was found that the rate of recidivism gradually decreased in proportion to the increase of the length of the imposed term of confinement. For this reason, the optimal upper limit of imprisonment was determined at 9 or 10 years.[33]

Similar findings were reported in Poland by Wasik with the qualification that ef-

[28] Uusitalo, *op. cit.*

[29] Mannheim and Wilkins, *op. cit.*

[30] S. Benson, "Prediction Method and Young Prisoners", *British Journal of Delinquency,* September 1959.

[31] H. A. Weeks, *Youthful Offenders at Highfields,* (1958).

[32] Avanesov and Rutgajzer, *op. cit.*

[33] G. A. Avanesov and G. Tumanov, "O vernykh granitsakh nakazaniya i vide lisheniya svobody", *Sotsialisticheskaya Zakonnost'* No. 7, 1969.

fectiveness decreased in the period between 3 and 18 months then increased significantly again.[34]

The effectiveness of short term imprisonment (under 6 months or one year) is commonly doubted, and therefore the restriction of its application, or its abolishment, is proposed.[35] According to the dominant view, in certain cases short-term imprisonment may be effective, mainly against first offenders.[36]

The Research Department of the Ministry of Justice of Japan also reports that no significant favourable changes have occurred in the behaviour of offenders during the implementation of short-term sentences; on the contrary, in many cases negative tendencies have developed.[37] One can read of similar unfavourable effects in the works of certain Soviet authors.[38]

In the sphere of *long-term* prison sentences (more than one year), determinate and relatively indeterminate sentences are judged differently from the point of view of effectiveness.

A number of investigators have concluded that *relatively indeterminate sentences* are somewhat more effective.[39] The higher effectiveness is due to a significant extent to the fact that offenders have an interest in forming their own position and future, and this form of punishment provides better opportunities for eliminating the antisocial attitude of the offenders.

It is a uniform experience of criminological investigations that *first offenders,* should they be sentenced to any kind of punishment, will commit new offences at a lower rate than recidivists, that multiple recidivism increases the chances of a new offence and that in youth (under 30) the rate of new convictions is higher than in older age, independently of the kind of punishment imposed.[40]

The majority of criminological investigations into the effectiveness of the penal systems of our age, of the various penalties, particularly imprisonment, show no significant difference in the special preventive effects of the various kinds of punishment. There are, however, a few investigators who optimistically consider these findings good, like the Danish Christiansen, when he sees only a good opportunity for selection. The majority, setting out precisely from the data, are doubtful of the

[34] Wasik, *op. cit.*

[35] N. A. Struchkov, "Nakazanie kak sredstvo borby s prestupnost'yu", *Sovietskoe Gosudarstvo i Pravo* no. 11, 1969.

[36] Davidovič et al., *op. cit.*

[37] T. Yamonato, "Research Concerning the Effect of Short-Term Liberty Depriving Penalty", *Bulletin of the Criminological Department,* 1964.

[38] See N. A. Struchkov, *Sovietskaya ispravitel'no-trudovaya politika i ee rol' v borbe s prestupnost'yu,* Saratov, 1970, p. 189.

[39] F. Meyer, *Rückfalls Prognose bei unbestimmt verurteilten Jugendlichen,* Bonn, 1956; M. von Hinüber, *Untersuchungen über die Lebensbewärung unbestimmt verurteilter Jugendlicher,* Göttingen, 1961.

[40] Hood, *op. cit.;* D. Glaser, *The Effectiveness of Prison and Parole System,* New York, 1964.

special preventive effects and wishes to change the system of punishment according to the requirements of general prevention, the protection of society. The ineffectiveness of the Swedish prison system providing almost perfect objective conditions of education has only intensified the doubts concerning special prevention or even justified the denial of such effects (about two-thirds of the discharged prisoners commit new offences.) This explains why it is becoming a generally accepted idea in Holland and in the Scandinavian states that if the various forms of prison sentence served in penal institutions do not differ from each other in their effectiveness, then, considering the requirements of humanism and economy, short term loss of freedom sentences not longer than half a year are the most expedient, since the requirements of general prevention are effectively satisfied in this way as well. For example, in Sweden, in 1970, 69 per cent of offenders sentenced to imprisonment were sentenced to a term of less than four months, 22 per cent were sentenced to terms of between 4 and 12 months, and 9 per cent were sentenced to one year or more.[41] In Holland, in 1970, 60 per cent of loss of freedom sentences were shorter than 3 months, 80 per cent less than 6 months.[42]

The studies of effectiveness described so far measure and compare the effectiveness of the kinds and forms of punishment already existing. The Danish study comparing two groups of offenders sentenced to imprisonment is materially different from them.[43] In the first group, intensive and consistent measures of education were taken in order to ensure the re-education of the offenders and adequate assistance was provided for their re-socialization, i.e. the objective conditions for the realization of the intention to adapt were ensured for them. The members of the other group were left under the usual, traditional conditions. There was a significant difference between the rates of recidivism of the two groups. Only a small ratio of those who had been under intensive care committed new criminal offences and even they did so within a short time after their discharge from prison. This fact shows these recidivists did not yet have the intensive intention of adaptation at the time of their discharge, either because the term of imprisonment had been incorrectly determined by the sentence, or because the educational means used had not been in harmony with their personality.

The findings of the Danish study programme demonstrate that imprisonment may be rendered a more effective punishment, as long as the conditions of resocialization are created. Soviet authors, too, frequently mention that the present conditions of the implementation of prison sentences do not always exert a favourable influence on offenders. V. Shmarov, for example studying the phases of the process of social adaptation, observed in one of his papers that the pedagogical and psycho-

[41] *Kriminal varden* (Statistical Yearbook), 1972, Stockholm: S.O.S. 1973, p. 11.

[42] D. Van der Grient, *The Treatment of Offenders and Their Rehabilitation. Some Experiments in the Netherlands,* The Hague, 1973.

[43] See Christiansen, *op. cit.*

logical atmosphere in the period preceding release is not good, owing to the indifference or roughness of various educators, and in such situations the intention to abide by the law can hardly be formed in the offenders. In addition to creating the proper psychological and pedagogical atmosphere, the author considered the introduction of gradualness extremely important, i.e. that offenders should spend a period before their release in a grade of deprivation of liberty close to the conditions of free life, in the so-called "settlement colony".[44]

Criminological studies have made it evident by now that under the conditions of closed prisons it is impossible to prepare the inmates for free life, it is impossible to make them practice the forms of behaviour, the solutions of situational problems, which could make them prepared to satisfy social norms in the conditions of free life. For this reason, it seems right if we do not regard open and closed penal institutions primarily as independent forms of the implementation of punishment but as various grades of the homogeneous system of institutions of punishment implementation. This, of course, does not exclude that a certain group of offenders, particularly those with a short-term sentence, should serve their full time in the same institution.

Hungarian studies of the effectiveness of prison sentences also bear witness to the fact that the present system is not effective enough, that it could be made much more effective through the intensified use of the means of criminal pedagogy. According to the findings of an investigation carried out recently, the intention of social adaptation has not been formed in about 30 per cent of offenders just before being released. A definitely favourable effect of the punishment could be demonstrated only with 40 per cent of the offenders. In the remaining percentage the intention of adaptation developed due to other factors (family, place of work, friends).[45]

It has also been found in the examination of general prevention that it is not so much the length of the term of confinement as the punishment itself, (independent of its quality and measure) and social condemnation entailed by the establishment of criminal responsibility and other kinds of unpleasant events (interrogation, trial, etc.) that have restraining effects.

The creation of the intention and ability to adapt socially is only one of the preconditions of resocialization. The other indispensable precondition is after-care, the creation of the objective conditions. Hungarian and foreign experience prove beyond doubt that the establishment of responsibility is incomplete without adequate after-care. For this reason, at present, resocialization has two clearly distinguished phases; the one within and the other after release from the institution.[46] The

[44] I. V. Shmarov, "Sotsialnaya adaptatsiya osvobozhdennykh ot nakazaniya", *Sovietskoe Gosudarstvo i Pravo,* No. 11, 1971.

[45] Vigh and Tauber, *op. cit.*

[46] See Shmarov, *op. cit.*

Danish survey mentioned also shows the perspectives of effective punishment in this respect. But we could refer to Hungarian findings too. Where the official network of aftercare has been properly used to serve the interests of juveniles, favourable results are necessarily shown.[47]

If the effectiveness or ineffectiveness of various kinds of punishment are studied, the question arises whether the known kinds of punishment and their varieties are properly used. In my opinion, Dr. Hood says correctly in his quoted work that one kind of punishment may be beneficial for certain offenders and may be absolutely ineffectual for others. Penal codes frequently prescribe the same penalty for perpetrators with different personalities and these penalties are usually applied in the same way. Similarly, it is not rare either that people with the same attitudes receive deferring penalties as a consequence of the act-centred approach.[48] The demand for complete individualization evidently cannot be realistic but the more differentiated application of the various penalties is a realistic demand.

At first glance, studies carried out in the sphere of effectiveness do not seem to have helped in finding the perspectives of the system of punishment; rather, they seem to have enforced the idea of denying the present system. A number of questions have been raised and the answer to them is still lacking.

No doubt the traditional views on criminal justice, and the institutions that are in harmony with them, are in crisis, as pointed out by the theses of the XI. Congress of the International Association of Penal Law.[49] But the recognition that the penal system that is built on the freedom of the will, or on the relative freedom of the will, and is primarily concerned with retribution, repression, no longer satisfies social requirements brings up the possibility of creating a new, better system of penal measures. For specialists who have a sense of history, the change in the nature of measures applied against offenders which has been experienced during the last two decades, and the new reform tendencies concerning criminal law, outline the directions of development. It is possible to surmise the theories on which the new system of establishing responsibility is going to be built and the new institutions in which the establishment of responsibility is going to take place. In my opinion, the theoretical basis can only be the universal law of causality and the principle of determinism which are accepted as theoretical bases in the socialist philosophy of law. The consistent putting into effect of these is preconditioned by the introduction of a wide variety of penalties with preventive aims and a pedagogical content. The struggle for the resocialization or social adaptation of offenders will create the

[47] I. Babay, "A fiatalkorú visszaesők helyzete és a hivatásos pártfogók működése" (The Position of Juvenile Recidivists and the Operation of Probation Officers), *Belügyi Szemle* No. 1, 1975.

[48] H. J. Eysenck, *Crime and Personality,* London: Routledge & Kegan Paul, 1964.

[49] E. Cséka, "A Nemzetközi Büntetőjogi Társaság budapesti kongresszusának várnai és freiburgi előkészítő kollokviuma" (The Varna and Freiburg Preparatory Colloquium of the Budapest Congress of the International Association of Penal Law) *Jogtudományi Közlöny* No. 4, 1974.

measures that will best serve the preventive aims. Good examples of this are the forms of establishing responsibility that are closely connected to society, and penal measures taken with the assistance of society, which are widely used methods in the socialist countries.[50]

In the socialist countries, Hungary among them, in the sphere of crime prevention, the possibilities that follow from the social conditions are naturally far from being adequately exploited (e.g. social tribunals, aftercare at the place of employment.)

The formation of new ways of establishing responsibility and new punitive measures is significantly influenced by the movement of the "new social defense" which denies all forms of retributive measures and strives to make measure with preventive aims and a pedagogical content general. However, there are favourable tendencies, we must not forget that we may create, as we certainly will, a better and more effective penal system, but the reduction of crime and recidivism is to be expected only if the objective conditions of social adaptation are gradually created, parallel to the improvement of the system of establishing criminal responsibility, and if favourable changes take place in social relations and in the interrelationships of people.

[50] See A. Senchin, "A fiatalkorú jogsértőkre kiszabott büntetések hatékonysága a Szovjetunióban" (Effectiveness of Punishment Applied for Juveniles in the Soviet Union), *Magyar Jog* No. 8, 1973.

V Some Problems of Sentencing

1 The Powers and Function of the Court

The methods and means used for the resocialization of offenders, to restrain them from committing new offences, are defined by statutes, primarily by the provisions of criminal law. The provisions of criminal law, however, are different in different countries. Some of the differences concern the means applied. There are countries where the penal system is based on imprisonment while in others punishments not involving confinement come to the fore. The circumstance of how wide a scale of penalties may be found in a particular country and with what aims they are applied depends above all on lawmakers. From the point of view of sentencing, however, the differences apparent in the powers of the courts, i.e. how much discretion the courts have in the selection of the penalty and its measure, are more important. Some laws grant broad discretionary powers to courts (e.g. certain Scandinavian states, or England) for the individualization of the punishment, while others strongly limit judicial individualization of the punishment. The school of criminological penal law that strives for the creation of a penal system with preventive aims and a pedagogical content, necessarily demands that courts should have "broad discretionary powers", as Professor Christiansen of Denmark puts it, in choosing the penalty and its extent corresponding best with the personality of the offender.[1]

N. Walker considers one of the principles of sentencing that "Sentencers should be free, and should do their best, to choose for each offender the measure most likely to correct his tendency to break the law as he had done (or, in a more ambitious version, to break the law in any way at all)."[2]

The expansion of the possibility of individualization to this extent, of course, intensifies the demands on the court. The judge, in addition to determining the perpetration of the criminal offence and the possibility of establishing the responsibility of the perpetrator, has to study intensively the perpetrator's personality, the conditions of his life, and, considering all this, he has to reflect upon the applicability of the various penalties from the point of view of their effectiveness. If it is expected from the judicial sentence that the penal measure should exert a

[1] The contribution of K. O. Christiansen at the regional seminar of Central European countries; *Przeglad Penitencjarny i Kriminologiczny* No. 4, (Warsaw), 1972, p. 85.

[2] N. Walker, *Sentencing in a Rational Society,* Allen Lane, The Penguin Press, 1969, p. 119.

Simor's assertion, it is never possible to prognosticate future criminality with absolute certainty. Prognostication has of necessity only a lower or higher probability. And should there be even the smallest possibility of the offender's correction, this should not be left out of consideration—on the contrary, the penal measure should be applied according to that. Of course, it is a serious responsibility, because stereotyped sentencing has to be replaced by serious deliberation, by a way of sentencing where the offender's future is kept in view.

From the fact that there are hardened recidivists one may equally infer—incorrectly—their ineducability or—correctly—the inadequate special preventive effects of the penal measure. In my opinion, the data verify the latter. The survey among violent offenders carried out by the Department of Criminology of Eötvös Loránd University calls our attention to the necessity for the intensification of the preventive effects of punishments to be used in the case of offenders with a criminal record. The relevant statistical data may be of interest here, too.[11] (Table 17)

Table 18

The distribution of the studied violent offenders by their sentences and criminal record

Punishments	No record	Criminal record		Total
		recidivist	non-recidivist	
Death sentence	1	—	1	2
Imprisonment				
15-20	2	—	—	2
12-15 years	4	—	—	4
8-12 years	3	—	—	3
5- 8 years	8	4	2	14
3- 5 years	13	2	8	23
2- 3 years	17	8	8	33
1- 2 years to be implemented	17	5	10	32
suspended	2	—	—	2
30 days-1 year to be implemented	34	10	18	62
suspended	37	1	7	45
Corrective-educative labour	15	2	3	20
Fine	5	—	—	5
Total:	158	32	57	247

[11] J. Vigh, K. Gönczöl, Gy. Kiss and Á. Szabó, *Erőszakos bűncselekmények és elkövetőik* (Violent Crimes), Budapest: Közgazdasági és Jogi Könyvkiadó, 1973, p. 318.

The distribution of violent offenders is very remarkable. Of violent offenders those with no criminal record received heavier sentences than those who had been punished previously, although it would be natural the other way round even from the point of view of retribution. For example, among those who had a previous record there were none who received an imprisonment term longer than 8 years, while among first offenders the number of such offenders was 9. Although the number, i.e. nine, is not high in itself, it is not a random phenomenon, in my opinion, but real interrelations may be discovered behind it. These nine persons were convicted for homicide, rape and intentionally endangering life committed in the sphere of their occupation. It is a fact that these offences, or their varieties, are threatened with severe punishments in the Code, independently of the criminal record of the offender. This cannot, however, be an explanation in itself, since these offences could be committed not only by first offenders. The data, on the one hand,

Table 19

The distribution of the studied violent offenders by their punishments and by the number of their previous sentences

Punishment	No record	1—3	4—8	9 or more	Total
		previous sentences			
Death sentence	1	—	1	—	2
Imprisonment					
15–20 years	2	—	—	—	2
12–15 years	4	—	—	—	4
8–12 years	3	1	—	—	4
5– 8 years	8	5	1	—	14
3– 5 years	13	10	2	—	25
2– 3 years	17	12	3	1	33
1– 2 years to be implemented	17	10	5	1	33
suspended	2	—	—	—	2
30 days–1 year to be implemented	34	25	5	—	64
suspended	37	8	—	—	45
Corrective-educative labour	15	5	—	—	20
Fine	5	—	—	—	5
Total:	158	76	17	2	253

show that those who receive long-term prison sentences as first offenders try to avoid recidivism or the perpetration of offences for which they may receive long-term sentences. On the other hand, and this is probably the stronger factor, the so-called incorrigible criminals are not among the perpetrators of the gravest offences, i.e. not among those who were sentenced to long-term imprisonment but among those who received relatively short-term sentences.

Taking the data of the table into consideration, it seems the criminal record is not adequately measured, together with the gravity of the offence, in the process of sentencing; in other words, the requirements of special prevention are not given a proper place in sentencing. The correctness of this assumption is substantiated by the next Table. (Table 19)

It is clear from the data that the rise in the number of the previous sentences is in inverse ratio to the length of the imposed imprisonment terms. Such sentencing is possible only in a penal system where the principle dominates that punishment should be proportional to the act, and, consequently, the examination of the personality and the objective circumstances of the offender, and, therefore, the requirements of special prevention, are restricted to the background. The existence of unreformed offenders is necessary from the point of view of the sentencing practice as well. This does not mean, however, that they are also incorrigible, for, at present, even the institutions having the task of implementing prison sentences do not have a regime of adequate pedagogical content.

2 Mitigating and Aggravating Circumstances

Mitigating and aggravating circumstances also deserve mention in connection with sentencing. In a penal system determining the kinds and measures of punishment in their foundations, the personal circumstances of the offender, his personality traits, can mitigate or aggravate punishments only to a small extent. In turn, the application of penal measures with preventive aims and an educational content attributes intensified significance to this aspect. In the practice of Hungarian courts, the mitigating or aggravating circumstances are taken into consideration, apart from a small percentage of the cases.

According to the data of the mentioned survey of crimes of violence, the courts took only mitigating circumstances into consideration in 27.3 per cent of the cases, only aggravating circumstances were found in 6.7 per cent and both mitigating and aggravating circumstances in 62.2 per cent of the cases. We have no data concerning the extent to which these circumstances mitigated or aggravated the punishment that would have been imposed otherwise, or what punishments would have been imposed by the courts without these circumstances.

The frequency of taking the various mitigating and aggravating circumstances into consideration allows a glimpse into the structure of judicial deliberation.

Table 20
Mitigating circumstances taken into consideration in the case of the surveyed violent offenders[12]

Mitigating circumstances	number	per cent
Clean record	132	25.6
Confession	131	25.4
Married family status	109	21.1
Mental or other illness	37	7.2
Youth	26	5.1
The victim's own contribution	23	4.5
Disorganized family life	13	2.5
Good attitude to work	13	2.5
Old age	8	1.6
Causing minor damage	4	0.8
The offender being injured himself	2	0.4
Other	17	3.3
Total:	515	100.0

About two-thirds of the mitigating circumstances were accounted for by a clean record, married family status and confession. Other factors appeared only as a small percentage. In the evaluation of the frequency ratios it is a serious problem that we do not always have data showing in what percentage of the cases these circumstances are present and what their ratio is when the courts actually take them into consideration. For example confession was mentioned as a mitigating circumstance in 25.4 per cent of the cases, in other words, with 131 of the 267 persons surveyed. It is not known whether the other 136 persons confessed at all, and if they did, why their confessions were not considered to be mitigating circumstances, whether because they were not repentant enough or whether these circumstances could be taken into consideration from the point of view of qualifying the act. Married family status can be evaluated to a certain extent. 52.7 per cent of the offenders surveyed were married, in other words, in more than 2/3 of the cases the family status was considered a mitigating circumstance although 10 per cent of the families were childless and 21 per cent of the offenders could not adapt to the ties of the family.

On the basis of the data, it seems that married family status as a mitigating circumstance is mechanically accepted in a small percentage of the cases, especially if we keep in mind the finding of the Supreme Court, namely that "having several children, as a mitigating circumstance, benefits only a person who takes care of his family."[13]

[12] *Loc. cit.*, p. 32.; the data concern 267 persons.

[13] Supreme Court, Bf. II 750/1953. decision.

An opposite trend may be discovered in the evaluation of the attitude to work. The frequency of this mitigating circumstance was 2.5 per cent, i.e. it was mentioned with only 13 offenders. However, 74 persons, i.e. 27.7 per cent of the offenders, liked working. According to the practice of the court, liking work and good work are not mitigating circumstances.[14] Against that we have the opinion that conscientious, good work of many years, even if it has not produced an "outstanding" performance, should deserve more attention and ought to be attributed a more significant role in sentencing. It is particularly at the present stage of our social development that good work performance should be properly recognized.

A different evaluation of the attitude to work is needed in the realm of aggravating circumstances as well. According to the data of the survey, the most frequent aggravating circumstances were a criminal record and the frequent perpetration of the same offence.

The wrong attitude to work or a work-avoiding way of life were not even enumerated among the aggravating circumstances, although 14 of the violent offenders surveyed did not like working, and in their own words 18 of them had not done any work during the last five years preceding their convictions. From the point of view of preventive and educative penal measures, these factors must not be left out of consideration. However, it is self-evident that the punishment of a person liking work and that of a person who avoids work should be different not primarily in the duration of the term of imprisonment or in the amount of the fine, but in the kind of punishment imposed. It seems logical that a perpetrator who likes working and does his work conscientiously needs the application of different means of criminal pedagogy than the parasitic who avoids work, in order to teach him to adapt to social requirements.

A criminal or clean record have an outstanding role among aggravating and mitigating factors. These factors are commonly taken into consideration by the courts. A clean record was evaluated as a mitigating circumstance with about 50 per cent of the offenders, while the ratio of offenders with clean records was 64 per cent; at the same time, a criminal record was taken into account as an aggravating circumstance with only 23 per cent of offenders, although 36 per cent of the offenders had a criminal record. These data do not show more without a coefficient of reckoning than that neither of the factors are automatically taken into consideration.

In connection with the regular or chance nature of crime, we have already seen that the categorization of perpetrators as first offenders and repeaters (which basically corresponds to the categories of offenders with clean or criminal records) reflects the socialization of the perpetrator's personality only in a rough approximation. For this reason, it is more correct to operate in sentencing with the concepts of regular and chance perpetration. The concepts of regular or hardened criminal show

[14] Földvári, *op. cit.*, p. 342.

Table 21

Aggravating circumstances taken into consideration in case of the surveyed violent offenders[15]

Aggravating circumstances	Number	Per cent
Criminal record	61	21.0
The offence being frequent	55	18.9
The brutal way of perpetration	32	11.0
The offence caused grave injury	30	10.3
Alcoholic intoxication	20	6.9
Frequent hooliganism	19	6.6
Continuous perpetration	16	5.5
The victim being a family member	15	5.2
Cumulation of offences	15	5.2
The offence caused light injury	7	2.4
Other	20	7.0
Total:	290	100.0

most clearly where forced education is needed most. It was as a consequence of this recognition that the idea of relatively indeterminate prison sentences has arisen also in Hungary.

*

In our discussion of this topic we included only those main issues of sentencing that need perhaps the most attention from the point of view of passing preventive and educative sentences.

To avoid misapprehension, I consider it necessary to note that even if the intensified requirements set for sentencing are satisfied to the maximum extent we have to reckon with a certain number of faulty, ineffective sentences. A punishment with the aim of prevention always has the nature of prognostication, it is to ensure certain effects for the future.[16] From this it follows that the value of the sentences increases together with the increase of probability. Precisely for this reason, the work of a judge or the courts cannot be measured through the faults, or ineffectiveness, of one particular sentence, it is measurable only through the indices of effectiveness of a great number of sentences.

As can be seen, a certain percentage of error appears in sentencing, and in the implementation of punishment as well, and for this reason, the special preventive effect of the punishment cannot be complete in reality, i.e. it can be considered regular that the intention of social adaptation is not formed by a certain percentage of the offenders.

[15] J. Vigh, K. Gönczöl, Gy. Kiss and Á. Szabó, *op. cit.*, p. 325. The data concern 267 persons.

[16] See T. Király, "Valószínűségi elemek a büntetéskiszabásban" (Elements of Probability in Sentencing), *Jogtudományi Közlöny*, No. 1, 1971.

VI The Need for Developing Aftercare

Like the penal system with the aims of prevention and an educational content, the institution of aftercare can be traced back theoretically to the universal law of causality, to the principle of determinism. If we accept these principles we have necessarily to recognize that punishment with preventive aims and an educational content is not enough even in its most effective form to prevent the repetition of the offence, recidivism, in the case of a significant ratio of offenders, since the intention of social adaptation is only one of the components of the future behaviour of the offender. The second component is the objective conditions, as has already been discussed, that surround the perpetrator after the sentence has been imposed or implemented. Thus, it is an indispensable precondition of preventing the repetition of the offence that the objective conditions should render possible the realization of the intention to adapt. The recognition of these facts has led to the idea that assistance has to be given to offenders who need it, to promote their resocialization.

History proves that as punishment with preventive aims and a pedagogical content has gained ground and the determinative force of the objective conditions is admitted so the number of institutions providing help for offenders grows. It is juvenile offenders who were first declared, on a scientific basis, to be offenders in whose case punishment with a pedagogical content and various forms of state and social assistance may be used to ensure their resocialization. Thus, the special system of establishing responsibility has been created, and the institutions of patronage and aftercare have been formed. And the outlook that first appeared together with the struggle for reforms of penal law at the turn of the century and created the education-centred penal law of juveniles, all over Europe and even beyond Europe, is gaining new force nowadays and demands the complete re-structuralization of the whole system of establishing criminal responsibility. The demand for making the penal system with preventive aims and a pedagogical content general also for adults is more and more urgent and, together with that, the demand for the establishment of institutions that will assist convicts is becoming stronger, too.

Good examples of taking care of offenders may be seen in the Soviet Union (e.g. the taking of responsibility for the offender by fellow-workers) and also in other socialist countries. In a number of capitalist countries, a network of supervisors and aftercare officers has been created. In Sweden, for example on 1st January, 1972, altogether 2188 professional aftercare officers or supervisors and 10,053 volunteers were dealing with 22.895 offenders not in prison.[1] Similarly favourable ratios can be found also in England or in Holland.[2] In these countries the accepted view is that financial resources made available by the decrease in the number of persons sentenced to confinement should be used partially for the modernization of the institutions and partially for expanding the network of aftercare.

The patronage of juvenile offenders may be considered adequate in Hungary, too. According to the provisions of the Penal Code, a juvenile on probation, or who has been sentenced by the court to corrective-educative work, or whose prison sentence has been suspended, or who is on parole, who has been temporarily discharged from a corrective institution, is under the supervision of patronage. (Art. 100). According to the provisions of Decree No. 6 of 1969 MM, supervision of patronage may also be ordered if the juvenile offender is permanently discharged from the penal institution before passing his 18th year of age, if it is needed.

In order to improve the work of patronage, Decree No. 131 of 1970 MM rendered possible the employment of professional patronage officers. Their function is to perform the obligations of supervisors, to direct the work of volunteer supervisors, and to co-ordinate the measures taken by the agencies competent in this sphere.

It is Government Decree No. 12 of 1965 that first regulated comprehensively the assistance and aftercare of adult offenders. The Government Decree reflected the criminological view that taking care of offenders is a state and social task. According to Art. 3 of the Decree, aftercare was obligatory in the case of offenders under local banishment, multiple recidivists or hardened criminals, in the case of offenders who had been sentenced to a term of imprisonment longer than three years, who needed assistance or supervision in the opinion of the authority of the implementation of punishment, or who asked for assistance in finding a job.

However, aftercare under that decree was restricted to finding a job and providing minimal financial aid to the offenders. The Decree provided for the solution of the problems of finding a place to live, for solving family, cultural and other problems, related to adaptation. According to the Decree, aftercare was the responsibility of the apparatus of the local councils, which were overburdened with other types of cases, so that even these limited tasks were performed ineffectively, frequently mechanically, owing to the lack of personnel.[3] The experience of aftercare work done by social organizations (Interests Protection Committee of the Youth Organization, Group of Students of Criminology of the Eötvös Loránd University) prove

[1] M. Althar-Cedenberg, *Probation and Parole in Sweden,* Stockholm, 1972.

[2] J. Vigh, "A bűnözőkkel való bánásmód Angliában" (The Treatment of Offenders in Great Britain), *Magyar Jog* No. 11—12. 1971; *The Netherland Prison System,* The Hague, 1972.

[3] See T. Tavassy, "A visszaeső bűnözők szabadulás utáni helyzetéről" (On the Circumstances of Recidivists after their Release), *Kriminalisztikai Tanulmányok,* Vol. 6, Budapest, 1968.

that at the present level of the mentality of people and the educational effects of imprisonment, well-organized aftercare can do a lot to reduce recidivism.[4]

This was recognized by Law-decree No. 20 of 1975 of the Presidential Council of the People's Republic which regulated anew the aftercare of offenders discharged from prison. The Law decree took aftercare from the jurisdiction of local councils and made it the responsibility of the courts and ordered the establishment of a network of professional patrons operating under the courts with the assistance of volunteer activists.

A further significant step was taken by the Law decree when it prescribed that in addition to finding a job for released offenders social assistance had to be provided for them and they had to be helped in finding accomodation, i.e. the state helped the offenders released from prison in creating the basic conditions of life and thus it created the objective conditions of social adaptation, at least partially.

Aftercare concerns two categories of offenders, i.e. it involves

a) providing assistance for offenders released from prison if they need it and

b) the supervision and control of, and providing assistance, for persons convicted for intentional offences in whose case there is a reason to believe they may commit new offences.

Violations of the rules of behaviour prescribed for the aftercare period have been declared by the Law-decree to be administrative infractions and may be penalized with incarceration or a fine up to 5,000 forints.

On the basis of the experience of the work of aftercare being done by the Department of Criminology of the Eötvös Loránd University since 1965, we can classify the offenders from the point of view of aftercare into four groups;

1. The first group embraces the offenders who have the intention of social adaptation at the time of their release from prison and in whose case the objective conditions of social adaptation are also present. This group accounts for about 40 per cent of the released offenders. They do not need aftercare, it may be presumed that they will find their place among law-abiding citizens without any special assistance.

2. The second group embraces the offenders that have the intention of social adaptation at the time of their release from prison, but need the assistance of society, to put their plans into practice (they need a job, a place to live, etc.) This group represents about 20 per cent of those released.

3. The third group includes the offenders who are no longer dangerous to society at the time of their release from prison but in whose minds the active acceptance of the fundamental norms of social co-existence is not yet formed, i.e. they do not have firm plans and ideas concerning their future.

The objective conditions of adaptation are present for a number of them. In spite

[4] J. Vigh, "A börtönből szabadult fiatalok utógondozásának néhány tapasztalata" (Some Experiences of the Aftercare of Juveniles Released from Prison), *Acta Facultatis Politico-Iuridicae Universitatis Scientiarum de Rolando Eötvös Nominata,* Vol. IX, Budapest, 1969.

of that, they need aftercare supervision in our opinion. Their future behaviour depends to a great extent on what kind of people will constitute their environment, whether they will be able to form ties with their fellow-employees, families, law-abiding friends. The ratio of these convicts is about 15 per cent.

4. Finally, the fourth group embraces the offenders, in whose case imprisonment has not been effective, who leave the penal institution with a possibility or plan of committing new offences. This group is estimated to account for about 25 per cent of the offenders, and they usually do not ask for the assistance of society. They accept social assistance but try to hide away from officials so that they can live their own life according to their own norms.[5]

The estimated data show that about half of juvenile offenders sentenced to imprisonment need aftercare. Presumably, the ratio is approximately the same in the case of adults. If we take into consideration that not only some of those sentenced to confinement but a certain proportion of offenders sentenced to other kinds of punishment need assistance and help for their resocialization, the *raison d'être* of effective aftercare is perfectly clear.

Without discussing the problems of aftercare in detail or without making direct proposals as to its development, I should like to note some circumstances that have the significance of principle, of approach.

First, the activities of aftercare are significantly hindered by the view predominant among the general public concerning offenders.

The experience of aftercare shows that public opinion and the prejudice of fellow-workers frequently make the adaptation of offenders more difficult. The majority of fellow-workers receive released offenders without being helpful, with indifference, reservations or expressed antipathy. According to a Hungarian empirical study, only one third of released offenders were received with helpfulness by fellow-workers, another one third were met with indifference and about 15—20 per cent experienced aversion or contempt.[6] People usually consider the punishment which is proportional to the act to be just and do not believe that it will exert a favourable influence on the offender, particularly in the case of imprisonment. This outlook is based mainly on everyday experience. A significant proportion of offenders become recidivists. Hence, the aversion, withdrawal and fear on the part of law-abiding people are justified to a certain extent, and this could be changed only by an experience of the opposite. But it is not enough to make our penal system more effective in order to ensure the success of resocialization, but the way of thinking of

[5] J. Vigh and K. Gönczöl, "A társadalmi beilleszkedés objektív feltételeinek megteremtése a fiatalkorúak utógondozása során" (Creating Objective Conditions of Social Adaptation in the Course of Aftercare of Juvenile Offenders), *Jogtudományi Közlöny* No. 1, 1973.

[6] J. Vigh and I. Tauber, "A szabadságvesztés-büntetés hatékonyságának főbb jellemzői" (The Main Characteristics of the Effectiveness of the Imprisonment Punishment), *Jogtudományi Közlöny* No. 11, 1976.

people, their judgement of offenders should also be changed. It has to be made known to people outside the circle of specialists that offenders can be educated through the proper measures, through changing their circumstances and personality, to be law-abiding citizens, and that the means of criminal law are not sufficient in this work, that the assistance of the state and society also is needed, and the understanding and help of the family members and fellow-workers do not come last in this respect.

However, the creation of the organization of aftercare, which requires material and personal resources, providing significant help (financial aid, accommodation, assistance in finding a job, etc.) to offenders, is evaluated in various ways even by specialists. There are people who feel that taking care of offenders to this extent is exaggerated, particularly when even law-abiding citizens have housing problems and financial difficulties. It is a fact that the measures taken in order to prevent crime must not contradict the development of society, the financial potentials of society. We do not mean, however, to demand possibilities for offenders which are not ensured for the members of society. The requirement is only to create better possibilities for forming the intention of social adaptation and to ensure the conditions of its realization. If we take the struggle against crime seriously and we really want to reduce crime, we have to accept that we can only advance in this way. To be able to know that public order and safety exist and there is no reason to fear criminals is worth the extra expenditure required by the creation of modern means of the struggle against crime.

The introduction of new measures of criminal policy, however, must not be a question only of economy. We cannot take the position that the measure applied should be "economical", since life, bodily integrity, health, or public order and the feeling of security do not have a price, a value in terms of money. In the examination of the economic consequences of new institutions, what should always be kept in mind is whether with reasonable extra expenditure we can attain better results in protecting the life, property and safety of the public.[7] Crime is far from representing such a great danger to society in socialist countries as in the capitalist ones. But if we do not improve our system of establishing criminal responsibility, our system of aftercare, parallel to the development of society, if we do not find more effective measures, crime may represent an increasing danger for us, too. And, in any case, we may expect offenders to become useful members of society, people to follow the laws, only if we create the necessary subjective and objective conditions.

[7] See the material of the Warsaw seminar of Central European countries: *Przeglad Penitencjarny i Kriminologiczny* (Warsaw) No. 4, 1972. Several speakers at the seminar discussed the economy of crime and surveyed the methods that can be used to demonstrate the financial consequences of crime and the struggle against it.